LADIES
of the
GRAND TOUR

—❦—

BRIAN DOLAN

Flamingo
An Imprint of HarperCollinsPublishers

Flamingo
An Imprint of HarperCollins*Publishers*
77–85 Fulham Palace Road,
Hammersmith, London w6 8jb

www.**fire**and**water**.com

This paperback edition 2002

1 3 5 7 9 8 6 4 2

First published in Great Britain by HarperCollins*Publishers* 2001

Copyright © Brian Dolan 2001

The Author asserts the moral right to
be identified as the author of this work

ISBN 0 00 710533 9

Set in PostScript Linotype Adobe Caslon

Printed in Great Britain by
Clays Ltd, St Ives plc

For Dorothy

Contents

Illustrations

A Woman in Blue Reading a Letter, by Jan Vermeer, 1663–4. (Photograph © Rijksmuseum, Amsterdam)

Elizabeth, Lady Webster, later Lady Holland with her spaniel Pierrot, by Robert Fagan, 1793. (Private Collection)

Henry Richard, 3rd Lord Holland. (Portrait by François Xavier Fabre, reproduced by courtesy of the National Portrait Gallery, London)

Hester Thrale Piozzi. (Portrait by unknown artist, reproduced by courtesy of the National Portrait Gallery, London)

Henrietta, 3rd Countess of Bessborough.

Mary and Agnes Berry from a painting by Johann Zoffany, ca 1783.

Ellis Cornelia Knight by Angelica Kauffman, 1793. (Photograph © Manchester City Art Galleries)

Portrait of Mary Wollstonecraft Godwin, after a painting by John Opie, 1802. (Bridgeman Art Library)

Frederick Hervey, 4th Earl of Bristol and Bishop of Derry, with his granddaughter, Lady Caroline Crichton, later Lady Wharncliffe, by Hugh Douglas Hamilton, ca 1790–3. (National Gallery of Ireland)

The Customs House at Boulogne, by Thomas Rowlandson. (Yale Center for British Art, Paul Mellon Collection, USA/Bridgeman Art Library)

Gavin Hamilton leading a party of Grand Tourists to the archaeological site at Gabii, by Giuseppe Cades, 1793. (Photograph © The National Gallery of Scotland)

The Manner of Passing Mount Cenis, by George Keate, 1755. (British Museum)

Rome Seen on a Grand Tour, by John Feary. (David Ker Fine Art/ Bridgeman Art Library)

The Falls at Tivoli, by Jacob-Philippe Hackert, 1770. (Leeds Museums and Galleries (City Art Gallery)/Bridgeman Art Library)

The Return from a Masquerade – a Morning Scene, by Robert Dighton, 1784.

Acknowledgements

This project began as a file that I started to compile while researching another book on travel in the age of the Enlightenment. I had in mind to write principally about women travelling for their health but became fascinated with the many other proclaimed benefits that continental travel offered eighteenth-century British women.

I would like to thank my colleagues in the Wellcome Unit for the History of Medicine and the School of History at the University of East Anglia, particularly Roger Cooter, for providing a stimulating environment in which to work; the staff at Cambridge University Library, the British Library, the Wellcome Library for the History and Public Understanding of Medicine, and the London Library for all their assistance. At Cambridge University: my friends and colleagues in the Department of History and Philosophy of Science and at Hughes Hall – especially Robin Boast for reintegrating me to that community. I would like to thank the excellent team at HarperCollins: Michael Fishwick, Kate Johnson and Caroline Hotblack, for all their advice and assistance. I am grateful to my literary agent, Peter Robinson, through whom I met such an enthusiastic publisher, and to Kathleen Anderson in New York for introducing me to Hugh Van Dusen.

I have been lucky to receive comments and criticisms from a number of keen readers, without whom I would easily have lost the confidence necessary to move as broadly as I have done through the various themes of this book. They include Jan Bensley, Jeff and Kay Brautigam, Janet Dolan, Nancy Ernst, Sandra Evans, Bob Hatch, Gale Hennelly, Kathy Keenan, Roy Porter and Janet Todd. I would like to thank Julian Holmes for his research assistance.

Finally, I express my heartiest and deepest gratitude to Dorothy Porter, for tolerating all those loft evenings.

The world is a very good world, but you must seek it; it will not do to neglect it,
The advice of Sydney Owenson, Lady Morgan, the first woman writer to be given a pension (£300 per annum from 1837)

It makes my mouth water to hear of abroad; we have no chance till next year,
Lady Holland to her son, 15 December 1826

I shall be glad I have been at Paris even when I have left it,
Elizabeth Montagu to her brother, Morris Robinson, from Paris, 1776

I would not do in England what I think it no harm to do in Paris,
Hannah More, *Moral Sketches of Prevailing Opinions and Manners*, ix, (1819)

They may say what they please but a handsome English Woman is a thousand times superior to a handsome Foreigner,
Frances Crewe's conclusion during a trip to Paris, 1785

Hell stalks abroad,
Mary Wollstonecraft, *Vindication of the Rights of Men*

Belles Lettres and Black Swans

The Enlightenment & Travel

*With your wings, Madam, you must fly: but have
a care, there are clippers abroad,*
> Dr Johnson's advice to Hester Thrale

*Lady Tancred's accounts were by no means invit-
ing, tho' I made due allowance for a traveller whose
peregrinations for several years before had been
confined to the road between London and
Ramsgate,*
> Mary Berry to Bertie Greatheed,
> on hearing about conditions of travel in
> France, 1798

UNBEKNOWN TO MARY BERRY, two days before she wrote to her confidant Bertie Greatheed in Göttingen, Admiral Nelson's fleet had destroyed Napoleon Bonaparte's army in the battle of the Nile, quashing the French Egyptian expedition and effectively ending French plans to aggravate Britain further by thrusting at India. As far as Mary Berry was concerned, writing from her home in Mayfair on 2 August 1798, Napoleon was still running riot in Europe; the prospect of a French invasion of Britain was on everyone's lips, and the Continent was closed off to travellers. Twelve months earlier, Mary thought she would by now be on the Continent – her much looked forward to third trip there – conversing personally with Bertie Greatheed. But, alas, she was stranded, left to lament through correspondence her inability to escape. 'Most thoroughly,' she wrote, 'do I begin to feel the want of that *shake* out of English ways, English whims, and English prejudices, which nothing but leaving England gives one.'

This was hardly an appropriate time to condemn 'English ways' and a desire for the continental lifestyle. Mary Berry could have been accused of being a French sympathiser – a Jacobin (a radical activist in support of the principles of the French Revolution), or, with equivalent indignity, a Catholic. Mary was politically aware, but her restlessness with forced domestic residence overrode her sense of discretion. And anyway, she could have claimed with some justification, when *was* there a good time for a woman to talk about shaking loose 'English prejudices' and broadening her intellectual horizons?

By 'English prejudices' she was in part referring to a deep-rooted antagonism towards women's enlightenment. Mary felt confined, both physically and intellectually. The world seemed to be shrinking around her and without a change of air, and marooned in England she feared intellectual suffocation:

> After a residence of four or five years we all begin to forget the existence of the Continent of Europe, till we touch it again with our feet. The whole world to me, that is to say the whole circle of my ideas, begins to be confined between N. Audley-Street and Twickenham. I know no great men but Pitt and Fox, no king and queen but George and Charlotte, no towns but London. All the other cities, and courts, and great men of the world *may* be very good sort of places and of people, for aught we know or care; except they are coming to invade us, we think no more of them than of the inhabitants of another planet.

Just a few years earlier, before relations with France disintegrated completely, another English woman abandoned London and headed for Paris. Mary Wollstonecraft had longed to visit the Continent for some time. She had dreamt about it for over a decade, while pursuing a catalogue of occupations open to middle-class women, before taking pen in hand and daringly writing herself into a new career as an author. By 1792, with her authorial voice and confidence gathering strength, she published the work for which she is most well known: *A Vindication of the Rights of Woman*, written while intoxicated on the champagne fizz of the French Revolution. In this work she expressed a desire to see the revolutionary principles of *liberté*, *égalité* and *fraternité* apply to women as well as to men. Things were happening abroad; the Continent was a model of change and liberation. 'In France or Italy, have women confined themselves to domestic life?,' she asked her readers. 'No!' England was behind the times. 'I long for *independence!*,' she cried. 'I will certainly visit France, it has long been a desire floating in my brain.' Within months of the publication and immediate success of her book, she had embarked on her journey.

Mary Berry and Mary Wollstonecraft had much in common. Both

were from middle-class backgrounds, but had seen the prospects of family wealth squandered by rogue relatives. At the time of their travels, neither was married. Both had overcome prejudices against female advancement and become published authors. And both would find the experience of foreign travel stimulating and cathartic. It is no accident that the metaphor of travel has long been used to represent the twists and turns, discoveries and drudgery of intellectual and psychological development.

Travel and the knowledge collected along the way gave currency to the metaphor of 'the path to enlightenment'. By the end of the eighteenth century, the term was taken much more literally, and directed many women in their quests for improvement to the Continent. Letters and journals recorded their responses to life abroad, and in turn their discoveries about themselves. Travel writing, which included letters written home, presented a rare opportunity for Georgian women to articulate views on the world around them and their responses to it. Partly personal, biographical and intimate, their writings were often also political, descriptive, forthright and polemical. Through travel women of a certain status could fashion themselves into informed, discriminating observers, acute social commentators and listened-to cultural critics.

Berry and Wollstonecraft were but two of a wide range of women determined to elevate themselves through travel. By the end of the eighteenth century, 'ladies of letters' had begun to settle into their pursuit of a 'life of the mind': continental travel allowed them to carve out niches in the intellectual geography of Enlightenment England. Many women who had the chance to travel were changing the course of common assumptions and showing others how travel could help them arrive at a new position – personally and socially – in polite society.

A number of 'bluestocking' women, noted for their intellectual accomplishments, also left the droning world of polite drawing-room conversation to exercise their minds, enjoy social independence and cultivate new tastes, and romances, abroad. Travel helped women to develop views on the opportunities and rights to education; it guided those seeking separation from unhappy domestic circumstances; it worked to improve mental and physical health abroad and turned many into writers, arbiters of fashion, and *salonnières*.

Above all, travel was inspirational. Who would not be impressed with classical landscapes who had read *The Iliad* or the *Odyssey*, or by Italy who knew any history, wondered Lady Webster, as she absorbed the glories of the past? 'The first and strongest sensation one feels on entering Italy is the recollection of those historical events that from childhood are impressed on the mind,' she wrote. And seeing the scenes first-hand allowed her to realise new levels of literary appreciation: 'Florence of all places is the most calculated to inspire a taste for the pursuit of modern literature.' Affection for anything foreign was fast becoming the fashion. Hester Piozzi described to her daughter how her friend, Mrs Greenland, was positively 'mad after Belles Lettres, modern Languages, Accomplishments &c., doting on the Italian Artists'.

While abroad everyone seemed to acquire and cultivate refined judgement, which they eagerly flaunted when they returned home. Cornelia Knight, lady companion to Princess Charlotte, used the tastes she had acquired during her lengthy residence in Italy to size up the state apartments at Carlton House in London. 'They were well lighted, and were superior to anything I had seen in England', she thought, 'but the classical taste and sober dignity of Italy, with the grandeur of its spacious habitations, eclipse in my mind all I have seen elsewhere, and render Carlton House nothing more than a nobleman's dwelling expensively furnished'. This trenchant judgement certainly contradicts the assessment of one Swiss visitor, César de Saussure, that 'I do not think there is a people more prejudiced in its own favour than the British people, and they allow this to appear in their talk and manners. They look on foreigners in general with contempt, and think nothing is as well done elsewhere as in their own country.'

It was often exactly the desire to abandon homespun prejudices and escape the gossip and foolish attitudes towards foreign manners that compelled many Georgian women to travel. 'I think one very considerable benefit arising from seeing other countries besides our own,' opined Lady Anna Miller in 1770,

> is the eradication (by the testimony of one's own senses) of many prejudices and littlenesses of thinking, which insensibly have taken so deep a root in our minds, as to render it almost impossible to judge in an impartial way and liberal manner of our fellow-creatures, who happen to live at a great distance from us, and whom we imagine must differ from us in every respect, in proportion to the number of leagues that separate us from them.

Despite continental wars periodically erupting and relations with France rapidly disintegrating towards the century's end, such intellectual outlets were increasingly available to women. The Continent was no longer considered the exclusive playground for Gentlemen's Grand Tours.

But this was a recent development. The standard view was still that women were not expected to stray from their homes. 'Men,' it was stated in *The Art of Governing a Wife* (1747), were supposed 'to get; to go abroad and get his living; deal with all men; to manage all things without doors'; while the duties of women were 'to lay up and save; look to the house; talk to few; take of all within'. Discussions of the benefits of foreign travel had rarely included considerations of women, and when they did they merely expressed the belief that such an experience could benefit women's marriage marketability. Women travelling blurred the distinction between male and female activities, violated the division of labour that governed Georgian society and angered many male critics.

Unless eloping with a lover or hired by an aristocratic family, middle-class women previously had had no real chance for escape. And 'escape' was often the way they viewed going to the Continent. This was true even for aristocratic women who had long possessed the financial means for foreign travel and, progressively through the eighteenth century, were taking advantage of such privileges.

When twenty-two years old, Lady Elizabeth Webster (later Lady Holland), who, having been married at fifteen, had already spent seven years suffering an unhappy and ill-conceived marriage, was able to relish the time she spent travelling abroad, distancing herself mentally and physically from her youthful foibles: 'experience and a better knowledge of the world makes me laugh at menaces that used to terrify me out of my senses', she declared. The need to flee undesirable domestic circumstances and seek emotional refuge abroad motivated many other women of Elizabeth Webster's generation. The weight of domestic pressures was expected to be borne with silence and modesty: husbands were masters; marriages were arranged by rank and fortune; love and affection were subordinate to duty and honour. Continental travel provided a chance to break free.

On Monday, 19 June 1769, forty-three-year-old Lady Mary Coke was returning to her Notting Hill home having visited friends in Chelsea, when she suddenly found herself in a scene straight out of Macbeth. Riding slowly along in her carriage, she saw three women – gypsies – boiling a cauldron under a hedge; they immediately approached her. One wished to tell Lady Mary's fortune. 'You have been very Unfortunate,' said the gypsy, 'yet you are not born under an unlucky planet; you are now going into Foreign parts; this will prove a prosperous Summer; you will never dye in anybody's debt, but others will dye in yours; take care of a lady; you have had bad friends; you have been disappointed in an attachment.' Lady Mary rode on, reflecting on what the gypsy had said, thinking that her visions revealed a great deal of truth.

The gypsy was right about Lady Mary's past: she had spent two years in a turbulent, tortuous marriage before separating from her husband, and, after his death four years later, she remained a widow, growing increasingly distressed with court society of which she was part. Perhaps the gypsy had sensed something in Lady Mary's bearing or disposition. But there was nothing to indicate that Lady Mary would travel in the future. True, more British women had begun travelling to the Continent since the end of the Seven Years War, in 1763, but for a woman already presumed to be in unhappy domestic circumstances, the prospects of a pleasurable trip abroad were surely not good. That a mystic fortune-teller alluded to Lady Mary's future travels is symbolic of the fact that explorations into the unknown by women were not taken for granted in Georgian society. For men, however, prospects of foreign travel were far from mysterious, vague or uncertain. The latter half of the eighteenth century was the apogee of the age of the Grand Tour, and it was, we are overwhelmingly told in histories of the eighteenth century, a man's privilege.

So how did men respond to ladies on the Grand Tour? 'You have travelled enough,' Horace Walpole playfully wrote to Lady Mary Coke, who was now on her second continental trip since her encounter with the gypsies. '[You] ought to have the Magi come to see you, instead of wandering yourself after every Star.' Although probably writing in jest, elsewhere in his correspondence with Lady Coke, Mary Berry and others, Walpole betrayed a complete lack of understanding of women's motivations to travel. He was not the only one. 'They must have thought me a strange person,' laughed Lady Webster, referring to the onlookers she encountered when trekking through Italy, 'young, pretty, and alone, travelling merely to see the quarries of Carrara! It was perhaps an odd freak.' She may have mused about what kind of solitary spectacle she had made of herself in this instance; but she was not 'alone' when she managed to dodge her undesirable husband and arrange a rendezvous with her lover.

Men and monarchs wondered what foreign society had to offer women that society at home did not. They knew that men left home in order to understand better where they left – to compare and inspect, to collect and converse. Political society, like the natural world of shells and plants, was best understood by rational, comparative analysis. But such activities were considered far beyond the capacities of women.

It was an uncomfortable truth for men to come to terms with the fact that English women were leaving because they saw home as somehow inadequate. Georgian Britain was run as a gentleman's club; the Continent offered the most amenable environment in which women could explore and develop their own interests and abilities.

Foreign soil held the promise of freedom from the strait-laced laws and customs of their own society.

Of course foreign society was by no means exemplary for women's rights. Far from it. Despite Mary Wollstonecraft's assumptions about French and Italian liberties, British women were often fault-finding in their accounts of fashionable society. Hannah More described the 'encomiums of modern travellers, who generally concur in ascribing a decided superiority to the ladies of this country [England] over those of every other', adding that such was the state of foreign manners that even the comparison was an injury to English women. Lady Northumberland, who fell out of favour with the British royal family in the 1760s and so decided to frequent their continental equivalents, remarked that the court at Bonn was 'intriguing, insomuch that a virtuous Woman is here almost as rare a Bird as a Black Swan. All have their Lovers and too often those of their own Family.' A few years later, Lady Catherine Hamilton, the first wife of Sir William Hamilton (British Ambassador to Naples), wrote to her niece mentioning that they took a house in the country, to distance themselves from the Neapolitan court, and 'where we live as English a life as we can make it'. But after Lady Hamilton's death in 1782, when Sir William remarried to the free-spirited Emma Hart (later lover of Admiral Nelson), English society at Naples partied in an orgy of passion and pleasure.

If it was not virtue and honour that were sought by travelling abroad, it was for some at least the freedom of being able to join a mobile society that lived by its own rules. It was exactly this emancipation, for example, that convinced Hester Piozzi to go and live in her new Italian husband's homeland. Having married a Catholic, she found fashionable society in Britain less than happy. 'I *must* either quit you for Heaven or for Italy,' she wrote to her friend, Fanny Burney, 'and which is nearest?' There were personal as well as practical reasons for going abroad. She desired to 'show her girls' the sights, and it was a place where 'we will live cheaper and with more respect'. But to her estranged companion, Samuel Johnson, Italy was simply a lurid destination; only 'phantoms of the imagination seduce you to

Italy,' he bitterly wrote to her. Having abandoned her religion, friends and fame, what could be worse than abandoning her *country*?

Gentlemen Grand Tourists fashioned themselves as connoisseurs and collectors of desirable objects while simultaneously asserting themselves the caretakers of high-culture civility and sensibility, whilst women had more complex motives for travelling. Travel generated profitable rewards for men eager to conquer new fields, appropriate new curiosities, and capture emblems of empire. Not for them were quests for 'equality'; their intoxicating vision was acquiring future fortunes and that was something that men had every interest in keeping within closed ranks. So, the legacy of the Georgian travellers is dominated by accounts of self-styled travelling dilettante such as William Ponsonby, 2nd Earl of Bessborough, but not his daughter-in-law, Henrietta, Lady Bessborough, who travelled on the Continent a number of times between the 1770s and 1790s; similarly, the stories about the exemplary connoisseur Sir William Hamilton are well known, but not those of his niece, Mary Hamilton – though she travelled on the Continent in the 1770s and then became a favourite in King George III's court.

Whereas men's travel accounts are preoccupied with conquest, connoisseurship and domestication of the wild, women's narratives record more diverse experiences concerned with individual growth, independence and health. Travel provided education, entertainment, physical exercise, and an escape route for a wide range of women throughout the eighteenth century. The educational writer Maria Edgeworth travelled to France desiring to breathe in the intellectual atmosphere in the salons of so many famous *lumières*. Later her sister, Fanny, toured Europe and returned home to Ireland more 'rational' in her appreciation. 'She has been in London, Paris, Geneva with me for many months,' wrote Maria, 'and lately with her sister Fox and Barry Fox at Rome, Florence, everywhere abroad, and has had more than her share of admiration, but she is quite unspoiled by this and returned to her own country and own home, preferring them after comparison and all home affections and occupations to all others.' Exploring the Continent was a way not only to develop one's sensibilities, but was a way to explore foreign relations as well. Like any gentleman was expected to do, gentlewomen who travelled through Europe were also conscious to build up a bulletin of contemporary events, and contemplated whether Europeans shared their nation's interests while simultaneously assessing the civility of their neighbours. As Lady Anna Miller wrote of the Italians she met on her 1770 tour, they 'seemed well acquainted with political affairs, the interest of Europe, the balance of power, the real private characters and manner of life of the potentates of Europe, the trade, commerce, and interest of England, the parties there, &c. &c'.

Women travellers provided other women with contemporary social and political knowledge that was not formally bestowed on them. After discussing fears of a French invasion at her 'Ladies Circle' in Llangollen in 1796, Eleanor Butler asked 'To what part of Europe can we now turn our eyes in which we shall not meet the embryo images of future woes?' These were women who would cull information from other women's travel books, consulting Anna Miller's *Letters from Italy* (1776), Hester Piozzi's *Observations and Reflections made in the Course of a Journey through France, Italy, and Germany* (1789), or Marianna Starke's *Letters from Italy* (1800). Each decade saw more women transcending self-deprecation, overcoming feelings of vanity, considering themselves justified to write about their experiences abroad.

Women were still the minority amongst travel writers, but they provided models for other women. It began as admiration for the French *salonnières*, the famous Parisian hostesses such as Julie de Lespinasse, Madame Geoffrin, or Madame du Deffand, who provided more stimulating intellectual alternatives to increasingly corrupt court culture. Hannah More astutely compared the activities of the English 'Bluestocking Circle' in the latter half of the eighteenth century to the famous salon run in the Hôtel de Rambouillet, revealing a parallel that helped mould the identity of British learned ladies. And by the end of the eighteenth century, there were enough women travellers and travel writers for a new image of the 'literary traveller' and learned lady to emerge. An ensemble cast helped to fashion the Georgian 'lady of letters'. Ways to lead a 'life of the mind' were carved out collectively. The experience of travel and the exploration of foreign ground were integral to this enterprise.

'If anything could inspire an unpoetic imagination . . .'

Education & Improvement

We went this Morning to wait on Madame de Bocages, who meant I am sure to be extremely civil to us, and ought to express her meaning more perfectly for She has written & has travelled.

Hester Thrale, writing in her journal
from France

You fear that the minds of women should be enlarged and cultivated, lest their power in society and their liberty should consequently increase. Observe that the word liberty, applied to the female sex, conveys alarming ideas to our minds, because we do not stay to define the term; we have a confused notion that it implies want of reserve, want of delicacy; boldness of manners, or of conduct; in short, liberty to do wrong.

'Answer to the preceding letter from a gentleman',
Maria Edgeworth, *Letters for Literary
Ladies* (1795)

For most British women in the eighteenth century, Europe was a fantasy, an 'imaginative geography' represented in landscape paintings, narrated in books or described in letters, the backdrop to exotic episodes from history, as depicted by artists in allegorical scenes of Europe's past.[1] What was not represented visually was described in history books or oral lessons. Women as well as men knew the stories. 'Oh there is no Comparison between one's Sensations at home and those one feels at Naples,' declared Hester Piozzi, travelling in Italy with her new husband in 1785, before launching into an effusive, Gibbonesque blast of Italian history, trampling through its tumultuous past:

> Royalty demolished, and Empire destroyed; Power unlimited once, now changed to a childish display of empty splendour; and Riches *heaped up* as the Scripture says, *without knowing who was to gather them* are the Images with which Rome impresses one's Imagination.[2]

But these could not convey the sense of distance that travellers traversed, or the splendour of the landscape.

'I love the notion of seeing all the places one has read of in Roman history, where great men have been and great things done,' wrote Caroline Lennox to her sister in 1766, when preparing for her third continental trip which would take her to Italy for the first time. And thirty years later, Lady Elizabeth Webster struggled to remember the history she had learned in order to enjoy the places she felt privileged to visit: 'those classical sentiments that one strives both from vanity and taste to bring back to memory'. Sometimes the surrounding scenes were overwhelming, 'when the turbulence of the imagination subsides, and a long residence in the country familiarises one with objects so attractive, modern Italy, her poets, historians, and artists, arrest the attention very justly by the admiration to which they are entitled'.[3]

Imagination was needed to fill in the empty spaces of knowledge, sometimes leading to fanciful projections of reality. Once, the much-travelled Hester Piozzi took her friend, a twenty-seven-year-old woman who had never been 10 miles beyond London, to the Sussex coast.

'And well, Child!,' Hester exclaimed, 'are you not much surprised?'

'It's a fine sight, to be sure,' answered her friend, with a cool calm, 'but . . .'

At which point Piozzi interrupted: 'But what? You are not disappointed are you?'

'No,' replied her friend, 'not disappointed, but it is not quite what I expected when I saw the ocean.'

'Tell me then, pray good girl, and tell me quickly,' urged a puzzled Hester, 'what did you expect to see?'

'Why I expected,' her friend replied in hesitation, '*I expected to see a great deal of water.*'[4]

Maybe she dreamt of a wall of water, or more visible depths. For those who had never travelled, anything could be expected.

Despite the limitations of formal schooling, many women of status were fluent in European languages, had studied history, acquired artistic skills, and were keen to engage in intellectual debate.[5] Travel offered a rapid education in taste and manners which bypassed the traditional (all-male) route to refinement. Men had long taken for granted the many associations between travelling and self-improvement. But such quests for personal enlightenment were seen as unseemly and unsuitable subjects for women's attentions, and few women openly spoke about it. One exception was Mary Berry.

'Considering the education given to women,' she complained, 'and (according to the present system) the subsequent and almost necessary idleness both of mind and body, I am only astonished that they are not more ignorant, weaker, and more perverse than they are.'[6] Her protest against the 'present system' of women's education was stirred by the concern that *she*, regardless of her later wealth and commitment to the improvement of her mind, might have ended up in much more disagreeable circumstances than she did. 'Every expense of education in the acquirement of talents was denied us,' she wrote in her autobiographical recollections.[7] Central to this neglect was one 'blood-boiling' point to which she repeatedly returned – that due to family politics and social customs, financial constraints prevented as full an education as she and her younger sister, Agnes, desired.

Mary Berry was born in March, 1763, fourteen months earlier than Agnes, who was born in May 1764. Neither she nor her sister married during their long lives, and they remained inseparable until they died – within eleven months of each other – in 1852.[8] Mary was strong-willed, and held in high regard women's intellectual powers. The stages of her life – as a traveller, writer and bluestocking – demonstrate her determination to tackle head-on her concerns about her lack of 'systematised' education.

It is well known that in the eighteenth century British genteel society placed influence and affluence in the pocket of its eldest sons. By the right of primogeniture the fortunate son would inherit all the wealth and land in the immediate family (or extended family, if there was no direct male progeny), distributing to his siblings at his discretion parts of the estate not already entailed. Mary Berry's father, Robert, was that fortunate son. His wealthy uncle, who had no children of his own, had built a fortune of about £300,000 as a merchant in London. In 1762, Robert – after being educated for the Bar and embarking on his own Grand Tour – married Elizabeth Seton, the poor daughter of a Scottish widow. Tragedy struck five years later when Elizabeth and their third child, another daughter, died in childbirth. Mary was four.

During these years Robert Berry's younger brother, William, had been endearing himself to his wealthy uncle. William was adept at business, had married a woman of respectable wealth whose dowry brought him about £5,000, and, to his greater benefit, his first two children were boys. It soon became obvious that fortune favoured William. With only two daughters and therefore no heir apparent, and unwilling to contemplate remarriage straight away, Robert fell out of favour with his uncle.

Mary later reflected with disbelief on her great-uncle's conduct: her father had been left to 'starve' on an allowance of £300 per annum, while his younger brother 'was living in ease, indulgence, and luxury'. When the great-uncle eventually died in 1781, aged ninety-three, William was left virtually everything. 'To my father,' wrote Mary, 'a bare legacy of £10,000, with no mention *at all* of his two children.' No property, no linen or china. 'For many years afterwards,' Mary wrote, she could not think of the reading of the will 'without my blood boiling in my veins, and lamenting that I had not been present to support and reply for my father.'⁹ Mary was eighteen years old and away visiting a family friend when this episode occurred. Her rage and determination to 'reply' for her father, tell us much about her character – described by the same family friend as 'Sober, Honest, Virtuous & Industrious'. Thereafter she made clear her presence and voice in the masculine world that she believed had already overlooked her.¹⁰

From the moment that her father 'silently acquiesced' to such terms, Mary Berry gained an acute sense of responsibility. She had no mother. She was growing up in a world where, because she was female, her father and her sister had been 'choused' or cheated out of their inheritance, and, to add insult to injustice, William added only £1,000 per annum annuity to his brother's inheritance, again ignoring Mary and Agnes, since 'he concluded', thought Mary, they 'would marry, and be thus got rid of'.¹¹

William was wrong, and Mary determined to take charge of her own destiny and her family's future. When Mary's mother was eighteen, she once told someone who commented that baby Mary would grow into a handsome woman that she would prefer her to develop 'a *vigorous understanding*'. When her father first told her the story, Mary was greatly struck by it: '[it] has impressed on my mind ever since all that I must have lost in such a parent'. Mary intended to make good her mother's hopes and expectations, and travelling was her resolve. 'I was now eighteen,' she wrote, 'and began to long to see that world of which I had been picking up all sorts of accounts from much desultory and often improper reading'.[12]

Her 'improper' reading was a consequence of her father's inability to afford her a governess until the age of twelve, thus leaving Mary and her sister 'to our own devices – to be as idle, and to read what books, and choose what other employments we pleased'. They veered from the conventional commitment to religious instruction. 'It was in the middle of the age of Voltaire,' Mary later explained, 'and his doctrines and his wit had been adopted by all the *soi-disant* Scotch wits,' referring to Scottish philosophers such as David Hume. The reference to Voltaire by Mary (whose family was of Scottish origin) reveals an early sense of affinity with the intellectual *esprit* of the French *philosophes* who bestrode the 'age of Enlightenment'.

Voltaire, who lived most of his life in exile from Paris for his radical views on religion and philosophy, resided briefly in London, after which he published what is considered the first direct assault on the theological dogma of the *ancien régime*, his *Lettres philoso-phiques* (1734). Voltaire saw England as a land of civil liberties, where free trade and commerce promoted social intercourse between people of different nationalities, leading to religious toleration, peace and prosperity.[13] *Philosophes* such as Voltaire, Montesquieu (another trav-eller to England), Diderot and others, created the 'moment of Anglo-mania', as Mary called it, where England was revered with a 'respect for those who had so long preceded her in the enjoyment of civil liberty'.[14]

British relations with France (the usual country of entry for travel-lers to the Continent), were strained during the eighteenth century – the two countries spent nearly four decades at war with each other. Yet it was no secret that French *philosophes* held British philosophers (especially the 'trinity': Francis Bacon, Isaac Newton and John Locke) in high regard. Radicals abroad hailed Britain as a model for developing a rationally governed and egalitarian society.

In certain ways, then, it is ironic that travel to the Continent would become such a fashion when European sophisticates were looking to England with such admiration.[15] But clearly England was not a model for everyone. The *philosophes'* esteem of English civil liberties, for instance, said nothing of the exclusion of women from Enlightenment goals of asserting their 'natural rights' to equality. The view of the place of women in eighteenth-century Western culture, held by theorists such as the *Encyclopédie* editor Denis Diderot, the Scottish historian John Miller or the Scottish physician William Alexander, was that women were, at least, happier than their primitive, savage ancestors, and in modern society they could afford the time to support the family. Women were, in Montesquieu's poignant phrase, 'domestic slaves' – a better position, he added, than 'real slavery'.[16]

According to Locke (who had travelled through France in the 1670s), young men should travel the Grand Tour to finish their education and 'compleat the Gentleman' – and then return to flaunt their freshly polished sense of self-worth. British women were never publicly instructed on what benefits foreign travel might hold for them, but the most frequent criticism of women's status in Enlightenment society was the lack of education given to them. One solution arrived at by many women was to go abroad *to begin* their education.

No matter how many philosophers celebrated England as a path-finder to Enlightenment principles ('As I have passed a good deal of my time with the Litterati at Paris,' wrote Elizabeth Montagu in 1776, 'you may imagine I heard much of the manner of Mr Hume's taking leave of the world'), for British ladies, *foreign women* were models of the benefits to be had from pursuing enlightenment in modern society.[17] Women in countries such as France and Italy engaged much more actively in philosophical debates and were able to elevate themselves in civil society. Despite the contemporary insistence of associating woman with the 'natural occupations' of childbirth and familial care (or 'domesticity') and men with culture (mostly political debate and economic management), even the continental *philosophes* began to acknowledge that they themselves were increasingly breathing an intellectual atmosphere conditioned by the women of the house. 'Women accustom us to discuss with charm and clearness the dryist and thorniest subjects,' admitted Diderot. 'We talk to them unceasingly: we listen to them: we are afraid of tiring or boring them.' The ladies of the Grand Tour went abroad to meet and learn from them.

Male observers too were struck by the 'women of quality' abroad, but not always favourably. Writing to Lady Hervey during his stay in Paris in 1765, Horace Walpole explained some of his prejudices about France and French women, owning that 'Paris can produce women of quality that I should not call women of fashion: I will not use so ungentle a term as vulgar, but for their indelicacy, I could call it still worse.'[18]

Being 'indelicate' rather than 'fashionable' meant talking freely about unseemly topics (at least 'in my English eyes', he thought) such as Walpole had experienced during evenings of entertainment at the home of the famous wit and salon hostess Madame du Deffand. This *grande dame* engaged with the best of the revolutionaries, and held views that were noted as being radical, irreligious, republican, and pro the American War of Independence. On visiting Paris a couple of decades later, Thomas Jefferson was captivated by the candid conversation he encountered between men and women in the salons, and learned from the wealthy Philadelphian Anne Willing Bingham what some American women thought of the growing spirit of equality amongst the women of Paris.

> The state of Society in different countries requires corresponding Manners and Qualifications. Those of the french Women are by no means calculated for the Meridian of America, neither are they adapted to render the Sex so amiable or agreeable in the English acceptation of those words. But you must confess that they are more accomplished, and understand the Intercourse of society better than in any other country. We are irresistibly pleased with them, because they possess the happy Art of making us pleased with ourselves; their education is of a higher

Cast, and by great cultivation they procure a happy variety
of genius, which forms their Conversation to please either
the Fop or philosopher.

Another American abroad, the commercial agent Governeur Morris,
agreed: France was 'the Woman's country'. Even Fanny Burney's
six-year-old son shared such views (no doubt influenced by his French
father's insight), declaring that 'Ladies govern there entirely.'[19]

Mary Berry, who was a close friend of Horace Walpole, was quite
familiar with the character of French women such as Madame du
Deffand as well as with Voltaire's views. Rather extraordinarily she
edited for publication du Deffand's personal correspondence, which, in
1780, had been bequeathed to Walpole (who passed them on to Mary),
enabling her to read through hundreds of letters written to the *grande
dame* by Voltaire, Rousseau, Montesquieu, de Staël, and others. These
were radical writers whom Mary Berry, for the sake of her reputation
in England, needed to distance herself from, declaring in her Preface
to the published letters that she should not be 'associated either in the
principles, the opinions, the taste, the merits or the demerits' of du
Deffand. But those who knew Mary Berry and her fondness for foreign
philosophy would see through such disclaimers. The evangelical writer
Hannah More for one (while trying to proselytise Walpole) worried
about Mary Berry's intellectual inclinations. 'Spoke boldly to Miss
Berry,' she scribbled in her *Memoirs*. 'Made her promise to read some
of the evidences of Christianity, and the New Testament. Oh Lord!
Do thou follow with my blessing her resolves, and show her the truth
"as it is in Jesus." Open the blind eyes!'[20]

But Mary Berry's eyes were wide open, and focused on the Continent. There, life was full of wonder and intellectual vigour. When
she was as young as eight years old she had been seduced by stories
of life abroad by relatives returning from their travels. 'The accounts
my young ears heard from them of the beauties and charms of Italy,
first impressed on my mind the strong desire of seeing what they
described.' A decade later, equipped with the modest inheritance from
her wealthy uncle and burning with a fever to escape England, her
moment had arrived. She 'persuaded' her father to give up the house

in London and 'to go abroad'. 'This had long been the first object of my wishes.'[21]

In May 1783 Mary, Agnes and their father, Robert, set off on their first trip to the Continent. They stopped in Rotterdam, where some of their extended family – some of her Uncle William's in-laws – lived. Mary was overjoyed to be abroad, and recognised immediately the rewards she was reaping. 'I have always looked back to those three weeks as the most enjoyable and most enjoyed of my existence, in which I received the greatest number of new ideas, and felt my mind, my understanding, and my judgement increasing every day, while at the same time my imagination was delighted with the charm of novelty in everything I saw or heard.'

After only a few months, she felt she had matured, and gained a new understanding of herself and her role as the eldest female in the family. 'I began to feel my own situation, and how entirely dependent I was on my own resources for my conduct, respectability, and success,' she wrote. Her father, devastated by the loss of his wife, neglected to see that it was his duty to nurture the motherless daughters into accomplishment and happiness. It was a role that Mary, now of age and maturing, felt she must take over. Her mission was to guide her family on life's journey.

> I soon found that I had to lead those who ought to have led me; that I must be a protecting mother, instead of a gay companion, to my sister; and to my father a guide and monitor, instead of finding in him a tutor and protector. Strongly impressed as I was that honour, truth, and virtue were the only roads to happiness, and that the love and consideration of my fellow-creatures, and the society in which I was about to live, depended entirely on my own conduct and exertions, the whole powers of my mind were devoted to doing always what I thought right and knew would be *safe*, without a consideration of what I knew would be agreeable, while I had at the same time the most

lively sense of everything that was brilliant and distinguished, and the greatest desire to distinguish myself.

The route to the improvement of her mind, to becoming 'distinguished', and to preparing herself and her sister for 'society' took them across the Continent, through Holland, Switzerland and Italy, where Mary encountered others with like ambitions. In Lausanne, she met the sixteen-year-old Madame de Staël, the future author who spent her youth involved with her mother's salon; in Rome, she was presented to the Pope; and in Naples she was invited to the court of Caroline, daughter of the Austrian Empress Maria Theresa and sister of Emperor Joseph II.[22] On subsequent trips she would converse with the famous mathematician Pierre Simon Laplace, and be personally introduced to Napoleon Bonaparte.[23]

Europe was buzzing. Pierre Ambroise Choderlos de Laclos's *Les Liaisons dangéreuses* (1782) was entertaining readers; Mozart's Mass in C minor was performed for the first time in Salzburg; and Immanuel Kant's *Was ist Aufklärung?* (1784) was hot off the press. And as if this was not enough to excite the nerves, one could always lose oneself in the scenery. Switzerland was a favourite destination for many travellers, inspired by Rousseau's *La Nouvelle Héloïse* (1761) and the home of luminaries such as Voltaire, Gibbon and de Staël.[24]

At Chamouni, near Geneva, Mary walked over a glacier, under waterfalls, and gazed at mountains and valleys. Here she found her heart's content, venturing that 'If anything could inspire an unpoetic imagination, it would surely be the scenes which surround this delightful valley.' Even the local people seemed nicer than anywhere else. She could barely believe her thoughts. 'I am hardly a romantic,' she confessed. 'God knows! and I am far from supposing that there anywhere exists a society of men free from the mean passions and frailties incident to human nature,' but at Chamouni, the people were convincingly in 'good fellowship with one another'.[25]

Mary Berry's travels, 'the first object of my wishes', were central to her autobiographical reflections. In the wake of the family crisis sprang her initiative to travel. Subsequent references to continental journeys also featured in her writings, whether in regular correspondence or in her politicised publications. Her self-governed education in her teens, and the fulfilment of a two-year Grand Tour also made an impression on others who came to admire her.

After returning from the Continent, Mary and her family moved to a house in Twickenham, near Horace Walpole's, whom they met in 1788. The Berry sisters, he observed, 'are returned the best-informed and the most perfect creatures I ever saw at their age. They are exceedingly sensible, entirely natural and unaffected, frank, and being qualified to talk on any subject.' Mary, he 'discovered by chance, understands Latin, and is a perfect Frenchwoman in her language'. He thought her more impressive than Agnes, who, however, 'draws charmingly'.[26] Already they were beginning to situate themselves in the fashionable circles of the London season. From his first meeting with them, aged seventy-one, Walpole grew more infatuated with the sisters with each passing year, calling them his 'twin wives'. Mary's relationship with Walpole would set her on the path to posterity, gaining as she did his literary patronage and posthumous 'presence' (Walpole left the Berrys his personal manuscripts which Mary edited). Did he see in Mary a young Madame du Deffand? In many ways she did come to resemble the politically minded Parisian hostess, later holding her own salon at her home in Audley Street, Mayfair, and hobnobbing with the likes of the distinguished socialite Elizabeth Montagu.

For Mary Berry, travel not only led to maturity, self-reflection, and the rational analysis of foreign cultures, but it was also the best way to broaden the mind. She felt sorry for her countrywomen who were disciplined into believing that travelling from the metropolis to their country estates was the route to happiness.

> All English women think it necessary to profess loving the country, and to long to be in the country, altho' their minds are often neither sufficiently opened, nor their pursuits sufficiently interesting, to make such a taste rational.[27]

For Mary, neither the countryside nor her own country was capable of opening the mind sufficiently to cultivate love, culture and rationality. She was not alone in this sentiment. Sir William Hamilton, the British Ambassador to Naples, struck a similar chord when he tried to persuade his niece, Mary Hamilton, to visit him. He 'wished us to come to Naples', Mary wrote in her diary, '& said many things on the advantages of travelling & nothing opened the mind more, it was beyond conception how it furnished ideas to those who had natural taste & observation'.[28] She, however, remained and ventured no further in her life than Belgium.

In 1752 Sarah Scott turned twenty-nine, and for reasons that others speculated involved domestic violence or illicit affairs on the part of her husband, George Lewis Scott, the couple separated. Sarah assumed residence at the home of a friend, Lady Barbara 'Bab' Montagu, in Batheaston, near Bath. Here she led a charitable and methodical life, as described by her sister, Elizabeth Montagu (no relation to 'Bab'): 'My sister rises early, and as soon as she has read prayers to their small family, she sits down to cut out and prepare work for 12 poor girls, whose schooling they pay for.' Sarah gave particular attention to promising pupils, volunteering to teach them writing and arithmetic. On Sundays, the twelve girls, joined by twelve young boys, would visit Sarah's house before attending church to read the catechism, some chapters, and to 'have the principal articles of their religion explained to them'.

This was an increasingly common lifestyle for women of the employing class through whose efforts the charity school burgeoned in the eighteenth century. Women such as Sarah Scott devoted themselves to moulding their pupils into sober, industrious and competent workers: the girls were being prepared for a life of a maidservant or maybe a position in cottage industry, and eventually to be well-mannered wives.[29]

While living on a small income and denying themselves 'unnecessary expenses', Sarah and Lady Barbara Montagu managed to enjoy the 'reasonable pleasures of Society', attending plays and occasionally even a ball in Bath. Hoping to heal the 'wounds of disappointment' that she acquired from her ill-conceived marriage, she was now living a life that her sister thought would at least 'lead her to truth'.[30] Even though Elizabeth – three years the elder – acknowledged that Sarah 'seems very happy', there are moments in their correspondence when she affectionately reaches out to her sister, almost in the hope of removing her from her routine life.

One August day in 1776 Sarah opened a letter from Elizabeth, writing from Paris, which treated her to a glimpse of how her days might be otherwise consumed.

> I desire you to follow me on Sunday to Madame Neckers, dine there with Monsr de Bouffons and many learned Academicians, and take a gentle walk with them in ye evenings along ye banks of ye Seine, which is the most discreet of all rivers … On Tuesday you shall dine with us at Col Drumgolds, and hear him read some composition of his, made for ye Royal family in France when they were young. The delicacy with which he conveyed virtue and truth into things so tender as young minds, and royal minds, wd please you. That night you shall sup at la Marquise de Defants [du Deffand] with Russian Princes, French Princesses, beaux esprits etc.[31]

It was a thoughtful, and playful, invitation to her sister who, after reading her letter, would not only have a mental picture of daily life for a lady traveller abroad, but would be encouraged to think of herself as a fellow traveller. Like many Grand Tourists, Elizabeth walked her correspondents through foreign streets and took them into the homes of local society figures. Her philosophy was that 'When friends are at a great distance, the proper subject is, where they have been, where they are, how they are, and what they are doing.'[32] Striving for intimacy in writing helped close the distance between correspondents while also educating others about the routes and rituals of life abroad. Such epistolary exchanges between travellers and friends and family generated the most widely received views of foreign travel in the eighteenth century (postcards were a late nineteenth-century solution to keeping in touch). Particularly for women, for whom the art of letter writing was an essential part of a well-born education, creating a literary legacy was a central element to the Grand Tour. Without this the history of the ladies of the Grand Tour would have been lost.

Such letters made seductive reading for the fireside voyagers who, from the familiar surrounds of their own home, followed the path of their own foreign correspondent. Travel was about time rather than space – time apart from a friend or lover, time spent anticipating the next letter. Maps, even those laid out to plot the path of the voyager, could never tell the whole story. The image must have been familiar. It was depicted by Jan Vermeer in his painting *Woman in Blue Reading a Letter* (1663/4). A pregnant woman stands tranquil, self-absorbed and engrossed in a long letter. Behind her, above an empty chair, hangs the parchment of a large map of Holland, a pronouncement that her thoughts often dwelt on distant places and on absent voices. For most women in England this is how the Grand Tour was experienced.

Letters from travelling friends and loved-ones were cherished. William Spencer Cavendish, future sixth Duke of Devonshire (son of Georgiana, Duchess of Devonshire), received letters from Mary Berry while she was touring France during the Peace of Amiens. 'You cannot think, my dear Miss Berry,' wrote the precocious thirteen-year-old to Mary (who had just turned forty), 'how much pleasure your letter gave me; everything you say about Nice will be news to me, as I have never had any correspondent there.' Young William was to receive news from abroad and already dreamt about conducting his own Grand Tour. 'I envy you very much upon your *tall personable* beast upon the mountains, whilst we (poor souls!) are shivering in great coats by the fireside. We are *certainly* to go to Paris this summer. Perhaps we shall meet you there on your way back.'[33]

In a distant branch of William Spencer Cavendish's family was Miss Sarah Ponsonby, who lived with her lover, Lady Eleanor Butler – the two being known in society circles as 'the Ladies of Llangollen'.

They lived in Wales in self-imposed exile from fashionable society, and their favourite evening's entertainment was discussing travel, books and continental curiosities. 'After dinner talked of Rome' with Mr and Mrs Whalley, Sarah recorded in her diary. The list of Sunday afternoon subjects continued: 'Talked of Rousseau. Switzerland. North Wales. The exquisite pleasures of retirement, and the Luxury of Purchasing Books.' Their guests would head for home at nine, leaving Sarah and Eleanor to romanticise about a richer life. 'My Heart's darling and I sat by the Kitchen Fire, talking of our Poverty.' Two days later, a Mr Bligh, who had just returned from the Continent, and his brother visited them. Again, conversation centred on life abroad. The traveller showed them his trophies of travel:

> Six views of Switzerland, washed drawings by Hacklet which I confess I want taste to admire. Two Rings, fine antique, bought at Rome for Mr. and Mrs. E. Tighe. An Eye, done at Paris and set in a Ring. A true French Idea, and a delightful Idea, which I admire more than I confess for its singular Beauty and Originality.

And where did their conversation lead them? 'Geneva, its Government. Poor Rousseau. That detested Voltaire. Rome, the walls of an apartment which the Bishop Derry purchased there and sent to Ireland. Vienna . . .' Other visitors informed them of the practical details of continental travel. Lord Milton, fresh back from a two-year tour of the courts of Berlin and Brunswick, relayed stories of the 'Mode of Travelling in Germany . . . The Inns horrid . . . Mutton, half a hare, pieces of goose that had been heated over several times. Performances at the Theatre,' and so on, throughout their days as recorded in Sarah's diary.[34]

Before she toured Belgium on her single trip abroad, Mary Hamilton – when not attending the soirees of her London bluestocking friends such as Elizabeth Vesey or Mary Delany – found regular interest in conversation with Lord Stormont, who had recently returned from his continental travels. The traveller 'inform'd me of ye stile of living at Vienna, wch was when he resided there ye most polish'd court in Europe. We talk'd a good deal abt the great difference of expense in *every article* between living abroad & in England.' Several weeks later she saw him again, and once more he 'entertained me very much by describing the different *stiles* of *manners* in foreign Countries & particularly the *"bon ton"* etiquette in France'.[35]

Travel was a recurrent subject of conversation for the chattering classes. Everyone could be entertained by a returning traveller, intrigued by a book of published travels, and impressed by letters received from abroad. The instalments were informative as well as intimate. It was through reading such accounts that many women began to think of travel as a virtue – as a stimulant to the mind and an avenue to intellectual 'improvement', and in the words of one of a closely supportive and intellectually ambitious circle of friends surrounding Elizabeth Montagu, the best way to develop 'our natural abilities'.

In the 1750s, it was Elizabeth Montagu's ambition to make her marital home on Hill Street, near Berkeley Square, 'the central point of union' for all the intellectual and fashionable people in London. She began hosting evening assemblies for the discussion of literary topics, from novels and poems to paintings and plays. She drew a crowd: members of Samuel Johnson's Literary Club were regulars, such as the Royal Academy painter Sir Joshua Reynolds, the actor David Garrick, the president of the Royal Society Sir Joseph Banks, the political economist Adam Smith, the historian Edward Gibbon and the writer Oliver Goldsmith. It was an eclectic mix providing an intellectual forum for women as much as men. Many of the women, besides Elizabeth Montagu, were highly accomplished, and such was their fame that many were depicted by Richard Samuel in his painting *The Nine Living Muses of Great Britain* (1779), including the artist Angelika Kauffmann; the writers Hannah More, Elizabeth Carter and Charlotte Lennox; the historian Catharine Macaulay; the educational writer and poet Anna Laetitia Barbauld; the actress and playwright Elizabeth Griffith; and the singer Elizabeth Linley.[36] In the 1750s Elizabeth Montagu formed a social circle that included Elizabeth Carter, Catherine Talbot, Elizabeth Vesey and Frances Boscawen; they began to be referred to as *salonnières;* their *petticoteries* being seen as the British equivalent to the Parisian salon culture – arenas of sociability that began to appear amid England's tightly packed male club culture.[37]

These women became known as the 'bluestocking' ladies. While today this generally refers to any woman with intellectual ambition, in the eighteenth century the term 'bluestocking' was used with nuance. Coined in 1756 by Elizabeth Montagu, it was first used in reference to a particular gentleman acquaintance who frequented her soirees bedecked in blue, rather than black, stockings. Through the 1760s, however, the term evolved to apply to any man whose friendship with a woman was valued for his encouragement of her intellectual interests, as well as coming to represent a certain intellectual outlook, a 'blue stocking Philosophy' (as used by Elizabeth Montagu). What is little known is that the term was also used in a pejorative way as a reference specifically to women who violated the taboo against ladies being learned.[38] (Thus, the modern, common tendency to think of a bluestocking as an esteemed eighteenth-century learned lady is often historically inaccurate, and leads to grouping women together who did not see themselves as one of 'the Blues', such as Hester Thrale, later Piozzi.)

What is notable is the existence of the term at all. It identified certain women who possessed intellectual characteristics: they became in particular ways identifiable, indicating that the trait of 'intellect' was not as transparent or ubiquitous among women as it was considered to be in men. However, it is clear that the term was never entirely stable and the leading figures within the bluestocking circle were always changing.

The character of the bluestocking – built on literary accomplishment and sociability – generally conflicted with conventional views about the appropriate conduct of a lady in public; this generated criticism from some quarters, but also considerable admiration. The evangelical writer and educational theorist Hannah More, for example, wrote her poem, 'Bas Bleu; Or, Conversation' (1786), as a tribute to the bluestockings, and dedicated it to Elizabeth Vesey. Vesey's salon in Clarge Street 'rescued the ravag'd realms of Taste' from 'Whist ... that vandal of colloquial Wit' – in other words it aimed to rescue polite conversation from the drinking and card-playing culture of gaming society. Hannah More praised Vesey for her 'sensibility', referring to the dignity and virtue she had for possessing emotional feeling as well as intellect (a particular late-eighteenth-century way of linking the emotional and moral faculties). The blue-stockings' intellectual companionship and conversation allowed them to explore their feelings and their natural sensibilities, to develop their own voices. This was not a private collusion, and to be accepted as intellectuals in public meant they had to run the gauntlet, face criti-cism and risk ridicule. Their unity led Horace Walpole to dub the bluestocking circle 'the first female club ever known'.[39]

Yet this 'club' maintained no consensus about the means of achiev-ing women's intellectual advancement. While to speak of the improvement of *men's* minds often involved an explicit reference to the benefits of travelling, for women improvement was usually con-nected with a regimen of religious contemplation. Hester Chapone's (anonymously published) *Letters on the Improvement of the Mind* (1773), for example, stressed the study of the scriptures, and later linked proper learning with decorum, economic housewifery and a general knowledge of history. Yet Hester Chapone was not antagonistic towards more enlightened avenues for women. After all, she had put the time in to her studies, writing (at twenty-two) 'I have (and yet I am still alive) drudged through *Le Grand Cyrus*, in twelve huge volumes, *Cleopatra* in eight or ten, *Polyxander*, *Ibrahim*, *Clelia*, and some others, whose names as well as all the rest of them I have forgotten.' Some-times referred to as the 'bluest of the Blues', she collaborated on translation projects with Elizabeth Carter, and dedicated her edu-cational tract to Elizabeth Montagu (who urged her to publish it).[40]

Thirty years later, Mary Wollstonecraft was unable to accept such a conventional blueprint for women's education. The French Revolution breathed new life into radical defences of equal rights across the ranks of society. The very event that had kept Mary Berry at home, but longing to travel, was that which provided Mary Wollstonecraft with her own battle cry. The face of 'Reason' promised to cut off the 'dark hand of despotism' of the *ancien régime*, she wrote, raising her glass to the promotion of the principles of *liberté, fraternité* and *égalité*.[41] But frustratingly, these principles did not yet apply to women. When Wollstonecraft read Talleyrand's plan for national education in France, she was disappointed to find that it failed to mention women. How was it, she wondered, that the new-found rights of humanity applied only to men? Her response, dedicated to Talleyrand, was *The Vindication of the Rights of Woman* (1792).

Mary Wollstonecraft discarded an inventory of writers who 'have rendered women objects of pity, bordering on contempt'. Out was Rousseau ('What nonsense!' she cried at one point in reference to *Emile*); dismissed was the old-familiar Dr James Fordyce (who recommended, in his *Sermons to Young Women*, that women should be meek, timid, complacent, and retain 'a propensity to melt into affectionate sorrow'); Dr Gregory was tender but wrong-footed; Hester Chapone escaped lightly: 'I cannot, it is true, always coincide in opinion with her, but I always respect her,' and Catharine Macaulay's writing, where 'no sex appears', was mature and profound.[42]

Wollstonecraft's book pressed against the bruise on the British aristocracy's faith in social stability. Already shaken by the loss of the American colonies, the British governing classes now feared their own revolution, a forewarning of which was offered in the eagerly consumed *Reflections on the Revolution in France*, by Edmund Burke. Whereas Mary Berry celebrated growing up in the 'age of Voltaire', Wollstonecraft was writing in the middle of the 'age of anxiety': parliamentary reform was being debated, and the year the *Rights of Woman* was published was the year that the first democratic organisations with representatives from the artisan and working classes entered British politics.[43] The fear of the spread of 'infectious spirits' that were being agitated by English radicals such as Thomas Paine, author of the *Rights of Man* (1791), and now Wollstonecraft, made any proclamations on women's equality or rights to education and intellectual improvement particularly pungent.

Hannah More is remembered for her apparent attack on the 'radical' Wollstonecraft despite the fact that, as their contemporaries noted, their philosophies were similar, something that even More – who certainly voiced her disagreements with Wollstonecraft's approach – recognised.[44] More is often seen as a conservative figure, a critic of women's abilities and their intellectual potential. (Statements such as, 'Far be it from me to desire to make scholastic ladies or female dialecticians ... for by shewing [women] the possible powers of the human mind, you will bring them to see the littleness of their own', lend themselves to such an interpretation.[45]) Yet, the subtleties of her campaign for educational reform remain overlooked. Despite being 'much pestered to read the *Rights of women* [sic]', she refused to on the grounds that 'I have as much liberty as I can make good use of, now I am an old maid.'[46]

More's own writings may not have been infused with such strong sentiments of liberation and rule-breaking radicalism, but she too was able to evade the trappings of the feminine world of domesticity and live by her pen. Despite relying on male patronage, her writings carried subtle messages about how women could improve themselves. She believed in the righteousness of evangelical philanthropy as a means of improving individuals who were godly, regardless of gender. The danger with fashionable society was its potential for corrupting morals through overindulgence in luxury, fatuous discourse, and aristocratic snobbery. If pious and disciplined, however, any man or woman could create a more civil society. Within Hannah More's vision of civil society, women had the potential to develop morally and intellectually. Her philosophy for improving women's education was underpinned by evangelical values and her belief that it would reinforce the moral probity of the nation. Education was 'a school to fit us for life, and life be a school to fit us for eternity'.[47]

Her life was a chapter in such capacities for accomplishment. Hannah was born in 1745 to a family with humble origins and raised with her four sisters near Bristol, where her father became a school headmaster. Hannah and her sisters were educated by their father (the mother being absent from this role, and subsequently absent in most biographical or analytical accounts of Hannah More's life). When Hannah was twelve, she and her sisters (the eldest being nineteen), set up a boarding school for girls that concentrated on moral improvement through Bible reading. Her career as an author began when she wrote stories for her pupils, and by the age of seventeen she completed her first play, *The Search after Happiness,* published in 1773. In her early twenties Hannah met and became engaged to a local high-born country gentleman. This proved an unlucky courtship – he failed to appear at their wedding on three different occasions. Disgraced but recompensed with an annuity of £200 from him, Hannah packed up and, with a spirit for independence, ambition, and the manuscript of her play in hand, headed for London.

Hannah More lived until her eighty-eighth year and enjoyed an immensely successful literary career. Amidst her poems and plays was her educational tract, *Strictures on a Modern System of Female Education* (1799), which reached five editions and sold 19,000 copies. It held out the promise of improved education for women without challenging men's 'superiority'. *Not challenging* masculine culture was different from remaining deferential towards it. There was reason to support intellectual growth in women despite their overall genius being subordinate to men's; 'that women have equal *parts*, but are inferior in *wholeness* of mind, in the integral understanding', she suggested. Men, she continued, should be less inimical to women's improvement, not least since men 'themselves will be sure to be gainers by it'.[48] They would gain better companions who were thoughtful, considerate, and sympathetic – not antagonistic.

> Their knowledge is not often like the learning of men, to
> be reproduced in some literary composition, nor ever in
> any learned profession; but it is to come out in conduct.
> A lady studies, not that she may qualify herself to become
> an orator or a pleader; not that she may learn to debate,
> but to act ... The great uses of study are to enable her to
> regulate her own mind, and to be useful to others.[49]

Like Hannah More, Maria Edgeworth was from a middle-class background and became a novelist as well as an educationalist. She took up the issue of women's intellectual growth in her first publication, *Letters for Literary Ladies* (1795). Unlike Wollstonecraft's earlier *Rights of Woman*, however, Edgeworth's *Letters* was not written as a polemic. It is an epistolary fiction, a hypothetical exchange of letters between two gentlemen discussing the future education of one correspondent's new-born daughter. One of the points she pursued through the voice of the gentleman who opposes women's education, was that they could not attain an equivalent intellectual status as men due to society's 'customary' (and therefore somehow legitimate) exclusionary practices. 'We mix with the world without restraint,' wrote the antagonistic correspondent, referring to men like himself.

> We converse freely with all classes of people, with men of wit, of science, of learning, with the artist, the mechanic, the labourer; every scene of life is open to our view; every assistance that foreign or domestic ingenuity can invent, to encourage literary studies, is ours almost exclusively. From academies, colleges, public libraries, private associations of literary men, women are excluded, if not by law, at least by custom, which cannot easily be conquered.[50]

Maria Edgeworth used this fictional character to underline how ingrained such customary mechanisms were in men's minds, and how impotent they were to change the situation. Her point echoed that made over thirty years earlier by a reviewer who admired the bluestocking Elizabeth Carter's translation of the Greek *Works* of Epictetus (published in 1758), who noted that if 'women had the benefit of liberal instructions, if they were inured to study, and accustomed to learned conversation ... if they had the same opportunity of improvement as the men, there can be no doubt but that they would be equally capable of reaching any intellectual attainment'.[51]

This point again suggested that women were not by birth 'irrational' creatures or incapable of learning, but that the exclusionary practices of society wrongly deprived them of their chance to prove themselves.[52] *If only*, however, still seemed to be followed by *but*. The gentleman who advocated women's education in Maria Edgeworth's tale pointed out that it was illogical to exclude women from literary studies and then ridicule them for their lack of accomplishments. 'After pointing out all the causes for the inferiority of women in knowledge,' he wrote in his reply, 'you ask for a list of the inventions and discoveries of those who, by your own statement of the question, have not been allowed opportunities for observation.' He polished off his retort by adding: 'With the insulting injustice of an Egyptian task-master, you demand the work, and deny the necessary materials.'[53]

Despite the limitations of formal education, some women privately pursued an intensive self-education. Bluestockings were bookworms. Elizabeth Montagu's busy bookishness led her friends to nickname her Fidget, especially since one night after a ball and still in formal dress she chose to relax by reading the 'Ajax' and the 'Philoctetes' of Sophocles, wrote commentaries on both, then went to bed.

Similarly, after returning from dinner on a spring evening in 1768, Lady Mary Coke wrote in her journal, 'I am now going to read. I laid out yesterday eleven guineas in Books.' Books on prints, history, religion, travel – all lined her shelves; they were passed between friends, or borrowed from the newly established town libraries (the first lending library opened in Liverpool in 1758, with many others opening in the following decades). On a frosty and foggy evening the next January Lady Coke 'read Sherlock upon Providence, & then the fourth volume of Mrs Macaulay's History'. Visiting her friend Lady Charlotte Finch a few months later they 'had some conversation upon Books. She recommended two to me upon religious subjects, I shall send for them to Morrow.' Her appetite for reading was liberally catered for: 'I have laid out in books since I came to Town above fifty Pounds,' she once wrote, but this was by no means unique to her.[54] Some women built up a personal library that became their pride and joy. The writer Charlotte Smith, separated from her philandering husband and economically abandoned by him, regretfully sold her collection of 500 books to help ends meet after single-handedly raising her seven dependent children. And if there was ever any question that they bought without discriminating taste, a London bookseller could settle that. 'There are some thousands of women, who frequent my shop,' reported James Lackington in 1791, 'that know as well what books to choose, and are all well acquainted with works of taste and genius, as any gentlemen in the kingdom, notwithstanding they sneer against novel readers.'[55]

By the century's end, women's learnedness and measure of accomplishment could be related to various educational systems. 'I have had so strange an education,' wrote Lady Holland (formerly Lady Webster), 'that if I speak freely upon sacred subjects it is not from an affectation of being an *esprit fort* [freethinker], but positively because I have no prejudices to combat with.' Holland's education was self-directed.

> My principles were of my own finding, both religious and moral, for I never was instructed in abstract or practical religion, and as soon as I could think at all chance directed my studies; for though both my parents were as good and as virtuous people as ever breathed, and I was always an only child, yet I was entirely left, not from system, but from fondness and inactivity, to follow my own bent.

She could have lived a life of idleness but, she declared, a quest for knowledge and intellectual improvement guided her course. 'Happily for me I devoured books, and a desire for information became my ruling passion.' But with contemporary prescriptions for educational conduct, such a Rousseauvian route as hers was not recommended. 'The experiment of leaving a child without guidance or advice is a dangerous one, and ought never to be done; for if parents will not educate it themselves they should seek for those that will.' As a twenty-seven-year-old, she continued to voraciously devour books. In late June 1798 she recorded in her diary:

> I have read since Xmas the D[uke] of Marlbro's *Apology*, Burnet's *History*, ye *XIII. Satire of Juvenal*, Hearne's *Travels into N. America*, Smith on ye figure and complexion of ye human species, Bancroft on dying, some desultory chemistry, *Roderick Random*, *Lazarillo de Tormes*, Leti's

Life of Sixtus V., various German and French plays, novels, and trash, Cook's *Third Voyage*, Wolf's *Ceylon*, part of Ulloa's *Voyage*, and some papers in ye memoirs of ye Exeter Society. Frequent dippings into Bayle, Montaigne, La Fontaine, Ariosto. Read ye three first books of Tasso; Ld. Orford's works.[56]

A good start for 1798, but by the early nineteenth century other budding intellects were already lost in the growing libraries. The national library at the British Museum (which, under the privilege of copyright deposit, acquired a copy of every work printed in the United Kingdom – a privilege vested to this day) was the most over-whelming. By 1811, Princess Charlotte's companion, Lady Charlotte Bury, accompanied a royal entourage to the Museum, and was taken aback by the staggering display of bound knowledge. 'I was interested in walking through the magnificent library, and in looking at the statues; yet whenever I view these collections my mind is depressed,' she confessed in her journal.

> I devoured with greedy eyes the outside of the volumes, and wished – oh! how vainly – that their contents were stored in my brain. A whole life of learned labour would not suffice for that; what chance have I then, in the middle of my days [she was thirty-six], of accomplishing such a wish?

In a further self-effacing tone, she lamented that 'I shall leave nothing to excite one emulative sigh when I am gone! I shall die, and nothing will tell of my existence!' In fact, the next year she began writing, and left numerous novels and her *Diary* published for posterity.[57]

It was not uncommon for women to express feelings of frustration in their intellectual stagnation and the desire to inquire into new forms of knowledge. Elizabeth Wynne, who on her seventeenth birthday reflected on her accomplishments thus far in life, determined she wanted to be 'more philosophical'.[58] Attaining this goal might involve learning a science. Lady Holland recorded in her diary her perusal of chemistry books, but pursuing natural history more generally was a prevailing fashion for women as much as for men. In the 1780s

Mary Hamilton – the niece of the British Ambassador and dilettante collector of antiquities, Sir William Hamilton – spent time with the bluestocking Mary Delany. Together they 'arranged a Glass Cabinet of fossils, Spas & Minerals for her, she gave me a few specimens'.[59] While most societies and institutes were open to men-only membership, by the early nineteenth century lectures in various subjects of natural philosophy were offered to women in private homes or, in some examples, public forums. The Royal Institution, founded in 1799, quickly attracted curious people 'of the first rank and talent – the literary and the scientific, the practical and the theoretical, bluestockings and women of fashion; the old and the young, all crowded – eagerly crowded – the lecture room'.[60] Lady Holland, however, was unimpressed – dismissing the Royal Institution as 'a very bad imitation of the *Institut* at Paris; hitherto there is only one Professor, who is a jack-of-all-trades, as he lectures alike upon chemistry and shipbuilding'.[61]

Here again the Continent provided more inspiring examples of learning for women. Italy was famous for having at least one noted scientifically learned woman in its cultured cities, such as Laura Bassi, professor of Newtonian physics and mathematics in Bologna; Maria Gaetana Agnesi, mathematician in Milan; and Cristina Roccati, tutor in physics to the patricians in the Veneto. Women were featured as interlocutors in popular scientific pedagogical tracts from Fontenelle's *Conversations on the Plurality of Worlds* (1686) to Francesco Algarotti's *Dialogo sopra l'ottica neutoniana* [*Newtonianism for Ladies*, 1737], to Giuseppe Compagnoni's *La chimica per le dame* [*Chemistry for Ladies*, 1796]. They were also respected translators of scientific treatises, including Guiseppa Eleonora Barbapiccola's 1722 translation of Descartes's *Principles of Philosophy* or Emilie du Châtelet, whose acclaimed translation of Newton's *Principia* was published in France in 1759.[62]

Despite Lady Holland's criticisms, public science lectures in Britain, such as those offered at century's end at the Royal Institution, introduced women to new realms of exploration, inspiring some – such as Maria Jacson, Jane Marcet, or Rebecca Delvalle – to write what became immensely popular catechisms on subjects including botany, chemistry and mineralogy. The late-eighteenth- and nine-teenth-century marketplace for such books provided unprecedented opportunities for women to pursue enlightened subjects. It was not unknown for these educational books to make it on to the recommended list in reformed systems of education for women. Erasmus Darwin, grandfather of Charles, suggested Maria Jacson's *Botanical Dialogues* as part of his *Plan for the Conduct of Female Education* (1797), an author also recommended by the Edgeworths in their *Practical Education* (1798).[63] Some of these were approached with caution, and sometimes confusion. Upon reading that 'every well educated person is expected to know the Botanical names of plants', Maria Edgeworth's American friend Rachel Lazarus wrote to her asking whether the great educational theorist thought 'that Latin ought to form a part of female education', since, of course, botanical nomenclature was in the scientific language of Latin.[64] Intriguingly, Maria Edgeworth remained silent on this question.

Central to the issue of women's educational development was the question: how could women learn, but remain feminine? How were they to engage with men, but not be too 'public' or too aggressive about it? The message of James Fordyce's *Sermons to Young Women* (1766) lingered in inquiring minds: women should not let 'education' lead them to 'display' themselves publicly or lead them to aspire 'to shine anywhere but in [their] proper sphere'.[65] The learned woman was expected to maintain her 'femininity' but learn in the 'masculine' style. Hannah More's father dealt with the 'problem' of her aptitude for mathematics by halting her lessons in that unwaveringly masculine field. Ironically, Fordyce's words were echoed in Hannah More's first play *The Search after Happiness*, where one character advises a female friend to rein in her intellectual ambitions, 'for a woman shines but in her proper sphere'.[66] Such censures led to a culture in which women chose to conceal their personal achievements.

Sarah Dickenson, writing to Mary Hamilton (also a friend of Hannah More's), understood the problem. She admired Hamilton for spending her 'whole time in the Improvement of your Mind', and doing it with enough humility to preserve her from pedantry, a characteristic which is the cause 'why a wise Woman is in general disliked'.

> The Men wou'd have no Rivals in Knowledge & are very angry at every Woman who shall attain it, but the truth is, our Sex are very apt to be *proud* of what they know, & *this* is the true cause, why we are despised.[67]

But Mary Hamilton took heed to her insight. A year later Mary, then sixteen, cautiously decided to let her cousin and guardian, William Napier, in on a closely guarded secret: she was studying Latin. 'I thank you for your *Secret* & be assured I'll keep it to myself,' he reassured her, 'tho I own had you asked my advice . . . I should most certainly have persuaded you *not* to do it.' He knew her better than to presume she would stop. Therefore he wrote: 'I beg you will keep it a dead secret from your most intimate friends, as well as from the rest of the World, as a Lady's being learned is commonly looked on as a great fault – even by the learned.' But why, Napier wondered, could she possibly want to learn Latin? In ages not too long past, any proficiency in the language shown by women was a sign of demonic possession. And, Napier pointed out, it was reserved for 'what is called the learned Professions' of divinity and medicine, '& all the books in that language, proper for your reading, (as many are very improper for Ladies) are translated into English'.[68]

Just as the content of books written in learned Latin was deemed 'improper' for ladies, so the study of foreign languages could create an undesirable, unpatriotic and cosmopolitan mentality. Despite the fashion in the eighteenth century to engage with the arts and literature of European nations (particularly France), there nevertheless remained an underlying anxiety about Britain's cultural pre-eminence in relation to her continental neighbours. This sometimes led to the suppression of foreign influences and the encouragement of the view that 'home was best'. Just as Napier hoped that Mary Hamilton would settle for books translated into English, others similarly wished that gentlewomen would prefer England to *anything* else. Increasing one's linguistic skills could be interpreted as a symptom of over-fondness for foreign life, and cultivating such desires was therefore more comfortably pursued in private.

Some women, however, dared not to be so secretive. The bluestocking Anne Damer (née Conway), Mary Berry's closest friend who resided in Lisbon, wrote to Mary congratulating her on her linguistic skills, 'I rejoice that you follow your Latin so closely.' Anne Damer was of the opinion that her friend's proficiency in Latin would equip her with a new ability to expand her taste for literature, particularly the classics, which few people understood properly. 'Many *construe* Homer, Virgil, Plato, and Cicero, but few read them. With your taste,' Damer continued, 'this will be a constant source to you even of something more than amusement.'[69] Cornelia Knight (later companion to Princess Charlotte) recollected that when she was growing up in Neufchâteau, in the Champagne region of France, an 'excellent master', Monsieur Petitpierre, 'taught me French, Latin, the elements of Greek, and of the mathematics, with geography and history'.[70] Near contemporaries of Hester Piozzi (dubbed the 'light blue stocking' by later biographers) openly admired and sometimes exaggerated her linguistic prowess. 'She not only read and wrote Hebrew, Greek, and Latin,' wrote the Revd Edward Mangin in 1833, twelve years after her death, 'but had for sixty years constantly and ardently studied the Scriptures and the works of commentators in the original languages.'[71]

By the early nineteenth century, some women had created strict regimens for intellectual improvement. The following week's 'plan for the improvement of time' was arranged specifically for the winter season by Margaret Gray, from a humble York family whose parents were devotees of Hannah More's writings.

MONDAY
Prayers a quarter before eight. Breakfast at a quarter past eight. Read Psalms etc. At half past nine go to Mrs. L. [for French, Italian, Drawing] until one. Walk until half past two, if fine (if not read and work). Read till dinner time (quarter before four). Music from five until tea-time

(quarter past six). In the evening music working and reading.

TUESDAY
Read Psalms etc. Italian till eleven. Music and reading until one. Walk till half past two. Read till dinner-time. Music from five till tea-time. Evening as usual.

WEDNESDAY
Dr. C. [for music lessons] from a quarter past nine till ten. Read Psalms etc. From half past ten till twelve, Mrs. L. Read till one, and from half-past two till dinner-time. Music after dinner, Church at seven. From eight, reading and working as usual.

THURSDAY
Psalms etc. Italian, Music. Read and work till one. Tracts. Walk. Read from half past two until dinner-time. Music from five till tea-time. Evening as usual.

FRIDAY
Psalms etc. Mrs. L. from half-past nine till one. Walk till half-past two. Read till dinner. Music as usual; after tea read and work.

SATURDAY
Read Psalms etc. Dr. C. from a quarter before ten to half-past. Italian. Miss D. [collecting for Church Mission-ary Society] from eleven till twelve. Italian till one or half-past. Walk till half-past two. Read. After dinner, music. Evening as before.

She continued her schedule with her 'plans for reading at present':

HISTORICAL
An hour in a morning, read Prideaux' 'Connections' to myself.

INTELLECTUAL
In an evening, and at other times when practicable, read Watt's 'Improvement' to my mother.
For miscellaneous reading, Jowett's 'Researches in Syria'.

And in religion, Chalmers, and Thomas A. Kempis, (French).

For ornamental reading, one has always both time and inclination.

Practice Music at least one hour a day. Singing about half an hour.[72]

Such repertoires were not unique amongst bluestockings, and as this schedule shows, learning languages was increasingly routine. Nevertheless, learning languages as an educational ideal for women in this period was considered problematic. Both sexes aspired to be 'accomplished' and 'perfected'; but for women, accomplishing too much betrayed their 'politeness', virtue and 'sensibility'.[73] Over-education led to lewdness in the 'weaker' sex; bluestockings, therefore, attempted to scotch such suspicions by turning learned women into paradigms of moral probity and virtuosity.[74] But would that work, if, for example, they advocated proficiency in French – the tongue of a country with (it was alleged) a lack of morals?

Some, such as Hester Chapone, thought not. In 1773, she was of the opinion that 'dancing and the knowledge of the French tongue are now so universal, that they cannot be dispensed with in the education of a gentlewoman'.[75] French remained a language that was associated with attempts to emulate the Parisian salon – a culture synonymous with pre-revolutionary political rantings and with women exposing the bare bones of their philosophical radicalism to the *haute bourgeoisie*. Even if British women were not tarred by such associations, fluency in foreign languages might indicate something worse: a lack of national pride and an unhealthy interest in continental customs and points of view.

If learning languages led to problems associated with cosmopolitanism, just as women were supposedly not 'strong' enough to learn mathematics, science, or other masculine subjects, what of pursuing knowledge about the Continent through direct experience? Mary Wollstonecraft had no such qualms. Through travel she felt she could shrug off the burdens of decorum, her critics, and her failed love affairs. Educational writings were vague on the purpose and benefits of travel.

Therefore travelling abroad had to be approached with caution, lest such adventures were associated with some form of impropriety.

Travel did not, for instance, rate highly in Hannah More's view of an improved system for educating women. Even though she was writing with 'a view to domestic instruction' for the 'middling sorts', the occasional reference to 'the higher walks of life' reveal what she thought of the over-inflated sensation of 'seeing the world'.

> Even the children of better families, who are well instructed when at their studies, are yet at other times continually beholding the WORLD set up in the highest and most advantageous point of view. Seeing the world! knowing the world! standing well in the world! making a figure in the world! is spoken of as including the whole sum and substance of human advantages.[76]

Aspiring to experience 'the world' for character-building was symptomatic of vapid ambition or misadventure. For More, 'knowing the world' was 'to know its emptiness, its vanity, its futility, and its wickedness', it was to 'despise it', and in this view, 'an obscure Christian in a village may be said to know it better than a hoary courtier or wily politician'.[77] She feared that travelling to foreign countries would corrupt morals and lead to impiety. France, its 'infidels' such as 'Voltaire and his associates' whose 'grand aim' was to 'destroy the principles of Christianity in this island', was particularly dangerous.[78]

Yet others learned to compare what they saw of educational systems at work in other countries with their own ideals. Mary Berry, for example, was critical of the misdirected exercises for the mind in post-revolutionary France and closely allied regions, which she visited (for the fourth time in twenty years) during the Peace of Amiens, in 1803. Mary Berry's comments are laced with her distaste for revolutionary politics. Did the French or their sympathisers comprehend the goals they were fighting to achieve?, she wondered.

The problem with the French Revolution, she thought, was that it relied upon an 'impossible combination' of combat (which led to 'idle profligacy in manners') and well-ordered liberty (maintained by a new government). Somewhere buried within this was supposed to be the improvement of one's mind and morals. Unhappily the revolutionary spirit appeared to her to have adversely affected life in Switzerland (at this time a confederation of which Napoleon was named protector), whose residents 'looked up to the French as their models in everything'. She was disappointed by Lausanne, where she thought the frequent passage of French troops had corrupted the Swiss character. The men forgot about their trades, abandoned their shops, and 'loitered about in groups, talking the politics of their country'. The women were equally idle: they entirely missed the philosophical point about freedom and fraternity for citizens, which embraced intellectual equality. The women 'consider *liberty and equality* as an equal right for everyone to read *novels from morning till night, which they do,* from the lowest *servante* to the first *citoyenne* in the town'. She reckoned that such hollow works were all that must be available. The cost of war exhausted the potential for printing good works, and books brought in from Paris were morally bankrupt. 'Impoverished by their revolution', decent works were yet another casualty of war. With no intellectual order, reading itself could be hazardous to health. 'If ever anything could persuade one to consider being taught to read as a disadvantage to the lower order of people,' Mary Berry concluded, 'it would be here, from the often vile, and always absurd, use which is made of it.'[79]

Lack of direction in reading was like travelling without a map. After filling in some casual hours reading, Lady Holland reprimanded herself for her lack of intellectual discipline. 'I have been reading French literature of a desultory sort and in a desultory way, both pernicious to the mind,' she wrote. She was convinced that reading improper literature – particularly French novels – damaged her memory and destroyed her powers of understanding, presumably fearing the inevitable consequences of confusing literary fiction with historical fact. An action that was frequently taken to guard against such misinterpretations of literary content was for women to read aloud to others, where correct meanings of the text could be derived through consensus, or to be read to by a man, who could censure the inappropriate parts.[80] 'I can speak from experience,' Lady Holland continued

– somewhat betraying her own claim to intellectual instability – 'as I have completely obscured my faculty by too great an avidity to read, or, rather, devour books, without any method in my pursuits.' As evidence of her lack of 'method' in satisfying her craving to read, she later scribbled how she managed to squeeze into her busy schedule 'half of Bernier's *Travels into Hindostan*, and about as much of Pennant's *Hindostan*, a part of a great work called *Outlines of the Globe*.'[81]

Clamping down on reading travel literature was akin to preventing one from preparing for the beginning of a journey. Mary Berry complained about the lot of women, like herself, whose wealth and ability afforded them the means of attaining intellectual distinction, but they were forbidden to do so by social convention. Girls were either sent to boarding school or, depending on the family's wealth, were educated at home by a governess. However, the encounter with 'formal' education was altogether too brief. 'Our education (if education it can be called) is nearly ended by the time that our minds begin to open and to be really eager for information,' Mary Berry wrote (in a letter to a male friend). 'When you men are sent to college we are left (such of us as are not obliged to gain our bread, or to mend our clothes) to positive idleness, without any object, end or aim to encourage any one employment of our mind more than another.' This was the bitter bone of contention: women were led to the fireside at the age when men had the world opened up to them.

This, for Berry, was also ironic: the natural abilities of men and women were in her mind suited for role reversals. Women, being more creative than men, should be encouraged to explore, whereas men were suited to solitary activities in their studies. 'Our imaginations are naturally more lively than yours,' she wrote, 'our powers of steady attention, I think less than yours. What would you have us do?' A rhetorical question. She knew that books were their only resources. As Maria Edgeworth's correspondent in *Literary Ladies* (in favour of women's education) pointed out:

> Women begin to taste the pleasures of reading, and the
> best authors in the English language are their amusement,
> just at the age when young men, disgusted by their studies,

begin to be ashamed of alluding to literature amongst their companions. Travelling, lounging, field sports, gaming, and what is called pleasure in various shapes, usually fill the interval between quitting the university and settling for life'[82]

Like Lady Holland, Mary Berry was aware that 'desultory reading during the first years of (mental) life does often much mischief', and thus was a waste of time. In this context reading could only be good for one thing for women: it could be counted upon as a resource 'in those days when the attractions of the world and of society fade as much in *our* eyes, as our attractions fade in *theirs*'.[83]

For Mary women's 'marketability' for marriage was as short-lived as their formal education.[84] Perhaps that contributed to the antagonism felt towards the idea that women should travel before marriage, and then, maybe, with their husbands (unless, like Maria Edgeworth, the woman was taken abroad by her father in the hope of marrying her off).[85] But Mary Berry was not to be confined by the mechanisms of the marriage market, and her views on educational development and intellectual maturity would be forever tied to her commitment – and opportunity she created for herself – to travel.

The expanding world of print had allowed greater access to books which helped broaden women's intellectual horizons. Besides the first-hand accounts or letters from correspondents on the Continent, travel books were also widely used as sources of information about life abroad. Read aloud or in private, passed around to friends or discussed at parties, such books were a genre of 'useful knowledge' that could both educate and entertain – so long as one clearly understood the messages that were legitimately to be taken away from the text. Cornelia Knight, for example, suspected that a book she read when she was young, the *Voyage en Italie*, written by the French astronomer (and later director of the Paris observatory) Jérôme-Lefrançois de Lalande and criticised by a Venetian senator as an inadequate description, did not meet the standards of John Eustace's

A Tour through Italy (1813). Seemingly a straightforward enough assessment, until we realise that the books in question were written by authors with unconventional motives for writing, and which, according to some contemporaries, were corrupt.

Lalande's *Voyage* was part of a scientific campaign that used archae-ology and history to inspect antiquity and to demonstrate 'scientifi-cally' France's superior understanding of ancient culture.[86]

Eustace's *Tour through Italy* was likewise written to expand the increasing stock of knowledge relating to antiquity gathered from new finds which the *English* could boast as their own superior know-ledge. But there was a problem. Eustace was a Roman Catholic, writing about a Catholic country, therefore he needed to allay poten-tial criticism of this lethal combination by stressing that his aim in publishing his book was to support the ideals of a liberal education. He wrote for an audience (albeit mainly Protestant) that he assumed would be preconditioned with a proper education to understand the technical dimension of his research. 'As these pages are addressed solely to persons of a liberal education,' he wrote, offering his clearly masculine readership a bit of laconic advice, 'it is almost needless to recommend the Latin Poets and Historians.'[87]

Science and politics, national identity, ancient languages, religious toleration – these subjects, which were interwoven into travel narra-tives – were not 'feminine', nor considered appropriate points of contemplation for women. 'To read,' warned Edmund Burke, the leading critic of the French Revolution, 'is to lay oneself open to . . . Contagion.' What might look educational and innocent enough might in fact be infected with infidel messages. They could lead the inquiring pupil to a world of blasphemy and unbelief. Who would suspect the potential for 'destruction which lurks under the harmless or instructive names of *General History, Natural History, Travels, Voyages, Lives, Encyclopaedias, Criticism* and *Romance*'? asked Hannah More, later dismissing the growing fad for anything foreign by advis-ing that 'Religion is our Compass'.[88]

The irreligious stench that was released from such writings was contagious. Foreign philosophy was a vehicle for vice, and it was not only the French one should fear. 'Listen to the precepts of the new German enlighteners,' she continued, displaying her own disbelief at their secular assertions, 'and you need no longer remain in that situation in which Providence has placed you!' Countries close to home were known for their heathenish immorality, but who knew what was concealed in farthest corners of the world? Lest the developing intellect be exposed to uncensored accounts, More sternly advised her pupils to 'guard against a too implicit belief in the flattering accounts which some voyage-writers are fond of exhibiting of the virtue, amiableness, and benignity of some of the countries newly discovered by our circumnavigators . . .' Such accounts were prone to mislead or confound the imagination, leading to the over-excitement of young women's intellectual passions. Instead, she should be taught 'that human life is not a splendid romance, spangled over with brilliant adventures, and enriched with extraordinary occurrences, and diversified with wonderful incidents'; in short, More recommended she learn 'that human life is a true history, many passages of which will be dull, obscure, and uninteresting'.[89]

Priscilla Wakefield, a travel writer for children, took a different view. Her *Family Tour through the British Empire*, published in 1804, was written to provide pupils with a range of useful information about distant parts of the British empire, such as topography, manufacturing and customs. Was such information legitimate for these budding intellects? A contributor to the *Imperial Review* was happy to report that the 'fair author' took care 'to avoid every thing that might excite improper ideas' in the youths' minds, and allowed that the book could therefore be 'safely recommended' to them.[90]

Less 'misleading' or exciting, perhaps, but nonetheless not for women's indulgence was the professional world. Both Lalande and Eustace took for granted that scholars reading their works would know Latin and Greek.[91] With such warrant, it is clear that travel books often required more than reading through a record of distances between towns or a listing of scenic sites. Most travel books were laden with the political or scientific interests of the author, at times making them controversial reads, and more often written for a masculine audience. What seems more intriguing, however, is that Cornelia Knight was not unique for being a woman reader of such travel books. Thus, despite concerns about the content of travel literature and it being a genre ostensibly geared to supplement a gentleman's 'liberal education', women were also avid readers in this field. And they increasingly took to the field in much more resolute ways than mere reading allowed.

'The real subject of my journey'

Liberty & Independence

*We had a very pleasant journey together, and find
'tis possible to travel comfortably without that
lordly person – Man!*
    Anne Donnellan, referring to her continental
     travels with Anne Pitt, 1739,
     in a letter to Elizabeth Robinson
      (later Montagu)

E DUCATED WOMEN often either cultivated their talents privately and secretly, or risked ridicule by priggish critics who saw women's forays into the masculine world of intellectual discourse as an affront to polite feminine etiquette. The road to enlightened improvement for men was expected to involve university education and continental travel; for women, it involved bible study and child-rearing. Women were educated and raised to be companions, not connoisseurs; they were ideally suited to complement men, not compete with them.

However, social conventions were not always strong enough to contain certain individuals. Some women's radical attempts to assert their independence – in terms of their intellectual as well as cultural conduct – left them castigated as outcasts; others chose to leave Britain and live on the Continent. Mary Wollstonecraft is a good example of the more extreme case. 'You know,' she wrote to her sister, 'I am not born to tread in the beaten track.' Turning on her heel she determined to write what she wanted and travel where she desired.[1] Others had less outspoken, but equally dedicated, commitments to break loose from domestic unhappiness.

Wollstonecraft picked apart the easy assumptions made about women as 'naturally' different from men – physically weaker, possessing reproductive functions, and so on – and the alleged associated characteristics of weak minds and 'natural' social inferiority. She dismissed as irrelevant the Rousseauvian images of natural woman since society was not primitive but civil.

It appeared to Wollstonecraft that to be a civilised woman meant no more than conforming to the limitations on intellectual development and social interaction set by conduct books, fathers and husbands. 'Civilised women are, therefore, so weakened by false refinement, that, respecting morals, their condition is much below what it would be were they left in a state nearer to nature.'[2] In other words, given the artificiality of the construction of the 'civilised' woman, which was equivalent to how they were ideologically constructed as proper wives, women were morally worse off than if they were in the Rousseauvian 'natural', 'primitive', or uncivilised (pre-ideologically constructed) state. Women, in short, were not constructing *their own* images of what being a civilised woman, or a 'companion', meant for themselves.

Unlike the writer of advice books John Gregory, for one example, who was unsettled by the apparent tendency of companions and wives to become 'less amiable women', Wollstonecraft condemned the notion of the 'amiable woman' as exactly that which degraded their social position. Could there not be an 'amiable female companion'? She knew that the common answer to that question was that men saw women who sought to be intellectual companions as indulging in intellectual liberties – 'liberties to do wrong', as Maria Edgeworth quipped. Rousseau, whom Wollstonecraft cited, shared the same sentiment: give women the right to reason, and they will abuse it; 'women have, or ought to have, but little liberty; they are apt to indulge themselves excessively in what is allowed them. Addicted in everything to extremes, they are even more transported at their diversions than boys.'[3] In Wollstonecraft's view, women had as much right to liberty as men, and developing their own faculties for reason and intellect paved their road to Enlightenment. 'Reason is,' she wrote, 'the simple power of improvement; or, more properly speaking, of discerning truth.'[4] If one only recognised that there was nothing 'natural' about the position of women, and that their 'civil' self was, as she said, 'arbitrary', then they could learn to effect change.

Who was to provide the model for change? Wollstonecraft provided one answer. Establishing a new civil woman meant reforming the concept of 'mutual esteem', and she recommended that change be swift and decisive. 'It is time to effect a revolution in female manners – time to restore them to their lost dignity,' she wrote; women needed to take on the task of 'reforming themselves to reform the world'.[5] Women at the highest levels of society, the women of fashion, who were as subject to social constrictions as others, needed to act: 'It is a melancholy truth; yet such is the blessed effect of civilisation! the most respectable women are the most oppressed; and, unless they have understandings far superior to the common run of understandings, taking in both sexes, they must, from being treated like contemptible beings, become contemptible.'[6] For inspiration, one could look to the Continent. 'In France or Italy, have the women confined themselves to domestic life?' No. And in such places there were further lessons to be learned about self-improvement and social emancipation.[7]

Mary Wollstonecraft's commitment to the principle of 'rational love' had left her stranded outside the marital ties surrounding the object of her desire, the artist Henry Fuseli, and his wife, who in 1792 rejected Wollstonecraft's suggestion of a *ménage à trois*. 'I intend no longer to struggle with a rational desire,' she wrote to Fuseli's friend William Roscoe, referring to the failed relationship, 'so have determined to set out for Paris in the course of a fortnight or three weeks.'[8]

A journey to France had for some time been on her mind, and the fact that she went alone was a realisation of years of longing for 'independence'. Her father had squandered away his inheritance, and his extravagance had destroyed any chance of social improvement for her family. When Mary was eighteen she left home and gained employment in 1778 as lady companion to a Mrs Dawson in Bath; she then became a seamstress, and four years later she opened a school in Islington with her sister and two friends. At the age of twenty-six she became a governess to the Lord and Lady Kingsborough's children in Ireland. That same year, 1786, she wrote her first book, *Thoughts on the Education of Daughters*, published by her new friend, the radical publisher Joseph Johnson; who just over two years later also published Wollstonecraft's first novel: *Mary: a Fiction*.

Thus, in a dynamic decade, Wollstonecraft had pursued about as many respectable jobs as a middle-class woman could have in the eighteenth century. She also provided personal support for her dying mother and friends with troubled marriages, while creating a career for herself as an author.[9] 'In the course of near nine-and-twenty years, I have gathered some experience, and felt many severe disappointments – and what is the amount?' she wrote to Joseph Johnson. 'I long for a little peace and *independence*!,' she cried.[10]

Independence she shortly received when Lady Kingsborough dismissed her from her position as governess. Earlier that summer she had been 'trying to persuade Lady K[ingsborough] to go to the Continent but am afraid she will not'. This had frustrated Mary, who wrote to her sister ridiculing the mentality of her employer: 'You cannot conceive my dear Girl the dissipated lives the women of quality lead.'[11] The year after her dismissal, Mary was still committed to the idea. 'I am studying French,' she wrote to that same sister who was at that time residing in Paris,

> and wish I had the opportunity of conversing indeed, if I ever have any money to spare to gratify myself, I will certainly visit France, it has long been a desire floating in my brain, that even hope has not given *consistency* to; and yet it does not evaporate.[12]

Meanwhile Mary remained committed to working towards higher levels of self-education and intellectual enlightenment. 'While I live, I am persuaded, I must exert my understanding to procure an independence, and render myself useful,' she wrote to Joseph Johnson, while working on a translation of a German text. 'To make the task easier, I ought to store my mind with useful knowledge.'[13] 'So the author of the Rights of Woman is going to France!,' wrote one of Mary's sisters to another, not concealing her annoyance at her neophyte sister's virile ambitions. 'Well, in spite of Reason' – of course, meaning that most masculine of traits – 'when Mrs W reached the Continent she will be but a woman.'[14]

Wollstonecraft's notoriety as an author was fast soaring to the heights occupied by such famous radicals as William Godwin and Thomas Paine. Her *Rights of Woman*, while not selling at the rate of some of her contemporaries (only a few thousand copies sold in the first five years, compared to Hannah More's *Strictures on Female Education* which sold over 10,000 copies within its first three years), nonetheless attracted much attention, and was quickly translated into German and French, and published in Paris and Lyons.[15] Mary felt her moment of independence had arrived (though, indebted to a host of creditors, not quite yet 'very flush with money', as she put it). As William Godwin wrote, in his *Memoirs of the Author of a Vindication of the Rights of Woman* (1798), she 'conceived it necessary to snap the chain of this association [with Henry Fuseli] in her mind; and, for that purpose, determined to seek a new climate, and mingle in difference scenes'.[16] She borrowed some money from her sisters and set off for Paris.[17]

Despite all the mutations of the body politic in revolutionary France, Mary Wollstonecraft found that upon her arrival Paris seemed tranquil, reaffirming her regard for the country. 'All the affection I have for the French is for the whole nation,' she wrote to a friend. And even if the Parisian streets were neglected and too filthy for her to walk for fresh air, this did not lessen her opinion of the people. 'I am almost overwhelmed with civility here, and have even met with more than civility.'[18]

Part of her appreciation of civil society was her intellectual involvement with those engaged in national reforms. For example, she mentioned that she was 'writing a plan of education for the Committee appointed to consider that subject'.[19] What might have been 'more than civil' was the love affair she had just begun with the American entrepreneur Gilbert Imlay.

Before leaving for Paris, Mary had chaffed that while there she 'might take a husband for the time being, and get divorced when my truant heart longed again to nestle with its old friends'.[20] Her sudden relationship with Imlay went some way towards satisfying this scheme. In contrast to the 'rational' love she achieved with Fuseli, she now indulged in pure desire. 'I obey an emotion of my heart,' she wrote in a night-time love note to Imlay.[21] And such emotions would become a motive force directing her future travels, written about in her *Letters* from Scandinavia.

We must leave Mary Wollstonecraft in Paris for the moment.[22] Thus far she had shown that she was prepared to take her own advice and liberate herself from conventional society. Her 'advice', of course, was far from the standard eighteenth-century prescriptions for the behaviour of women. Feminine passivity, moral probity, courtesy and companionship were characteristics expected in women in the domestic sphere. But such confines had already driven some women out of the country. As Hester Piozzi stated: 'Tis more Sullenness towards one's Own Country than delight in any other that makes People ever contented in a foreign Nation – supposing equal Degrees of Kindness, who would not prefer that of their native Land?'[23]

'Most *men* are commonly destined to some profession,' stated Hannah More, in her explanation of what she thought women of the middling ranks could do with their lives. 'The profession of ladies, to which the bent of *their* instruction should be turned, is that of daughters, wives, mothers, and mistresses of families.' There were certain appropriate ideas, habits and principles with which women should, she felt, be acquainted to prepare for such roles. For

> when a man of sense comes to marry, it is a companion
> whom he wants, and not an artist . . . it is a being who
> can comfort and counsel him; one who can reason, and
> reflect, and feel, and judge, and act, and discourse, and
> discriminate; one who can assist him in his affairs, lighten
> his cares, soothe his sorrows, purify his joys, strengthen
> his principles, and educate his children.[24]

And if the woman happened to have any unique talents, that was a bonus, so long as they did not interfere with the rest of her 'professional' duties.

Middle-class women in the eighteenth century were caught between a world of particular duties and obligations and the idealisation that all women shared universal traits and characteristics of intellectual potential and spiritual purity. Each woman was required to adapt immediately to the tastes and circumstances of their husband's world. Women needed to be 'particular' enough to engage with one man often chosen for them, while the universalist ideal cast women as possessing characters adaptable to whoever she may end up with. Thus, any woman, as long as she was of acceptable birth and social status, was potentially fit for any particular man, but once married, she needed to become specifically suited to that individual. A successfully accommodating wife effortlessly danced to her husband's tune, as apparently did James Boswell's:

> I know or fancy that there are qualities and *compositions of qualities* (to talk in musical metaphor) which in the course of our lives appear to me in her, that please me more than what I have perceived in any other woman, and which I cannot separate from her identity.[25]

However, women were not supposed to dance with spirit, but to bury their emotions, as Boswell's wife must have done when overlooking his incessant infidelity. Much more widespread, however, was the unhappiness caused by 'mercenary marriages', where women were contracted to a gentleman specifically to promote economic welfare. The most many women could hope for was the respect or esteem of their husbands rather than love. Mistresses were commonplace for men, and women were powerless to complain about infidelity or even certain degrees of physical abuse. If a woman had an extra-marital affair, however, that was grounds for divorce, and, equally damaging, social ostracism. But some fortunate women managed to find a more acceptable path to emancipation.

In the eighteenth-century notion of 'companionship', women were specially prepared for positions that earned a wage – such as being employed as a lady companion or, more prestigiously, a lady of the royal court;[26] women were also groomed to be companions in order to make them more pleasant wives.

Companionship was made to order. Advice books recommended that women, not knowing what interests their future husbands might pursue, should not overly concentrate on one area of 'self-fashioning'. As Maria Edgeworth acerbically pointed out in her *Letters for Literary Ladies*, 'No woman can foresee what may be the taste of the man with whom she may be united; much of her happiness, however, will depend on her being able to conform her taste to his: for this reason I should therefore, in female education, cultivate the general powers of the mind, rather than any particular faculty.'[27] Thus women were forbidden to excel in any one area for fear they become over-intellectualised and strong-headed companions. If the wife was not to become too particular in her own tastes, she could not distinguish herself intellectually – nor stand out as a pioneer or excel in a career. A professional wife knew how to adapt to changing circumstances and how to manage a diversified household.

She also followed her husband's lead, was able to converse unidioti-cally on a range of subjects and listen sympathetically to her spouse's problems. A wife should think of herself, advised Hester Chapone, as a friend, since 'marriage [is] the highest state of friendship,' and therefore, 'the qualities requisite in a friend, are still more important in a husband'. Although a woman was deemed capable of choosing her female friends, the choice of a husband was too significant and complicated a decision to be left in her hands, since 'young women know so little of the world, especially of the other sex, and such pains are usually taken to deceive them, that they are every way unqualified to choose for themselves, upon their own judgement'.[28]

So long as the management of marriages was seen as an affair of the mind and not the heart, women had to submit to a chain of command, where their fathers controlled who they married and their husbands decided how they would live.[29] The greatest fiction, women were encouraged to believe, was that marriages were based on love. Never mind what they read in novels. Conduct books cried out that the best a woman could do was to understand the concept of a companionate marriage, to approach her position rationally. 'What-ever romantic notions you may hear, or read of,' warned Hester Chapone, 'depend upon it, those matches are almost always the happi-est which are made upon rational grounds – on suitable character, degree and fortune – on mutual esteem, and the prospect of a real and permanent friendship.'[30]

Happy, companionable marriages of this sort created and reinforced what was regarded as civil society. 'Civilisation', however, was prone to contract diseases, not only in epidemiological, but also ideological terms. As pre-Romantic 'primitivists' such as Jean-Jacques Rousseau suggested, civilisation, with its over-indulgence in luxury, its vices, slovenly habits, and indolence, was by its own construction unhealthy, in contrast to the arduous and pure lifestyles of the 'noble savages' from non-civil society.[31] Lasciviousness, a notoriously unbridled passion of the upper classes, was one disease that threatened the sanctity of civilisation. Whilst the aristocracy could make and play by their own rules, the middle classes were deemed 'uncontrollable'. Promoting rational, friendly companions as spouses was the antidote to this. Lord Hillsborough, speaking in the House of Lords about the Marriage Act of 1753 – designed to eradicate reckless, clandestine marriages – opined that mutual love was certainly 'a very proper ingredient' for a marriage, but it was 'a sedate and fixed love, and not a sudden flash of passion which dazzles the understanding'.[32]

The Enlightenment emphasis on rationalising love thus made marriages of 'mutual esteem' part of the civilising process. The companion or wife was ideally equipped with an impartial, rather than impassioned, view of her domestic circumstance, which embodied the tenets of 'civility'.[33] Women were often cast in this role as if in a proclamation of friendliness and male civility: 'I have always considered your sex, not as domestic drudges, or as the slaves of our pleasures, but as our companions and equals,' wrote John Gregory in his own advice book to women.[34] But Mary Wollstonecraft, for one, was sceptical of such reasoning. Gregory's definition of companionship rendered women unequal to men since being a good companion made them, as he described them, 'less amiable as women', a distinction which Wollstonecraft mobilised against the unwitting author. 'This desire of being always *women*,' she retorted, 'is the very consciousness that degrades the sex.'[35]

The wife, Gregory and Wollstonecraft both agreed, was part of the construction of civil society. But Wollstonecraft's *Vindication of the Rights of Woman*, which she defined as a treatise 'on female rights and manners', called for women to refashion themselves as civil members of society. For her, this meant seeking out the best models of civil society, which she suspected would be found abroad.

To outsiders , the ladies of the royal courts and bedchamber – 'women of fashion' may have had 'liberties' that seemed enviable, but court culture – where rules of etiquette were strictly regulated and enforced – was often disconcertingly claustrophobic. Court nevertheless provided a rare environment in which women from the upper levels of society could be gainfully employed. Ambitious husbands or pressures on the family purse often made it impossible to refuse such offers of employment. The ladies of the bedchamber were among the highest born women in England, and their selection to this position at court added considerable eminence to both the woman's family of birth and the one into which she married. They were adjuncts to the Queen, companions at outings and ornaments to flank royal entourages in public. These were positions of showmanship that carried an annual salary of up to £500, and could lead to other material rewards and privileges for the women themselves and their family and friends. Through royal favour or through contacts with government and court officers who kept company in these prominent social circles, pensions could be secured, new posts assigned, patronage granted, marriages arranged, reputations boosted and recognition gained across Europe.

Many of Queen Charlotte's ladies-in-waiting complained that they were required to relinquish their independence, their 'liberty' as some described it. When in 1761 Princess Charlotte of Mecklenburg-Strelitz moved from Germany to Britain to marry the newly crowned King George III, she acquired a new family. Its members included her ladies-in-waiting: the Duchess of Ancaster (Mary Bertie), Mistress of the Robes and first lady of the Bedchamber; Lady Egremont (Alicia Wyndham); the Duchess of Hamilton (Elizabeth Gunning); Lady

Effingham (Elizabeth Howard); Lady Northumberland (Elizabeth Percy Seymour, later Duchess of Northumberland); Lady Weymouth (Elizabeth Thynne), and Lady Bolingbroke (Diana St John).

Traditionally, court culture was the epitome of ceremonial pomp. Regal splendour was symbolic of national wealth, power and prestige. But after England's Glorious Revolution, with the creation of the constitutional monarchy and the fragmentation of the alliances between political power and royal patronage, court culture began to lose its lustre. Gone were the days when the court was the fount of fashion, grand masques and sexual promiscuity (Charles II in particular was said to have seduced numerous ladies of court). By the reign of Queen Anne (1702–14), court culture was, contemporary consensus confirms, 'dull'.[36]

The Georgian court was no better. Under Queen Charlotte (until her death in 1818), court culture ran on strictly regulated routines and rigid rules. Rather than entertaining and celebrating state affairs in style, the court was aloof from the fashionable world. The assemblies at the Queen's 'Drawing Rooms', the twice-weekly socials at St James's, were less a fête than a customary formality where introductions, a young woman's 'coming out' and polite conversation took place. The staid atmosphere stifled any spirit of gaiety and left the ladies of the bedchamber with less a sense of honour and devotion than one of duty. Lady Egremont considered her position 'a very triste affair', complaining that the women were 'tired of each other's clothes by seeing them so often; that they got by heart everything they wore by sitting in a circle and having nothing else to look at'.[37] Lack of stimulation at court reflected the retired disposition of the royal family. 'The King & Queens manner of life was very methodical & regular,' remembered Lady Northumberland. 'Whenever it was in their power they went to Bed by 11 o'Clock.'[38]

Some ladies of the bedchamber such as Mary Hamilton and Fanny Burney sensed that they were, as Mary Wollstonecraft put it, 'the most oppressed'. They longed to be back outside and part of the intellectual world that stretched beyond the walls of Windsor and St James's, and beyond the Channel. Travel proved much more alluring and educational than court life – whether as an option pursued in place of a position at court (as in the example of Elizabeth Carter, who opted against joining the royal household and travelled to the Continent with her bluestocking friend Elizabeth Montagu), or an activity pursued immediately after leaving court.

In terms of social dynamics and intellectual stimulation, the prim court events paled in comparison with the salons run by the bluestockings. Mary Hamilton ('Hammy' to her friends), upon quitting court as sub-governess to the princesses in 1782, was relieved to reacquaint herself with the bluestocking circle that congregated at Elizabeth Vesey's home. 'I find it is a very agreeable circumstance to live so near the Veseys; their house being exactly opposite, & I have the liberty to go to them whenever I choose,' she wrote in her diary. She went from the stoical and austere court to the variety of society that fit any mood:

> viz: the Learned, the witty, – the old & young, the grave, gay, wise & unwise, the fine bred Man & the pert coxcomb; The elegant female, the chaste Matron, the severe prude, & the pert Miss, but be it remembered that you can run no *risque* in Mrs. Vesey's parties of meeting with those who have no claim to respect, as is too often the case in mixed assemblies in London.[39]

Mary Hamilton finally was able to live a life apparently not amenable to court culture. Even the Queen had recognised (apparently with some regret) that Mary Hamilton 'wished to appear a Bas Bleue (Manqué)'.[40] Mary obviously felt that the hodgepodge company in the salons was more attractive than the personalities at court. Even young George, Prince of Wales (the future King George IV), who at sixteen was enamoured of the twenty-three-year-old Hammy, had failed to seduce her. This was despite his flattering compliments to her ('I see Beauty, Person, accomplishments, every thing in Short in you, that could make my life happy'), and his flattering description of himself. Writing in the 'impartial' third person, he saw himself as:

now approaching ye bloom of youth, he is rather above ye common size, his limbs well-proportioned, & upon ye whole well made, tho' rather too great a penchant to grow fat, ye features of his Countenance are strong & manly, tho' they carry with them too much of an air of hauteur, his forehead well shaped, his eyes tho' none of ye best, & tho' grey are yet passable, tolerable good eyebrows, & eyelashes, ... a good mouth tho' rather large, with fine teeth, a tolerable good chin, but ye whole of ye Countenance is too round. I forgot to add my ugly ears.[41]

He also later confessed that he was 'rather too fond of Wine & Women', and soon gave up his pursuit of Mary Hamilton in favour of the Drury Lane actress, Mary Robinson (who managed to procure a promissory note for £20,000 payable when the Prince came of age!).[42]

Mary Hamilton grew intimate with her new society, including Frances Boscawen, Charlotte Ord, Elizabeth Montagu, Hannah More, Elizabeth Carter and Fanny Burney. Just as Mary Hamilton was coming out of court, Fanny Burney was about to enter it. Her bluestocking friends Anna Ord and Mary Delany delivered her to the Queen's Lodge and her new life of 'cabals and rules and timidities' in 1786.[43] Learned ladies may have been eager to engage in intellectual conversation, but court culture was not a place for the bluestocking character. And unsurprisingly Fanny, whose diaries during her five years as part of the royal household provide the most intimate portrait of court life under Queen Charlotte, constantly complained about her new life. What was worse for Fanny Burney was that her 'cabal' was not even part of the prominent sect of ladies of the bedchamber. She was appointed Second Keeper of the Robes, part of a more intimate, 'professional' tier of women who, along with their assistants, the 'wardrobe women', received less pay than the ladies of the bedchamber (Fanny received £200 per annum), but were unmarried and resided permanently with the royal household.[44] These women, there 'for life', or so the Queen hoped, were closely involved in the private service of the Queen's toilette, helping her dress in elaborate gowns, styling her hair, and draping her in diamonds (which she was famous for wearing). But this unglamorous position was not to Fanny's taste, as her association of it with an iniquitous marriage makes clear: 'I am married,' she wrote. 'I look upon it in that light – I was averse to forming the union, & I endeavoured to escape it, but my friends interfered, – they prevailed, & the knot is tied.'[45]

For Fanny, being tied to the confines of the royal household was even more disturbing since her writing talents had already gained her public notoriety, making her one of the very few women who could forge an alternative career for themselves. By the time of her court appointment, her first two novels, *Evelina* and *Cecilia*, had already been well received; even the King and Queen were eager to meet the celebrated writer. She, on the other hand, was less enthusiastic, writing in her journal how in court she was

> lost to all private comfort, dead to all domestic endearment.
> I was worn with want of rest and fatigued with laborious
> watchfulness and attendance. My time was devoted to
> official duties and all that in life was dearest to me – my
> friends, my chosen society, my best affections – lived . . .
> in my mind only.[46]

There was the one exception when the royal family left her while they took a brief sojourn in the country. In January 1788 Fanny dashed out to Queen Anne Street, in Cavendish Square, where Elizabeth Ord had gathered 'an assembly at her house of my old friends, purposely to indulge me with once again seeing them in a body' – Mrs Garrick, Mr Pepys, Sir Joshua Reynolds, Elizabeth Montagu, and others.[47] But Fanny's knot was not yet untied, and back to court residence she went.

To Fanny's mind being part of the Queen's household was a job that seemed to betray all sense of personal engagement or fulfilment. In Burney's *The Wanderer; or, Female Difficulties* (1814), Juliet, a lady's companion, must 'be always at hand, early or late . . . Success was unacknowledged, though failure was resented. There was no relaxation in her toil.' Juliet, 'the wanderer', therefore continues on her travels, searching for her liberty. This was something Fanny Burney herself managed to secure, however, in 1791, when she finally quit court.[48]

Life regulated by someone else's demands, desires and time was considered too restrictive for others besides Fanny Burney. Elizabeth Gunning, the Duchess of Hamilton, had consistently irritated the Queen by turning up late to events, prompting the latter to give her a diamond-studded watch, saying, 'She hoped She wou'd never be too late again.'[49] The Duchess's flamboyant court etiquette was also said to have created tensions between her and the Queen. However, contemporary reports of this nature were probably prone to exaggeration since the Duchess offended some aristocratic sensibilities by being a commoner by birth.

Aristocratic conduct was governed by strict social protocol, and if prejudice against one's birth was prone to offend some, it was certain that sexual improprieties would swiftly meet condemnation. Adultery by women brought acute social stigma. The Duchess of Hamilton's daughter, Elizabeth (Lady Derby), was disgraced when in 1778 she left her husband and children and eloped with the Duke of Dorset, a character notorious for his affairs. The Duchess of Hamilton once again demonstrated her disregard for social codes when, after this event, she tried to secure for her daughter a place in the royal household. It was out of the question. Any woman who even brushed with public scandal was shunned by court. Having fallen from the Queen's grace, the Duchess of Hamilton decided to leave court, citing 'ill health', in 1784.

Those who already knew that the court environment was less than stimulating managed to avoid the call-up altogether. Elizabeth Carter, whose friends attempted to persuade her to accept a position in the royal household under George II, managed to secure her father's permission to decline the offer. Elizabeth was an admired translator and poet, and was mid-way through translating the complete works of Epictetus, a Roman Stoic much admired by the *philosophes*.[50] Life as a governess in the royal household, she feared, might prove fearfully drab. What, she asked herself, would she be doing there? 'If it be only to teach the children to read,' she wrote, mocking a pretence to seriousness. 'Would it not be a more eligible life to be a country schoolmistress *with apron blue?*' She observed also that the royal household was not noted for its displays of erudition. 'Of Latin and Greek indeed I might perhaps be able to give them some notion; but this surely cannot be the scheme; for since the days of Queen Elizabeth and Lady Jane Grey, who ever thought of teaching princesses Latin and Greek?'[51] Lady Charlotte Bury, the Duchess of Hamilton's youngest daughter who was appointed lady-in-waiting to Caroline, Princess of Wales, was inclined to agree. She sardonically reiterated some of the princess's 'prattle', complete with phonetic spelling to stress the princess's heavy German accent. 'Sometimes, the Princess philosophizes,' Charlotte wrote, 'here is a sample of her philosophy:'

> She said one day, 'Suspense is a very great bore, but we live only de poor beings of de hour – and we ought always to try to make us happy so long we do live. To tell you God's truth', – her favourite expression, not always used appropriately, – 'To tell you God's truth, I have had as many vexations as most people; but we must make up *vons* mind to enjoy de good, spite of de bad; and I mind now de last no more than dat' – snapping her fingers.[52]

On 19 January 1784, Mary Hamilton found herself 'not *envying* ye fine folks at ye Birthday (Queen Charlotte's) but enjoying *my liberty*'. She later reflected on her period as part of the Queen's court, between 1777 and 1782:

> My health and spirits suffered very much from leading a life of constant restraint, I felt myself unequal to it and regretted my loss of liberty – the situation became irksome and I had few opportunities of enjoying the society of many most dear and valuable friends – for it was totally inconsistent with the place I was in, to ask for permission to live so much as I wished with those persons I loved.[53]

The Duchess of Northumberland, while one of the first ladies of the bedchamber to Queen Charlotte, felt similar constrictions on her liberty. Her position was further complicated by personal difficulties with the Queen. Similar in some ways to Elizabeth Gunning, the

Duchess of Hamilton, the Duchess of Northumberland had ruffled the Queen's feathers with her own penchant for pageantry. Contemporaries noted the Duchess's fondness for the 'show and crowds and junketing' reminiscent of the old court, and her habit of moving about with a larger retinue of servants than her Majesty prompted the Queen directly to reprimand her.[54]

The Duchess's style thus cramped, she decided to leave court. Eventually an opportunity arose 'making it much more eligible for me to be no longer a dependant,' she later wrote, 'a State I ever detested.' During the 1760s, her husband, Sir Hugh Smithson, began to climb the political ladder, and, gaining wealth and the patronage of the Crown, was honoured with a dukedom by the King in 1766. The Duchess no longer needed her position at court in order to keep up appearances. In 1770, 'longing to enjoy my Liberty', the Duchess of Northumberland resigned her post as lady of the bedchamber.[55]

The Duchess had never believed that her role as a lady of the bedchamber, despite it being a position to which she was called by birth and estate, was meaningful enough. She was born foremost a woman of independent spirit, a trait amongst the women in her family that would shine through any restrictions placed upon her.

Her grandmother, Elizabeth Percy, was sole heiress to the estates belonging to the Earldom of Northumberland. She had been thrice married. Pestered into marriage first at twelve years old to the sickly Lord Ogle, she had been widowed six months later. Her second marriage at fourteen years of age to Thomas Thynne, a wealthy man of disreputable character who was known as 'Tom of Ten Thousand' (a seventeenth-century allusion to his wealth), was more ignominious. No sooner was the marriage ceremony over than Elizabeth fled to the Continent in fear for her life. Subsequently an assassin hired by Count Königsmark, a Swedish suitor of Elizabeth, murdered Thomas Thynne. The following year, 1682, Elizabeth married her third and final husband, Charles, the 6th Duke of Somerset, and became lady of the bedchamber to Queen Anne.[56]

The Duchess of Northumberland not only inherited her grandmother's name, estates and title, but it seems her sense of liberty.

And from her mother, Frances Thynne (a cousin of 'Tom of Ten Thousand'), she acquired a taste for learning. Indeed it appears that Frances was disapproved of by her father-in-law, the 6th Duke of Somerset, for being too learned. Other contemporaries, however, respected Lady Frances Somerset's qualities. Elizabeth Carter, writing to the 'Queen of the Bluestockings', Elizabeth Montagu, in 1759, recalled with admiration Lady Somerset's house, which she remembered 'with great respect and veneration, not without a strong mixture of regret, that what was once the elegant abode of virtue and genius, and honoured by the conversation of the Duchess of Somerset and [the poet] Mrs. Rowe', and was now, only five years after Lady Somerset's death, 'so disorderly'.[57]

Her daughter, the Duchess of Northumberland, was in no doubt about what to do with her rediscovered liberty after leaving court. Immediately after withdrawing from the royal household, she 'left London in order to go to Vienna to meet my youngest Son Lord Algernon & to be present at the Feasts given there on account of the Marriage of the Archdutchess Antoinette with the Dauphin of France'.[58] She had been to the Continent on at least two occasions previously: in 1766 to Holland and briefly to France in 1769 to attend another royal wedding. But this adventure, taken on her own initiative, was to prove the ultimate contrast to the cloistered, prosaic existence of court life.

Her journey, departing from Dover on 20 March 1770, began uncomfortably. 'We had a snowy and disagreeable Passage with Rain & Snow,' she recorded in her diary, and matters only got worse. 'The Snow grew more violent & such a storm arose as the Captain said he had not in 35 years using the Sea seen the like of it, and we every moment expected to be swallow'd up by the Waves.' She gingerly made her way to her cabin, but the boat heaved over a wave, throwing her to the ground and breaking her finger. 'I rose up & was once more on my Feet when the force of another Wave gave such a Shake that I fell backward' into her cramped cabin, hitting her head upon a locker, 'whilst my Legs lay over the Seat of the Post Chaise which happened to stand across the Cabin'. Her candle blew out, and she lay prostrate, shouting for help. 'I call'd to them to beg for Gods sake' that her servants exercised caution while struggling to reach her in the dark, 'that they wd sit down on the Locker at the entrance, and by that means as it surrounded the Cabbin they might get safe at me.' To her obvious relief, her footman was able to reach and comfort her.[59]

For all the trauma of her brief voyage (the ship, forced to turn around, made it back to the safety of the English coast), the Duchess was nevertheless able to attend a fashionable 'feast' and ball in London two days later, where she, no doubt, provided the story of the evening. The *Annual Register* offered the following embellished account:

> Her grace the Dutchess of Northumberland, in crossing the Channel from Dover to Calais, very narrowly escaped being drowned. By the violence of the waves the cords which lashed her chaise to the vessel were burst, and, had it not immediately been discovered, the next returning sea would have carried her grace over board. She was on her journey to the court of Vienna, to be present at the nuptials of the Archdutchess with the Dauphin of France; but being driven back, & with the utmost hazard landed near Folkestone, her grace's design has been frustrated.

The court too was provided with a surge of gossip. For others who were planning their 'escapes' abroad, the fact that the Duchess had such an adventurous, albeit hazardous, start to her new life probably stimulated their desires even more.

Lady Mary Coke was in Paris in 1770 when news of the Duchess of Northumberland's close encounter with death reached her. As close friends (she knew most of the ladies of the court well), Lady Coke was genuinely alarmed, and it must have reminded her of an earlier incident involving the Duchess, who had long been outspoken about her desires to travel abroad. In 1767 she told a party of women at court of her plans to dash off to Paris and Brussels for a few weeks before returning in time for the Queen's birthday, and in 1768, Lady

Coke, who had just returned from a similar trip, found herself discussing the familiar topic of continental travel at a dinner with her. 'The Duchess,' Lady Coke wrote, 'has laid aside her intention of going to Paris, but is still determined to go Abroad, & consulted me where She shou'd go to that was not very distant, & where there was something worth seeing.'[60] She recommended the south of France or Bonn.

When the Duchess set out, however, an attempted road robbery thwarted her trip, and discouraged her until she could arrange better security, eventually making it to Germany a few weeks later. Better prepared with security and servants but not for the weather, she set out again the next year, and the incident in 1770 was perhaps, thought Lady Coke, a result of the Duchess's hasty 'determination' to get abroad.

She dryly exclaimed that that must be the risk to one who was so anxious to get to Paris to see the ceremonial celebrations surrounding the Dauphin's (the future Louis XVI) forthcoming marriage. 'Tis a proof that I am older in disposition than the Duchess of Northumberland,' reflected Lady Coke, who believed that her lavish tastes, her desire to seek sociable society and to attract attention were the driving forces behind her departure from court and voyage abroad. Lady Coke, on the other hand, was more sombre in her devotion to travel. She preferred subtler occupations. This attitude stemmed from uncomfortable circumstances she met with two years earlier when a regular visitor to the English court.

Lady Mary Coke was the youngest daughter of John Campbell, 2nd Duke of Argyll. Her older sister, Caroline, Lady Dalkeith, was presented at the court of George II, but later turned down an offer from Lord Bute to be a lady of the bedchamber to Queen Charlotte. Mary and her two other sisters were admitted into the parlour, and Mary later continued to frequent the court of George III.

In 1746, when she had just turned twenty, Mary's father reached an agreement with Lord Leicester in a plan to marry his daughter to Leicester's son, Lord Coke. It was common practice to arrange marriages, based on barter rather than romance, and women had very little say in the matter once the father had struck the deal. Mary was to receive a £2,500 per annum jointure (money to support her in the event of his death), and £500 per annum 'pin money' (an annual allowance), while her dowry to the groom was £20,000.[61] It was far from a marriage made in heaven. Mary, who reluctantly accepted the 'proposal', confided in her sisters her discomfort with her situation, but refused their well-intended but futile advice to break off the engagement while there was still time.

No sooner had the wedding ceremony ended than the marriage turned sour. Lord Coke had been gaining a reputation advancing towards that of his father, as being a profligate who lacked any principles. His regular bouts of gaming and drinking quickly led to the demise of any semblance of a relationship with Mary. Even his father, Lord Leicester, acknowledged his son's 'Brutish' and 'Beastly' behaviour towards his new wife, though he admitted he was not surprised, hinting at his son's past problems. 'Before he was married, I had fears that he would relapse,' he wrote to Mary, in an apologetic tone.[62] Things became most agitated a year later, when Lord Coke took his wife to Holkham, his parents' Norfolk estate, where Mary was forced to live in confinement for almost a year. During this time Lord Coke left the estate, giving power of attorney to his father, enabling him to control the domestic arrangements regarding Lady Coke as he wished. For her part, Mary pretended to be sick. It was not long before Lord Leicester severed completely all Mary's connections with the outside society including those she had invited to receive privately.[63] Lady Coke's domestic servants were dismissed without discussion; her physicians and apothecaries were refused further consultation, and, in a supreme act of insult to her family, Lord Leicester even refused permission for Mary to receive her mother, who had long been sceptical of the character of her daughter's in-laws, knowing of Lord Leicester's notoriously fiery temper.

This final act prompted Mary's mother, the Duchess of Argyll, to take legal action with the guidance and support of James Stuart Mackenzie, who had recently married Lady Coke's sister, Caroline.[64] They obtained from the judges of the King's bench a writ of *habeas corpus*, ordering Lord Coke to present his wife to the Chief Justice, which he did in November 1749. At the same time Lady Coke filed for divorce *a mensa et a thoro* (literally, separation 'from table and bed'), which would allow separation, but not remarriage, in cases of adultery, sodomy or cruelty. The possibilities for divorce for eighteenth-century women were few – permitted in certain cases of proven insanity, impotence or excessive violence from the husband; men had the additional permission to sue their wives for adultery, when, if successful, Parliament would dissolve the marriage, allowing for remarriage. Lady Coke's case against her husband, citing cruelty and seeking legal separation, was typical of the imbalance of judicial power when weighing the claims of women against the defences of men. How was 'cruelty' to be defined? Sir William Scott, judging on a case in 1790, was to provide one famous answer:

> It is the duty of courts, and consequently the inclination of courts, to keep the rule absolutely strict. The causes must be grave and weighty, and such as shew an absolute impossibility that the duties of the married life can be discharged. In a state of personal danger, no duties can be discharged; for the duty of self-preservation must take place before the duties of marriage ... What merely wounds the mental feelings is in few cases to be admitted where they are not accompanied with bodily injury, either actual or menaced. Mere austerity of temper, petulance of manners, rudeness of language, a want of civil attention and accommodation, even occasional sallies of passion, if they do not threaten bodily harm, do not amount to legal cruelty.[65]

But long before this decision, crowds were eager to see how courts would resolve the case. The courtroom was packed with spectators from all ranks of society. On Lady Coke's side were women from the royal court, relatives sobbing and fainting, and on Lord Coke's side were wild rakes and condescending wits jeering at the exhibition. She testified she was treated 'barbarously' and 'in the most cruel manner but not content with that he struck me on my arm! And tore my ruffle all to pieces ... I thought myself in danger of my life.'[66] But she was vague in her stories of their confrontations, and according to society's codes, Lord Coke had not, in fact, overstepped his 'rights' as a husband.[67] Lady Coke might have been verbally abused, but this did not matter to a court. Her case reiterated the decision that what 'merely wounds the mental feelings' was inadmissible.

Verbal abuse did matter, however, to the socially governed life of the aristocratic realm. A gentleman's agreement was for this reason reached between the two warring parties. In exchange for pin money and 'freedom' to live at her sister's house at Sudbrook, Lady Coke would withdraw her suit, pay all legal expenses, and live in quiet exile from fashionable London society (a reduced sentence to the initially proposed banishment from within twenty miles of London and her having to 'confess' publicly that she lied about her claims). To a quiet life on the margins she thus retreated.

Her world turned around, however, three years after this settlement. 'There is a report that Lord Coke is dying,' Elizabeth Montagu – who had enjoyed a rare chance to socialise with the exiled Lady Coke – wrote to her husband. 'She is extremely pretty, her air and figure the most pleasing I ever saw. She is not properly a beauty, but she has more *agrémens* than one shall often see. With so many advantages of birth, person and fortune, I do not wonder at her resentment being lively, and that she could ill brook the neglects and insults of her husband.' Within a month Lord Coke had died. In September 1753, Lady Mary Coke once again entered society. With the new royal household emerging in the 1760s, life for Lady Coke – now independently wealthy and thirty-four years old – began anew. But, as some of her new friends were discovering, even court life had its moments of crisis.

Horace Walpole once described Lady Coke as having 'a frenzy for Royalty', and when in the 1760s she formed a special acquaintance with one of the royal family, it appears her enthusiasm might have taken a turn towards the indiscreet. Edward, the Duke of York, was King George III's brother, and almost thirteen years Lady Coke's junior. It seems she encouraged the impression that she and the Duke were on intimate terms. Once she allegedly defended the seeming impropriety of being alone in an apartment with the Duke by demanding that her mother (who caught them) recognise her as the 'Duchess of York', an event that may have prompted her mother later to confess that she believed they were secretly married.[68] Others doubted that it was more than a fancy in Lady Coke's mind, since, after all, the Duke was known as a bit of a rake. Lady Coke's friend the Duchess of Northumberland characterised the Duke as 'remarkably plain, [a man who] had great Vivacity but with a Mind so devoted to pleasure & so little regard to propriety as robb'd him of his Dignity & made him rather a trifling than an amiable Character'.[69] But such dismissive characterisations were not as entertaining as a royal romance, and any gossip would liven up court life, happily interrupting the boredom of official functions. On one occasion, for example, Lady Coke recorded an episode when she joined a royal outing to the opera but decided to sit in an undesignated spot:

> But I immediately saw the King observed it, & when the Duke of York came into the Box, & placed himself behind me, I saw a whisper in the Duchess of Bedford's Box, & in some others. 'Twas plain they all thought I had particular reasons for changing my place, but the truth is I had none . . . & was myself surprised when I saw the Duke of York come in, it being unusual for HRH to go any where in the Opera House in sight of the King, Unless he went in form.

Despite her demur regarding her choice of seat, even the King joined in the banter. He had asked Lord Hertford whether Lady Coke chose to be further back in the box to escape early for another engagement, but then playfully added that this could not be the reason since she had not gone after the opera. 'I little thought so trifling a circumstance wou'd give occasion for so much suspicion,' she observed.[70]

But the 'friendship, or whatever it was', as the author of her *Memoirs* put it, came to an abrupt end when the Duke died in 'immoderate pursuit of pleasure and unremitting fatigues in travelling', as the typically searing Horace Walpole surmised, in Monaco in 1767, a tragedy which sank Lady Coke's spirits to disquieting depths.[71] She forbade any of her company from mentioning the Duke's name and sobbed at the sight of Westminster Abbey, where his body lay in a royal vault. She experienced repeated nightmares about being at the Abbey:

> & the Funeral service was performing for the poor Duke, that I had not resolution to go into the Chapel, but sat down on a Tomb in another part of the Abbey, where I thought the figures on the Monuments moved. I then seemed to be left alone, & fancy'd I was shut up, but on walking down one of the great Isles I saw a door open, which I went out at, & was then perplex'd walking about the streets.[72]

She mourned his death feeling alone and confused. But others found it hard to see things from her point of view. Her sister Anne, Lady Strafford, wrote to her warning that she was at risk of being 'censured' or 'ridiculed' by the world. Perhaps it was to coax her sister into rationalising the situation, as Lady Coke began to do when she replied 'that being unmarried, & the Duke a single Man, I cou'd not see why my concern was to draw the censure of the World, & as to redicule, tho' uninstructed by me, the World knew enough not to find any room for anything of that nature'.[73]

Princess Amelia, the Duke's aunt, was the only woman it seems in whom Lady Coke had confided about her mixed emotions for the Duke. She confessed that from two months after their first meeting, 'I had begged of him to put an end to the acquaintance,' but he refused, and 'in a few Years he grew too agreeable to me to make me wish for it'. Then her feelings turned again, when it seemed he had forgotten her after being abroad for six months, in 1764, and not having written to her. As a way finally to end the tease, she claimed she was contemplating marrying someone else. But then the day came when the long-awaited letter from the distant traveller finally arrived, so she 'laid aside all thoughts of marriage, & determined to spend the summer Abroad, as he told me he shou'd return to England in the Autumn'. So to Spa, in Belgium, she did indeed go, where she received intelligence of the Duke's coeval tour of Italy.[74] After their return to England, she was happy to see that 'his inclination seem'd to be as strong as ever'. But it was clear that his 'inclinations' never met Lady Coke's expectations or desires, and her affected displays of distress at his death and her lengthy convalescence grew irritating to others, including Princess Amelia. After encouraging her to shake loose from sorrow and re-enter the world, the Princess hit Lady Coke with the blunt statement that: 'if you did but know what a joke he always used to make of you, I promise you would soon have done crying for him'.[75] It seems that being shown a packet of affectionate letters from the Duke did not dissuade the Princess of her assessment.

It did not matter to Lady Coke what others thought of her view of her relationship with the Duke, believing that she had enemies who were out to do her harm, and so 'I submitted most humbly to the will of God, that had thought proper to cooperate with them in putting an end to all my hopes of Happiness in this World.'[76] Thus, once again removed from society and 'retired from the world', she found comfort at home reading 'Mrs Macaulay's History' and 'a large Volume of Travels'.

She passed the next year gradually reacquainting herself with society and increasingly attending court functions. Finally, enough strength regained, in mid-1769 she arranged plans to head for the Continent. She paid off her debts, organised her retinue of servants, and briefed Princess Amelia on her schedule. 'My journey abroad brought on a very painful subject, which, tho' ever present in my mind, I never talk of to anybody but HRH.'[77] The subject was the Duke's death. His picture was impressed on her mind, and in turn cast upon the map of Europe, wedged between France and Italy. If, as she lamented in her diary, seeing the Duke of York's favourite gambling table made her blurry-eyed, then she certainly would not want to plan a retreat to the Continent that followed in the Duke's doomed footsteps. 'You wonder why I don't go to Nice,' she wrote in response to a query from her mother, who followed her daughter's progress through Europe, 'but you who are looking over maps must have observed how near it is to Italy, & to a Town that I can never think of without sorrow . . .', meaning Monaco, where the Duke died, only nine miles away from Nice, which was much too close to her heart for her comfort.[78]

Lady Coke's plan to travel abroad ostensibly stemmed from her desire to spend a winter away from England in the pleasant environs of Aix-en-Provence, where 'I am assured that till January one may dine out of doors'. But the added attraction was that the granddaughter of the celebrated writer Madame de Sévigné had taken residence there, and Lady Coke felt 'some pleasure in the thoughts of being acquainted with her, as I shall have a thousand questions to ask'.[79] Madame Marie de Rabutin-Chantal, Marquise de Sévigné (1626–96), was an author much admired by the bluestocking circle in England. Her letters were published in various editions in the first half of the eighteenth century, and her animated, witty style provided a model for the way women would write their own correspondence.[80] When Lady Coke arrived, however, she was disappointed to hear that the granddaughter, Comtesse de Vance, had died six weeks earlier, a death, she tormented herself by saying, that was probably hastened by her longing to meet her, 'for you know I am disappointed in everything I wish'.[81]

Lady Coke's foremost desire on this trip was to escape from the English court and enjoy some peace of mind in different company. She looked to the Continent's scenery and society to improve, fundamentally, her mental health. She was not looking for mere 'rest': as she told her mother, 'being in my bed at Notting Hill wou'd not have answer'd the end for which I came Abroad'.[82] Alas, the company with whom she associated abroad probed her for the reasons for her travel and the other English travellers created a satellite society of gossip and rumour. What, they wondered, could be the reason for an independently wealthy, forty-three-year-old woman deciding to travel abroad, 'alone' (excepting, of course, her retinue of servants), during the social season in London?

The most prominent English visitors to Aix with Lady Coke were the fabulously wealthy Lord and Lady Spencer, with their children, the eight-year-old Henrietta (or 'Harriet', the future Lady Bessborough), her older brother George (Lord Althorp), and Georgiana, the older sister (later Duchess of Devonshire). Lady Spencer had just lost her daughter, Louise, an infant who died at only a few weeks old, and, having three years earlier lost a new-born daughter the family resolved to travel in an attempt to escape depression.[83] They had a reputation for travelling in grand style (something easily accommodated by Lord Spencer's spectacular £700 *weekly* income), and upon their arrival in Aix Lady Coke pondered where they might stay, 'for there is but one very good Inn, & that not large enough to contain so many people, for Ld & Ly Spencer travel with as great a suite as usual'. Lady Spencer was also acquiring a reputation for obsessive gambling – a vice that affected (to a lesser degree) Lady Coke as well. It appears that in the course of Lady Spencer's socialising some tattle was spilled regarding Lady Coke that pricked the curiosity of the local French socialites.

'I don't know whether I have observed to you,' wrote Lady Coke to her mother on New Year's Day, 1770, 'that the French have a great deal of curiosity, & very soon after my arrival, as they wou'd not believe I came here for my health, they were curious to the last degree to find out what had brought me here'. As we know from her own confessions about choosing only to confide in Princess Amelia about 'that painful subject', it comes as no surprise that she tried to dodge the question, and diverted attention away from her personal affairs.

> I am not as you know very communicative with regard to my own history, tho' thank God I have nothing to reproach myself with, but tho' determined to say nothing that cou'd instruct them of the real subject of my journey, I was often puzzled to know how to answer their questions, but as they were convinced I was not happy, I hoped they wou'd cease to say anything that might be disagreeable. Ly Spencer, however, by something She said, renew'd all their eagerness to be better informed.

Apparently while travelling through Marseille, Lady Spencer had let slip that Lady Coke's unhappiness 'proceeded from an Attachment for a person who had married another Lady', which Lady Coke assured others had no foundation, but she was 'impatient to know what it is Ly Spencer has said that can have given room for such an idea'.[84]

Such disturbing conversation cancelled out the effects of the bright sunshine in the south of France, which 'is certainly a service to the spirits, but upon the Whole,' she was sorry to report, 'I don't think my journey has had the effect that I hoped an intire change of scene might have brought about.' Matters were not helped by a change for the worse in the weather, topped with some losses at whist, but these proved only temporary setbacks. If this journey did not prove particularly therapeutic, she was not prepared to give up: over the next five years she continued to spend lengthy winters abroad, often only returning to England on brief summer visits to see her family and settle household matters.

This trip, however, was coming to an end. Summer was approaching, and by April 1770 she was back in Paris, waiting for a sudden bout of bad weather to pass before setting 'out for England, as I will never again undertake a journey in such weather & I see no prospect of its changing'. Her friend, the Duchess of Northumberland, had not exercised such caution. At that moment she was on the other side of the English Channel caught in the storm en route to France that gave the court in England another dose of amusing gossip.

'We live as English a life as we can make it'

Fashionable Society & Foreign Affairs

Lady Shadwell saw Lady Mary Wortley Montagu at Venice where she now resides, and asked her what made her leave England; she told them the reason was people had grown so stupid she could not endure their company; all England was infected with dullness; by the bye, what she means by insupportable dullness is her husband, for it seems she never intends to come back while he lives,

Elizabeth Robinson, in a letter to a friend,
22 July 1740[1]

4

'IN JUNE 1791 I left England and went to Paris.' So begins the *Journal* of Lady Elizabeth Webster (née Vassall).[2] But unlike the widowed Lady Mary Coke, who travelled to the Continent to escape memories of her unhappy marriage and then short-lived romance with the Duke of York, or Mary Wollstonecraft, who fled to the Continent initially to escape a failed love affair, Lady Webster did not travel independently. Despite the deliberate and liberal use of the first person singular pronoun 'I' throughout the journal of her travels, she was for much of the time travelling with her husband. What she did share with Mary Coke and Mary Wollstonecraft, as well as many others, was the desire to travel to soothe away personal unhappiness. Eventually, her *compagnon de voyage*, as she at best referred to her husband, returned to England on his own, whilst she continued her tour, having been granted a most welcome 'geographical independence' from him. Like Mary Wollstonecraft, Lady Webster discovered she was not averse to taking up the occasional lover while abroad.

Adultery amongst the aristocracy in the eighteenth century was far from unusual; one need only pick up an issue of the short-lived *Female Tatler* (1709–10) or the later *Town and Country* magazine for a monthly account of the sexual exploits and stories of the mistresses kept by one or another gentleman or nobleman. Despite the emphasis on female chastity and virtue, aristocratic women did pursue their own romances. Meanwhile writers encouraged the view that innocent women ran a high risk of being shamelessly misled down an improprietous path by licentious men. 'Thousands of women of the best hearts and finest parts have been ruined by men who approach them under the specious name of friendship,' thundered John Gregory in 1774.[3] Women were advised that a study in chastity would give them the strength to defend themselves against the sharpest arrow ever shot from Cupid's bow. Some conduct books even proffered moral advice to such hapless beauties who might be subjected to 'the poison of life, and scourge of civil society', such as Wetenhall Wilkes in his 'Dissertation on Chastity':

> Chastity is a suppression of all irregular desires, voluntary pollutions, sinful concupiscence, and of an immoderate use of all sensual, or carnal pleasures. Its purity consists in *abstinence* or *continence*. The first is properly attributed to virgins and widows, the other to married women. It is the proper office of this virtue, to resist all impure and unclean thoughts; to mortify all unchaste longings, and to avoid all alluring objects. This is a sublime virtue.[4]

Chastity was a 'natural' state for women, Wilkes explained, and therefore a woman who committed adultery must lack womanhood. In short, an 'immodest woman is a kind of monster, distorted from its proper form'. But more and more 'monsters' were crawling out of the bedsheets. In 1779 a civil attorney wrote that 'conjugal infidelity is become so general that it is hardly considered as criminal; especially in the fashionable world'.

But while the legal eye might have turned away, the real crime committed by a woman's adultery was the threat it posed to her husband's property. As an anonymous writer on the 'real causes' of unhappy marriages put it, only women could commit the 'crime' of adultery since she 'imposes a spurious Breed on her Husband's family; makes a Foreigner Heir to his Estate; depriving sometimes his real Children begotten afterwards, of their just Inheritance'.[5]

Indeed, a woman's chastity seemed to matter most when confusion of progeny threatened estate legacies – that 'constitutes the essence of the crime', the great cataloguer of the times Samuel Johnson reaffirmed.[6] Still, some families lived the lie, and illegitimate children were accepted into the household. Lady Harley, the Countess of

Oxford's children were known as 'the Harleian Miscellany', and Georgiana, Duchess of Devonshire, brought up the daughter of her husband from his mistress Charlotte Spencer, while Georgiana's own illegitimate daughter was raised by the family of her own lover, Sir Charles Grey.[7]

While there was a modicum of discretion in their affairs, aristocratic lives were far too crowded with family, friends and servants to keep secrets. Occasionally, the pressure of public awareness of their lewd activities forced the issue of divorce – especially amongst a public becoming increasingly disdainful of aristocratic conduct, seeing their personal lives as a reflection of their political debauchery. In the 1760s Sarah Lennox's multiple love affairs became a very public scandal; stories rapidly circulated in the tabloid press, and her marriage eventually ended in divorce.[8]

But divorces, as Lady Coke's painful experience demonstrated, were not easy options. Divorces on the grounds of adultery were only permitted when the woman's indiscretions pushed the husband to such legal proceedings; if he was having an affair, women were advised to adjust their attitudes – part of the flexibility they were required to have in making themselves acceptable companions. Separation, when initiated by either spouse for whatever reason, was far more likely to discredit the wife than the husband.[9] In addition to the inequality of rights afforded to men and women in initiating proceedings and the publicity such cases attracted, divorce trails could be exremely expensive when testimonies had to be gathered from witnesses living abroad. There was suggestion even that unscrupulous wives brought groundless suits against their husbands in order to land them with hefty legal costs, asking 'a commission to examine witnesses in Italy, although there are no witnesses in Italy'.[10] The same could occur in reverse, but the legal bill for an unsuccessful claim would still need to be paid for out of the husband's purse. The combination of cost, fear of humiliation, but also a genuine commitment to marital values, meant that early modern England was not a divorce society. Until about the middle of the eighteenth century divorces were extremely rare, and even in the following decades there were only three or four a year.[11]

The actual union between husband and wife was also closely monitored. The match had first to be approved by the woman's family and, to some degree (depending on who the woman was) society, lest she be ostracised. Certain social codes were expected to be followed. For instance, in eighteenth-century Protestant England marrying a Catholic or a foreigner was frowned on. When Fanny Burney finally left court at the age of forty, she fell in love with Alexandre d'Arblay, a French Roman Catholic émigré. She worried that she might lose her pension from the Queen if she disapproved and she also needed her father's blessing (this her father grudgingly gave, but he refused to attend the wedding).[12]

Acquaintances could not understand Fanny's actions. 'What is Sense good for?' asked Maria Holroyd, daughter of Lord and Lady Sheffield, upon hearing of the marriage of the respected novelist. 'Nothing at all I am convinced to Women, for it is the sensible Women who do the Most foolish things.'[13] Polite society, and her family, were shocked too when Hester Thrale married the Italian musician Gabriel Piozzi, in 1784. For Hester, Italy – where she went to live immediately after her marriage – became a land of renewed life; but for her close friend Samuel Johnson it remained a lurid destination: 'only phantoms of the imagination seduce you to Italy', he taunted her.

Images of the prim and proper eighteenth-century woman tend to gloss over the capacity many possessed for breaking free from sexual conventions – pursuing their desired romances and dealing with their unsatisfactory marriages by asserting independence of sexual spirit abroad. Some believed that the conduct of ladies was deteriorating; certain male critics cited the slow but steady increase in cases of divorce as evidence of this. Lady Mary Coke had heard that the King consulted Lord Camden, the Lord Chancellor, being 'desirous that something shou'd be thought of that might be likely to prevent the very bad conduct among the Ladys, of which there had been so many instances lately'. The proposed solution was a bill to prevent divorced adulterous ladies from marrying their lovers, but four attempts to pass it were defeated in the House of Commons.[14]

What could be enforced, however, was the rule forbidding undesirables from visiting court, such as was noticeably imposed on Lady Waldegrave and any of her visitors after she secretly married the Duke of Gloucester against the King's wishes in 1766.[15]

It was also noted as a matter for concern that *English* ladies were succumbing to moral lapses normally associated with 'abroad'. After all was not the Continent the seat of lewd and lascivious behaviour, where every lady had her *cicisbeo* – a man chosen by a married lady who, as an astonished Englishman in Italy learned, 'attends on her to all publick places & wherever she goes, sits in her box at the playhouse, attends her in her coach, and the husband never thinks it necessary to be jealous'?[16] Was that not the apparent root of Samuel Johnson's disapproval of Hester Piozzi's flamboyant flight to Italy? And was this not also why venereal disease was colloquially known as the 'French pox', or why the libertine actions of Valmont and Madame de Merteuil captured the spirit so well in de Laclos's sensational *Les Liaisons dangéreuses*?

Women travellers had long commented on the levity of conduct of women across the Channel. The English author and librettist Frances Brooke pondered on the differences between manners at home and abroad. 'I have said married women are, on my principles, forbidden fruit,' she wrote in her *History of Emily Montague*. 'I should have explained myself; I mean in England, for my ideas on this head change as soon as I land at Calais.' Continental women had 'different mores', so that 'coquetry is dangerous to English women, because they have sensibility; it is more suited to the French, who are naturally something of the salamander kind'.[17] In 1771, Lady Coke reported from the royal court in Vienna that the Princess D'Auersperg – Maria Josepha Rosalia – was 'a very pretty Woman, but more than suspected of being the late Emperor's Mistress, nor is She intirely free from suspicion of having had too much compliance for others'. Still, Lady Coke went on to note, 'excepting that failure in her Character, all the rest is amiable' – particularly when she consciously, quickly and exactly paid off the gambling debt owed to Lady Coke.

Touring on the Continent at this time was Lady Coke's friend the Duchess of Northumberland, who was similarly appalled by the standard of behaviour displayed by the ladies of the court at Bonn. She told of one in particular to illustrate her point, though it was not the most remarkable example circulating in local gossip: 'The Comtesse Fugger who is not reckon'd one of the worst told Mrs Cressener that the Grand Ecuyer by whom she is now kept (or rather I believe she keeps him), was her 49th *Gallant*,' (meaning her *lover*, as 'gallantry' was a borrowed French euphemism for amorous behaviour).[18] This, in fact, was one of the features that made travelling the Grand Tour so attractive to young men and so agonising to their mothers. When Lady Stafford advised her son, the young Lord Granville Leveson-Gower, about how to prepare for his Grand Tour, she let her anxiety slip:

> For I think your future situation and Figure in Life depends so much upon your Conduct and Connections when Abroad that I look upon it as a matter of the *greatest* Consequence to have it settled properly. *Most* of the Young Men who travel had better remain in their own Country; they learn follies and contract Vices in Foreign countries without getting either knowledge or Improvements ... How many of them lose all Idea of Religion; they hold the Government of the Passions in Contempt, connect themselves with married Women, and return what the World calls a fine Gentleman.

Surely her own son must possess the reason and resolution to guard against such evils, if not for his sake, then for hers? 'My dear Granville,' she added, 'if these were to be the consequences of your foreign travel it would break my Heart.' She even thought it prudent to mention an acquaintance of theirs, Mr Anson, who was presently courting the fourteen-year-old daughter of the Earl of Leicester, 'whose quietness and mildness have inspired him with the idea that she will be a *Stayer-at-Home*', which, thought Lady Stafford, was a good thing, 'not like the London Ladies who make Dissipation their Business'.[19] Alas, as we will see, her son indeed went on to break his mother's heart. But sons were not the only ones causing familial anxiety.

Lustful male youths sought and found libidinous pleasure while Grand Touring and often with *English* women, also touring. Worse still, some English ladies abroad failed to find their compatriots as stimulating as their foreign counterparts. This was one of the apparent 'dangers' suggested by those opposed to women's freedom to travel, such as a writer for the *London Journal* who, in 1731, thought that 'it is highly probable, that by means of our ladies travelling, some of our noble families may be honoured with a French dancing master's son for their heirs'.[20] And here again we see the source of the offence: women's 'liberty', the freedom to act for themselves, to take lovers or even to travel, was regarded less as a menace to morality than a fundamental threat to English gentlemen's property.

'I was left *alone* at twenty years old in a foreign country without a relation or a real friend,' so Lady Webster bemoaned her circumstances in the summer of 1792.[21] She and her husband, Sir Godfrey Webster, had embarked on their travels the previous summer, when his parliamentary duties ended. Soon after there emerged a dispute over his defeat at the polls which, at the urging of his political patron Thomas Pelham, required Sir Godfrey's prompt return to England. Despite her apparent protest – being left '*alone*' – Lady Webster, in fact, was relieved to be rid of him. As she immediately made clear, after his departure she was left with 'some of the least miserable, I might add the most happy hours, of my life'.[22]

Lady Webster was born Elizabeth Vassall in March 1771. She came from an affluent family who had reaped the rewards of their ancestors' interests in the New World, dating from the *Mayflower*'s voyage to Massachusetts – a ship that was part of the merchant fleet owned by Samuel Vassall. Thereafter they amassed their wealth from the slave trade, Jamaican plantations and New England estates. Elizabeth, an only child, became moneyed at the age of eight. From then on, events in her life moved rapidly.

Elizabeth soon attracted suitors, and in 1786 Godfrey Webster wrote to her parents extolling Elizabeth's merits and expressing his sentiments towards her; whilst acknowledging that her parents 'wld not be v. ready to part with Her', he asked for their consent to marriage. Presumably after weighing up the advantages of the union – taking into account Elizabeth's wealth, title and position in society – they decided they were indeed prepared to do so, even though she was merely fifteen and Webster forty-nine.

However, such age discrepancies were not uncommon in a time when mercenary marriages were being regularly created. When the bluestocking Mary Granville was seventeen, her uncle, George Granville, Baron Lansdowne, vied for a political alliance by forcing her into marrying sixty-year-old Alexander Pendarves. Mary recorded the moment when she first feasted her eyes on her husband-to-be: 'I expected to have seen somebody with the appearance of a gentleman,' she wrote in her autobiography, 'when the poor old dripping, almost drowned, Pendarves was brought into the room, like Hob out of the well. His wig, his coat, his dirty boots, his large unwieldy person, and his crimson countenance, were all subjects of great mirth and observation to me.' Her family attempted to soothe her dismay by organising a grand wedding ceremony the following summer, but it was hopeless. 'I was married with the greatest pomp,' Mary recollected. 'Never was one dressed out in gayer colours, and when I was led to the altar, I wished from my soul I had been led, as Iphigeneia was, to be sacrificed. I was sacrificed. I lost not life, but all that makes life desirable – joy and peace of mind.'[23]

Fortunately for Mary, the gouty, drunken squire died seven years later, and, at the age of forty-three, she met and married a more amenable match – an impoverished aristocrat named Patrick Delany – although she had great difficulty securing her family's approval.[24] Her personal situation made her highly critical of the undue anxiety felt by mothers to marry off their daughters. To her, the whole 'race' that women 'too-young' were set off to run in life, where 'a husband is to be the prize', earned them miserable rewards.[25]

Elizabeth Vassall would surely have agreed. Since she was still a minor at fifteen, a special marriage licence needed to be obtained from the Archbishop of Canterbury. Her marriage to Sir Godfrey Webster took place on 26 June 1786, but she never forgot that unhappy day. On her seventh wedding anniversary she wrote in her journal of how that 'fatal day seven years [ago] gave me, in the bloom and innocence of fifteen, to the power of a being who has made me execrate my life since it has belonged to him'. This she wrote when she was travelling with her husband in Italy. However, she was beginning to feel that there was a way out. 'Despair often prompts me to a remedy within my reach. "To enjoy is to obey,"' she recited, adding 'to be wretched is to disobey.' Was this situation set in stone? Could she take charge of her own destiny? She wondered: 'If Providence interposes not for my relief, may I not seek it?' Her remorse concerning the loss of her 'innocence' to Sir Godfrey and consignment to the shackles of a loveless marriage led her to contemplate an escape much more serious than a change of social scenery:

> My mind is worked up to a state of savage exaltation, and impels me to act with fury that proceeds more from passion and deep despair than I can in calmer moments justify. Oftentimes in the gloom of midnight I feel a desire to curtail my grief, and but for an unaccountable shudder that creeps over me, ere this the deed of rashness would be executed. I shall leave nothing behind that I can regret. My children are yet too young to attach me to existence, and Heaven knows I have no close, no tender ties besides. Oh, pardon the audacity of the thought![26]

Lady Webster's gloom was more deeply embedded than anything that could be attributed to a seven-year itch. In fact the relationship had been on the decline right from the beginning, when her husband began suffering from severe bouts of depression and started excessive drinking and gambling. To this was added fits of jealousy.

Before Sir Godfrey returned to England, the travelling party was joined in Lausanne by Thomas Pelham – who appears not to have turned his doting eyes from Elizabeth from the moment he first saw her. Maria Holroyd, who also travelled with the group to visit the glaciers at Chamouni in Switzerland, witnessed the apparent rivalries among the men. 'It will be a true Party of Pleasure,' she wrote to her aunt:

> in other words, the most unpleasant thing in the world. The Party consists of Sir G. and Lady Webster, Severy, and us. Sir G. is more cross than you can imagine; in short, he has just discovered that he is married, and that Mr P. has a great regard for his Lady.[27]

For aristocrats – male and female – to travel in groups with a large travelling retinue was quite the norm in the eighteenth century. Lady Mary Coke reported that Lord and Lady Spencer were renowned for travelling 'with as great a suite as usual'. When Lady Coke's cousin, the 5th Duke of Argyll, was planning to take his wife Elizabeth Gunning (who by this time had already left George III's yawning court), for Italy, he had to expand the size of the travelling retinue, since she 'loves a train, [and] carries Lady Augusta and Mrs Clavering with them'. Meanwhile, the Berrys travelled more moderately, requiring transportation enough only to carry 'my sister, myself, and our maid, a mule for my father and another for one of the servants, while the other was left to come over with the carriage' that probably carried the luggage.[28]

Accommodation along the Grand Tourist routes could also be problematic: 'The sitting room of our inn opened into the stables, there was no room in the inn, so my sister & I were wrapp'd up in a blanket, & lay on the floor,' wrote eleven-year-old Harriet Spencer of her and her sister Georgiana's night in Saintes, western France. But, she was keen to point out, she was not complaining: 'Papa says girls of our age should learn not to make a fuss but sleep anywhere.'[29] If she truly did not fret over those conditions, then she must have been a pleasant travelling companion, perhaps fit enough to dissuade Sir William Hamilton of his harsh conviction that 'of all Women in the World, the English are the most difficult to deal with abroad'.[30]

Women had their own ways of overcoming the discomforts of the road. Elizabeth Montagu – who unremittingly complained about the 'evil odours' in foreign lodgings, 'the collected perspiration I suppose of ten thousand travellers' – passed her time reading and writing letters:

> Many a measured mile and letterd post have I passd insen-
> sibly, and unheeded, by being engaged in some frolick
> with Tom Jones, or absorbed in the wonderful adventures
> of Robinson Crusoe. I can with great truth assure you, I
> shall look on my long journey with much less apprehension
> by having Cecilia for my fellow Traveller. If Cecilia has
> half the sense, and half the amiability of Miss Burney, I
> shall find improvement and delight in her company. Per-
> haps you may think my considering these kind of works
> chiefly as travelling companions shews a degree of con-
> tempt for them, but it arises from a very different principle,
> a persuasion that they have power to interest and amuse,
> and that nothing can hinder sympathy with the circum-
> stances and situations, but the intrusions of business or
> company. Interruptions and intrusions of other objects are
> fatal to sympathy, and Fiction fades away in the importu-
> nate solicitations and presence of Realities.[31]

What else would one expect from the Queen of the Bluestockings than to absorb herself in books!

When Sir Godfrey Webster returned to England in late 1791, he left Lady Webster with their three-year-old son and at least one *valet-de-chambre* and a maid (although servants are rarely mentioned in journals). In Nice just a few months later, Elizabeth Webster began to make new acquaintances. 'In Feb 1792,' she recollected, 'the Duncannons, Dowr. Lady Spencer, Dss. of Devonshire, came to Nice: my friendship begun there'.[32] This was a motley crew. The 'D[uchess] of Devonshire' was Georgiana, who arrived – in fact in March, not February – in Nice with her 'Dear friend,' Lady Elizabeth Foster. One year earlier Georgiana had been exiled to the Continent by her husband, the Duke of Devonshire, where she gave birth to her illegitimate daughter, Eliza – the result of her affair with Sir Charles Grey. Along with Lady Elizabeth Foster was *her* illegitimate six-year-old daughter, Caroline St Jules – interestingly, the result of Foster's affair with Georgiana's husband.[33] The Duncannons (the future Lord and Lady Bessborough) were Frederick and his wife Harriet, Georgiana's sister; and the said Lady Spencer was Georgiana and Harriet's mother, who kept a close eye on the behaviour of her daughter, hoping for a reconciliation between her and the Duke of Devonshire.

Georgiana, Harriet and Lady Foster were confidantes. 'I believe there never existed a stricter confidence and friendship than there has for many years between my sister, Ly. Elizabeth, and myself,' Harriet confessed, attempting to smooth over an alleged indiscretion of 'betraying' some secret revealed by her correspondent.[34] The three women needed to protect each other, not least to ward off excessive rumours steaming through society about their graceless behaviour. Lady Spencer might have been fervent in her supervision of Georgiana, but the others too had had their own censurable relationships. On a break from her relationship with the Duke of Devonshire, Lady Foster travelled to Italy and seduced a Swedish diplomat, Count Fersen. In Paris a few years later – whilst pregnant with the Duke of Devonshire's child – she had become involved with the Duke of Dorset, and a few years after that, once more pregnant, she had an affair with the Duke of Richmond, provoking speculation about who the father was this time. Lady Foster's love life did not stabilise until after Georgiana died, when she married the Duke of Devonshire.[35]

Harriet, Georgiana's sister, was not much more settled. In the 1780s she had had affairs with Charles Wyndham, Lord John Townshend, Richard Fitzpatrick, and the playwright Richard Brinsley Sheridan.[36] Her sister's London estate, Devonshire House, was the venue for many of her liaisons – a place which attracted company that even Lady Spencer desired her daughters would mix with less frequently. 'I could not help thinking that a few such acquaintances . . . agreeable people' such as the 'young Mrs Montague' or Lady Mary Palmerston, 'were just what I wish'd for you & your sister,' Lady Spencer wrote to Harriet.[37]

Although much of the Devonshire circle seemed aware of her

activities, her husband, Lord Duncannon did not. Not immediately, at least. When he did find out, in 1788, about his wife's affair with Sheridan, it looked as though their marriage would end. Lord Duncannon started divorce proceedings, a motion that piled stress upon many close to the turbulent triad. 'You will imagine that this affair gave me no little uneasiness,' wrote Eliza Sheridan, Richard's wife (who had known for some time about her husband's philandering, but was anxious to see an end to it).[38] However, Duncannon succumbed to family pressure and decided not to pursue the divorce.

To add insult to his already injured pride, Lord Duncannon then learnt that he was required to pay thousands of pounds of debts incurred by his wife. In the summer of 1790, family tensions became further strained when Georgiana, Duchess of Devonshire, nearly died in childbirth.[39] In 1791 events finally became too much for Harriet: she collapsed, suffering temporary paralysis of her left side. It is likely that she had had a stroke, but there are no detailed accounts of her illness, and the cause of the convulsions she also experienced was a mystery. Anne Seymour Damer, relaying the gossip about Harriet to Mary Berry, described it as a 'violent illness, the precise cause of which the Physicians could not account for'. Perhaps it was 'some inward disease', since Anne was under the impression 'she was breeding' at the time. Damer had heard that others were more speculative: some thought 'that she was not ill at all, but confined by her husband; some that she was mad; some that she had poisoned herself, and assigned all the necessary and plausible causes'.[40] Such was the uncertain state of medical knowledge in the eighteenth century, though her later symptoms suggest that she was suffering from tuberculosis or 'consumption'.

Others believed Harriet's illness was the consequence of her husband's uncontrollable temper. Besides turning into a gambler and a drinker, reports had it that Lord Duncannon was, like Sir Godfrey, also prone to jealous fits and abusive behaviour. Concerns had been voiced about Duncannon's moody disposition at the time of his marriage to Harriet. Before the ceremony, Harriet's mother bestowed some prudent advice, telling her to be judicious over the management of her money and preserve her piety, and she spelled out conduct appropriate to a companionate marriage:

> I will not suppose it necessary to caution you not to give [Lord Duncannon] the least foundation for jealousy by your behaviour to men. Reason & religion, even without your affection for him, will make you always, I trust, think of such an idea with horror . . . we are all but too fond of admiration, & many a woman has fallen a sacrifice to the snares it has held out; your own good sense will easily furnish the best means of discouraging such foolish & improper conversations, if you really are as desirous as you should be, to put a stop to them.

As for the bond with her female friends or family, that too was likely to provoke her husband:

> But there is another kind of jealousy which it will be more necessary you should be aware of, a jealously arising from your husband being conscious how much he loves you & fearing you have more confidence in your sister, your family, or even some female friend, than in him; this would be an unfortunate weakness, but is not an uncommon one in people of great sensibility.[41]

It soon became clear that Lord Duncannon was guilty of such 'weaknesses', a condition perhaps aggravated by the fact that Harriet surrendered to the emotions that her mother so earnestly wished she would resist, placing more confidence in her friends than her husband.

Harriet was nineteen when she married, afterwards she confided to her sister:

> I wish I could have known him a little better first but my dear Papa and Mama say that it will make them the happiest of creatures, and what would I not do to see them happy, to be sure the connections are the pleasantest that can be . . . when one is to choose a companion for life (what a dreadful sound that has) the inside and not the out is what one ought to look at.

When she did begin to know him, she grew frightened of his temper. Not long after their marriage, Lord Duncannon erupted at a ball, yelling at Harriet, according to shocked spectators, in an apparently unprovoked attack. 'I never felt more ashamed or hurt than I did for you, and I must tell you that your Behaviour did not escape the notice of the Company who heard it as well as myself with astonishment,' Lord Duncannon was told by his cousin, the Duchess of Portland. 'The cards were getting to your mind, nothing had happened to put you out of your humour, but upon Lady Duncannon's coming into the Room, as I thought very properly dressed, your temper was immediately ruffled because she had put on her diamonds.'[42] It was a humiliating public spectacle and apparently not the first. Harriet's mother, Lady Spencer, started to comment on her son-in-law's liking for gaming, while others from their circle began to express their dislike for him. According to Anne Damer, Lord Duncannon was merely 'a peevish little mortal', and 'abuse has been lavished on Harriet, without reserve'.[43]

When the party embarked on their continental tour in late 1791, Lord Duncannon believed it was to help alleviate Harriet's ailments. Unbeknown to him, Georgiana was then pregnant with Charles Grey's child and she sought a temporary escape from her husband until she gave birth. Initially she and Harriet contrived to use Harriet's sickness as an excuse to travel. Georgiana's husband discovered the truth, however, and presented his wife with an ultimatum. 'We must go abroad – immediately,' Harriet insisted, knowing that the Duke had threatened separation, and had cast Georgiana out until she gave birth.[44]

Once abroad Lord Duncannon quickly grew bored by the Grand Tour and concerned with obligations back in England, occupied his mind writing idle observations about the condition of European society and the slow progress of his wife along the road to recovery. 'Harriet bears the journey as well as could be expected,' he reported to his father.[45]

Shortly after their arrival at Nice in May 1792, Duncannon returned, albeit temporarily, to England, leaving Harriet to continue her convalescence. Lady Webster and Lady Duncannon were relieved to be away from their husbands. Lady Webster was now accompanied by her son, Godfrey Vassall Webster, and Lady Duncannon by her only daughter, seven-year-old Caroline. She was saddened, however, at being apart from her five-, nine- and eleven-year-old sons (the eldest ones resided at Harrow). 'I told you I was not well,' she wrote to them in December, '& I believe the lowness of my spirits that I felt, was a good deal encreas'd by recollecting that on that day year, I quitted you all, my dear loves.' She had been on the Continent for over a year, but the year before that she also spent mostly away from home. 'I hope you still remember me & continue to love me, but I should be very sorry [if] your little hearts should ever feel the bitterness I have suffer'd at this long separation from you'.[46]

Lady Webster meanwhile was rejoined by her husband, and determined, partly for her own protection, that they would continue travelling in a large party. 'As I had experienced very cruel usage from the unequal and oft times frantic temper of the man to whom I had the calamity to be united,' she explained in her journal, 'it was the wish of my mother, Lady Pelham, Ly. Shelburne, and those I most respected, that I should never venture myself in a journey alone with him.'[47] (Glimpsing ahead in their travels we can see why; her journal is littered with accounts of bursts of his rage, particularly in reaction to his wife's desire to be alone: 'My companion in a paroxysm threw the book I was reading at my head, after having first torn it out of my hands . . .' – this was not an atypical tantrum.) Thereon the travelling itinerary was arranged to coordinate with those of the Duncannons and Devonshires, and for the following few months they rendezvoused at various places – Turin, Rome, Naples – along their route.

Despite the protection afforded by the company of others, Lady Webster again fell into dispute with her husband, mainly over the issue of the pace at which they travelled through the country. In June, after leaving Milan, they 'skirted Lodi, famous for its cheeses and deep sands', but when a violent thunderstorm hit, Lady Webster 'stopped; and notwithstanding abuse and threats I was resolved to stay and not risk my life and my child's with hot horses near a deep river during a heavy storm'. Neither was she prepared to risk the life of the baby she was carrying, due in seven months' time (as far as we know she and Sir Godfrey it seems shared a moment of reconciliation upon his return to the Continent).

When the travellers arrived in Dresden in July, they found 'a numerous society of English', including the shy but charming Lord Henry Spencer, who was on his way to Vienna. Elizabeth Webster was immediately impressed by him. Lord Spencer 'was very witty, and possessed a superabundant stock of irony', she wrote, eagerly recording the crux of her excitement. 'In short, he became ardently in love with me.' He was twenty-two; she had just turned twenty-one: 'and he was the first man who had ever produced the slightest emotion in my heart'. Thereafter Lady Webster attempted to move in circles in which she could avoid her husband. Lady Webster's and Lord Spencer's flirtatious romance continued, becoming especially 'embarrassing', she recorded, when, during an evening at court, Prince Antony mistook the frolicsome couple for husband and wife, and in front of a crowd, complimented Lord Spencer upon her beauty, adding 'I see by your admiration and love for her you are worthy to possess her.' It was, Lady Webster blushed, 'too painful to bear'.[48]

If Sir Godfrey had any suspicions about his wife's activities, they would have only increased when, in early August, the party followed Lord Spencer to Vienna, or, even more indiscreetly, when Lady Webster decided to make an excursion to Budapest. 'Ld. Henry was there,' she entered in her journal. 'We parted on September the 25th or 26th, not later.' Did Sir Godfrey wonder how her 'excursion' went? Or who gave her the gift of her new companion, a spaniel she named Pierrot (shown in portraits of her painted in Naples)?

Naples was always a seductive spot for Grand Tourists, made more so towards the end of the eighteenth century by the glamorous parties thrown at the house of the British envoy Sir William Hamilton. 'The English, of whom we have a large flight this year,' he reported to his nephew, Charles Greville, in 1775, 'have felt the good effects of my being on such a good footing at court.' He told of how 'one or two of the set' took it upon themselves to decide for the rest when it was time to pursue 'the Arts, gaming, whoring, or drinking'. The previous year, he remembered, everyone followed the arts and gaming, this year, 'drinking and gaming' were the prevailing passions with the English. Little had changed in the habits of the British abroad, as the Websters and their companions were to discover when they arrived in Naples at the beginning of 1793.

'The English society was composed of many of my friends,' wrote Lady Webster, including Harriet and her husband, Lord Duncannon; Lady Spencer; the Duchess of Devonshire; Lady Foster; Sir Godfrey's colleague, Thomas Pelham; and Lady Palmerston (who Lady Spencer had once reckoned might be amongst the 'agreeable people' her daughters should mix with). In February, without ceremony, Lady Webster gave birth to a son, whom she named Henry; soon afterwards she resumed her morning walks 'to see the objects most worthy of notice', and passed the evenings with friends. She walked amongst ruins, recalled the Latin poets, studied the architecture, and, as her twenty-second birthday crept nearer, spent the nights by herself, thinking of her situation in life.

> I walked upon the terrace before my window and enjoyed the beauty of the night; the moon shone bright, which added to the lulling sound of the waves [and] filled me with every pleasing and melancholy recollection. Tho' separated by land and sea from some objects too dearly cherished, yet I was tranquil. Prudence satisfied me that all was for the best.[49]

At about this same time, Harriet and Lord Duncannon received word that their circumstances had also changed. In March 1793, Harriet's father-in-law, old Lord Bessborough, died, making her husband Earl, and he headed back to England to settle his estate. For a brief while, the English society that remained in Naples entertained themselves with long soirees. During the days, the tired group would take leisurely sojourns to see local sights. 'Unfortunately the late hours of

Devonshire House are transferred to the Chiaia,' joked Lady Webster whilst waiting for her travelling companions before a visit to a convent in the country, 'so we did not begin our expedition till six o'clock,' finally arriving just before the sun's fiery rays sank behind the promontory of Circe. Such occasions – wandering amidst Elysian fields, gazing at the 'yawning volcano', or relaxing in the balmy Italian summer night air – were what filled Lady Webster with the greatest feelings of tranquillity:

> I never in my life experienced the degree of happiness enjoyed: it was the gratification of mind and sense. The weather was delicious, truly Italian, the night serene, with just enough air to waft the fragrance of the orange flower, then in blossom. Through the leaves of the trees we caught glimpses of the trembling moonbeams on the glassy surface of the bay; all objects conspired to soothe my mind and the sensations I felt were those of ecstatic rapture. I was so happy that when I reached my bedroom, I dismissed my maid, and sat up the whole night looking from my window upon the sea.[50]

In nearby apartments, her English compatriots continued to enjoy each other's company, perhaps, Lady Webster thought, a little too much. As she prepared to leave Naples, she wondered what was in store for her new friend, Lady Plymouth, who was courting the interest of the young Grand Tourist Lord Berwick (whose Cambridge tutor, Edward Daniel Clarke, was too busy climbing Mount Vesuvius to worry about Berwick's affairs). 'I was sorry at leaving Ly. P.,' she wrote, 'because tho' I am not very prudent, I think she is less so, and I might have kept her out of the scrape she is on the brink of falling into, for Ld. Berwick remains the whole summer.'[51]

Once back on the road the atmosphere soured for both Lady Webster and her friend Harriet (now Lady Bessborough). In Rome, Lady Webster was eager to see the sights, and to admire the city's art and antiquarian collections. To her frustration Sir Godfrey was impatient to keep moving. 'In all the collections much escapes me,' she complained in her journal, after jotting some notes about paintings, 'as

I am always accompanied by one whose impetuosity compels me to hasten from objects I would willingly contemplate, and whose violence of temper throws me into agitations that prevent me distinguishing the objects when they are before me.' Sir Godfrey was not only bored with sightseeing; he was fed up with being abroad altogether. 'The present reigning grievance is the being from home,' concluded Lady Webster; particularly irksome to Sir Godfrey was 'my determined love for being abroad.'[52] She drew the crucial distinction and perfectly divided the emotions: he was upset at being *away from home*, away from his seat of power; she relished *being abroad*, where she could gently gain greater self-determination for herself.

When Lady Harriet Bessborough arrived in Rome, Lady Webster thought that she looked 'ill, very ill'. Leaving the breezy Neapolitan air, she ventured, may have troubled her consumption. Although her husband commiserated, expressing his 'disappointment' at her ill health ('It is a sad disappointment your having any more spitting of blood,' he wrote from England), he needed to clarify some issues about her outstanding debts, which did not make her feel any better. He discovered that she owed one firm £1,100, 'which I wish you had told me of'. But having paid off this debt several further claims landed on his desk. 'For God's sake tell me all your debts, there is no use in concealing them,' he demanded with a note of rising anxiety. 'I don't say I can pay them, but we might make some arrangement of them to make them less ruinous.' Over the next few weeks Lord Bessborough paid out upwards of £3,000 to help clear Harriet's debts. (No matter how much of a spendthrift Harriet was, her liabilities fell worlds short of Georgiana's staggering debt approaching £100,000.)[53]

With her financial affairs now out in the open, Harriet's tensions began to recede. With winter approaching she determined to return to Naples for the sake of her health. Before the year's end, she and her daughter Caroline were reunited with Willy, her six-year-old son, who had travelled out with Lord Bessborough. Willy ran around Naples wide-eyed and excited. He dictated a letter home to his siblings:

Brothers, I have seen an irruption on Mount Vesuvius. I have not yet been up Mount Vesuvius though. My sister sends her love to you. I have been to Virgil's tomb, if you know any such person, he lived about 1800 years ago. We are at Naples. Virgil wrote poems.

While Lady Bessborough was enjoying the family reunion (climbing up the volcano with her mother, Lady Spencer, and gathering a lava collection), Lady Webster was becoming more melancholic. She was travelling north; Sir Godfrey was coaxing her into returning to England, while she invented delays. Was all of her comfort destined to be left behind, her desires banished to an 'imaginary happiness'? In the serenity of her evenings, she longed for someone with whom to share her emotions.

> For in spite of my cold maxims of solitary comforts I feel a strong desire to be dependent upon another for happiness. The want of passion in my constitution will always save me from the calamity of letting my heart run away with my reason, but what will be my resource if both head and heart accord in their choice?

Lord Henry Spencer might have been the first to arouse her passions, which she managed to suppress, but, with the threat of returning to a life of domestic boredom in England, what if reason and romance combined to overthrow her situation? She wondered if she had enough strength to do it. Travelling had given her knowledge of the world and had sharpened her perspective. 'A revolution has happened in my whole system; my opinions are more formed, and tho' I am conscious that they retain still a portion of absurdity, yet I have adopted some that will be useful.'

Pressures to return home became almost irresistible, however, when she received news from England that her father was gravely ill and wished to see her. What would she do? Returning to England might put an end to any hope of happiness; she dreaded being locked away once more in her husband's home, secluded and denied any hope of escape. 'All human miseries must have a termination,' she cried in her journal, 'this consoles, tho' at 22, it is a melancholy consolation.' She determined she would not return to England without a guarantee that she could return to the Continent, 'a pledge for my return', as she described it.

The fear of being locked away in the family home was not unique to Lady Webster. Unless forbidden through a clause in a separation deed, husbands had the right to 'seize' forcibly and confine – but not 'imprison' – their wives; ('confining' a wife was not declared illegal until 1891).[54] As a writer on the *Hardships of Laws on Wives* wrote in the 1730s, 'Wives may be made prisoners for life, at the discretion of their domestic governors, whose power ... bears no manner of proportion to that degree of authority which is vested in any other set of men in England.'[55]

But the legislation of such behaviour was inadequately enforced, and men found more flexibility in the legality of their actions than women were able to find remedies against ill treatment. In 1769, when Princess Amelia heard that Lady Sarah Bunbury (née Lennox) had given birth to an illegitimate child, she speculated to Lady Coke about her options, concluding that 'her running away from him wou'd give him a right to lock her up for the rest of her life' if caught. Lady Coke, however, was under the hopeful impression 'that times were alter'd, & I was persuaded she wou'd not be lock'd up, tho' I remember'd when people were locked up for no fault at all.'[56] When there was 'reason', there was little restraint on the man's behalf. In 1770, for example, Jonathan Collet brought an action against his wife for having committed adultery 'with diverse strange men', 'particularly a man in a meadow, dressed in a scarlet or red coat'. Furthermore, her taste for liquor allegedly fired her temper, requiring her husband to administer a few blows to calm her down, even though he was 'not a person of a cruel and malignant temper and disposition'. When that did not work she was put in a madhouse for a couple of weeks. Once back home, she still needed to be restrained. One witness testified that the husband needed to borrow a handkerchief, with which he tied her hands behind her, but she soon got loose again; and afterwards he chained her with a little jack-chain to the floor, but she soon got loose; and he afterwards chained her with the same chain for near a fortnight; that she got loose sometimes, and he let her loose upon her promise of behaving better; but when she got loose she would throw the first thing she met with at the said [husband]; and then he said she should suffer, and confined her again; but she did not seem to mind it, and contrived to get loose.

'Getting loose', of course, would lead to her being returned to her spot to 'suffer' more, so this logic dictated she must not have minded the recurring process. The court sympathised with the husband's predicament, and a divorce was granted on grounds of adultery.[57]

Lady Webster was already loose and determined not to be further constrained. 'How much I detest the prospect of a residence in England, even though it be but for a few weeks,' she fumed upon her decision to return, for however brief it would be: 'country, climate, manners, everything is odious to me'. Leaving her children behind in Italy (her 'pledge' and guarantee to return), 'comfortable, established in a good house with proper attendants', she and her husband headed home.

'I turned my back on Italy with regret,' she wrote ('dear, dear Italy' as she would refer to it). Happiness was now suspended for the duration of her expedition home. 'Every step that approaches me to England lowers my spirits. Oh! how I abhor the thoughts of living in that country. No friends! No relations!' Lady Webster was carried over the Alps backwards, always keeping her eyes fixed in the direction of her beloved Italy. She heard dogs – 'known for their sagacity in seeking the bewildered traveller lost under a mass of snow' – barking in the distance as they searched for missing bodies. The snow on one side of the mountain was very deep, and her porters 'waded through it with great labour; they often fell, but I was neither hurt nor frightened'.[58] But she was not bothered. She claimed to feel 'indifferent' about life, and able to jettison petty fears of falling or the bitterness of the piercing wind. One wonders what attitude towards life her porters had.

'Dover, 1st December, 1793 – Occupation and vexation prevented me from keeping anything like a journal during the whole of my stay in this odious country.' Therefore Lady Webster spent a few moments jotting down from memory what had occupied her time during the three months she had been required to stay in England. Before going to their family home in Battle ('where I languished in solitude and discontent the best years of my life'), she visited her father in Windsor, where she optimistically reported he was 'better, tolerably cheerful, but very weak'. She then spent some time at the home of Thomas Pelham's parents in Stanmer, where he was also staying at the time. He was 'of course enchanted at seeing me', she wrote.

Whilst with 'Tom', she met up with her neighbours, Lord and Lady Sheffield, whose daughter, Maria Holroyd, was less than impressed with Elizabeth's continental affectations. 'Her Ladyship has entirely adopted Foreign Manners and Customs,' she commented after observing Antonio, Lady Webster's Italian servant, washing her mistress's feet before she retired to bed. While she had only been in the country for a couple of weeks, Lady Webster was already making plans to return to the Continent: 'she says she means to go abroad in ten days, and Heaven grant she may keep her Resolution!', sighed Miss Holroyd.[59]

She did; but her flight back to the Continent was less than straightforward. Each week the French armies gained more victories – most recently over the Prussians and Austrians. The French monarchy had been not only dethroned but decapitated, and England was again at war with France. 'The accounts from Paris make one shudder,' wrote Lady Webster, relieved at having safely circumvented France, via Belgium, Germany and Switzerland. 'The guillotine is active, and hundreds daily perish by that horrible machine of death.' Despite the extreme turbulence of the times, she had managed to fulfil her commitment to return to the Continent and to reaffirm her 'determined love for being abroad'.

By mid-January 1794 Lady Webster was back in Florence, 'and found to my supreme delight both my dear children perfectly well'. She also found that continental passion was just as pronounced as it was when she left. ('Ld. H[ervey] implies his love for Ly. B.,' Hervey had confided to her, 'I shut my ears, as I abhor these sort of confidences.') But before long, she found herself submerged in a *comédie de mœurs*. On the first of February, two twenty-year-old English gentlemen arrived in Florence: Lord Granville Leveson-Gower and Henry Richard Fox, the 3rd Lord Holland.

Leveson-Gower had previously met Lady Webster in Dresden, at the time when she became entangled with Lord Henry Spencer. When he mentioned their first encounter to his mother, she (in an attempt to prevent any besmirching of her son's reputation) used the opportunity to denounce Lady Webster's character: 'I have seen Lady Webster,' she wrote,

> she was a very pretty, innocent looking woman, but I saw her in bad Company, with bad Connections – I mean bad for domestic Happiness – and her Husband never near her, and I then fear'd they would not long continue happy. When you get a Wife, I trust you will *go* and *come* together, and not think it necessary that she should live with the fashionable bad Wives about London.[60]

Now, a year and a half on, it was Leveson-Gower's fresh face and devilish charm that enticed Lady Webster. 'He is remarkably handsome and winning,' she wrote. He was no longer his 'mother's little boy'; over the last 'year or two', Lady Sutherland had presented him in Parisian society as her *beau beaufrère*, and 'initiated him to the orgies of gambling, an acquisition he has maintained'. His travelling companion, Lord Holland, did not at first strike Lady Webster's fancy. Despite having come from Spain with a Mediterranean tan and in good health, she felt that 'Ld. H. is not in the least handsome.' Yet, after attending a few dinners at which he was present, his good nature began to grow on her. 'Ld. H. quite delightful; his gaiety beyond anything I ever knew; full of good stories.'[61]

While Lady Webster's amorous affections were warming to the new company, another recent arrival had fallen for her. 'Surprise and embarrassment have completely overset me. Oh! what vile animals men are, with headstrong passions.' An old acquaintance of Lady Webster's, Sir Gilbert Elliot, had been shipwrecked near the coast at Leghorn (Livorno) and had arrived in Florence suggesting to her that all the danger and excitement had aroused his prurient passions. 'Pécher en *secret*, n'est point pécher,' – a secret sin is not a compromising sin – he whispered to her. 'I told him it savoured of his Jesuitical education,' she retorted, but she was all the more shocked since she – along with most other English who held their company – knew that he usually preached his own maxims of morality and domestic virtue. Lady Webster at first reasoned away his behaviour:

> His long absence from home, perfect seclusion, and the
> strong impression of delight at meeting a countrywoman
> who brought back the remembrance of past scenes – this
> complicated feeling made him deck the object who revived
> the recollection in glowing colours, and in him created a
> violent and, I hope, a transitory alienation from sense and
> propriety.

After this first awkward encounter, she did not quite know how to shake off Sir Gilbert's advances. And when he attempted to seduce her when returning home in a carriage one night, Lady Webster recorded that she 'was compelled to get out of the carriage to avoid his pressing importunities.' At this moment Sir Gilbert quickly came to his senses, and became alarmed that his wife might hear of his actions and his reputation for conjugal felicity would be ruined. In his retreat he pleaded 'Be *kind* and *discreet*.'[62]

She found herself where she left off on her way back to England five months earlier – contemplating the powers of her own 'passion in my constitution'. Back then, at a dinner party in Lausanne she flirted with the 'clever, very handsome, and very captivating' Lord George Morpeth, but soon realised that his interests lay elsewhere. 'If I were addicted to coquetry I believe I could easily become her rival,' Lady Webster wrote with an air of condescending confidence. 'A pretty young woman is always sure of as many lovers as she chooses, but to *me* there would be more humiliation than glory in such a train.' So – in fitting fashion – she 'amused' herself by attending a ball thrown by the ageing libertine, Casanova.

On the road a few days later she was 'extremely irritated' to find that a certain Mr Douglas had decided to pursue her from Lausanne. 'I knew that a timely check might rid me of his company for the journey.' So, she stopped her carriage, 'spoke to him with cold civility' and sent him on his way. Her strategy worked. 'He looked embarrassed, took the rebuff, and turned back.' But during these episodes her mind remained preoccupied with Lord Henry Spencer. When she arrived in Belgium on her way to England she met with the first true test of controlling her passion. There, she received a packet of letters from Lord Spencer, who 'talks of coming to meet me', but it was not easy as 'he can be absent from The Hague [where he was Secretary to Lord Auckland] only by stealth'. She determined this time that her head and heart were on the same terms. 'Wrong as it will be, my inclination would get the better of my reason if I had the measure to decide upon, but as I have *not*, it must take its chance.' Alas, at the last moment Lord Spencer was sent to Stockholm and they failed to meet. Sadly, that proved their last opportunity: he died two years later in Berlin, aged twenty-four.[63]

While the occasions of courtship and rejection upon her return to the Continent might by then have seemed all too familiar, Elizabeth Webster was nonetheless developing a new romantic intrigue. At the end of February 1794 she proceeded with a gaggle of flirtatious English men and women to Naples. There she was reunited with Lady Bessborough and Lady Spencer, along with 'a numerous band of young Englishmen from college; gambling and gallantry filled up the evenings and mornings'. She also caught up on the gossip about the previous summer's romances: 'Ld. Berwick behaved shockingly to poor Ly. Plymouth: she is very unhappy'; 'Ld. [Edward] Digby fell in love with Ly. Bruce, who only coquets with him.' Lady Webster did not abstain from the entertainment, but she had trouble deciding whose company she preferred most. 'My favourite, Ld. G. Leveson-Gower, used often to come to me in the evening, as I sat at home a good deal on account of my *grossesse* and disliking the card parties.' But his companion, Lord Holland, who 'is quite delightful' was rapidly gaining favour. She wrote a lengthy paragraph in her journal outlining all the mature, agreeable points about his political philosophy, which others had reckoned 'very like his uncle' – referring to the political hero Charles James Fox.[64] 'Though so zealous,' she summed up, 'he is totally without party rancour; in short, he is exactly what all must like, esteem, and admire.'[65]

Also in Naples and hobnobbing in society generally was Charles Beauclerk. It was no secret that he was in love with Lady Harriet Bessborough. During a large party excursion to Tivoli, near Rome, Beauclerk's attraction apparently overstepped the boundary of discretion, provoking Lord Bessborough to erupt in a fit of jealousy, causing the party to return to Rome. Harriet and Lady Webster probably found this amusing, for they both knew that Lady Bessborough had other admirers.

Ladies Webster and Bessborough were fast becoming close friends – spending every morning together and embarking on local excursions. They also became confidantes, for Lady Webster had made up her mind about which of the gallant duo she was more interested in. Therefore, accompanying them on their local excursions was Lord Holland, and their trips provided a modus operandi for the development of their affair. Lady Bessborough was happy to provide their alibis; after all, she had fallen in love with Lord Holland's closest friend, Lord Leveson-Gower. It appears the couples pulled off their covert affairs with great aplomb. The only bystander who fostered any suspicions was Charles Beauclerk, who, as Lady Webster detected, 'abhors Ld. Granville, who is his rival'.

Harriet Bessborough's frolic with Lord Leveson-Gower proved to be relatively short-lived. In May, after their brief visit to Rome and Beauclerk's last attempt to woo Lady Bessborough, she headed back to England. She longed to see her sons from whom she had been apart for over three years and her husband was anxious to get back to attend certain parliamentary debates. But the English society in Italy as a whole was breaking up. The French armies were ripping through Belgium and the English were massing arms to defend against what was increasingly feared to be an imminent invasion by the French. Most of the men who had enjoyed 'lounging and talking' amongst the fashionable Neapolitan circles, including Lords Granville, Digby, Boringdon and others who were militia officers, were required to return to their regiments in England.

Lady Bessborough and Lord Leveson-Gower parted with the '*half* promise' that she would write to him. Within a month of their departure, when she was temporarily in Rome and he was back in England, her half promise proved sincere. She wrote that Lady Webster left for Florence, followed by Lord Holland, and added that she now wanted a letter from him in return, with 'a list of sins you will have to confess before we meet again, if you retain me for your confessor, and put yourself in the *palais de la verité*'.[66] This was the first letter in a stream of correspondence connecting them in a union that would last until Lady Bessborough's death, twenty-seven years later, in 1821 – a relationship that bore the lovers two children.

As soon as Lady Webster arrived in Florence, she took up residence in 'a palace' and was shortly joined by Lord Holland, who 'assured me he came merely to make me a visit'. On 12 June, Lady Webster gave birth to her third child. Lord Holland stayed in Florence long enough to see the christening of her new daughter, whom she named Harriet Frances (the first two names of Lady Bessborough, who was also one of her 'sponsors'). The child had been conceived when Lady Webster was in England, staying with Thomas Pelham at his parents' Stanmer estate. Pelham, who was still promoting the political career of Lady Webster's husband, knew that he was the father of the child. 'Thank God that all has ended so well in Florence,' he feverishly wrote. Sir Godfrey, however, apparently suspected nothing, and believed himself to be the father – a belief obligingly encouraged by Pelham. 'I will certainly exert myself to the utmost,' he wrote to Lady Webster, for you have often said that any marks of Friendship shown to Sir G. have been attended with good effects on his conduct towards you and I shall continue as far as I may be able to keep him in that sort of temper as may make his séjour with you in the particular situation you are now in as comfortable as possible.

Thomas Pelham would have done anything for his lover. 'To promote yr. happiness is so decidedly the object of my life, that the only difference or hesitation that can ever arise must be about the means'. Sadly for him, another courtier had already stolen Lady Webster's heart.[67]

With Lord Holland temporarily away, Lady Webster passed her time quietly in Florence, taking 'solitary expeditions' and mixing with company she had never met before. 'They must have thought me a strange person, young, pretty, and alone, travelling merely to see the quarries of Carrara! It was perhaps an odd freak.' By the following summer, 1795, Sir Godfrey finally set off, without his wife and children, for England. Soon afterwards, Lady Webster took up residence at the Lucca Baths near Pisa; nearby was Lord Holland, who 'dined and supped with me every day' along with various other visitors. From then on their relationship grew uninhibited.

In April 1796 a crisis emerged. Lady Webster was two months pregnant with Lord Holland's child and she needed to decide what action she should take. There was no doubt that Sir Godfrey would discover the illegitimate child and divorce her. Would she be able to withstand the public humiliation of facing adultery charges in court? More agonising still, could she bear to lose all her children in the divorce? Her fears were well founded. A woman who had committed, or was believed to have committed adultery, would inevitably face separation from her children. Fleeing to, or remaining on, the Continent was the surest way of keeping her children.

Lady Webster's anxiety drove her to extreme measures. She vowed to at least keep two-year-old Harriet Frances, who 'required the tenderness of a mother'. Should she take the baby and run away, 'retire and bury myself in some remote corner'? If so, would she be able to bear hiding and absolute isolation? But she equally feared involving Lord Holland in a custody battle. The decision that she was compelled to make, 'out of *necessity*', was that she would 'give up' her daughter. But she did not intend to give Harriet Frances to Sir Godfrey. Her plot was much more sinister.

If a baby at this time developed measles, it often led to further complications – fevers, sweating, faintness, even leading to coma and death itself. Such illnesses developed quickly, with each deleterious stage following an all-too familiar and predictable pattern. Measles and fevers were epidemic; only a few weeks earlier Lady Webster needed to isolate her son, little Godfrey, from the children at the royal palace in Caserta who were suffering from measles. The danger seemed to lurk in every town. After separating from Lord Holland at Prato, Lady Webster, with her children and servants, headed for Modena. On the road, she anxiously called out to her servants that little Harriet had been taken ill and was developing measles. As the travellers detoured to a small village the fear was confirmed when the nursery maid caught a glimpse of red spots on the baby's arm. Hurriedly, she and the other servants were ordered to escort her sons, Henry and Godfrey, on to Modena, leaving Lady Webster and baby Harriet behind. Once alone, Lady Webster transformed her guitar case into a small coffin, filling it with rocks and pillows, and placing a mask inside – which customarily indicated the death of a diseased child. A footman was ordered to carry the coffin to the British consul in Leghorn with instructions for its burial. Wiping the red paint off Harriet's arm and dressing her in male clothes, she then ordered a maid to proceed with Harriet and her own child to an address in Hamburg and await further instructions. Lady Webster then rejoined the others in Modena, relaying the tragic news that Harriet had died.[68]

The daring plan was successful. Sir Godfrey seems never to have questioned the death of the little girl whom he had believed to be his daughter (neither, apparently, did Thomas Pelham), while Harriet in fact lived on secretly in England. Only later, in 1799, did Lady Webster reveal the truth to her own mother.

When Lady Webster finally returned to England in June 1796 (now four months pregnant), Sir Godfrey promptly initiated divorce proceedings. Since his wife was an adulteress, the law permitted him to sue her lover for 'criminal conversation' with his wife, seeking money for 'damages' to his property.[69]

Initially Lady Webster and Lord Holland rented part of Brompton Park House – the Victoria and Albert Museum now stands on its site – where Lady Bessborough hoped they would quietly remain until after the baby was born. They contemplated eloping abroad, but Thomas Pelham recommended that Lady Webster go on her own and 'reflect – for a few days at Lausanne'.[70] But her pregnancy was not concealed, and the affair was made public. When Lord Granville learned about the ruckus, he wrote to Lady Bessborough, encouraging her to exercise caution in her friendship with Lady Webster. 'You know by this time how unnecessary your cautions on poor Ly. Webster's account were,' she replied to him. 'I knew of her situation before her arrival in England,' and as an unselfish friend, no 'motives of personal prudence [could] have prevented my doing every thing in my power to conceal it, to soothe her and endeavour to dissuade her from the rash step she has now taken' of planning to elope with Lord Holland. When Lord Granville's parents heard the flamboyant lovers' plans, his father – concerned about the political future of his son – wished a message be clearly conveyed to him. 'He desired me to observe *to you* the Misery, Disgrace, and Ruin that follow such Connections,' wrote his mother. 'Ruin' – possible. 'Disgrace' – perhaps; but eighteenth-century aristocrats seemed to be capable of swiftly rinsing off the emotional stains in the whole continuum of guilt, shame, embarrassment, humiliation and disgrace. Lord Granville replied philosophically, hoping to allay his father's fears about his own conduct – a gesture his mother saw right through. '*I say* you are a little cunning Villain,' she wrote,

> You *know* what is right . . . *But* do you not act according to this Persuasion? Are you not drawn on and on by a Passion that absorbs all your Faculties, that employs your every Thought, and that draws you from every laudable

worthy Pursuit, and weans your affections from all those who are not connected in this unfortunate Affair?'[71]

In November, Lady Webster gave birth to a son, Charles Fox Vassall. Lord Holland's sister, Caroline Fox, and Lady Bessborough were both eager to be godparents. Eight months later (and on an appropriate date) Elizabeth was finally divorced from Sir Godfrey. 'My wretched marriage was annulled by Parliament on the 4th July,' she wrote. The divorce would be the scandal of the year – at the social functions she attended for the next couple of years she waded through whispers and giggles. But she showed no embarrassment and never let concerns over unconventional behaviour break her stride. 'I never could Convince Her of the necessity of Conformity to Established Rules,' admitted Sir Godfrey. 'She always looked upon them as formed by Dull People.'[72] Sir Godfrey profited from the settlement: Lord Holland was ordered to pay £6,000 in criminal damages, and Lady Webster signed over her fortune to him (about £7,000 per year revenue from the West Indian estates), save £800 per annum for her own use. But he lived an unhappy life, gaining an enormous gambling debt. Three years later, in June 1800, Sir Godfrey was found dead in his study with a pistol lying beside him.[73]

Two days after her divorce Elizabeth, Lady Webster, married Henry, Lord Holland. 'I was twenty-six years old. Ld. H. was twenty-three. The difference in age is, alas! two years and eight months – a horrid disparity.' She beamed with happiness. 'I never saw creatures so happy,' wrote Lady Bessborough to Lord Leveson-Gower of the day of the wedding. 'Such perfect happiness as theirs scarcely ever was instanc'd before.'[74]

In a society where the marriage contract was held to be sacrosanct, a failed marriage was seen as a failure by the woman to fulfil the most important role of her life. The termination of marriage was a high moral offence, and for any marriage that was ended by wifely adultery, the woman's social life was effectively terminated. For example, when in 1767 Lady Sarah Bunbury grew bored with her marriage and went to Paris, flamboyantly flirting and gambling; her bawdy behaviour led to widespread speculation about moral transgressions. Back home, a year and a half later, and following the birth of an illegitimate daughter, the truth emerged about her affairs. Her marriage to Thomas Charles Bunbury ended and so shortly afterwards she was excluded from society. Whenever it appeared that her 'natural vivacity' was beginning to shine through her 'life of penitence', her sister implored her to 'use disguise enough to look grave'.[75]

Travel provided not just a way out of unhappy marriages, but could emancipate women from restrictive social conventions. Lady Bunbury's elder sister, Emily, Duchess of Leinster, pursued this path. For the greater part of twenty-five years she had been steadfastly devoted to her husband, James Fitzgerald, Duke of Leinster, but following his death in 1773, forty-three-year-old Emily turned squarely towards her son's tutor, William Ogilvie, with whom she had begun a covert love affair just two years previously. There could hardly be a more scandalous match than between a Duchess and a mere tutor. But the solution was decided upon in January 1774, when she determined to take her family abroad. Later that year in Toulouse they were married, and, free from the shackles of social conventionality (and in a less expensive country to boot), they settled in their new lives. For Emily, it could not have worked out better: she was with her lover and was going to live in style.[76] That is something only a newly fashioned life on the Continent could have provided.

The Duchess of Leinster's marriage to Ogilvie was not an elopement, the kind of furtive escape of the sort Lady Webster contemplated, but legal records show that continental elopements were not unknown, as in the case of *Horneck vs. Horneck*. In 1775 Charles Horneck, Esq. sued for divorce from Sarah Horneck (née Keppel, daughter of the Earl of Albemarle), for having committed adultery and eloped to the Continent with John Scawen, the owner of a house in which the married couple temporarily lodged. While no illegitimate children were born and cited as proof of the affair, the 'party proponent' (plaintiffs) provided testimony of servants – often key witnesses used to 'prove' paternity – who were taken with Mrs Horneck and Mr Scawen to France and Italy, where they 'constantly passed for man and wife' and laid in the same bed together, 'and their cloaths lying in the room by the bed-side'.

But even those of less wealth, not so concerned about codes of etiquette or social gossip, fled to the Continent to pursue new lives. In 1777, for example, the Exeter merchant George Degen brought action for divorce against Catherine Degen (née Furlong). After consummating the marriage 'by carnal copulation and the procreation of three children', Catherine fell in love with 'John' Baptiste Larreguy, a recently arrived French tradesmen. Two years after meeting Larreguy, Catherine became pregnant and moved to a house in Holborn, under the alias Mrs Dunning with a housemaid named Mary Osborn. The maid testified that 'Mr Dunning', as he called himself, 'lay with her every night naked and alone in one and the same bed'. Larreguy, however, stopped visiting, so Catherine ordered her servant to buy her a man's suit, and disguising herself with it, she, her illegitimate daughter and the maid travelled back to Exeter, 'within a stone's throw' of her actual husband's house. Reunited and reconciled with her lover, she told the servant 'she was going to France', and that *a* 'Mr. Larreguy had been arrested by her husband, but that he had got off, for he was arrested by a wrong name'. Believed to have fled to France, the couple were never seen again.[77]

The Continent provided an escape from English laws and customs; a refuge from gossip and ostracism; it could even provide a higher standard of living in an alternative society. It could enable some to break away from an unhappy marriage and pursue love affairs. Some simply enjoyed a continental romance; others eloped.

Of course, not all romantic experiences involved making or breaking marriages. In 1783 the spinster Mary 'Moll' Carter and the younger, widowed Louisa Clarges (with her four children), set off on a three-year tour of Europe together. There was a twenty-year age difference between them, but various people suggested they might have been travelling as lovers. They certainly enjoyed a close friendship, and expressed to each other profound love, although there is no indication of a physical relationship – no testimony from eaves-dropping servants, for example. But in a world of social etiquette that adhered to strict formalities in relationships (such as family members referring to each other by their titles), a bond could become 'intimate' if it merely penetrated beyond the spiritless 'rules of engagement' – beyond parlour room introductions and polite conversation.

Unlike the bluestocking Ladies of Llangollen, Miss Sarah Ponsonby and Lady Eleanor Butler, who, deeply in love with each other, lived together in self-imposed exile from fashionable society, Moll Carter and Louisa Clarges parted company, but remained close friends, after their Grand Tour. Moll continued to travel, returning to the Continent in the 1790s, meeting in Italy with the Ladies Webster, Duncannon and Spencer, et al., and risking life and limb by climbing mountains with Lady Palmerston for the sake of adventure. 'Few women but such trampers as we are go there,' she wrote.[78]

If social conventions at home restrained unhappy spouses from separating or from remarrying, one solution was to escape to a different society, especially when there was another lover involved who would offer support. But this is not to say that divorce or adultery only took place abroad. Indeed, puerperal flights abroad or pre-court escapes to the Continent seemed to be rather common. In 1792 the *Town and Country* magazine reckoned that a man being sued for criminal conversation from an affair in England 'prefers a residence in some other country rather than pay a sum which would reduce him almost to penury'. This was reported in a decade when more marriages terminated through actions against 'criminal conversation' than any other decade in its existence (the legal action was abolished in 1857), and by the same time England far surpassed European countries such as France, Austria and Norway in 'private separations'.[79] But for all its 'freedoms', being taken to the Continent could also occasionally work against individual liberties, such as in the case of abductions and forced marriages. The Grand Tour could provide exile as well as a means of enforced change for men and women; it could lead to greater independence and a better education, as well as a loss of innocence, chastity and social mores.

Lubricious behaviour abroad was said not only to undermine the sanctity of the family by threatening the legitimacy of an heir's claim to an estate, but also that such behaviour ultimately chipped away at the foundations of civil society. At least, that is, so long as a woman's chastity was presented as one of the pillars of traditional society. If women failed in marriage and lost their chastity, writers such as Thomas Pollen suggested, then society itself risked the loss of its virtuousness and thereafter Britain would stumble towards inevitable decay in its imperial edifices. Preceding Gibbon's diagnosis that the Roman Empire fell in part as a consequence of its diseased morals and vanishing virtuousness, Pollen lamented that 'as virtue has dropped, so vice has reared its head . . . Where luxury has gained ground, there effeminacy has done the same . . . Where lasciviousness reigns, there flows in a torrent of debauchery, to the destruction of private families and to the insult of public laws.'[80] But for many ladies of the Grand Tour, continental travel did not threaten family integrity so much as fulfil their own desires for liberty and personal enlightenment.

'Air gives us powers over our Own Lives'

Sea Breezes & Sanity

Among the therapeutic agents not to be found bottled up and labelled on our shelves, is Travelling; a means of prevention, of cure, and of restoration, which has been famous in all ages,
Daniel Drake, *Western Medical and Physical Journal*, 1827[1]

In 1792, Mariana Starke, a thirty-year-old London play-wright who had been raised in India where her father was governor of Fort St George in Madras, accompanied a consumptive relative to Italy for a seven-year period of recuperation. Having already used her insight into Anglo-Indian relations as material for her dramas, she took the time while abroad to reflect on her overall experiences as a traveller in charge of the care of another, and recorded practical details for the benefit of future travellers. Knowing that the warm Mediterranean south was the desired destination for those in search of good health, she prepared a list of 'things most requisite for an invalid, and indeed for every family to be provided with on leaving England':

> A cot, so constructed that it may be transformed into a
>   sofa-bed
> Two large thick leather-sheets, two pillows, two
>   blankets
> Two bed-side carpets, pillow-cases, towels, table-cloths,
>   napkins (strong, but not fine)
> Pistols, knives
> A pocket-knife to eat with
> Silver table spoons
> Soup, tea, and salt, spoons
> Sugar-tongs
> A silver or plated tea-pot, a block-tin tea-kettle
> A travelling *chaise-percée*, made to fit the well of a
>   carriage

A block-tin lamp, made to serve for the night, and for
    boiling water, soup, coffee, &c

A tea and sugar chest

Irons and an ironing cloth

Tea, loaf-sugar, fish-sauce, essence of anchovies,
    curry-powder, ketchup, soy, mustard,
    Cayenne-pepper, ginger, nutmegs, oatmeal,
    portable-soup, sago

Pens, pen-knives, wafers, razors, strap, and hone;
    needles, thread, tape, worsted, pins

Saddles and bridles, whether for men or women

Gauze, worsted stockings, flannel waistcoats, and
    drawers to wear next the skin, with new sets of each
    to replace the old

Cork or common double-soled shoes and boots, which
    are absolutely needful in order to resist the chill of
    brick and marble floors – elastic soles

The London and Edinburgh Dispensatory

Buchan's *Domestic Medicine*

De la Lande's *Account of Italy*, Duten's *Itinerary*

A medicine-chest with scales, weights

A rhubarb-grater

An ounce and half-ounce measure for water

A small marble mortar

A knife for spreading blisters

A set of instruments for cleaning and filing teeth,
    tooth-brushes, and leaf-lead

James's powder, castor-oil, bark, harts-horn, sal volatile,
    aether, pure opium, liquid laudanum, paragoric elixir,
    ipecacuanha, emetic tartar, vitriolic acid, spirits of
    lavender, camomile-flowers, antimonial wine, calomel,
    salt of wormwood, essence of peppermint, magnesia,
    blistering salve, yellow basilicum, caustic, lint,
    arquebusade, opodeldoc.[2]

The extent of the equipment, travelling accessories, and cautionary
paraphernalia reflects the complexity and predicaments of travel. All
this was useful advice, offered by an experienced traveller who had
conscientiously made notes – possibly embellished after a rummage

'A Woman in Blue Reading a Letter', by Jan Vermeer, 1663-4. A woman is absorbed in a letter from an absent lover, which brings forth expectant thoughts of distant places – an image recalling the fact that for most women the Grand Tour was an epistolary experience.

Twenty-two-year-old Elizabeth, Lady Webster, later Lady Holland,
with her spaniel Pierrot, by Robert Fagan, 1793.

Henry Richard Fox, 3rd Lord Holland, whom Lady Elizabeth first met in Florence whilst touring with her husband Sir Godfrey Webster.

BELOW Henrietta, 3rd Countess of Bessborough, in classical attire, reflecting the ambience of the ancient Italian lands that so attracted Grand Tourists.

Hester Thrale Piozzi. During her second continental tour in 1785 she sat for a portrait in Rome, where she thought she looked like a 'motley Creature', 'for my Riding Habit was bought at *Rome*. . . my Hat & Shirt at *Naples*; my Shoes at *Padua*, my Stockings at *Brescia*, my Ruffles at *Genoa*, one of my Petticoats at *Milan*, & the rest of my dress in *England'*.

LEFT Mary and Agnes Berry from a painting by Johann Zoffany, *ca* 1783. The inseparable sisters travelled to the Continent together nine times.

BELOW Portrait of Mary Wollstonecraft Godwin, after a painting by John Opie, 1802. After declaring that she was 'not born to tread the beaten track' Mary Wollstonecraft set off for revolutionary Paris to see how citizens' rights could be extended to women.

LEFT Frederick Hervey, 4th Earl of Bristol and Bishop of Derry, with his granddaughter, Lady Caroline Crichton, later Lady Wharncliffe, by Hugh Douglas Hamilton, *ca* 1790-3. They stand in the gardens of the Villa Borghese, where ladies of the Grand Tour such as Mary Berry met artists including Gavin Hamilton, Jacob More, and Jacob Hackert.

Ellis Cornelia Knight by Angelika Kauffman, 1793. In 1785 she moved to Naples with her widowed mother who thought they could live more comfortably in Italy.

'The Customs House at Boulogne', by Thomas Rowlandson. Customs houses and passport controls were always lamentable stopping points for travellers as searches could cause considerable delays; Elizabeth Montagu for one complained about Boulogne's 'wretched Inns' while being detained there.

'Gavin Hamilton leading a party of Grand Tourists to the archaeological site at Gabii', by Giuseppe Cades, 1793. Here, the Scottish artist and connoisseur Gavin Hamilton is acting as a *ciceroni*, taking British Grand Tourists to view treasures bound for the art market at a newly-excavated site.

'The Manner of Passing Mount Cenis', by George Keate, 1755. Traversing the Alps involved leaving one's coach and being carried in a *chaise à porteurs* – the traveller would try to avoid catching a glimpse of the 'vast profundity' over the mountains' precipices.

'Rome Seen on a Grand Tour', by John Feary. Rome in the eighteenth century was the entrepôt of Europe, an obligatory passage point for Grand Tourists and a thriving cosmopolitan centre for artists from across Europe.

'The Falls at Tivoli', by Jacob-Philippe Hackert, 1770. Few Tourists failed to visit the scenic falls at Tivoli, in the Sabine Hills, near the ruins of Hadrian's Villa – an ancient retreat for Roman poets. In 1785 Hester Piozzi described the 'violent roar of the dashing waters' as she walked in the grotto carved into the rocks: 'so sweetly elegant, so rural, so romantic'.

through her kitchen pharmacopoeia – to help others travel with advantage.

Prospective travellers could also benefit by consulting the appendix to Mariana Starke's *Letters from Italy*, published in 1800, just after her return to Britain. Judging from how many horses were necessary to haul the travellers' belongings, such advice was eagerly consumed and closely followed. Besides the practical necessities, it was obviously desirable to make travelling as comfortable as possible. To this end, and sparing no cost, ladies of the Grand Tour travelled with masses of furniture, from specially designed writing tables to 'portable' wardrobes. But no number of guidebooks, accoutrements or spices could truly prepare the fledgling Grand Tourist for the on-the-road realities of continental travel.

Travellers suffered a catalogue of problems in transport. 'The journey very unpleasant,' wrote Elizabeth Montagu to her sister when just arrived in Paris. 'The horses are so bad, ye postillions so awkward, the rope harnesses so rotten, the Inns so nasty, that I think no one wd ever travel 10 miles in this country if they cd help it.' On disembarking from the cutter at Calais the first order of business for the Grand Tourist was to procure horses – fourteen in Elizabeth Montagu's case: six for the coach carrying belongings, four for the chaise carrying herself and the servants, and four 'for my horse men' (on short runs or evenings out, a snug coach – called a *vis à vis* – was normally used). Obtaining the complement of horses took longer than expected, and Elizabeth was forced to pass the night in a 'wretched' Inn at Boulogne. 'Turn up your nose, pinch it very hard, go into a bad bed,' she wrote in a sardonic letter to her sister.

> Don't shut your eyes all night, but rejoice when the dawning blush of Aurora salutes them. Get early into your Chaise, look often behind you, to see, that your Coach with six horses does not proceed less than 3 miles an hour. You are to stop every six Miles (for the sake of expedition) to change horses; to Add to the advantage of this continual change, the most awkward Animals of Postillions are to tye a thousand broken cords together, to tye their Horses

to the Carriages, and these connexions, not being formed
on more sound and firm principles than our party connexions, are very apt to break.

From one 'Hog sty' to another, the traveller would crawl towards
their destination. 'No, No. Instead of sleeping you are scratching your
left arm, and driving away the Vermin as often as they have the
insolence to encamp on your forehead.'[3]

Then there were the inevitable irritations of bureaucracy. In the
eighteenth century national boundaries were rigorously policed, and
customs officers contemptuous. After the French Revolution erupted
in 1789, security checks were especially vigilant and suspicious eyes
cast in everyone's direction. Each region had posts where passports
were required. Having had her possessions and herself thoroughly
checked at a French control point in 1790 (during her second continental trip since her uncle's death), Mary Berry feared perpetual
delays. 'I really began to dread being searched at every village,' she
wrote.

Once permitted to pass through territories, travellers then faced
problems of the route itself. Carriageways were patchy and there were
few turnpikes. There was no such thing as a smooth passage. Riding
on the rough road from Italy to Vienna made Cornelia Knight sick.
'I cannot say that I enjoyed the journey,' she bluntly reported in her
diary, 'for I was dreadfully fatigued, far from well, and uneasy on
many accounts, besides being a good deal injured by the carriage
being overturned in which I was travelling.'[4] Earlier, when Lady Anna
Miller suffered a carriage crash en route to Italy, she unhappily faced
the additional problems of haggling about a blacksmith's cost for
repairs. He asked for six vaches. '*Six Vaches*, cried I with astonishment!
The peasant, who felt the cause of my surprise, smiled, and said, he
means eighteen fols – which in this country goes under the appellation
of *six cows*. Our host charged us five livres for four eggs; pray how
many cows does that make?'[5]

Cornelia Knight likewise considered local finances a singular
inconvenience. 'The money of many different countries was current
in Genoa,' she noted, 'but changed in value every week. This at first

puzzled us not a little, but a gentleman of our acquaintance afterwards used to call upon us every Saturday at noon, and tell us the rates of exchange for the following week.' Still, she considered it a matter of some trouble when paying a bill to calculate the different values of Austrian, Papal, Piedmontese, Tuscan, and French coins.[6]

Rough estimates put the cost of hiring horses for one chaise at around four shillings for every six miles; to reserve a seat on the diligence (public coach) from Lille to Paris in the 1770s cost 55 *livres* (approximately £2 5s at the time), including provisions and accommodation en route. Servants, such as the *valet de chamber*, cost about a *sequin* per head per day. Lodging, food, drink, tips, local transport, clothes and sundries all quickly added up. In only a few weeks during the winter of 1766/7 the Countess of Fife, with the 2nd Earl of Fife, spent over £1,700 in order to live 'in the first company in Paris' while buying furnishings for their London home. On a short trip to Spa the Earl complained that accommodation was costly, 'no less than 16 shilling a day'. In 1785 the Cambridge don and gentleman's travelling tutor William Bennet estimated that 40,000 Britons were then abroad, and alerted the prime minister to his conservative calculation that at least £4,000,000 was being drained from the British economy each year as a result.[7] Whatever the exact sums, it is clear that at the end of a continental sojourn, many tourists faced a mountain of debt.

But first they had to negotiate the Alps. They were awe inspiring – in the words of the poet Thomas Gray, 'There are certain scenes that would awe an atheist into belief.'[8] Travellers were astonished that they could climb higher than the clouds, but were wary of its dangers. Even in early summer the Alps remained cold, the peaks streaked with melting snow. Travellers piled on fur caps, warm greatcoats and half-boots lined with hareskin. The peasants who lived in the mountains, Hester Piozzi was told, were unhealthy and short-lived. She read other travellers' reports that there were regions 'of the air so subtle as to extinguish the two powers of taste and smell'. Still, it afforded the 'most magnificent scenery in nature'. 'Every step,' she wrote, gives new impressions to the mind each moment of one's passage; while the portion of terror excited either by real or fancied dangers in the way, is just sufficient to mingle with pleasure, and make one feel the full effect of sublimity.

The dizzying heights naturally led to apprehension. At least one English traveller, Adam Walker, confessed to jumping off his horse and running to the other side of the path 'to avoid seeing the vast profundity below'.[9] Hester Piozzi figured that only with 'frequent reiteration' of the journey would fear of the dangers die away. 'The men who carried me seemed amazed that I should feel any emotions of fear,' she wrote. To her commands of *prenez garde*, take care!, the men would ask *Qu'est-ce donc, madame*, what's the matter, my lady? But the least slip, she was alarmed to imagine, would be fatal to them all.[10]

Lady Webster descended the Alps sitting in a *chaise à porteurs* that was carried with 'great labour' by two men, wading through deep snow; 'they often fell, but I was neither hurt nor frightened', she wrote, with utter emotional disengagement. 'My intrepidity is more owing to an indifference about life than to natural courage. I have nothing to love, so life is not to me invaluable.'[11]

The standard mode of transportation was by mule, but, if one could bear the cost, the traveller could sit in a *chaise à porteurs*, like Hester Piozzi and Lady Webster, to be carried up and down the mountain peaks and crevasses. It was a simple design. The seat was matted with tree bark and ropes twisted together, which yielded to the weight of those it conveyed. In place of legs, the chair was fixed to two long poles, and hauled on the shoulders of a number of men. Sometimes travellers observed the porters applying a composition of wax and rosin to the soles of their shoes to prevent them from slipping. Only rarely was the chair enclosed. Besides the troublesome weight it would add, sudden gusts of wind might carry the planks of wood away like a kite. 'I liked this manner of travelling very much,' admitted Lady Miller, 'you are conveyed along surprisingly fast on the plain [where] the porters run rather than walk.' Her husband, however, grew bored with being carried, offering that the road was not incommodious for a person to walk along. 'You know how humane he is,' Lady Miller wrote to her mother, noting that he had walked three quarters of their expedition, 'and being carried by his own species is *no part of his system*.'[12]

Healthy travellers could find it hard to be romantic about the Alpine scenery when travelling with the worry of personal injury, let alone those who were already ailing. Mariana Starke's consumptive companion was luckier than most. The Dowager Duchess of Ancaster donated an enclosed sedan chair to the 'Director of the Mountain' on the border near Tende. It required eight men to carry her into Italy, but at least the passage was conducted in relative protection (still, however, there was no floor to the unit, leaving her feet dangling between the burdened biceps). They made it uneventfully to Turin, where they met the Duchess of Ancaster. Again the patient was the recipient of the Duchess's 'universal benevolence' (in Mariana Starke's consideration). Having 'in her suite a skilful English Physician', the Duchess agreed to share his services and consultation on the journey from Turin to Geneva – making a combined caravan (families, porters, guides and guards) of fifty-four people.

But Mariana Starke's ward was destined for Italy, where they finally arrived in the autumn of 1792, settling at Genoa and embarking on periodic excursions to various Italian states. In nearby Nice, where her family was originally advised to spend the winter, Mariana began taking detailed notes on the climates, amenities, and services available in the cities. Patients with respiratory disorders were her main concern, but she hoped her observations would prove beneficial to any in search of a salubrious and safe environment.

Her first offering to aching souls was the advice not to travel over-land. Go to Italy by sea – sail around the Iberian Peninsula and cruise through the Mediterranean to Leghorn. Arrive by winter, and if accompanying someone consumptive, go straight to Pisa – it was the best place in Europe from October till the end of April, she believed. If fireside voyagers at home worried about marshy ground and standing water rendering the place damp and unwholesome, they were remembering a Pisa long past. Enlightened medical reforms had since cleaned the city. Now there appeared a growing, glowing population that 'dispensed cheerfulness and health throughout this elegant city'. If anything, one should be cautious of overexposure to its illuminations. 'Never,' she wrote – putting her own sentence in quotation marks, distinguishing it as a kind of local lore administered to all new visitors – never 'sit, stand, or walk in the sun, without being defended by a parasol; [one is] always to prefer walking on the shady side of a street, and never to go out in a strong north-east wind'.

Environmental extremes, such as strong winds, might lead to disease, just as there was a risk posed to the body from extreme heat by allowing it to bake in the sun. Mariana's comments make it all too obvious that her medically inspired regimen was certainly not one that revered the bronzed body. She was clinical in her description of relaxing without the rays, 'insomuch', she wrote,

> that I have sat out of doors in the shade at midday, when the thermometer often rises to eighty-five and ninety, without feeling more warmth than is easily supported; and as the wind always abates when the sun declines, and the surrounding higher mountains of the Apennine attract the dews and noxious vapours, this situation is not liable to those strong and dangerous vicissitudes from heat to cold which are common in populous Cities of Italy, and particularly baneful to weak lungs.[13]

In her opinion, nothing compared to the healthiness of Pisa's situation and climate. Nice had too many of nature's forces in opposition to each other, being 'replete with electric fluid, and where a hot sun, and a cold, drying, and uncommonly sharp wind are perpetually combating with each other'. Naples, probably due to the volcanic eruptions from Vesuvius, had too much sulphur impregnating its air. But in the summer, 'when the lungs are so far recovered as to be free from ulceration', Rome was hard to beat, with Florence being favoured for the autumn months.

* * *

In 1764 during one of Lady Mary Coke's earliest trips to the Continent, the seas grew so rough near Calais that the ship's captain dropped anchor two leagues offshore. Anxious to set foot on land, Mary made the hasty choice to finish the voyage in a small boat, towards which the waves had 'little respect'. She arrived so bedraggled that, she concluded, she might as well have swum the distance, and the current carried the dinghy five miles down the coast from Calais.

> I was forced to walk all that way over very uneven Sands cover'd with pebbles, that cut so many holes in my shoes & stockings that my poor feet suffer'd very much, & notwithstanding my courage (of which you Know I have a good deal) I was obliged to sit down twice on the sands not able to bear the pain.[14]

Life as a traveller was never easy. But to help smooth the discomforts of travel were the hired help, the servants brought from home and the local footmen employed along the way. This was the support staff that was ordinarily enlisted and vetted by the gentleman's travelling tutor, but which women travelling under their own authority would often organise themselves (occasionally with the assistance from their senior servant or the local government attaché). Guidelines had long been drawn for recruiting as close to an ideal travelling servant as possible:

> a servant selected to accompany a gentleman on his travels should be conversant with the French language ... write a legible and quick hand, in order to be able to copy whatever is laid before him: know a little of surgery, and to bleed well in case his master should meet with an accident where no chirurgical [aid] is to be expected. Gentlemen should endeavour to attach such useful servants to their persons, by showing the same care as a father has for a child, and promise him a settlement for life on their return.

The ideal servant was trustworthy, educated and street-wise, a skilled and utterly responsible person. He could be a companion as well as a protector. Under him were often numerous footmen, maids, cooks, guards, translators, and sometimes a travelling physician (such as Dr Samuel Drew, who travelled with Georgiana, Duchess of Devonshire and her sister Harriet). Whatever the ideal type for each individual, it was more commonly found that tourists' servants matched different stereotypes, such as represented in Lord Byron's rant about one of his travelling servants:

> The perpetual lamentations after beef and beer, the stupid, bigoted contempt for everything foreign, an insurmountable incapacity for acquiring even a few words of any language, rendered him, like all other English servants, an encumbrance. I do assure you, the plague of speaking for him, the comforts he required (more than myself by far), the [dishes] which he could not eat, the wines which he could not drink, the beds where he could not sleep. . .[15]

New degrees of familiarity, even forms of intimacy, between tourists and their servants were forged while travelling, a situation lending itself to uncomfortable circumstances. Mary Wollstonecraft found the unrelieved presence of the maid she took into service at Le Havre in mid-1795 at times awkward. 'What can I say?' she scribbled in a letter to her lover, Gilbert Imlay. 'What can I write with Marguerite perched in a corner by my side? I know not.'[16] Elizabeth Montagu also had to adjust her relationship with a travelling retinue of servants. 'I have a family composed of English, french, German, Italian, and flemish persons,' she wrote in between feverish spells on a trip to Paris in 1767. 'All this does very well in the holyday of health but it is unlike my orderly domestick system in England.'[17]

Despite the eased circumstances brought by such an entourage, the Grand Tourist still had matters to manage whilst travelling: dealing with problems with servants; managing money; keeping abreast of news at home; monitoring their English estates, and so on. This was true for many ladies of the Grand Tour, where the business of travelling far from home rendered more visible their concern over accounts.

For Lady Coke, matters went a little awry when she decided to spend winters abroad. While clearly capable of managing accounts and organising a retinue of servants, various personal pressures had resulted in complications while travelling. After the Duke of York's death, she began her yearly continental retreats to distance herself from the English court and to 'ease her mind'. She felt she needed a change of air, but there was more egging her on. 'My journey Abroad this year is not like my others,' she confessed in her diary in 1769,

> Everything at that time pleased & amused me. I have no hopes of that now, but I think a clear Sky & perpetual Sunshine may dissipate some of those gloomy hours I shou'd have passed here: I have still another motive; I want to try the effect of new Scenes. I shall have no Objects that can recall to my mind the sorrows of my life.[18]

In 1773, during her third visit to Vienna, she learned that one of her servants, who had been in her service for over eight years, had been cheating her out of money. It was discovered that the culprit, named Deihens, had leased Lady Coke's lawn on her Notting Hill estate to a local farmer for cattle grazing during the autumn months, whilst she was away. When she received word of these underhand dealings, Lady Coke began monitoring the finances when they were on the road. Far from home, and attended to by unfamiliar servants who had been hired along the way, she found herself tied to and dependent on Deihens's services to buy provisions and settle local arrangements. 'Think of my distress,' she wrote to her sister, 'to be at this distance from England and this Man in my service, who I am obliged in some things to trust, as I have nothing but footmen.' She suspected the worse. 'I have reason to believe he cheats me in everything,' such as trimming money off daily transactions and pocketing a regular portion of accommodation charges.

Lady Coke was particularly upset because she had in the past paid off Deihens's debts, provided renowned physicians (including the Duchess of Devonshire's personal physician) to attend to him when he was ill, and had trusted him with increasing levels of responsibility. When confronted, he denied the charges, crying that Lady Coke was cruel for having even suspected him of such a thing. But, back in England the farmer had produced the receipt for rental of the lawns in the servant's handwriting. Facing undeniable evidence of his betrayal, he fled her company.

When Lady Coke was making these discoveries, the British ambassador to Vienna, Sir Robert Murray Keith, was temporarily out of town. He would normally provide assistance in such matters – arrest the servant, or arrange for his deportation to face charges in England. But in this instance his absence led Lady Coke to feel uncomfortably isolated. Feeling betrayed and stranded so far from home, she decided that in future she would need to invoke limits on her travels.

> The many disagreeable things I have mett with in this last journey, tho' it has not made me renounce travelling, has at least made me almost determine never again to go so far from England. France and Flanders will I imagine for the future be the boundaries of my travels.[19]

To make matters worse, one footman she employed in Vienna was always excessively drunk and new suspicions arose regarding the behaviour of a French maid in her employment. A week after learning about Deihens's deceptions, a set of Lady Coke's pearls went missing. A month later, in November, having moved from Vienna to Venice, one of her 'Winter Silks' went missing, and she found that yet another new servant had been betraying her by citing inflated accommodation prices at stops along their journey and pocketing the surplus. When asked to leave her service, he refused to refund what remained of the advance of a year's salary. Following this, a conscientious footman in her service confessed to her his knowledge that the suspect French maid had been passing on to Deihens incoming letters to Lady Coke from England for his examination and possible confiscation to prevent her learning about any further foul play.

Lady Coke grew increasingly distressed and paranoid, even fearing for her life and believing that the ill-treatment she was receiving from the stream of servants was at the Archduchess of Austria, Maria

Theresa's command. By the time she reached Florence in mid-November, she dared to write about the conspiracy:

> Those Servants who have been taken since [the discovery about Deihens] have proved the greatest Wretches imaginable, and have now made demands upon me that are very extraordinary and under hand. Tho' their Roguery is well known they are supported against me, for 'tis no longer time to conceal that the Empress persecutes me in every thing.[20]

She intimated that Maria Theresa (Holy Roman Empress, 1745–65) – or 'the Empress' as Lady Coke called her – was an organising force behind all her 'open and secret enemies', and proclaimed she felt it imminently necessary that she would need to 'shun every place in her Government, or under her influence' to escape further harm. To onlookers, Lady Coke seemed close to becoming hysterical. At the inquest to examine her servants' behaviour towards her, she lost control. The consequence, as reported by the British envoy at Florence, Sir Horace Mann, to Horace Walpole, who had long been fond of Lady Coke, was that the 'height and violence of her temper exposed her to being summoned before the tribunals'. Lady Coke believed that the servants' 'rogue' behaviour was being covered up by allies of the Empress. Observers claimed that she became obsessed with her conspiracy theory, and Sir Horace Mann privately intervened in the proceedings to 'save her', being 'forced to make use of means which, were she informed of them, would appear an unpardonable crime'. He later remarked to Walpole about Lady Coke's conviction that she was being persecuted.

> Your Scotch Princess is quite mad upon the article of Empresses and their descendants, whose Emissaries, from their first Ministers and courtiers down to the lowest of the servants, lay traps for her and persecute her every hour of the day, which she, poor creature, who cannot (as she says) be in the wrong, is forced to submit to, not knowing how to get away.

Lady Coke for her part was not welcoming of Mann's interventions, writing in her journal that he 'was very false to me, & certainly in the secrets of my enemies: he appears to me a true Florentine'.[21]

The trials of travelling far from home and of being dependent on a team of treacherous individuals, then questioning the motives of absolute monarchs and believing that one's own life was in peril, all conspired to cause in Lady Coke what we might now call a nervous breakdown, although contemporaries had no precise medical definition for Lady Coke's distressed condition.

Since the Duke of York's death in 1767, Lady Coke had sunk into severe depression. After the incident involving Deihens and the mismanagement of her Notting Hill estate, she once again reflected on life's adversity: 'The great misfortunes I have mett with in life, and the perpetual disagreeable and vexatious incidence that forever attends me,' she sighed, 'has I think almost inured me to sorrow; I feel surprised when a day passes without some trouble or disagreeable event.' These were clearly the sentiments of one suffering melancholia. Lady Coke went as far as to diagnose her condition as being a case of 'hurt Nerves' and speculated on a potential cure: 'my journey to Italy will I hope mend them', she wrote, just before departing Vienna.

The reference to 'nerves' as a physiological basis for her emotional responses to life's misfortunes was the product of a medical philosophy developed in the seventeenth century that anchored 'sensation' to the spinal column, linking mind and body through the new study of 'neurologie'.[22] Increasingly in the eighteenth century, reference to the 'causes' or roots of diseases from melancholy to madness relied on such physical explanations; 'lowness of spirits' was as much a bodily as a mental alteration, which explained why people felt physical pain when severely depressed.[23]

Lady Coke, while obviously not an expert in diseases of the nervous system, was nevertheless *au courant* with some of the diagnostic languages in medical theory. As a chronic sufferer, she found comfort in compassionate company, perhaps being aware that it was recommended therapy (by some) to *talk* about their conditions.[24] She found such company in the person of Joseph, the Holy Roman Emperor (and joint ruler of the Austrian lands with his mother, Maria Theresa), with whom she sat during an evening at Madame D'Harrach's country estate outside Vienna. 'The conversation turned upon Nervous disorders and lowness of spirits occasion'd by misfortunes,' she recorded in her diary. The Emperor admitted then that he was occasionally attacked with a 'complaint' that started after the death of his first wife. The cure he preferred was rather peculiar. Feeling an attack coming on, he hid in a closet and read 'some trifling book' by candlelight until the disorder passed. What 'bizarre behaviour', thought Lady Coke. 'I shou'd recommend a quite different method for dissipating those complaints in the health occasion'd by great misfortunes,' she mused, 'but different minds require different methods, and perhaps I am an improper judge of these things having never cured myself.'[25]

Lady Coke's preferred approach was to travel. Along her journey she visited tourist attractions and sampled cultural offerings, attending the opera in Colorno (near Parma – a building which later became a lunatic asylum). Some of her early descriptions of the scenery she encountered shortly after leaving Vienna for Italy seemed promising. 'The Scenes in Stirie are very beautifull; mountains cover'd with wood; fine pasture grounds beneath, with numbers of cattle feeding; Rivers, falls of water, and vineyards.' However, a violent rainstorm quickly descended on Lady Coke's parade, and she, having climbed out of her coach until it was manoeuvred past an obstacle, was left unassisted by her hard-hearted servants, and ended up falling 'in all the water and mud, it rain'd at the same time so violently that I was wet through all my Clothes'.

When she finally settled 'in the boasted climate of Italy', matters did not improve. The weather remained 'perfectly cold'; the Italians, she thought, were 'very bad people' and even other Britons abroad, she suspected, were colluding with 'my enemies' to do her harm.[26] Whether by malicious arrangement (as she would have it) or not, Lady Coke's travels never cured the occasional bouts of nervous disorder and melancholy that she would continue to suffer and lament.

* * *

Unlike modern medical theory – which typically conceives disease itself as a specific entity (a germ or virus, for example) – in the eighteenth-century, *dis-ease* described the body's whole reaction to bring about a cure for *dis-equilibrium*. Rather than looking microscopically inwards to search for signs of a pathological entity within the body, those looking for the cause of illness looked outwards, to external features or elements of the surrounding environment that needed to be carefully controlled to maintain good health.

Physical diseases were not always considered distinct from mental diseases. Melancholia and hypochondriasis, for example, were related to an imbalance in bodily 'humours' (specifically four different kinds of fluids found in living organisms, including blood and phlegm), or to environmental influences. Disequilibria in these produced deleterious effects on health, prompting the English moralist John Brown to believe that 'Our effeminate and unmanly Life, working along with our Island-Climate, hath notoriously produced an Increase of low Spirits and nervous Disorders.' Echoing this estimation, Hester Piozzi wondered 'is there any Foundation for the Idea prevalent among us that we are the only Nation where Hypochondriac Diseases are frequent? And that the French are almost wholly free?' She was soon to answer her own question by travelling abroad, while John Brown later committed suicide.[27]

From the late seventeenth century, largely as a result of the work of the English philosopher John Locke, doctors began defining mental disease, particularly the concept of 'madness', according to a theory of the 'disorder of the imagination'.[28] Rather than it existing divinely, 'Reason', when corrupted produced madness. Locke saw the mind as composed of sensations acquired through experience. 'Passions' of the mind, therefore, were given shape by past experiences of pain and suffering, pleasure and sympathy. If these experiences were somehow confounded or misconstrued, if a person pieced together their life from 'false principles', it was a sign of mental derangement. According to this analysis, medicine was no remedy. Rather, lifestyle management – breaking bad habits and altering 'evil associations' – was the solution.

Disregarding the common image of the lunatic confined in a straitjacket and padded cell, various forms of madness (mental disorders, including hypochondria, hysteria, mania and melancholia were often considered indistinguishable) were thought to be treatable through travel. Travel could help ease the mind by providing active mental stimulation. Even those bent on providing a physical explanation for madness – pointing to the spleen as the source of mental irritation, for example – believed travel could be beneficial since bad weather often influenced the affliction. If suffering from melancholia, removing the patient from the context of harmful associations could help boost spirits. To Robert Burton, who wrote the pioneering *Anatomy of Melancholy* (1621), travel was a central part of a therapeutic regimen. In short, according to Burton, there was 'no better physick for a melancholy man than change of aire and variety of places, to travel abroad and see fashions'.[29] A century and a half later, the famous Edinburgh physician, William Cullen (who coined the term 'neurosis'), echoed the prescription. If those who suffered from melancholy 'can call off their attention from the pursuit of their own disordered imagination, and can fix it a little upon some others . . . a journey, both by its having the effect of interrupting all train of thought, and by presenting objects engaging in attention, may often be useful'.[30]

In short, travelling distracted people; this did not necessarily mean that it somehow soothed over a somatic illness, but rather that travel made people forget the *idea* that they might have an illness. Hypochondria itself was perceived as a species of disease. Excessive worry about getting ill led some voluntarily to self-dose and search for unnecessary cures. The eminent physician Erasmus Darwin (Charles's grandfather) wrote to a concerned correspondent explaining: 'Your brother's complaint seems to me to be hypochondriasis. It is very apt to last long and is but very little under the influence of medicine. He should endeavour as much as he can to amuse his mind among objects which are new and interesting & by travelling in foreign countries.'[31]

Travelling was thus not necessarily a cure for anything bar worry – or an obsession of the mind. Although in some physical distress (suffering from an attack of gout), Lady Northumberland found that the natural beauty of Switzerland lifted her spirits. The scenery from Mount Jorat, overlooking the Castle of Ripaille, Lausanne, Geneva and Savoy, was the most stimulating:

> Travelling in this country affords a most pleasing Variety as the Road is now and then close to the lake, then thro pastoral, cultivated grounds & Vinyards, now over immense mountains, steep, rocky & high, & then thro the gloomy Obscurity of Forrests of straight Tall Pines, & neat villages ... About half way up the mountain the scene was immensely beautiful: a verdant valley with a clear stream wandering thro it; the Chateau & Pont d'Issy, Cornfields, Horses & Cattle feeding, Rows of Pines, Fruit Trees, &c.[32]

The picturesque environs had the desired effect. 'It pleased me so much,' she wrote, 'that I forgot my Gout & got out and walk'd part of the way.'

Patients understood the associations between maintaining mental health and travelling, and planned their trips accordingly. When seventeen-year-old Princess Charlotte, King George III's grand-daughter, became depressed after the loss of her long-term attendant, Mrs Gagarin, it was noted by Cornelia Knight, Charlotte's lady companion, that attempts were made to improve her spirits. She wrote in her diary that they took 'long airings' before and after dinner while in residence at one of the royal households, and did 'everything that could divert her thoughts from the loss she had sustained'. Distraction, 'anything that could cheer her up', was thought especially prudent since the Princess's 'life was so monotonous, that any other young person must have felt it excessively dull'. Feeling melancholy, Princess Charlotte wrote to her father, the Prince Regent, asking permission to travel to the seaside, which 'all the medical people said she ought to visit every year till she was five-and-twenty'. Her request was denied (her relationship with her father was notoriously fraught).[33]

However, travelling had proved beneficial to Hester Thrale, whose immediate family had a medical history of nervous disorders. Doctors had diagnosed her daughter, Sophie, as having a 'nervous constitution', anxiety about which Hester's close friend, Samuel Johnson, attempted to dispel: 'Do not let them fill your mind with terrours which perhaps they have not in their own'; dismiss the disquisition on 'hystericks', for doctors 'are the bugbears of disease of great terrour but little danger'.[34] Some years later, after the death of her son and her first husband, ill health again drove Hester, this time with her new husband, Gabriel Piozzi, out of London. Their destination for 'the Season' in 1791 was Bath, since Hester 'had some Pains in my Stomach, and Mr Piozzi says (truly enough) that the Water will cure them'. Her husband would also benefit. 'Change of Air too will carry away his little Nervous Complaints.'[35]

Part of the healing process in which the Piozzis would find themselves engaged was 'taking' the waters – whether pumped, drunk, swum in, or simply soaked in. It also involved sociability. In fact, as Jane Austen was well aware, the presence of the Georgian elite in particular areas not only proved them healthy places to be, but generated an economy based on tourism for local areas: they were salubrious, popular, and fashionable. 'Here I have good Air and good Water and good Company – and at last – *good Nights* so that I mean to be among the merriest immediately. The Place is full, and the pretty Girls kind as my Master Says,' wrote a reviving Hester Piozzi, shortly after arriving in Bath. It was not the first time she had recovered there with the help of friends. Just the year before, the eminent physician Sir Lucas Pepys had 'saved my life', she wrote to her friend Samuel Lysons, whom she afterwards met while recuperating in Bath, where 'the Waters and your Friendship preserved it – assisted by Mr James's amiable Family, and uncommon Talents sweetened by cordial Kindness'.[36]

In order to receive fully rounded therapy, a change of company was considered necessary in addition to a change of air. On the Continent, health resorts were becoming extremely fashionable amongst the nobility and aristocracy, who flocked to mineral waters and spas to take advantage of the medicinal qualities of fresh elements.

Approaching one of the most popular of such resorts, Spa in Belgium, travellers were treated to the 'solemn and majestick character' of the scenery. 'The Town of Spa is situated in a little valley surrounded every way by mountains,' wrote Elizabeth Montagu in 1763, but paths cut into the mountainside were accessible, 'by which you are carried to the summit by an easy ascent'. From that vantage point, one looked down to a town so 'irregularly built one might imagine it had been raised in the first beginnings of architecture'. But it was the company that was the main attraction. 'Here you meet all the various orders and professions in which mankind are classed,' she wrote while she and Elizabeth Carter accompanied Lord Bath to Spa. They found it not only teeming with European princes and princesses (including the distinguished Princess Esterhazy, widow of a Hungarian prince, who held court for a number of years in the town), but also 'a great number of the English nobility'. They settled in for just over a week, before heading on to nearby Aix-la-Chapelle (Aachen), in Germany, dining, socialising, gambling, and having their 'health fortified by the waters'.[37] 'If it pleases God to continue to us our health, we shall have pass'd our time very agreeably,' admitted Lady Montagu.[38]

In 1767, Lady Mary Coke discovered that little of the social landscape of Spa had changed since Lady Montagu's visit, she being one of a multitude of British aristocrats engaged in monitoring the health of others: she found Lady Gore, Lady Sarah Bunbury, Lady Spencer, Lord Southwell and his sons (the eldest unfortunately 'in such a declining state of health, I think,' wrote Lady Coke, 'he will hardly survive another winter'). There was Lord Fortrosse, the Duke of Roxborough, and Sir Charles Hotham, among countless others. The balls were in full swing in the evenings, and the gamblers (Lady Coke a regular) trying their luck until early morning. On agreeable days, Lady Coke climbed on horseback and rode 'to the fashionable Fountains, on purpose to see the company'.[39]

Aix-la-Chapelle, where 'the Sun makes every thing chearful', was the fashionable place to pass the Spring. Even better, Lady Coke had befriended Madame de Saint Trope and her husband, who owned a considerable estate in the province, and, 'as they are very rich, they like nothing better than giving entertainments'. Although abroad for the benefit of her health, Lady Coke prioritised society over climate when deciding which places to visit, writing to her mother, 'I am not tired of Aix, tho' there are things that do not please me: the Society I am in is agreeable . . . [and as] for the climate I think it Heavenly'.[40]

In 1776, Mary Hamilton took a break from the claustrophobic ranks of court and accompanied Lord and Lady Dartrey to Belgium where they intended to improve their health by taking a course of waters. While there, they went book buying, dined well, attended the opera, and occasionally danced until dawn.[41] It seemed healthy to be lavishly entertained. And in 1783, after two years of having 'given warning', Mary decided to resign from her position in the royal household. But when sympathetic friends thereafter descended on her doorstep, the pressure of continual company began to overwhelm her. 'If I did not deny myself to Visitors sometimes in a Morng I shd never have a moment to myself . . . besides it is good for one's *Mind's Health* to be alone some part of the day.' Similar concerns prevented her from joining in the society surrounding her uncle, the ambassador Sir William Hamilton, when he called upon her during a return visit to England. 'As Sr Wm understands that my *Nerves*, & *State* of *Mind* will not admit of my being in their Society,' she wrote, 'I now feel *relieved* from all *difficulties*; They have continual Company.'[42]

At least one writer, concerned about the effects on the female sex of metropolitan amusements, would have agreed with Lady Hamilton. In 'such places, the predominant spirit is thoughtlessness', grumbled Thomas Gisborne, worried about the underlying discomforts of excessive socialising. Moving from one society to the next engendered restless spirits and 'stimulates the inherent love of entertainment'. This was not good for health-troubled travellers. Rather than curbing an illness, 'the contagion spreads . . . to many persons who are come in quest of health; and often affects them so powerfully, that the hurry of the evening more than counterbalances the salubrious influence of air and waters'.[43] But for many, such cautions seemed to blow away with the wind.

Such 'environmental' views of health were put forward in eighteenth-century protean medical manuals that stressed the importance of a personal regimen: diet, exercise and regular patterns of bedtimes and bowel movements. Was one getting enough sleep? How about the diet – were red meat and wine consumed in moderation? Was the patient getting enough exercise? Was the patient evacuating enough – for if not, excess urine in the system, for example, could lead to dropsy, making the body immensely distended. Such concerns showed an appreciation that lifestyle had an effect on health, as opposed to more antiquated views that demonic possession was a major cause of illness. Individuals were thus increasingly learning that good health was dependent upon their own self-discipline: the body was God's temple, and it was the duty of each person to preserve it.

Such preaching reinforced the idea that a legitimate recourse upon falling ill was to attempt to heal oneself by reviewing then reforming one's personal regimen – to attempt to regain bodily balance by looking at the effects that the immediate environment might be having on one's health. This sometimes led to complicated measures. Air, for instance, was not so easily 'controlled', but it had a powerful potential to provoke disease, and therefore its 'management' was central to the theory behind travelling to maintain or reinstate good health.

Since antiquity, physicians saw links between the weather, seasons, geographical place (hot and humid or bracingly cold areas in the extremes) and bodily health, so that understanding weather patterns was thought to provide indications of the prospects for good health. In the late seventeenth century, the English physician and father of modern environmental medicine, Thomas Sydenham, known as the 'English Hippocrates', revived these theories. Sydenham emphasised that in order to understand the causes of disease in people, one needed to understand the potential effects that the environment – particularly the qualities of air and the seasons – could have on the body's internal humours. If 'airs' were creating a deleterious effect on health, those that could were encouraged to change them by changing their scenery. This forged the associations between health and travel.

From the doctor's point of view, it often did not matter where patients travelled, just as long as they were travelling. (Elizabeth Montagu's friend Mrs Donnellan, however, had a curious machine built 'for galloping and trotting' for stationary 'exercise'; 'if I could get him to make me one that could move me from one place to another, with how much pleasure could I mount my chariot to make you a visit', she quipped to Elizabeth Montagu.[44]) Long journeys of horseback riding were one of Sydenham's favourite prescriptions – and he would sometimes use manipulative means to get patients to follow his directions. After attending one wealthy patient in London for several months without alleviating his symptoms, Sydenham advised he seek the services of a certain Dr Robertson of Inverness, who had cured many others suffering with a similar malady. Following the advice, the patient set out for Inverness – on horseback – and searched for the physician. To his dismay he learned that no one knew or had any memory of a Dr Robertson in that city. Upon his return to London the patient heatedly asked Sydenham why he was sent on such a long and fruitless journey, to which Sydenham replied: 'Well, are you any better in health?' 'Yes, I am quite well now, no thanks to you.' 'No,' said Sydenham, 'thank Dr Robertson'.[45]

By the eighteenth century people were much less sceptical about the professed advantages of travelling for health, partly because travel as a means of self-improvement in educational terms had already set trends in Grand Tourism. Many more felt free to offer their advice about the benefits of travel, such as Samuel Johnson, who told his acquaintance, John Perkins, who was planning a 'very long Journey' to restore his health:

1. Turn all care out of your head as soon as you mount the chaise
2. Do not think about frugality, your health is worth more than it can cost

3. Do not continue any day's journey to fatigue
4. Take now and then a day's rest
5. Get a smart seasickness if you can
6. Cast away all anxiety, and keep your mind easy
   This last direction is the principal; with an unquiet
   mind neither exercise, nor diet, nor physick can be of
   much use.[46]

Complementing the environmental view of improving one's health, weather patterns were increasingly being identified and predicted by world travellers who accumulated data, contributing to the emerging field of 'medical meteorology'. This provided more detailed insight into the possible dangers lurking in the weather. Atmospheric extremes and rapid atmospheric changes were often associated with disease. Winds that ripped through towns were related to the occurrence of certain ailments. This could even apply to drops in temperature at night, posing a risk for people on a night out in town. A Miss Weeton, for example, recorded in her diary what happened to her after she returned home from tea at Miss Dannett's one evening:

> The heat of the room [in which we sat] was such, that on coming away and plunging into the cold night air, I received a violent cold, and was for several days in a burning fever; and at the same time an inflammation in my mouth, and gathered gums. By Saturday following, I was recovered.[47]

Inside or outside, the air could easily become close, fetid, rank, stale, and in numerous other ways generally, unhealthy. Open windows, fresh breezes, air currents, and so on were helpful if carefully controlled. Lady Mary Coke, when not crying conspiracy against all those she believed were persecuting her, often perturbed her hosts whom she visited by throwing open all of their windows, declaring that she was a 'friend to air'.

Unseasonably hot or cold weather, high winds, even thunderstorms and lightning flashes were suspect events. Such environmental concerns also generated a 'map' of health that traced the contours of urban and rural settings, forming a sort of 'medical geography'. This led the Georgian gentry to wonder whether living in town or country was best suited to their health. The sociable thrived on city life, especially in the spring and the season, the time of year when being in the city was associated with the calendar of parties for the fashionable high life. But they were also aware that cities were generally less salubrious than the country. Poor water supplies, insanitary conditions, overcrowding, 'city stench' and the mere proximity to an unhealthy regimen (such as the excessive drinking areas depicted by William Hogarth of 'Gin Lane' or 'Beer Street') precipitated epidemic disorders.

Certain diseases – such as bronchitis, asthma, consumption and rickets – were especially associated with the city. Is it any surprise that even the fashionable chose to avoid 'the season' and stay away from the city, or flee the fog for fear of illness or for recuperation? Could concerns over one's health overcome the social pressures of needing to be in the right place at the right time? Travelling (away from the city and 'season') for health *was* understandable, so long as their absence did not lead to the perception that one's home company was intrinsically unhealthy, or otherwise inadequate. Lady Coke's experiences illustrate the tensions between being sociable and staying healthy.

No one in court society questioned Lady Coke's decision to remain abroad during the winters, so long as it was clearly for the benefit of her health; however, extended sojourns gradually gave the appearance that she was beginning to favour foreign *society* and not just its seasonal climate. The cool but 'civil' reception given to Lady Coke by the royal family during a brief return to London in the summer of 1772 sounded a caution not to abuse foreign travel. The King, Lady Coke found out, had been inquiring whether she intended to stay in England throughout the winter, a question he also put directly to her. 'I answer'd that His Majesty had done me the Honour to ask if I wou'd pass the winter of the year '72 in England, & that I had said I wou'd & never broke my word.' Did Lady Coke, the King questioned, continue to like Vienna on her successive visits as much as the first?

At this point Queen Charlotte let her own opinion be known: 'I had stay'd [abroad] longer than She expected,' Lady Coke recounted, '& that She grew a little angry with me'.[48] Clearly, whatever the benefits of foreign soil to one's health, there were also limits that such fashionable travellers were not expected to exceed.

Going abroad could also be interpreted as being unpatriotic, implying that home – with its own thriving resorts, such as Bath or Bagnigge Wells in London – was, literally, unhealthy. When Fanny Burney heard that her sister, Susanna Phillips, was heading abroad to improve her health, Fanny – anxious not to lose a cherished companion – complained 'must it be to the Continent? – the division by sea – how could I cross it were you ill?' Anyway, Fanny continued, what was wrong with England? 'You certainly have been well in various parts of England: Ipswich, Twickenham, Norbury – all shew the nation is not against you, just the clay soil.'[49] But when Fanny appealed to her friend, Hester Piozzi, for support, she received none from that quarter, Hester believed Susanna 'is in the right to try Continental Air'.[50]

Convalescing communities were growing abroad. Enthusiastic travellers and writers such as Lady Coke flocked to spas and helped to make it the fashion. One traveller, Henry Swinburne, in addition to reporting where people of rank and distinction were on his tour of the courts of Europe, cynically noted physicians' claims about the properties of different mineral baths, believing that their curative powers existed 'nowhere but in the idea or roguery of doctors'.[51] By and large, however, the population was far less sceptical. 'My friend Louisa Shipley,' testified a certain Mary Heber, 'has had a bad relapse again of her Cold & Cough soon after she left the balsamic air & charming Scenery' of one up-and-coming resort, Bristol-Wells. 'She has since been to the sea-side with her mother, where she entirely recovered again by constantly Riding & Sailing, & gained such a look of Health as She never had before. She has returned home scarcely above a week & this Surprising cold is beginning to come again.'[52]

Lady Coke might have preferred Spa in Belgium to Aix-la-Chapelle in Germany at certain times because of the seasonal visitors there, but each resort, she believed, offered specific recuperative benefits. For instance, when Sir Charles Hotham, who 'has intirely lost the use of both his Arms', arrived in Spa 'in hopes that these waters will contribute to his recovery', Lady Coke could not help but worry. Was this the most appropriate place to receive treatment? 'I shou'd have thought the Baths at Aix-la-Chappelle more likely to have succeeded,' but, she noticed, he appeared to be 'more chearful' in Spa than one would expect.[53] Perhaps Sir Charles should have followed Lady Coke's advice, for he died later that year.

Health-conscious travellers also became knowledgeable, or opinionated, about the Continent's most desirable regional climates. The rule of thumb was moderation: hot southern climates were best avoided in summer, and cold northern climates in the winter. Countries that fell in between were sometimes risky: occasionally one was caught by freak extremes in temperature (particularly cold spells in a southern climate for example). This happened to Lady Coke as she spent springtime in an otherwise favourable Aix-la-Chapelle. After a succession of frosty nights, during which she could only curl up at the fireplace, she complained that it was a region 'where they have rarely severe weather [so] no precaution is taken against it, which I now experience: there is not a window or door that shuts'.[54]

Lady Coke was by now a past master in seasonal migration through Europe, often securing her own accommodation days before the arrival of aristocratic entourages, and (usually) on the crest of glorified weather patterns. Others with more limited travelling experience learned about European environments of health as they went along. After years of living in Naples, Cornelia Knight saw Europe for the first time as she travelled back to England after her mother's death. She was amazed by the variety of lifestyles she witnessed as she travelled the regions, and attempted to identify the original 'influences' on everything from architecture to regional dialects and physiological appearances. She also noted the diversity of people's health. Most impressive, she thought, were the people of Sicily: whether it was because of their diet of wholesome prickly pears – or 'Indian figs' as they were called locally – or their preference for pure cold water as a remedy rather than 'scientific applications', the Sicilians 'generally enjoyed excellent health, and I suppose', concluded Cornelia, 'there is hardly any civilised country where so little medicine is taken'.[55]

Italy was regarded, among lady Grand Tourists at least, as holding the panacea to most ills of the body. When concerned about a decline in Lady Bessborough's health whilst in Florence, her friend and confidante Lady Webster remained optimistic: after all, 'what cures may not be received from this delicious climate!', she euphorically wondered.[56] And after leaving London in the hopes of improving Agnes Berry's health, the Berry family rushed to Italy. 'You will be pleased to hear,' her father Robert wrote to Bertie Greathead, 'that my daughters have already reaped the benefit from the change of air and exercise since they left England. Agnes has recovered her complexion, and I trust in God they will both return to England in better health than when they left it.' His assurance was based on the three weeks they had spent in Florence, where from the start they leisurely pursued 'the beauties of the fine arts and nature', and danced away the evenings at the *ballet champêtres*, which the Grand Priore threw for the local countryfolk. But the Berry sisters chose not to mix with the British socialites in Florence, preferring 'the mildness of the climate of Pisa', where they decided to spend the winter. Here, climate took precedence over company.[57]

When Hester Piozzi visited Italy shortly after her marriage to Gabriel Piozzi, she reflected on her earlier assessments of her own nation, when, 'foolishly' measuring it against ideas of 'Perfection', she thought it less than laudable. But now, having spent time travelling and 'drawing the Comparison with other States and other Climates', she was inclined to 'love, honour, and esteem' her home. 'The more I see of other Nations the more I respect my own,' as she simply put it. She arrived at this judgement while in Italy. But what could possibly be wrong with the Italian climate? She explained the anomaly of her view to her correspondent, Samuel Lysons:

You will wonder when I commend the Temperature of [England's] Air so loudly lamented by most People, but if its not particularly salubrious, it is at least not pestiferous like the Environs of Rome, sullenly unwholesome as about the Bagni di Pisa, or impregnated as here with fiery Particles, and Mineral Exhalations that hourly threaten the Lives of the Possessors.[58]

This she wrote from Naples on New Year's Eve 1785, where nature's discomforts were being expressed in full belch. From the terrace of her apartment on the Bay of Naples, Hester watched thunderstorms rushing in off the sea and Mount Vesuvius's vitriol spewing into the clouds above. It was an awesome spectacle, but her sense that the Neapolitan (or even Roman) environs were unhealthy was not without foundation.

Her grasp of environmental health was more particularised than most Grand Tourists', going beyond the mere association of temperature with health-giving properties. She saw nature's activities themselves as having an effect on human health. Once viewed as stable and bountiful, the environment began to be perceived as dynamic, decaying and dangerous. Besides being unpredictable, Mother Nature's mood swings were more alarmingly felt to pose a threat to human health. Winds and airs were always treated with caution, especially when they were thought to carry debris from the decomposition of substances embedded in the earth. Thus, Hester Piozzi's concern over the 'fiery Particles' and 'Mineral Exhalations' of Vesuvius was a concern to avoid breathing in the virulent gases thought to emanate from such eruptions. Similarly, marshy areas or stagnant waters – with their foul smells and decaying organic matter – were associated with dangerous 'miasmas' (a term vaguely corresponding to 'pollution') and the propagation of malaria (the term itself meaning 'bad air').[59] Local environmental defects, Hester was pointing out, posed a threat to the oblivious tourist.

Whatever her reservations about the environs of Rome and Naples, Hester Piozzi's opinions were more positive about the northern Italian regions. 'Well! what one *has* seen is certain, what one *is to see* is uncertain,' she stated, pleasantly surprised about both the culture and healthiness of Venice.

> The State of Venice is however most agreeable to inhabit of all Italy in my Mind: Verona is a heavenly Situation, the Society delightful, the Air wholesome, the Antiquities entertaining and respectable; while Nature has been lavish in her Gifts, and beautified its Environs with unequal and various Elegance, as Palladio has enriched her Streets with all the Charms of Proportion and Variety.[60]

While rare, she was not the only one to harbour such concerns. Despite all the 'boasting' (as Lady Coke put it) about the Italian climate, the chorus of opinion regarding the salubrity of southern Europe was not sung in harmony.[61] Medical writers increasingly urged travellers not to confuse the charms of antiquity and the seeking out of treasures with the pursuit of health. In fact, when the term 'malaria' was introduced into English usage in the early nineteenth century by John Macculloch, he was well aware of the paradox facing those seduced by the 'Paradise of Europe':

> This must suffice for the pure, the bright, the fragrant, the classical air of Italy, the Paradise of Europe. To such a pesthouse are its blue skies the canopy – and where its brightness holds out the promise of life and joy, it is but to inflict misery, and death.[62]

Although entire landscapes were never entirely rejected, travellers were beginning to understand that if environmental hazards were localised, then the trick was to learn to avoid them.

For many, travelling abroad was a matter of life and death. One of the few areas in medical research to have progressed in this period was 'medical climatology', or the study of the association between diseases and particular climates. To have a change of air was therapeutic, and by the century's end, environments became medicalised as much as the specific characteristics of 'airs' themselves ('oxygen', for instance, was a term coined in 1778). Chemists, who employed new techniques to analyse gases, helped define this relationship. Thomas

Beddoes, the Bristol physician who founded a 'pneumatic institute' for the study of gases in the hopes of curing lung disorders, was one of the better known: one result was the discovery of nitrous oxide, or 'laughing gas'. In 1794 he jointly published the results of early experimental trials with the engineer James Watt, in *Considerations on the Medicinal Use of Factitious Airs*. Just as travel literature was available and read by women, so too was medical literature. Streams of advice manuals instructed men as well as women about how to implement appropriate regimens to maintain good health.

For certain ladies of the Grand Tour, Beddoes's book seemed to suggest ways in which controlling one's environment could lead to emancipation. 'Have you read Beddowes' Book, Dear Ladies?' asked Hester Piozzi of the Ladies of Llangollen, Lady Eleanor Butler and Sarah Ponsonby. 'All about Oxygen Air and Gas, and how we have Power over our own Lives, and I know not what strange things. It is a curious Performance.'[63] This statement captures the spirit of how medicine – the controlling theory behind 'getting a breath of fresh air' and therefore travelling for health – could emancipate women from the constrictions of life at home. This starkly contrasted with popular medical opinion that sought to exercise control over women's bodies – with physiological theories enforcing a view that women were fragile and fit only for domesticity. Women also used the association between travel and health to find other ways to gain power over their own lives.

As a self-prescribed remedy, travelling for health provided not only the opportunity to improve oneself, but, unlike other forms of 'enlightened' activities by women, chasing health was a legitimate excuse to venture abroad. As Horace Walpole found out to his dismay, this was true even when such pursuits were undertaken at times of war, when the act of travelling itself posed its own health risks.

In 1790, when the ailing Agnes Berry was taken by her sister, Mary, and father to Italy, Walpole, ever protective of the wellbeing of his 'twin wives', was worried. 'You see by the papers that the flame has burst out at Florence – can Pisa then be secure? Flanders can be no safe road, and is any part of France so?' 'Horrors' were reported at Avignon, and riots in Madrid. 'Surely this is not a season for expeditions to the Continent,' he pleaded. What possessed them 'to so strange a fancy as that of leaving your country again, when it is, as appears to everybody else, the only country in Europe at present that one would wish to be in.' But Mary Berry remained undeterred, relaying her own news that two of her friends travelling abroad, Miss Crawford and Mrs Lockart, had met with no disturbances on their route. Walpole was forced to reconcile himself with his 'loss', left only with the sanguine hope 'that a winter in Italy, and the journies and sea air will be very beneficial to two constitutions so delicate as yours'.[64]

Travelling abroad for the sake of one's health was one of the few legitimate reasons women in Enlightenment England could use to escape domestic circumstances. Such was the attraction of these liberties that many sought shelter in the temple of health who did not require Hygeia's services.

Instances of eighteenth-century women giving the pretext of ill-health in order to justify travel abound. When Emily, the Duchess of Leinster, decided to go abroad with the family tutor, she used her children's ill-health as the reason for the voyage. Her sister, Caroline, went along with the deception. The south of France was delightful: 'All the physical folks agree a dry climate is the thing in the world for those humours: so pray go, sweet sis, and God Almighty send you success in an undertaking so worthy of your good sense, courage, and maternal tenderness.'[65] Lady Duncannon used the apparent advice of her physician, Dr Richard Warren, as an excuse to winter in the south of France, which obscured her ulterior motive of removing her sister, Georgiana, from her husband in order to give birth to her illegitimate son. The Duchess of Northumberland was not the only one to offer health as a suitable excuse to leave court and travel (although she did continually groan about her gout). Even the free-spirited Duke of Gloucester relayed a message to Princess Amelia that he was gravely ill and would miss a party for the visiting King of Denmark since he was going abroad to recover. The Princess was surprised since the Duke had appeared well at the opera a few days earlier, and Lady Mary Coke, who discussed the Duke's plans with the Princess, was even more surprised to find out he planned to convalesce for merely two weeks. 'I wonder what sort of illness it can be that the change in climate can cure in a fortnight,' she wrote in jest. Few would have been duped by his feigned illness, suspecting that he was intent on pursing either women or winnings there. 'So the Duke of Gloucester is at Paris,' Lady Coke would later write. 'I wonder after having made such disgraceful marriages that they cannot stay at home, as they certainly do nothing but expose themselves when they come Abroad.'[66]

Similarly when Lady Webster first met Lord Holland in the summer of 1795, with her husband anxious to return to England, sickness was a convenient excuse for her to stay behind. 'My health did not allow me to engage in travelling,' she proclaimed, 'and to say the truth I made as much as I could of that pretext, that I might not be forced to return to England, as I enjoyed myself too much here to risk the change of scene.'[67] In Rome, however, Hester Piozzi noticed that all such pretences were dropped: 'This is the first town in Italy I have arrived at yet where the ladies fairly drive up and down a long street by way of shewing their dress, equipages, &c. without even a pretence of taking fresh air.'[68]

'When a Man is sick, you are always sending him to the Continent,' a wary Hester Thrale once commented to Samuel Johnson. What an image of England this must communicate to the rest of Europe! 'Foreigners only get a Notion of England's being unwholesome by seeing such consumptive looking Creatures come out of its flock to Nice, Montpellier, &c. I dare say they think we are all so.' That, she guessed, was why – on her first trip abroad – 'the French Ladies [were] wondering at my healthy looks'.[69] But for some – such as Hester on her first trip abroad – the continental journey was intended to effect 'improvement' in areas other than health.

'*An ideal jaunt*'

Fine Art & Fashion

'*I'm sure it would be a very good thing if you'd go abroad yourself.*'

'*How will you make out that, hay, Madam? Come, please, to tell me, where wou'd be the good of that?*'

'*Where! Why a great deal. They'd make quite another person of you.*'

'*What, I suppose you'd have me learn to cut capers? – and dress like a monkey? – and palaver in French gibberish? – hay, would you? – And powder, and daub, and make myself up, like some other folks?*'

Madame Duval's advice in
Fanny Burney's *Evelina*

WITHIN FIVE HOURS – the duration of the sea crossing from Dover to Calais – the Grand Tourist had entered a different world. 'It seems strange,' wrote the young Mary Hamilton – having just arrived in France on her first trip abroad in 1776, 'that in the space of five hours every object should appear so different,' everything from 'building, language, to dress.'[1] Even the exhilaration of travel could be exhausting. Hester Piozzi, just arrived in Calais during her second trip abroad in 1784, laughed as she remembered how fatigued she had felt after her first Channel crossing. Turning to her travelling companion, 'to whom travelling was new', Hester informed her 'how she would be surprised at the difference found in crossing the narrow sea from England to France, and now she is not astonished at all'. How could she be? 'We have lingered and loitered six and twenty hours from port to port, while sickness and fatigue made her feel as if much more time still had elapsed since she quitted the opposite shore.' But watching the sun set over England helped turn exhaustion into excitement. She was now abroad.

Wonder inevitably grew as the traveller pushed into the interior of the Continent. Even for the seasoned traveller, little could compare to the feeling of arriving in a capital city – settling in at the hotel and visiting old haunts. Fatigue was mixed with anticipation. The Duchess of Northumberland, arriving in Paris in the evening of 9 May 1770, happily found herself 'extremely well lodged at the Hotel de Luxembourg, Rue des Petits Augustins', and the next evening went to the 'Old Boulevard' to people-watch – it was her favourite activity. 'I am always pleased with the chearfulness & whimsical variety of the spectacle,' she wrote, offering a glimpse of what one visitor called the 'moving tableau', where everyone from diamond-clad courtesans to tramps mixed along the tree-lined, hundred-foot wide and one-hundred-year-old rampart running east-west from the Porte Saint-Antoine to the Porte Saint-Martin.[2] The boulevards, 'a sort of Sadlers Wells' as Hester Piozzi described them, were 'places of public amusement for the ordinary Sort of People & consist of rooms, Arbours, Walks, &c.', filled with music but serving no alcohol, 'so that there is Gayety without Noise'.[3] Here the Duchess of Northumberland observed 'the confusion of Riches & poverty, Hotels & Hovels, pure Air & stinks, people of all sorts & conditions', from the Quality to the *Crocheteur*, the loafer. She saw common people in their 'sprucest dress' walking or junketing, '*beaux* parading on horseback, and People of Fashion sitting on chairs in little Parties of five & six'. Parisians were always whimsically dressed but one fashion was distinct – the garçon with the 'very clean white apron & Waistcoat'. The labyrinthine streets linked a vast network of markets and fairs, lined with busy merchants and buyers. The crowded walkways

> almost cover'd with Prints & border'd with Women selling Eggs, Loaves, Apples, Nosegays, Cakes, &c., others of both sexes running abt among the Voitures, & mounting on the Steps of them, offer for Sale Fans, Oranges, Sweet-meats, Dogs &c. Here a group of little Boys fighting, there a sett of Footmen round a Table drinking Beer, old Soldiers smoaking, Shopwomen & Abigails, bien Coiffée, with their Chintz Sacks & Lappels ... Puppet Shews, raree Shews, Monsters, Dancing Dogs &c &c &c. Crowds incredible.[4]

The contrasts were endless. Gradually entering Paris from the restful environs of the natural world the traveller rolled into noisy, cobbled streets. Landscape vistas turned into stone edifices, many still under construction. One Parisian spectator estimated that in the 1760s and 1770s, more than one third of Paris had been rebuilt, adding that, in the 1780s, 'immense blocks of building rise from the ground as if by magic and new *quartiers* are composed of the most magnificent mansions. This fever of construction gives the town an air of grandeur and majesty' from all sides.[5] In its expanding streets, there was already a distinct café society, nearly 3,000 cafés to choose from – in a population estimated at near 500,000.

If this was not enough to remind the traveller that she was again in Paris, the aroma would stir memories. Amongst the construction and the café-table chatter, wrote Rousseau, 'one is pursued by the unpleasant odour and infection from the places of ease' – the public latrines placed along the streets. To this was added the malodorous vapours emanating from cesspools, the horse dung laying in the streets, fish shops, the effluvia from excrement and refuse tipped into the Seine, and the hygienic aromas circulating around those hundreds of thousands of city dwellers. Curiously, perhaps, smells were rarely mentioned in the writings of Grand Tourists, and perfume was not yet commonplace for fear of the body's absorption of exotic chemicals.[6]

Five years after the Duchess of Northumberland's Parisian reflections, Hester Thrale entered the capital on her first trip abroad, accompanied by her daughter, Queeny (who celebrated her eleventh birthday abroad), Samuel Johnson (who celebrated his sixty-sixth birthday abroad), the famous linguist and part-time Italian tutor to her daughter, Giuseppe Baretti, and her then husband, Henry Thrale.

Immediately on their arrival, Hester recorded in her diary her impressions of the French cathedrals: 'let us never more talk of English Churches'. At Saint Omer, she studied the 'curious Ornamental part of this noble Edifice', and down the road in Arras, the twenty-year-old gothic cathedral was 'grandiose'. With high vaulted roofs and magnificent pillars, she approached the churches 'wondering where their splendours will have an End'. Nearby she spent an hour visiting the Benedictine monks' 'new Edifice', which had a refectory about the same size as Oxford's Christ Church and a library that reminded her of All Souls College. Her curiosity led her to loiter by the staircase, half desiring to sneak up to observe the private quarters, but she was reproved and removed by one of the monks who told her that their 'Dormitory was no place for Ladies'. Already her tour was making an impression. Leaving Arras, she reflected on how 'its Ornamental Churches, peevish Benedictines and Women in black Clokes will not be easily erased from my Memory'.

Foreign churches were a popular attraction for all Grand Tourists, which was something that the locals occasionally found amusing. 'You do very right to look at our churches,' an Italian 'lady of quality' once whispered to Hester Thrale, 'as you have none in England, I know – but then you have so many other fine things,' she continued, pressing Hester's hand to allay any offence, 'such charming *steel buttons* for example.'[7]

A notable dissimilarity between France and Britain besides the architectural majesty of the cathedrals was, of course, religion itself. Many in Britain were seething with anti-Catholic sentiment, encouraging many travellers to ridicule the rituals and beliefs abroad, and dismissing them as superstitious if not savage. Nevertheless, debates on religion were practically impossible to avoid. The routes of the Grand Tour necessitated a long trek through Catholic territory – a seemingly endless trial to the toleration of Protestant subjects. Critics preaching against the Grand Tour feared Britannia's sons and daughters would return from their travels, having been coerced into converting to Catholicism. Upon the subject of religion, wrote Edward Mellish – a British traveller through France in the early 1730s – 'the women of this country as well as all other countries often dispute about [it], for they generally think that their own religion is the best'. It was not easy to shrug off the confrontation with others' beliefs, and often Mellish felt urged to 'defend my religion against the Ladys, whose arguments and persons may be very powerful and persuasive in all cases except', adding condescendingly 'that of *religion*'.

No matter how aggressive the debates between people from opposite sides of the divide became, some travellers remained balanced in their outlook. 'I was now assailed on every side to become a Romanist, for *Catholics* I never would submit to call *them* who excluded from salvation every sect of our religion but their own,' Hester Thrale recounted in relation to a 'controversial chat' she had become embroiled in during a dinner in Italy. Eventually, she went on to note, the debates 'grew *very* wearisome and a *little* dangerous', though she would not allow herself to be converted.

Nunneries were particular sites of interest and intrigue for ladies of the Grand Tour, not least because of the numbers of British women who had renounced the outside world and chosen to live in convents abroad. They also wanted to understand the enigma of why *any* woman would choose to live a sequestered life. 'We visited Nunnerys in every town,' wrote Elizabeth Montagu during her French tour in 1763, adding that her travelling companion, Elizabeth Carter, was occupied 'expressing the greatest abhorrence of their strict vows' and limited lifestyles.[8]

In 1775 Hester Thrale showed a similar interest, but a more patient and compassionate approach. 'This morning my Curiosity was abundantly gratified by visiting two Convents of Religious Women,' she wrote in her diary on 23 September, six days after landing at Calais. The first were the 'Gravelines, or Poor Claires', with whom she and her daughter were only able to meet in their Chapel, but at least were able to speak to with ease, since 'they were all my Countrywomen & some still retained a strong Provincial Northern Dialect'. This was a poor convent, and the women were 'wretched'. They wore 'only one Petticoat, and that of the very coarsest Stuff, they were bare legged and bare footed, & had no Linen about them except a sort of Band, which was very dirty though I had Reason to think I was expected'. The health of the women whom Hester met was no better. Their disfigured fingers were knotted at the joints; their nails were broken; they were very thin and '*so cold* when one touches them; but no matter I will have another Touch with 'em tomorrow'. It was time to leave the English Poor Claires at Rouen, where she made a donation of a guinea, and continued on to 'a Convent of the highest Order', the Benedictine priory of Saint-Louis, to continue her investigations.

Receiving permission to enter the interior of the convent, she met with a number of nuns who were requested to 'satisfy the Curiosity of the *Dame Angloise*'. Accordingly, she was shown around by three sisters, 'as they call them', and visited the 'Refectory, Cells, Garden

& all Curiosities of the Place'. Here, 'they change their Linnen every day & are most delicately clean'. After the tour, she was invited to the apartment of the Abbess, where she met the prioress and four principal nuns and had discussions 'of Literature, of Politicks, of Fashions, of everything', and – in order to satisfy the curiosity of the nuns – Hester answered questions about the 'Cause of the Rebellion in America'.

'I have now acquired pretty good Notions of the Monastick Life,' Hester concluded the next day. The message she was able to carry away from Rouen, as she set off again for Paris, was that 'these Austerities are never chosen by any Women who have the least Experience of any other Mode of Life', but were forced into their lives of 'Ignorance & Superstition' by parents who want to be rid of their daughters. As such, one lesson already pencilled into Hester's diary of her Grand Tour was that foreign religions were led by, and perhaps pardoned as, 'involuntary Errors'.[9] Increasingly, the suspicion that the 'Romish Religion' was all pomp and show, without true devotion, was being reaffirmed by her encounters. Hester was hardly under any 'threat' of conversion to Catholicism. 'I am more & more delighted with my own dear Religion & Country,' she reassuringly wrote in her notebook.

On the rough roads to Paris, Hester's observations often turned to the countryside. It was, she had to admit, beautiful. So picturesque were the environs of Rouen – where wooded hills mingle among churches – that she dreamt 'it had originally been contrived merely to excite the Admiration of Travellers'. But elsewhere on the road she remarked on further contrasts with England. Where, she wondered, were the grand country houses? 'I could count but three Gentlemen's Houses between Saint Omers & Amiens,' she wrote. It seemed the French gentry all flock to the larger country towns to live, 'excepting the Richest & grandest amongst them', who preferred to reside in Paris, living off the rents of their country estates. The next day she happened to pass an estate owned by the Duke of Penthièvre which 'astonished' her due to its lack of 'Dignity or Ornament'. It was a plain, large, stone house. No garden, no park. 'How mean is such a place in Comparison of our Gentlemen's Houses in the distant counties of England?' Nowhere had she seen a Blenheim or a Chatsworth. Even 'Lord Bessborough's Villa at Roehampton is Paradise in Comparison' to Penthièvre.

While unquestionably *different*, France was so far not living up to expectations. 'Taste,' she declared, 'I have not yet found' – except, she qualified her remark, in cookery. Even French gardens were not quite right, in that they 'exactly resembled the English Taste of Fifty Years ago'. But it was early days; perhaps taste was 'confined to Paris', she wondered. 'We shall see one of these days.' Indeed, the closer Hester got to Paris the more appealing the landscape became to her. Travelling on the banks of the Seine on a sunny September day, she finally saw a vineyard and, while 'not half so pretty to the Eye as a Hop Garden', she nonetheless found it 'wonderfully pleasing' to pluck ripe grapes as they drove along. Following the winding river did offer beautiful views; 'the whole Country carries an Air of Fertility that is inexpressibly delightful', especially since the traveller was 'invited' by nature to indulge in the bounties of the nation, stocking up on fresh cherries, apples, asparagus, lentils and French beans.

Finally, on 28 September – just ten days after her arrival in France – Paris was in sight, the approach to which Hester considered 'very fine indeed and more than answered – exceeded my Expectations'. (She later wrote that the view from six miles out was magnificent – maybe not as good as approaching London 'when London is clear of smoke', she thought, 'but this Metropolis is always so, and you may distinguish every Spire in the City as clearly as the Houses at Hampstead'.)

Just as the Duchess of Northumberland had a few years earlier, Hester eventually settled in and enjoyed numerous evenings on the boulevards, writing of the vigour and vibrancy of the place, where 'Rope Dancing, Tumbling and Pantomimes preside – it was more entertaining than a Play' (though she did enjoy one performance depicting a mock engagement of men with muskets fighting women with clysterpipes: 'the Ladies conquered & were much applauded – so much for French Delicacy'). She found a daily rhythm, taking her daughter 'for a run' in Luxembourg Gardens, then strolling over the Seine past the Louvre and perusing the Palais Marchand – the stalls along the galleries of the Palais Royal. She too delighted in the excitement of the Parisian streets. 'I had a long Prance over them this Morning,' she wrote one evening, summarising the day's events. 'Coxcombs, Religious Habits, Wenches with Umbrellas, Workmen with Muffs, fine Fellows cover'd with Lace, & Old Men with Woolen Wigs make a Constrast & Variety inconceivable to a Londoner.'

Over the following days Hester excitedly visited one attraction after another, beginning with a call to the home of the French author Madame de Boccage, whose drawing room was adorned with monuments to England's illustrious writers: busts of Shakespeare, Milton, Pope and Dryden. She found Madame de Boccage, who 'sate on a Sopha with a fine Red Velvet Cushion fringed with Gold under her feet', a touch eccentric, her baroque home unkempt – for 'just over her Head [was] a Cobweb of uncommon Size, & I am sure great Antiquity' – and her manners, while appearing civil, were tainted with distasteful customs. 'A pot to spit in, either of Pewter, or Silver, quite as black & ill coloured, was on her Table; and when the Servant carried Coffee about he put in Sugar with his Fingers.' This habit also caused Hester's travelling companion, Samuel Johnson, to recoil in revulsion. 'The footman took the sugar in his fingers and threw it into my coffee,' he told Boswell. 'I was going to put it aside, but hearing that it was made on purpose for me, I e'en tasted Tom's fingers.' The others preferred tea, made *à l'Angloise*, but, observed Giuseppe Baretti, the 'literary lady of rank' produced an old china teapot with a clogged spout. Not considering it any impropriety, Madame de Boccage grabbed the teapot from the servant and, to the astonishment of the guests, 'blew into the spout with all her might, then finding it pour, she held it up in triumph, and repeatedly exclaim'd, "voilà, voilà"'.[10]

Things did not improve that evening when the travellers found themselves criticising the 'Dinner of the Day'. Hester described the hare on offer as 'not tainted but putrefied', the leg of mutton was 'put on the Spit the moment the Sheep was killed & garnish'd with old Beans', another dish was a meagre three sausages on a plate, and on another was 'nothing but Sugar plumbs'. Even the water 'disagrees with many People', noticed Frances Crewe, who visited Paris in 1786, suggesting to her friend 'if you ever come to Paris, pray remember that Circumstance, and put Lemon peel into it'.[11] Though most tourists knew that this was standard fare on the road, many felt compelled to comment upon what they considered adulterations of haute cuisine, 'No Meat here has the Taste of Meat in England,' concluded Hester; Johnson agreed:

> Onions & Cheese prevail in all the Dishes, & overpower the natural Taste of the Animal excepting only when it stinks indeed, which is not infrequently the Case: besides that every sort of Food being dress'd so very much, & no Flavour of the Food remaining, they are driven to the Necessity of superadding something else which is commonly Garlick, Vinegar, Cheese & Salt

In conclusion Johnson stated bluntly that he thought French food was 'gross'.[12]

Between France and Italy foreign travellers were rarely able to find food tolerable to their palates, as Lady Miller – though clearly an aficionado of English food – discovered. The predominant dish while making the treacherous crossing of the Alps was trout, but occasionally they ate shoulders of ram, 'as high flavoured as though it had belonged to a fox'. Like other travellers, they had frequently to force down liver and brains, 'to what animal they had belonged, I do not pretend to decide', but the Millers absolutely refused 'nose of Turk' and 'Tartar's lip' when offered to them at a small village near Florence. In Turin, however, they were delighted to imbibe good wine and mountain cheese, as well as bread and tasty butter, 'perhaps owing to the many aromatic herbs the cows find on the plain'. Lady Miller was informed that this was an exceptional delicacy:

> They asserted, that for nine months of the year they keep their cows in their kitchens, in order to make fresh butter for the English travellers. The wine is very pleasant, pro-

duced by the sides of the mountains, and is preserved in goat-skins. Had I seen this vessel before I had tasted of its contents, I doubt if I could have prevailed on myself to have touched it, for these skins have a dirty and disgusting appearance: the hair is off, but the skin looks black and greasy; where the feet and the head grew it is sewed up: the whole looks like some strange swollen monster.

Surely, she mused, when nature created goats she never intended wine to flow from such a 'tap'? In Genoa, they supped on boiled fowl, usually pigeons or partridges, with and without rice. Most meat obtainable on the road was not recommended, since 'after oiling the meat with a feather, they suspend it over a charcoal fire, until it is become so dry and brittle as to admit of pulverisation'. The only pleasant surprise was that gastronomy in Geneva was not as objectionable as they had been led to believe. 'As to what you have heard in regard to their eating cats,' Lady Miller informed her mother, 'if there is any truth in that report, it is not at Geneva that that animal is in vogue, but in the more remote and uncivilised parts of Switzerland'.[13]

Many travellers temporarily forgot the Continent's paucity of fine food and decorum once they feasted their eyes on its galleries and royal collections. Touring such sites was Hester Thrale's preferred occupation, though she was immediately unimpressed with Versailles, one of the first attractions she visited. She quickly grew bored with the menagerie, thought the positioning of the palace was undesirable, and could only marshal untailored praise for its gallery ('So spacious! So adorned!'). Much more to her satisfaction was the Duke of Orleans's Palace, where a cabinet of cameos, intaglios and other curious engravings 'of great Antiquity' impressed streams of visitors, many of whom would have agreed with Hester that the 'Collection of Pictures at this Palace is by far the finest I have ever saw', at least in Paris until 1792, when the pictures were brought to England and sold.[14]

When updating her journal later that evening Hester could not remember half the rarities she had seen at the Palace, but was determined 'not to forget the Head of Parthian engraved on some precious Stone with an Inscription in that Language illegible to the most learned Antiquarians. I was likewise struck with the Head of a Hannibal on Onyx, expressing the Anguish of that Eye which he lost in the Marshes of Italy.' Also not to be missed was the collection at Luxembourg, where, the following week, Hester 'saw the great Gallery filled with the pictures of Rubens – they perfectly dazzle ones Eyes'. Finally, the collection of rare gems at the King's Museum – the large cabinet of curiosities that had been arranged by the famous French naturalist, Comte de Buffon – was better, in her opinion, than Ashton Lever's museum in London.[15]

In addition to the public areas, she – in the company of a large party of fellow tourists and their 'conductor', Monsieur L'Abbé François – was invited to admire the interior of certain statesmen's homes. One was the home of the *intendant des Finances*, Monsieur de Gagni, which was richly furnished with jasper tables, china vases, crystals, corners packed with curiosities, and walls covered with Dutch paintings and silk damasks. It was a 'Fairy Palace', according to Hester, who was forced to leave quicker than hoped only because 'Mr Monville's House waited for our Inspection', but which, 'gave us no pleasure when we arrived'. The Hôtel de Bourbon, was notable, 'because of its newness, & the cleanliness of its furniture'.

In Paris, as in the provinces, Hester spent many days 'running about from Church to Church to see', as she ironically put it, 'the Splendour of the Romish Religion'. One stop was Saint Sulpice, 'the largest we looked at', which was 'well built in the modern Italian Taste – spacious & majestic'. She visited Saint Roque's Church, which ranked only second to the church in Amiens in its interior aesthetic appeal but which she chose not to dwell on in her diary, since its 'description is contained in every Book'. On the whole, however, churches never really quite caught Hester's fancy. It seemed the only thing as arresting as art in the capital was life in the convents – a topic which commanded more space in her journal than any other.

One encounter with a nun, a Miss Canning, who lived at the English convent Notre Dame de Sion in the Rue des Fossés Saint Victor, she found especially remarkable. This woman, she noted, was once 'a Beauty about London', was well-travelled and well-read, possessed a notable library in her room, desired to learn Latin, played the church organ and 'went over Handel's Water Musick with great Dexterity'. She was struck with the candour with which the abbess and other nuns felt able to converse – 'abusing the French Customs, wondering at the Hardships suffered by the Claires, telling & hearing in short whatever we had in mind'.

After this visit, she pondered this singular profession 'which at once inspires Compassion and Respect', but which was nonetheless governed by ambivalent vows of poverty, chastity, solitude, and obedience to their superior and perpetual enclosure. As to poverty, these nuns were well provided for and never felt the pressure of it; as to chastity, there was no social disgrace in it if one lived in a convent; as to solitude, 'few Women live in so much Society' as this community of some thirty nuns did, 'who pass their time in Prayer, Cards & Prattle just as these do' (the nuns, Hester noted, were amongst the most skilled chess players she knew). Obedience, however, was in principle the most objectionable vow, but since the nuns, rather than the King, elected their own abbess, it was made tolerable. In short, she learned that life in the convent could command her empathy, but lamented that the nuns could feel nothing about the outside world in return. Convent life, she concluded, was probably the best thing for those women. The problem as Hester saw it was that if a nun grew depressed, she tended to believe it was because she was a nun, 'whereas God knows', Hester opined, 'many of those I have seen today would have had more Misery by half had they lived in the World – what Happiness can there be in store for Women, young, friendless, ugly & poor?' Surely a convent was their safest refuge from the 'Shafts of Poverty & the Corrosions of Care'?

During Hester Thrale's first continental tour she began to develop a certain taste for continental cultural treasures. When she was half way through her stay in France, she summarised what had so far impressed her most. She was taken with the Duke of Orleans's collection of pictures, Monsieur Gagni's accumulation of costly rarities, and the serene situation and simple elegance of the royal residence at Choisy. Art was wonderful. As she said one night after returning from the Duke of Orleans's Palace, 'this has been my happiest Day hitherto; I have spent it with English Men & among Italian Pictures'. And when she was leaving Paris just a few weeks later, she once again summed up the benefits of the trip, 'where we have spent a Month of extreme Expence, some Pleasure & some Profit'. Her daughter picked up a little French and a great deal of dancing. But Hester had been most struck by the 'Chapel of the Invalides, the House of Monsieur de Saint Julien, the Disposition of the Alters in Saint Roque's Church, & the Pictures at the Palais Royal'. But Paris was only one stop on the Grand Tour, and Hester was still a novice.

Unlike male Grand Tourists, women travellers observed and wrote much about women. Local costume was one of the first features that caught their eye. How did the women dress? What were the current fashions – and how did they, or how did the traveller, measure up to expectations? Foreign fashions were almost always a matter of conversation. In 1742 the Duchess of Portland wrote to twenty-two-year-old Elizabeth Montagu, telling her that 'Mrs. Rook, an acquaintance of mine, is just come from Paris, and is come without a hoop, and tells me, except in their high dress, nobody wears one.' This was a valuable piece of information – it was important to keep up with the times – but the next snippet of information was additionally useful. 'Their sacks are made proportionally narrow and short, opened before with a petticoat and trimmed, and with a stiff quilted petticoat under.' For the Duchess of Portland, hearing about this adjustment towards comfort in the wardrobe was 'the only reasonable thing I have heard from France in a great while, and the only fashion I would wish to follow'.[16]

Because it was 'reasonable' to the Duchess, it was rather a relief.

It was not necessarily that one *enjoyed* following fashion, but a woman of her rank was expected to know current opinions of reigning styles. Self-presentation was a study in showing the trappings of distinction and power. Dressing to design identified the wearer with a particular social class. The Duchess of Portland noticed that even for those who had not been abroad during a certain season, having friends freshly returned from the Continent connected one to the latest styles. In London, a woman 'of fashion' was therefore able to associate herself with diverse continental locales and tastes in order to display that she was cosmopolitan. Dress enabled a woman to declare that despite not having travelled that season, her rank and fortune still enabled her to acquire a wardrobe in the style of the designs of the *marchands des modes*. In addition to the display of new attire donned by travellers on their return to England, examples were also carried across the Channel in the form of fashion dolls, the 'wooden mademoiselles' that wore replicas of the current *ensemble* with choice accessories.

Imitating foreign *coiffures*, ruffles, tassels, festoons and plumes also engendered a thriving trade for French milliners, mantua makers and tailors living in London. 'Nothing that is merely English goes down with our modern Ladies,' announced one successful mercer. 'From their Shift to their Topknots they must be equipped from Deare Paris.'[17] Similarly, attempts to ape the prevailing modes of dress in Paris put a premium on having a French maid, hired in all the most privileged households, who could suitably adorn her mistress.[18]

Much of what counted as acquiring 'taste' revolved around discussions of fashions that changed almost as frequently as travellers embarked on their Grand Tours. In order to emulate the fashions of the French court, the rich were required to purchase gowns in a catalogue of styles: *à la circassienne*, *à la Levantine*, *à la sultane*, *à la polonaise*, *à la créole*, and so on. Aristocratic dress was always in vogue: attention to the placement of a ribbon, the run of lace, embroidery or stitching, material for winged cuffs, or the braid or sprigs which ornamented skirts of petticoats, was critical. Determining whether a gown should be worn open at the front and worn with a petticoat, or whether a bodice and skirt should be worn with a *pet-en-l'air*, a loose-backed jacket fastened at the front, were also essential observations.

While travelling, however, such strict fashion etiquette was not always adhered to. Some women sported quilted satin travelling jackets, worn over a hooped petticoat, but the discomfort caused by the whalebones that stiffened the bodice made it an unattractive choice for long journeys. Women who removed their elaborate trappings in favour of the more masculine-style, short-cut riding costume, however, met with either disapproving glares or salutations of 'Sir', as did the Duchess of Queensbury who, during her European travels in 1734, was, to her brother's amusement, 'called *Sir* upon the road above twenty times'.[19]

The eighteenth century saw a greater coalescence of styles of dress than in either the seventeenth or the nineteenth centuries (by which time regional costume tended to fragment these unifying tendencies). Much of this was due to the Grand Tourists, and other 'people of quality', holding up mirrors to each other's fashions and tastes in the Continent's capitals and towns; here social order was worn on the sleeve.[20] Fashion helped classify groups of the population, making it possible to identify others of similar class and background. However during the French Revolution it became more difficult to categorise women as a group. Maria Holroyd, looking around during her trip to Paris in 1793, concluded that she thought 'all the French women look alike; the great objection I have to make against the beauty of the ladies is, that they have no "shape", as they never wear stays; they are an immense size, and a little French woman is quite as broad as she is long'.

Travellers were subjected to standards of social etiquette that encouraged conformity to, or at least some degree of consonance with, local dress codes. Fulke Greville's daughter, Frances Crewe, learned this when she arrived in Paris in 1785. Lady Clermont – already resident in Paris – immediately launched into detailed lectures offering the new arrival advice about 'Trades people whom *I must* use, and fashions *I must* follow.' Frances spent her mornings with a stream of artisans measuring for clothes, laying out samples of lace, and writing up bills, while her advisor spelled out the necessary accoutrements for the different social functions she would need to attend: 'Caps, Tippets, and Etiquettes of every Sort.' 'What a puzzling matter Dress is become within these two or three years,' Frances sighed.[21]

To be able to choose and change one's appearance according to the whims of fashion also reflected status. In contrast to the lavish costumes of polite society was the distinctiveness of rural dress. When the Duchess of Northumberland was on a tour in 1766, she regularly noted the appearance of the women in parts of Austria. The women in Achterbroek had

> Brown Skins, Black Eyes sunk in their Heads & bad Teeth. Their Dress is a Brown Stuff coarse snuff colour, Jacket, a Blue Frieze Petticoat, a roundabout Harden Apron, a Coloured silk Neck Handkerchief, a narrow black Collar with a kind of Gold clasp before. Not a Hair to be seen, a round Dutch Cap, edged Bodice, Grey Stockings & either Leather Shoes or Sabots.

Whereas her observations on the women's physical characteristics – their 'sunk' eyes or 'bad teeth'– was matter-of-fact, she was more critical of their self-presentation, where options were available, even if the means to decide were not. Their 'Brown Stuff coarse snuff colour' dresses and 'Grey Stockings' were telling features of their wardrobe, being cheap and common colours – a sure contrast to the brighter yellows and reds being produced with new expensive dyes for the wealthy.

The Duchess of Northumberland was more frank in her appraisal of the women in nearby Roefen, whom she described as 'ugly as the Devil'. She was surprised about their lack of jewellery. 'They wear plain Holland Dutch Cap, no Ear Rings nor anything round their Necks but a Blue & white Handkerchief.'[22] But fashion was not relevant to the lower echelons of society. Labourers' dress was dictated by necessity, not social distinction, and was worn as long as it remained functional. However, certain characteristics of local dress were notable, since, for example, the materials from which they were made were drawn from local resources.[23] Years later Lady Elizabeth Craven wrote in her *Journey through the Crimea* 'I am *femmelette* enough to have taken particular notice of [Turkish women's] dress – which, if female envy did not spoil every thing in the world of women, would be graceful,' going on to describe the jewellery, embroidered robes, *toilette*, the postures, and then the topics of conversation she had with the women she met. And, as Cornelia Knight recognised as she travelled through Italy in 1785, regional dress also reflected people's heritage, and customs.

In Naples, she observed that 'the dress of the common people was very slight, though very often exceedingly picturesque. The women wore their hair in the style of antique statues, and none of them had any stays.' They were then compared to women of a different class.

> Ladies even of the highest rank went about with only a ribbon tied round their head, and seemed by no means scrupulous as to etiquette. Many of them kept running footmen, but these were very dirty. A black petticoat and a mantle that covered the whole figure were generally worn by all women, except those of the lowest orders.[24]

In the increasingly commercialised culture of the capital cities, artisans and merchants began to tap into the burgeoning tourist economy. One rather sanguine statistic in a Paris newspaper gave the unbelievably high estimate that 32,000 Britons arrived in the capital each month, and another estimated that the average stay was two weeks, each visitor dropping thirty guineas into the local economy, making Paris the richer by 960,000 guineas a month.[25] The embryonic fashion industry also generated good business for haberdashers and tied the fashion-conscious English to regular and hefty expenditure. As if keeping one hand on his wallet, Lord Holland wrote a letter to Lady Upper Ossory during a trip to Rueil-Malmaison where he saw 'several beautiful women' appear as part of Napoleon's audience, who showed 'an expence, a display, and a taste in dress, which it is difficult to describe, and which it is as well that our ladies in London should be as ignorant of as they are'. This was a recurring refrain from those men who for the briefest moment contemplated the costs of maintaining high culture. 'The sums expended on dress are quite incredible, and the richness of the shops in those articles, as well as in furniture, exceeds not only all description we have ever heard in England, but anything the most expensive persons there can imagine.'[26] In Hester Thrale's 1775 critique of Parisian trade, she wrote that, 'The Shops here at Paris are particularly mean & the Tradespeople surly & disagreeable,' bitter also that, of the silks a mercer was willing to display, he refused to cut any. 'They run in pieces for Gowns & you are obliged to buy all or none.'[27]

Lord Holland's concern to 'keep the ladies in London ignorant' of the fashions abroad for fear of imminent insolvency had, it seemed, long played on men's minds. Consider the cautionary tale of the dangers of an Englishman taking his wife and daughter to Paris, written in 1753 by a fictional correspondent to the satirical rag, *The World*, published by Edward Moore.

The gentleman correspondent sought advice from one Adam Fitz-Adam, the alleged editor, who after forty years' travel through all parts of the 'known and unknown' world, was publicising his wisdom to help cure 'lying, cheating, swearing, drinking, gaming, avarice and ambition in the men; and envy, slander, coquetry, prudery, vanity, wantonness and inconstancy in the women'. But the problem presented here concerned domestic sensibility, and Adam Fitz-Adam printed the letter as a moral lesson for his readers. The tale began with a sketch of the customary education the gentleman afforded his son, to the point that the boy was sent abroad on his Grand Tour. It was at this point that he received an unusual recommendation from his wife, which he was struggling to come to terms with.

'My dear,' the gentleman's wife said, 'I think you do very right to send George abroad, for I love a foreign education, though I shall not see the poor boy a great while.' But instead of missing him, why not – she suggested – take the family and accompany the boy as far as Paris? The father sat silent while she volunteered reasons why it should not be a problem.

'The journey is nothing; very little farther than our own home in the north; we shall save money by it, for everything is very cheap in France'. But it would also serve an added educational function, 'it will form the girl, who is of a right age for it; and a couple of months with a good French and dancing master will perfect her in both', which would help her in the marriage market; after all, she reminded the father, 'husbands are not plenty, especially with only five thousand pounds to her fortune'.

The delicacy of the situation! Before the father could settle his thoughts – having had flashed before him a number of financial considerations – the daughter spoke up with enthusiasm. 'Ay, dear papa,' she cried, 'let us go with brother to Paris; it will be the charmest thing in the world; we shall see all the newest fashions there,' and as to the acquisition of airs and manners, 'I shall be quite another creature after it.'

The dumbfounded father took further convincing, however, admitting to the readers of *The World* that 'the absurdity of the proposal struck me at first, and I foresaw a thousand inconveniences in it'. The reality of it was, he confessed, that he had seen few *men* return truly 'improved' by their travels, and the women he had seen appeared 'ridiculous' after their foreign forays. Besides, as the wife pointed out, since the daughter was not of fine fortune, 'I saw no necessity of her being a fine lady.'

The next thing the father knew, however, he was in France and his fears had materialised: the spending spree had begun. For several days he sat in a lofty apartment, watching 'mechanics' shuffle in and out of the women's rooms, where they were at work 'disguising' his wife and daughter, until one day they entered the dining room 'different pictures of themselves'. 'But what hast thou done to thy hair, child?,' cried the father, looking at 'a complication of shreds and rags of velvets, feathers, and ribbands, stuck with false stones of a thousand colours, and placed awry'. The lamentable conclusion: 'My wife is become ridiculous by being translated into French, and the version of my daughter will, I dare say, hinder many a worthy English gentleman from attempting to read her' – and all at great expense.

Despite initial appearances, the moral of the story was not that the corrupting forces of the Continent worked only against women. The concerned father wrote back to the magazine about two months later, reminding readers that he was the one whose wife and daughter had '*run stark French*' (noting that they were perfectly recovered – since they could not keep up with the changing fashions). He now wrote with a similarly cautionary tale, of the 'wrong-headedness, the idle, and the illiberal turn of an only son' resulting from the Grand Tour.[28]

The supposed effects of foreign travel were widely represented in caricatures in the eighteenth century, but the fictional image probably proved so popular because the depictions of folly touched on familiar experiences. This was, of course, as true for the French as it was for any foreign visitor, as the seventeenth-century aristocrat and famous *epistolière* Madame de Sévigné once admitted after a visit from a 'pretty little farmer's wife', dressed in a fine white fashionable dress: 'Good heavens! thought I, when I set eyes on her, I am ruined: for you must know, her husband owes me 80,000 francs.'[29] But men were not unimpeachable.

'When an Englishman comes to Paris,' snorted Tobias Smollett, 'he cannot appear until he has undergone a total metamorphosis,' suggesting that the eagerness to spend was a result of men's as much as women's consuming passions. 'He finds it necessary to send for the tailor, peruquier, hatter, shoemaker, and every other tradesman concerned in the equipment of the human body.' For men and women, it was hard to escape, and, perhaps more worrying, following fashions was not the only costly pursuit abroad.

Not only did the fashion-conscious Grand Tourist travel from one couturier to another, but also from one art gallery to another, most especially in Italy. Italy in the eighteenth century was the training ground for artists across Europe.[30] Rome was especially cosmopolitan. Patronage in the city – the second largest in Italy next to Naples, with a population of about 175,000 (before the French invasions of the 1790s) – promoted various schools for artists of different nationalities, largely from Britain and France, to the extent that few well-known eighteenth-century artists were, in fact, Roman. 'If one thing more than another evinces Italian candour and true good nature,' wrote Hester Piozzi, thinking in particular of the talented artist Angelika Kauffmann in Rome, 'it is perhaps their generous willingness to be ever happy in acknowledging foreign excellence, and their delight in bringing forward the eminent qualities of every other nation' with their own.[31] Tourists commissioned historical or allegorical art and altarpieces from new modern talent, or bought restored or recently excavated ancient statues. The contrast between the displays of antiquity and the demands of modern craftsmanship was striking. 'Mingled with every crowding, every classical idea, comes to one's recollection an old picture painted by R. Wilson,' wrote Hester Piozzi upon entering Rome in 1785, referring to one of a series of drawings of the city by Richard Wilson commissioned by William Leg, the 2nd Earl of Dartmouth in the 1750s.[32]

One year earlier Mary Berry had also been in Rome, meeting with artists, and visiting the gallery of the Edinburgh-born landscape painter Jacob More – 'magnificent, ornamented with statues and busts alternately, and a vast number of pictures, some of the pictures beautiful'.[33] Praised by Sir Joshua Reynolds as being among the greatest landscape painters, More moved to Rome in 1773 where he spent the last twenty years of his life. This expert guide introduced Mary Berry to a few more prominent painters, and she began to learn about their work. She met Gavin Hamilton, another Scottish artist, art connoisseur and collector and dealer of antiquities, who lived in Rome most of his life. He started off as a portrait painter for British Grand Tourists but gained enough private income to turn his talents towards painting scenes from history such as episodes from the Roman republic and even eighteenth-century Scottish history in classical guise. Mary also met Jacob-Philippe Hackert, a forty-seven-year-old Prussian painter and engraver, who spent much of the previous twenty years painting the Italian environs and set new standards in landscape painting (Hackert was later appointed principal painter to Ferdinand IV, King of Naples).

Hamilton and Hackert were amongst the main artists commissioned by Prince Marcantonio Borghese IV in a massive undertaking to 'modernise' the Villa Borghese on the city's Pincio in neo-classical style. Although, Mary Berry was told, the Prince 'was not a man of taste', he had ambitions to make the villa a European attraction 'and lay a sum of money to be yearly expended, during his lifetime, in its embellishment' in the form of two refurbished rooms costing nearly 100,000 crowns.

One Friday morning in 1784, Mary had the opportunity to visit the Villa Borghese, enabling her to see the artists' plans and the work-in-progress. Approaching the villa she noted how its gardens were lined with rows of evergreen oaks and fountains, and populated with posing statues. The villa's exterior was ornamented with bas-relief and statues in niches; inside were more statues, and it was richly decorated with magnificent mosaics, marbles and pictures. 'At the first cursory view,' she wrote, 'one is dazzled and lost in the number of things worthy of observation.'[34] Mary found Hamilton and Hackert embroiled in painting murals in the villa. Hamilton was preparing a room where his paintings would narrate the birth, life and death of Paris and Helen with five works set into the ceiling. Meanwhile Hackert was decorating the villa's walls with contemporary scenic views of various Borghese property with small seascapes as overdoors. Jacob More was also employed on the villa's refurbishment: in addition to painting landscapes for the villa's interior he was charged with the not insignificant task of transforming the villa's park into an English garden.

A few days later, Mary accompanied More to the galleries of other artists – 'to Mr Dernot's, a history painter, to Mr Hamilton's, &c., and to a painter of fans', and added to her collection by buying 'two of the ruins of Rome' for a sequin apiece. For day upon day in her journal, Mary concentrated on relaying her judgements about the art, architecture and the places she had visited. Italy was without question a land of rich treasures, but she noted how much of it was in disrepair, or in continual maintenance. While any place she visited was likely to have some items worthy of praise, she was often uninspired and critical of the general appearances of things. Such was the case with the Palazzo Giustiniani, where 'the suits of apartments shown are not better kept than an *auberge*; fine pictures, all dust, against bare walls, without frames, and good busts in little niches, in windows where they cannot be seen, and placed without any order upon the floor round the room'.

Grand Tourists entered Italy with expectations of its grandeur drawn from a variety of literature, tourist pamphlets and poetry. Lady Webster, for instance, rarely let a scene pass without commenting on its merit relative to literary or artistic descriptions. In Paestum she saw the majestic temples which were 'precisely what I had conceived them to be from the drawings I had seen', and she agreed with Milton's views of Tuscany, who 'seems to feel a proper love for it'; 'nothing can be more lovely than the villas'. She was enthused with many of the scenic representations of Italy since it was, she felt, the natural beauty of Italy itself that inspired the artist. 'What a view lay stretched at our feet!' she exclaimed at Chiaia in 1793. 'Objects that would rouse torpor itself, and call forth the energy of the poet, philosopher, painter, historian.'[35]

Less magisterial landscapes would also find their way into guidebooks (often nothing more than sales catalogues), which told visitors to the city what to look for and even how to view the objects. In addition there were human tour guides – the *cicerones* – or local 'experts' eager to sell their services to help tourists find hidden treasures.

When the otherwise enthusiastic Lady Webster arrived in Cortona – one of the ancient towns of Etruria – after an exhausting nine-hour ride from Perugia, she was less than impressed with the welcome: 'a drunken *cicerone* conducted us to a mad *chanoine*', the latter named Celari, who was known as the master academician of Etruscan antiquities, but, Lady Webster reckoned, 'he himself is the rarest and greatest antiquity in the collection'. He was oddly shaped and oddly dressed, 'his head tottering from disease and imbecility', and he carried 'a dropsical paunch [which] gave him an uncouth waddle'. Worse, nothing he showed Lady Webster from the collection she thought remarkable, save a single bronze vase with curious bas-relief around the rim. Her luck, however, did improve. 'When I escaped from his clutches, I went to a very learned and civil advocate who has many chosen antiquities. A pretty Cupid in terra cotta, a shield embossed with figures, elephants' tusks found at Trasimene probably Carthaginian, a medal of Porsena, etc., etc.'[36]

But the real education was, of course, being able to see the objects for oneself. It was then that a lady might form a judgement on matters of taste. Mary Berry was not shy in stating her opinion of the artistic merits of works she encountered. Continuing on her ramble through Rome, she 'saw the pictures in the Capitol; many seemed to me very bad'. Those she enjoyed were noted in her journal. The seventeenth-century artist Guido Reni's *Fortune Flying over the Globe* she thought 'beautiful'; his *Saint Sebastian*: 'exquisite'. Rubens's *Wolf Suckling Romulus and Remus*: 'the wolf [was] life itself'. But the canon of quality art was still in the making; few eighteenth-century artists had attained a status so exalted that tourists felt obliged to pay homage to their work. Even for those who were recognised their place in the history of art was far from secure.

Speculating about the future of contemporary Italian painting in 1788, the Royal Academician Joshua Reynolds thought that 'Pompeo Battoni, and [Francesco] Raffaelle Mengs, however great their names may at present sound in our ears, will very soon fall into the rank of Imperiale, Sebastian Concha ... and the rest of their immediate predecessors' whose names had descended into what was little short of total oblivion.[37] Although masters such as Reynolds prescribed exact definitions of what made art appealing in his *Discourses on Art* (lectures delivered to the students of the Royal Academy), the fundamental technique for art appreciation in the eighteenth century was *staring*. When Mary Berry visited Saint Peter's in Montorio and saw Raphael's 'famous picture' of the Ascension, she wrote that 'like all Raphael's pictures, the longer you consider, the more you admire it'.[38] She warmed more quickly to a painting she saw a few days later, at the Convent of Santa Maria delle Grazie in Milan. 'In the refectory the Last Supper, by L. de Vinci, covering the whole end of the room.

It is by far the finest picture of his I have seen – the only one of composition ... the heads are fine, and struck me both in expression and colouring, like Raphael.' Slowly, the canon was being created.

Mary Berry's diary is fascinating not only because of the descriptions it offers of many of Italy's sites as they appeared in the 1780s, but also because it is proof of her enduring commitment to recording her daily excursions and opinions. But what of her days of rest? Occasionally, we get a glimpse of the torpor such Grand Touring created. On a day trip with a group of other English tourists to Capo-di-Monte, they had first to ascend a long steep hill to the palace. They initially thought it unimpressive. 'No beauty about the architecture; within is a labyrinth of quite unfurnished rooms, of which the bare walls are covered with innumerable pictures, some good, some bad, and many indifferent, all without frames, placed without order, and most wretchedly neglected.' Mary noted with some relief a sculpture of such exquisite workmanship that it 'exceeds description'. 'There is likewise a large collection of drawings,' she added, 'and so *many* pictures, that before I had got above half through the apartments I lost all power of observing anything particularly.'[39] After weeks of touring, observing, learning, absorbing and recording, Mary now was struck down with art fatigue.

So how to maintain one's attention? This was one of the few areas usefully addressed by the published travel guide which helped direct the Grand Tourist's attention and provided reviews ('pre-views') of major attractions.

Such guides became indispensable companions for both men and women. The only one penned by a woman Grand Tourist, however, was Lady Anna Miller's *Letters from Italy*.

In 1765 Anna Riggs, who had inherited a fortune from her grandfather, Edward Riggs, from County Cork, married John Miller, who inherited his family's estates from his brother, making him moderately wealthy. After building a home in Batheaston, the Millers, accompanied by Anna's mother, set off on a continental tour in 1770. From

Paris, where they left Mrs Riggs with their two children, Anna and her husband travelled to Italy.

Before leaving Paris, Mrs Riggs made one request of her daughter: that she write in enough detail to enable her to compare her daughter's observations 'with the best modern travels of French or English publication'. To this end, Lady Miller's epistolary reports attempted to be as accurate as possible – encouraging her to write up the day's observations even when utterly fatigued by her travels, or 'in moments unfavourable to precision', as she put it. It should not *really* matter, Lady Miller suggested, whether her remarks were truly precise, since they were written for private concern, or as the disclaimer in the preface to her book reads: 'by no means objects of information or entertainment to the Public'.

Although the original aim of her writings was to educate her mother, Lady Miller gradually became aware that her foreign travel accounts might be useful to the wider public: 'I think one very considerable benefit arising from seeing other countries besides our own,' she declared, 'is the eradication (by the testimony of one's own senses) of many prejudices' instilled by others. She set out, therefore, to provide as detailed a testimony as she could. Launching her correspondence, she invited her readers to 'follow me, then, in an *ideal jaunt*', which, if she was successful, would both help her mother imaginatively leave the confines of her Parisian armchair, and provide her subsequent readers with an ideal guide through Italy.

Of course, examples of detailed guides to Italian art already existed; Anna cited them: Jérôme Richard's *Description historique et critique de l'Italie* (1766), Jérôme-Lefrançois de Lalande's *Voyage en Italie* (1769), J.G. Keysler's *Travels Through Germany . . . Italy and Lorrain* (1756–7), and an Italian guidebook they picked up in Rome. What did she have to offer that these did not? After all, as she was ready to acknowledge, 'they made this journey with a view to writing and publishing their observations for the benefit of travellers', whereas she and her husband 'travel merely for our amusement'.

However, Lady Miller's travel writings were much more than this: she questioned the accuracy and thoughtfulness of other travel writers and provided a wealth of refreshing insights of her own. She thought Abbé Richard was overly favourable to much of Italy's architecture, and certain views admired by de Lalande she found did not in fact answer his descriptions. Kindly, Lady Miller reflected, *they* had probably been misled by previous travellers, on whose accounts they had based their tracts; otherwise, she thought, conditions had changed drastically. At St Michael, Lady Miller wrote late into the night, since 'the hardness and dirt of the bed does *not invite me to rest*'. How, she wondered, could J.G. Keysler have found the place attractive? He must have been doting when he wrote that 'there is very good accommodation in a spacious inn at Saint Michael'. 'Spacious it is indeed,' scribbled Lady Miller while glancing around, but with 'naked walls, and ill-paved floors; a few broken chairs, and straw beds'.[40] At least it was only for one night, she sighed with relief.

Disagreements among travellers provided a common reason for publishing more travel accounts. But Lady Miller's account offered a rare difference from what other travellers provided – namely, a female perspective. In fact, it was her gender that at times urged later, male, commentators to draw out specific distinctions between their work and hers. One example is the way in which the British travel writer John Moore contrasted his observations of the sculpture of *Hercules* at the Farnese palace with Anna Miller's. *Hercules* had for long been admired as 'an exquisite model of masculine strength', Moore established, but somehow 'it does not please all the world'. He was made unpleasantly aware 'that the women in particular find something unsatisfactory, and even odious' in the 'majestic' figure. To be sure, a woman he accompanied to the Farnese – he claimed – turned away from the figure in disgust. Pressed about her views on the sculpture, the woman likened it to a deformed giant, and could not accept that such a man 'could ever have been a reliever of distressed damsels'.

Moore's female companion served, if nothing else, as a rhetorical whipping block to ridicule feminine judgements about classical masterpieces. Moore's passage was in all probability a cloaked critique of Anna Miller, the woman 'behind' the woman, as it were. In her own critique, published four years before Moore's, she too described *Hercules*. 'It may be very beautiful, and the most perfect model of a man in the world,' Lady Miller allowed, 'but I am insensible enough to its charms to own, that if all mankind were so proportioned, I should think them very disagreeable and odious.' Moore had misread Lady Miller's responses to the statue and turned her qualified sentiment – '*if* all mankind . . .' – into the unanimous voice 'the women' who find the masculine form 'unsatisfactory'. Anna Miller, however, was ultimately triumphant in her aim to overthrow the 'prejudices and littleness of thinking' that male writers imposed on their public.[41]

Her detailed observations and comments about the objects on display, whether in the Medici estates or in the galleries, are testimony to her commitment to the principles of particularisation and accuracy. Lady Miller passed hours pausing in front of statues and paintings, taking meticulous notes. 'To avoid errors and omissions, I take my notes upon the spot,' she wrote in a letter, while tidying up her jottings, 'which I assure you is often very troublesome, as I am frequently obliged to write in my pocket-book standing, and at times supporting it on the pedestal of a statue.'[42]

Acquiring taste on the Grand Tour involved exercising both the mind and the body. At Palazzo Pitti in Florence, for example, Lady Miller characteristically paused to admire the paintings on the ceilings of the first-floor apartments:

> Pietro da Cortona and Ciro Ferri have exerted their genius
> in representing on these ceilings several allegorical subjects
> taken from ancient history, and from the heathen myth
> ology, applicable to the political history of the Dukes of
> Florence, and which would take up a volume to explain.
> I only wish you then to believe that they have great merit
> as paintings; that they are *symbolical*, *mysterious*, that I got
> a pain in my neck from looking up at them, and was tired
> to death at hearing them explained.[43]

Despite such trying circumstances, she was committed to commenting in brief on as much as she was able, later elaborating on select objects where her descriptions grew increasingly suave and sophisticated.

Her portable notebook critiques became a sort of rough guide to Renaissance art. Amongst the other paintings in the salons of the estate was a 'Holy Family, finely done, in which Saint John brings a lamb to the Infant, by Rubens. A portrait of a Lady in crimson sattin; the drapery beautiful, by the same. The Fates, by Michael Angelo; this picture is much blackened. A fine portrait of a Lady dressed in black, by Paul Veronese. A Magdalen emaciated by fasting and prayer: it is a very singular picture; she is draped in crimson velvet lined with fur; by Leonardo da Vinci,' and so she continues – the list is extensive.

In her published *Letters*, Lady Miller's 'editor' (most likely her husband) offered a caveat lest she appear 'reprehensible' for offering such extensive criticisms of Renaissance art. Her strong propensity to that 'science', the editor wrote, 'induced her treating it more largely than may be agreeable to some of her readers; and that he was prevented from suppressing any part, from a possibility of its being relished by those amongst them of a different taste, who may be unprovided with better or more recent accounts'. Further, the many simple catalogues of art that promoted the sale of paintings throughout Italy were often misleading and fortuitous. Thus, for the benefit of many a reader, Lady Miller's accounts were justified. 'Those in this country who commission persons residing in Italy (of which there are many) to procure them the best of such pictures as chance brings to market, may acknowledge some utility in critical disquisitions of this nature, if executed with a decent portion of truth and information; as serving to direct their choice upon the immediate objects of preference.'[44] Towards the conclusion of her book, she summed up the busy art market in Rome, offering simple recommendations. Pompeo Batoni was, 'I believe with justice esteemed the best portrait painter in the world'; the Pichlers, father and son, were 'admired by everybody of taste and judgement' for their abilities at gemstone engraving, their cameos and their intaglios (as well as reasonably priced); as to Giovanni Battista Piranesi, he was well known to be amongst the first copper-engravers, was wide-ranging and talented, and on a good day could be 'agreeable to strangers'; the best miniature portrait painter was 'Marsigli', as well as many other young, promising artists, who lived precariously on the whims and fancies of the trade from the Grand Tour.[45]

By the 1770s, the principles of artistic taste had been institutionalised in such establishments as the Royal Academy of Arts (founded in 1768). Its master, Sir Joshua Reynolds, and other champions of the arts made public pronouncements at this time about women's abilities to appreciate art: Theresa Robinson, Grand Tourist and promoter of elegance at Saltram House in Devon, Reynolds reckoned, was the only woman to have 'skill and exact judgement in the fine arts'. But Anna Miller, writing in the same decade, represents an early attempt by a woman to present a precise and systematic guide to Italian art and artists for future connoisseurs. This was a kind of book-keeping reminiscent of the record keeping of family expenditure that historians now know many women maintained, let alone the minute detail of foreign culture exchanged in correspondence, journals, and diaries.

On the Continent travellers experienced strange customs, were forced to sample culinary curiosities, and, of course, collected objects as their 'trophies of travels'. In the eighteenth century the great treasure houses of Britain were adorned with art and furniture brought back from the Continent. The image is familiar: the gentleman Grand Tourist heroically travels in order to spot emerging fashions, broaden his knowledge and hone his powers of discernment; he then displays his collections so he can be admired for his skill and taste as a connoisseur. But continental travel also cultivated women's taste and enabled them to become commissioners and consumers in their own right.

As part of this celebrated 'culture of connoisseurship', women reflected on foreign cultural ornaments and developed a sense of discrimination in taste and judgement. They too indulged in the glitz and glamour of the Grand Tour, stopping at the main attractions – cathedrals and royal estates – or stepping into local manor houses and catching operas and concerts. The correspondence between British women abroad and at home shows that they were critics of artistic talent, *au fait* with the character and dependability of local artists or

RIGHT 'The Return from a Masquerade – a Morning Scene', by Robert Dighton, 1784. Overindulging at foreign fêtes was a custom for Grand Tourists, especially in Naples, where Sir William Hamilton's position in the Neapolitan court afforded every opportunity for lavish parties; 'the late hours of Devonshire House are trans-ferred to the Chiaia' area of Naples, joked a fatigued Lady Webster in 1793.

BELOW Fan with views of Vesuvius and the environs of Naples, *ca* 1770. Painted fans were popular souvenirs among women Grand Tourists.

BOTTOM 'Nineteenth-century tourists fleeing Vesuvius'. Mount Vesuvius, the 'yawning volcano' towering above Naples, was a source of endless exploration and fascination for travellers such as Lady Bessborough and her mother Lady Spencer, who climbed it to collect lava and were forced to flee when it erupted.

ABOVE 'Company at Play', from 'Comforts of Bath', by Thomas Rowlandson, 1798, *and*

LEFT 'A Bagnigge Wells Scene', 1780. Travelling as a remedy for illness was highly recommended by contemporary doctors. Bath rose to fame amongst the fashionable who hoped to have their 'health fortified by the waters', as did Bagnigge Wells in St Pancras, London. On the Continent, Spa in Belgium and a number of other resorts including Aix-la-Chapelle vied to be centres of sociability and salubrity.

'La Salle des Saisons at the Louvre', by Hubert Robert, 1802-3. Artistic appreciation relied on *staring*: 'The longer you consider' a picture, opined Mary Berry, 'the more you admire it.' To train the eye, women took to sketching 'which I assure you is very troublesome', wrote Anna Miller, whose *Letters from Italy* was a celebrated guide to art galleries. 'I am frequently obliged to write in my pocket-book standing, and at times supporting it on the pedestal of a statue.'

ABOVE A cartoon parodying the hairstyles of the late 1700s, *and* RIGHT 'The English Lady in Paris', *ca* 1770. 'But what hast thou done to thy hair, child?' cried the father. English men frequently feared the 'translation into French' of their daughters and wives whilst abroad, even though men were equally susceptible to foreign manners and costume.

The Duchesse de Choiseul and Madame du Deffand, from a drawing by
Carmontelle, *ca* 1759. French *salonnières* such as Madame du Deffand,
shown here with her cousin and protégé the Duchesse de Choiseul, Julie
de Lespinasse, were role models for British bluestockings.

'The Nine Living Muses of Great Britain', by Richard Samuel, 1779.
A portrait celebrating women's contribution to English culture, represented here
are (*left to right*) Elizabeth Carter, Anna Letitia Barbauld, Angelika Kauffmann,
Elizabeth Linley, Catharine Macaulay, Elizabeth Montagu, Elizabeth Griffith,
Hannah More, and Charlotte Lennox.

RIGHT 'The Circulating Library', by Isaac Cruikshank, 1800-15, *and*
CENTRE 'The Novel', by Names Northcote, 1787. Women's thirst for knowledge was often quietly, if not covertly, satisfied by their eager consumption of books, ranging from romance novels (which were often condemned by critics for their questionable moral tales, forcing many women to hide such reading matter), to history books and 'voyages and travels'. The latter genre is shown on the top right shelf of Cruikshank's circulating library.

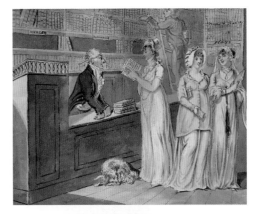

BELOW 'The Library at Holland House', from an engraving after the painting by Charles Robert Leslie, *ca* 1829. Here we see an aged Lady Holland holding a painted fan probably bought on the Continent; Lord Holland is seated opposite. Holland House was a hotbed of political debate, and Lady Holland 'reigned supreme'.

A mid-eighteenth-century quilted white satin travelling jacket and skirt. This would have been worn over a hooped petticoat; the bodice, stiffened with six whalebones at the back and two at the front, was an uncomfortable choice of garb for a long journey.

LEFT An example of a travelling medicine chest, which would according to Marianna Starke's suggestions, contain such paraphernalia as a scale and weights, a rhubarb grater, marble pestle and mortar, a knife for spreading blisters, a set of instruments for cleaning and filing teeth, toothbrushes, and leaf-lead.

craftsmen – opinions which informed their choices on commissioning artists.

Without spending a fortune, what, besides a journal, could women take away from their foreign travels? Women's skills at drawing – part of the celebrated 'feminine' qualities that were cultivated in their youth – were seen as being used to best effect when touring. Scenes would be eagerly sketched in an attempt to capture and record a view. While drawing was an important 'accomplishment' (it taught one 'to see', wrote one text-book writer, and was therefore 'beneficial to the mind'), no one fell under false illusions that their pen could portray the view as accurately as professional representations.[46] Still, drawing was a spontaneous and emotional response to the scenery. The view from Venice was such that it invited one 'never to stray from it', explained Hester Piozzi, 'and one sits longing for a pencil to repeat what has been so often exquisitely painted by Canaletti'.[47]

Just as modern tourists take photographs of places that are extensively represented elsewhere – in postcards and guidebooks – Grand Tourists felt compelled to represent the scene in their own way. The sketch was intimate, taken from a position and perspective unique to the traveller and could be used to rekindle memories. Such feelings led Lady Mary Coke, during a trip up the Rhine in 1767, to reprimand herself for her oversight in not opening her sketchbook. 'I have neglected very much my drawing,' she wrote in the relative comfort of a yacht, furnished with 'everything I cou'd want – Bed, table, Chairs, plates, glasses, & all kinds of provisions for my Voyage, & six bottles of wine'. After four days of floating past 'fine & beautiful scenes' of woods, vineyards, castles and ruins, she attempted to seize her remaining opportunities to redress her indolence, 'which I never repented so much as in this Voyage' – quickly making some sketches which 'I think I can have drawings taken from when I return to England.'[48] After taking her daughters on an educational trip to France, one Mrs Tighe was determined not to let their future drawing opportunities pass, and hired the eminent engraver and portrait painter, John Spilsbury (drawing master at Harrow), at the commanding sum of £300 per annum, to instruct the young girls in drawing.[49]

Cornelia Knight was known locally in the towns of France and Italy for studiously sketching and painting landscapes and ruins in the neighbourhood. She had had good training. As a child, she was a friend of Frances Reynolds, sister to Joshua. 'I used often to pass the day with her,' remembered Cornelia, 'when she would give me instructions in drawing, and as I was very intimate with her younger niece, we used to pass much time in rooms where the portraits of most of the celebrated beauties, men of letters, and politicians of the time, were exposed to view'.[50]

But for those desiring more material acquisitions, the same economy that led many Britons to live abroad comfortably enabled them also to collect everything from curiosities, to household furnishings, to paintings (the cost of commissioning a portrait in Italy was about a third of that charged by Sir Joshua Reynolds). Arranging for items to be sent home was fraught with difficulties, and travellers were endlessly cursing the customs officers. 'I have not got any of the things I bought last year at Paris,' complained Lady Mary Coke in 1768, 'it wou'd be some amusement to place them in my rooms, but I have not even that.' When, after another shopping spree, her tables and chairs finally arrived in England, she received the unpleasant shock of discovering that the duty and shipping costs had effectively doubled the cost of the items.[51] Her friend, the Duchess of Northumberland, was a noted collector (both at home and abroad) of engravings, pictures, miniatures, medals, coins, and anything else she desired.

In 1784, the Duchess of Portland ('intoxicated only by *empty* vases', quipped Horace Walpole) had formed her own museum of natural history specimens, rare manuscripts and medals. Looking to add some Etruscan vases, she bought a number of treasures from Sir William Hamilton, including collectibles that Sir William found difficult to put a fair price on: 'the Vase, the Head of Jupiter & my Picture of Correggio are the cream of all the Virtu I have ever possessed in my life, & I believe in my conscience there do not exist three finer Specimens of the perfection of Art'. He offered the Correggio painting to her for £3,000, and the rest for just over £1,000. She bought the lot.[52]

The purchasing power of women is a subject that has only recently begun to be examined by scholars.[53] The traditional view is one of men forming societies, such as the Dilettante Society, travelling and forming collections, which, like Charles Towneley's (amongst many others), later provided vital stock for the growing British Museum. Collecting antique statues, 'is that not a true Italian idea!' exclaimed Hester Piozzi, fresh back from her Grand Tour and looking at Towneley's collection.[54] But British women as well as men were increasingly importing the 'Italian idea', and acquiring a higher profile as collectors and decorators.

Collecting objects was a statement on taste. Mary Hamilton commented on the tastes and accomplishments of Mrs Walsingham, the widowed daughter of the 'very celebrated' Sir Charles Hanbury Williams, who enjoyed entertaining guests by reading from her manuscript collection, and was an esteemed painter. She was a woman of large fortune – Lady Hamilton heard she earned from her estates about £6,000 per annum: 'she has everything in stile, lives like a person of fashion; she is a good economist, & though she lives *expensively*, yet not *extravagantly*'.[55] And for any collection, the Continent seemed the greatest resource, or the fastest way to gain prestige.

Of course it was true that 'One comes to Italy to look at buildings, statues, pictures, people!', as Hester Piozzi declared, but Grand Tourists also came to buy. They travelled with an eye on commodities and a purse full of money. It did not take long for Hester Piozzi to see Voltaire's point when he opined that 'Italy was now no more than *la boutique*, and the Italians *les merchands fripiers de l'Europe* [the second-hand merchants of Europe]'.[56]

But not everyone could see the benefits of removing antiquities and showing them off in England. Hester Piozzi thought that the collection belonging to the Philharmonic Society in Verona was 'very respectable'. When she mentioned to the *cicerone* her opinion that they reminded her of the Arundel marbles at Oxford, the man replied 'Oh! That collection was very valuable to be sure, but the bad air and the smoke of the coal fires in England, have ruined them long ago.' Afterwards Hester was thumbing through the *Verona Illustrata*, and came across the same statement, at which point she concluded that this was an opinion reproduced merely by the authority of an Italian guidebook and was 'a very ridiculous prejudice'. After all, she went on to note tongue-in-cheek, the striking Greek remains and other monuments that she saw there were black, 'which look as if they had stood in our *coal smoke* for centuries'.[57]

Nevertheless, in 1786 Hester Piozzi, while resting with her husband 'in the midst of Luxuries cheaply purchased', was thinking it was about time to head home. She collected fossils for a friend back in England, and for herself various artefacts from Rome, including 'one Canaletti which one *must* love because tis the best Representation of *Piazza Saint Marco*, which, after all we have seen, still holds the first Place in my heart, for Elegance and Architecture'.[58]

In Naples in 1794, Lady Bessborough was busy acquiring a lava collection from Mount Vesuvius, vases, and other 'curious things' (noted her son). Lady Elizabeth Foster collected sheet music from Paris, which, according to Mary Berry, 'kept the young people in motion' at the morning dances at Devonshire House, and where, conveniently, many of the women present could practise the dancing they had learned at lessons in Paris.[59]

Travel encouraged some to compare different architectural styles. When an acquaintance of Lady Holland's, Mr Talbot, had an elaborate Grecian 'greenhouse' built to preserve some orange trees, she was dismissive about 'his adherence to the fashion of the times rather than his judgement in conceiving an appropriate decoration', but qualified her opinion about the architectural merits of the different, now fashionable, styles.

> Not that I am an enthusiastic admirer of Grecian architecture in any way but in a temple. There, indeed, the fine column, its slim shaft, rich architrave, cornice, and volute, surmounted with a graceful pediment, create a species of beauty which no other can. Indeed, the circular arch, as in the Pont de Garde, where they form a bridge and acqueduct by several tiers one above the other, is very grand; otherwise, in vast works, I like the Gothic architecture,

which, to use an affected phrase, is more *impressive* in loft structures.[60]

Visiting Lord Boringdon's Saltram estate in Devon in 1799, Lady Holland could acknowledge that it was 'excellent' – the apartments were adorned with many fine pictures and its view was very pleasing, but she had seen it all before. 'Switzerland, Italy, the Tyrol, and Nice have rendered me difficult about picturesque and grand views,' she liked to admit, 'therefore I am less inclined to be enthusiastic than most people.'[61]

Some travellers even bestowed praise on Italy in order to point out their distaste for architecture elsewhere in Europe. Writing from Prague toward the end of her continental tour in 1786, Hester Piozzi joked about how 'I fancy we shall take England for Italy at our return, so beautiful will Whitehall and even the Horse Guards look after German Architecture: and the Theatres here and at Vienna! What things they are!'[62]

As Hester Piozzi and many of her female peers believed, leaving home helps to understand better the place one has left. 'Where I hoped for Diversion abroad, I found to my much Amazement excessive great Comfort at Home,' Hester concluded, having returned to England in December 1786.[63] At its best, many believed, the foreign jaunt would reinforce patriotic feelings towards the homeland – a feeling alluded to by Cornelia Knight, who was in Naples when the English navy arrived on the heels of their victory against Napoleon. Bands played *God Save the King, Rule Britannia* and *See the Conquering Hero Comes*: 'No Englishman or Englishwoman can hear those airs without emotion in a foreign land, however trifling may be the effect they produce in our own country.'[64]

But some swayed the other way. After a three-week trip to Paris in 1774, Mrs Fitzroy was 'so charmed with every thing She saw', reported Lady Mary Coke, 'that She can talk of nothing else'. One of her principal interests was the French style of home decorating, which she (seeking the confirmation of her friends) thought 'much prettier', 'for nothing but what was done in France can please her'.

Such consequences of continental travel concerned Lady Coke: those who heedlessly favoured foreign fashions over everything else were not showing the *benefits* of their experiences abroad, but were merely being boastful. Those 'such as her [Mrs Fitzroy]', confirmed Lady Coke, 'shou'd not be allow'd to go out of their own Country; 'tis a sort of Affectation that is terrible'. But Francophilia was gaining ground everywhere she looked. Even immediately after her encounter with Mrs Fitzroy, Lady Coke attended a party where she entered to see the daughter and the granddaughter of the Duchess of Beauford 'both dressed *extremely french*'.[65]

This, critics cried, was the sort of malicious effect that foreign travel had on individuals and which could lead to the destruction of the moral, if not material, wellbeing of the country. Hannah More worried that this 'mania for whatever is foreign' would destroy England's domestic manufactures.[66] Worse, she feared, collecting new tastes might lead to the destruction of the fabric of the British constitution. Other women, dedicated to painting their own *tableau vivant* of life abroad, disagreed.

'A phantom falsely called Liberty'

Revelation & Revolution

*To the Women of Great Britain, particularly those
who have distinguished themselves by their writings in favour of the French Revolution.*
A toast, offered the evening of
18 November 1792,
at a banquet sponsored by the British Club
at White's Hotel, Paris[1]

7

FRANCE, 6 OCTOBER 1789. At around 5.30 a.m., an armed crowd of '*poissardes*' – a pejorative reference to working-class 'fishwives' and market women – joined by some men from nearby villages, found a weakness in the royal guard's defences and stormed the palace at Versailles, pushing all the way through to the royal apartments. The crowd was hungry and angry – grain barges had failed to deliver goods to the markets, no food was on offer, and they wanted the King, Louis XVI, and Queen, Marie-Antoinette, to answer for it.

It was alleged that inside the palace a guard heard a command from the crowd rushing towards the Queen's chamber to tear her heart out and cut off her head. Another guard at the Queen's door had just yelled out a warning cry when he was slain. The exact movements of the royal family or those who infiltrated the apartments are uncertain. But in his *Reflections on the Revolution in France*, the British politician Edmund Burke – who, even by immediate contemporary accounts, was perversely inaccurate in detail and wrote with theatrical flair – added the following description to the melodrama:

> A band of cruel ruffians and assassins, reeking with [the guard's] blood, rushed into the chamber of the queen, and pierced with an hundred strokes of bayonets and poniards the bed, from whence this persecuted woman had but just time to fly almost naked, and through ways unknown but to the murderers had escaped to seek refuge at the feet of a king and husband, not secure of his own life for a moment.[2]

Burke's passionate, if not deranged, attack against the revolutionaries was received by many (even those in his own Whig party) as a rather inexplicable manifesto. His largely hyperbolic argument was that Britons should beware, for it was entirely possible that they might soon find themselves in the middle of their own bloody revolution.

Others offered a very different interpretation of the meanings and events of the French Revolution. Not only did they criticise the inaccuracy of Burke's exposé, but they also disagreed about the extent of the potential threat from across the Channel.

Several political tracts, poems and pamphlets were published in the early 1790s addressing what became known as the 'debate on France'. Some women were amongst the most outspoken in the debate regarding individual rights and freedoms. Women such as Mary Wollstonecraft, Helen Maria Williams, Mary Berry and others, were sympathetic to the Revolution. French women such as Madame Roland, Madame de Staël, and even the more moderate Olympe de Gouges, and those who had run the salons of the liberal aristocracy, became role models for liberal-minded English women, some of whom went to Paris specifically to observe how the revolutionary changes might benefit them. They wanted to see the new rights that were being proclaimed for men extend to women, sharing the sentiment expressed in Olympe de Gouges's *Les Droits de la Femme* (*Declaration of the Rights of Woman*), published in 1791, a year before Wollstonecraft's *A Vindication of the Rights of Woman*. 'Women awake!' she rallied. 'The tocsin of enlightenment and reason resounds through the universe; recognise your rights.'[3]

In England, women fantasised about new freedoms and equalities, and wrote novels about the Revolution (such as Charlotte Smith's epistolary novel *Desmond*, 1792; but there was nothing quite like being there in person. For women who hoped to savour 'enlightenment' Paris in the early years of the Revolution was the closest they could get. Here, travel became inextricably bound to politics, when citizens were promised *liberté* and *égalité*. In the 1790s, continental travel became more hazardous and took on a new meaning.

In England, politicians and scribblers protested and quibbled that the recent eruption of reform in France was intent on invading the musty corridors of power of the *ancien régime*. Once again, diplomatic relations with France were on tenterhooks. It was less than a decade since France had sided with America in the War of Independence, and the Seven Years' War was still within recent memory. But unlike those who once sardonically complained that 'we take our fashions from the land we hate', travellers were now less interested in plumes than revolutionary politics, that 'object of curiosity so irresistible', in the words of one British visitor in 1789. Despite rumours in Paris that England was about to declare war on France, the Revolution only increased the desire in some, such as Mary Wollstonecraft, to travel there.

Having already expressed strong libertarian principles, it was precisely the new-found freedoms of expression abroad that Wollstonecraft found alluring. 'A spirit is abroad,' she wrote – addressing the British Prime Minister, William Pitt – 'to break the chains that have hitherto eaten into the human soul, which bids fair to mould the body-politic of Europe into a more proportional form, if we may be allowed the phrase, than has yet been seen on earth.'

A number of Wollstonecraft's writings concerned the wider implications of the French Revolution. But reading through her tracts one notices a change of heart regarding the practical implementation of revolutionary reform. The realities of revolution were more gruesome and distressing than were conceived in her reformist fantasies. When commentating from England she was able to sympathise with the grievances of the French people, to commend the principles guiding their revolution against unfair abuses of royal and religious power, and advocate the potential benefits of political reform to women. But, as a witness to the events in France, she was forced to reconsider her preconceived ideas. This shift can be seen in Mary Wollstonecraft's changing responses to Burke's 'reactionary' tome, *Reflections on the Revolution in France*, and, more intimately, in her reaction to the fate of Marie-Antoinette.

Burke's view of the French Revolution included one scene that Wollstonecraft found particularly offensive: his version of the events surrounding the morning of 6 October 1789 when the royal family was dragged from Versailles and placed under virtual house arrest in the Tuileries, the royal château in Paris.

Burke had attempted to show the vulgarity of the offenders by describing to his modest readers how a 'half-naked' Marie-Antoinette was stripped of her dignity and tormented by the mob. It was a shocking image. Symbolically, this was a vignette portraying a society stripped of its morals but it also represented human *equality*: removed from her luxurious trappings that so markedly distinguished her from the intruding proletariat, the Queen was rendered a commonly recognisable creature: like everyone else, an imperfect cast of God's image.

Burke's image of the Queen as a sexually vulnerable, threatened and passive victim of misguided, hot-headed revolutionaries provoked Wollstonecraft to offer her own narrative of events. Mary considered Burke's chivalric presentation of Marie-Antoinette utterly distasteful. Furthermore, whereas Burke on the whole supported the idea of aristocratic privilege, she loathed the patrician franchise.[4] If Wollstonecraft was to have an impact her rebuff needed to come quickly – Burke's nostalgic fondness for the *ancien régime* was being rapidly consumed as nearly 20,000 copies of his *Reflections* were sold in its first six months. Eager to put into print the issues she felt should be publicised about men's (and women's) civil rights, Mary penned her response in *Vindication of the Rights of Men* (1790).

The tears that Burke shed for the humiliation of the Queen, Mary considered, were 'vulgar sorrows'. She had no sympathy for the high-born who fed their bodies but not their minds: those, 'born in the lap of affluence' who 'by a necessity are, nine out of ten, the creatures of habit and impulse'. Where Burke saw splendour and joy emanating from the Queen's eyes, Wollstonecraft thought that 'neither virtue nor sense beamed in them'. His whole account of 'that infernal night', the 5th of October, was 'glowing' and 'exaggerated'.[5]

'The ruffians' to Burke were an irrational mob who attacked the Queen, not only as a royal figure, but a figure who symbolised the beautiful, simple, gracious and feminine qualities of society – all of which was under threat from the revolutionaries. Burke's 'almost naked' queen was not merely a disgraced leader, but represented the fall of an ideal. Wollstonecraft had a very different view, declaring that the Revolution was, in fact, a celebration of a future ideal *for* women as much as for anyone else.[6]

Most of the 'mob' were women. To Wollstonecraft, writing from her home in England, the women of the French Revolution had displayed a fine spirit of struggle. In contrast to Burke, Wollstonecraft wanted to show how women could support each other: 'I do not wish them to have power over men,' she wrote, 'but over themselves.'[7] Unlike any other moment in their history, Wollstonecraft concluded, women had the potential to ride their passion and discontent and assert their own rights to individuality in a free society.[8] But these freedoms had been attained at a high price.

Upon her arrival in Paris in December 1792, Mary Wollstonecraft found herself absorbed into the heart of revolutionary politics. She was stunned by the potency of the events surrounding her. For the past three years – since the forced removal of the monarchy from Versailles to the Tuileries – the revolutionary leaders were busy reconstituting the government, stripping away the King's authority, abolishing the nobility, and nationalising church property. By August, just four months before her arrival, the Revolution erupted to a new level. A group of revolutionaries, bent on removing the monarch from power altogether, took control of the Tuileries and imprisoned the royal family at the Temple (the former château of the Templar knights in Paris). With the loss of about 800 lives – mostly royal guards – France was now a fully fledged Republic, and the King was to be put on trial for treason, accused of conspiring with counter-revolutionary forces against his own people.[9]

Just after 10 a.m. on Wednesday, 26 December 1792, the beating of a distant drum echoed through the streets. Wollstonecraft looked out of the window of her room off the Boulevard Saint-Martin and watched the dethroned Louis XVI being driven in the mayor's coach to his trial. This was the day assigned for Louis's defence; only the second time he faced his accusers. Louis, on trial like an ordinary mortal, remained calm. Wollstonecraft sobbed 'insensibly' as she saw 'Louis sitting, with more dignity than I expected from his character, in a hackney coach going to meet his death . . .'[10] Indeed, there was little question of his fate. His 'defence' was tolerated as a mark of respect for legal procedure rather than for the possibility of his innocence. He knew this, even remarking to one of his counsel 'I am sure they will make me perish.'[11]

Regicide would stir the emotions of even the most republican spectators. The King was supposed to be all-powerful, possessed with the divine right to rule. Suddenly this once inviolable and sacred soul had been imprisoned and condemned to death by his subjects. 'For the first time since I entered France,' wrote Wollstonecraft to her publisher in London, Joseph Johnson, 'I bowed to the majesty of the people.'[12]

Less than a month later, on 21 January 1793, around 20,000 people packed into Place de la Révolution, near the Tuileries, where the six-foot scaffold had been erected for the guillotine. At 10.22 a.m., a thump sounded from the scaffold floor and the crowd cried: 'Long live the Republic! Long live Liberty! Long live Equality!' Raised in the executioner's hand, held high, was the head of 'Louis the Last'.[13]

Some contemporary witnesses believed that the King's execution was accepted even by the supporters of the monarchy, in the hope that his bloody end would 'shock the national feelings, awaken [people's] hereditary attachment', and turn the tide of opinion. At any rate, martyrdom was more useful to the counter-revolutionaries than an imprisoned king.[14] While 'tides' of opinion did not change, it is clear that the bloody end to the *ancien régime* shocked many, including Wollstonecraft, whose radical faith in the Revolution was ruptured. 'Before I came to France,' she confided in a letter to Joseph Johnson,

> I cherished, you know, an opinion that strong virtues might exist with the polished manners produced by the progress of civilisation; and I even anticipated the epoch when, in the course of improvement, men would labour to become virtuous, without being goaded on by misery. But now the

perspective of the golden age, fading before the attentive
eye of observation, almost eludes my sight; and losing thus
in part my theory of a more perfect state, [how could I
have faith] in the existence of God! I am not yet become
an atheist, I assure you by residing at Paris: yet I begin to
fear that vice or, if you will, evil, is the grand mobile of
action . . .[15]

This was from a woman who once was unconditionally committed
to condemning the monarchy and accusing aristocratic tyranny of
stunting the growth of civil society. Who now, she began to wonder,
were the bearers of humanitarian principles?

Sometime past midnight on a Monday in August 1793, Mary Wollstonecraft penned a love note from her rented cottage in Neuilly-sur-
Seine, a few miles outside Paris. The recipient was her lover, the
American Gilbert Imlay. Thinking of him, Wollstonecraft was able
to transcend the horrors of bloodshed that soaked the streets not far
away. During sleepless nights, she would 'obey an emotion of my
heart' and scrawl a short 'goodnight' letter to him. In these moments,
she was able to separate the personal pleasure she would find
'tomorrow' – anticipating a rendezvous with Imlay – and the fate of
the French who might wake to find themselves or their loved ones
being carried off to prison, or caught in the crossfire between opposing
factions of the new French government. Her lover was her protector;
with him she found peace. 'Cherish me with that dignified tenderness,
which I have only found in you,' she wrote, for, lifted by his love, 'I
cannot again fall into the miserable state, which rendered life a bur-
then almost too heavy to be borne.'[16]

As a Briton in France in 1793, Wollstonecraft was risking her
own freedom. In February war was declared against Britain, and all
nationals were imprisoned and their property confiscated. Here her
close relationship with Imlay was especially opportune. To parry the
authorities, Wollstonecraft was registered at the American embassy
as Imlay's wife.

In September, Imlay was called on business to Le Havre. While left alone in Neuilly, Mary reflected on the 'principles' of the now deceased moderate revolutionary leader Mirabeau (who, at the beginning of the Revolution, famously declared that 'When you get mixed up with directing a revolution, the problem is not to make it go, but to hold it back'), and had 'begun to form a new theory respecting men'. Like the 'moderate revolutionaries' themselves, she was becoming disillusioned by the course the Revolution had taken. What of the promise of liberation for women that the events of 1789 held? What, now, of her own principles – and of the security of her own freedom? She was in mental turmoil, pulled towards the comfort of her love but divided in her reflections on the Revolution. She was, as she put it, echoing the poet Thomas Gray, 'crazed by care'. The prospect of their retreat from Paris together held out the hope of calm. 'When we are settled in the country together,' she resolved, her heart would cease to be 'agitated by every emotion that awakens the remembrance of old griefs,' and will gain strength with 'that dignity your character, not to talk of my own, demands'.[17]

'The remembrance of old griefs . . .' Perhaps this referred to her own, personal sorrow – her failed love affairs in England. Or did her sentiments reveal her growing anguish for the suffering she witnessed in Paris? Her emotional turmoil, perhaps the prospect of peace in the country – away from the fright of the city – was enough to dissipate all those 'fumes of former discontent'.[18] At times she emphasised the parallels between her longing for repose and the prospects of political tranquillity. 'The face of things, public and private, vexes me,' she swore. The two seemed to stare at the same mirror of possibility. Writing to Imlay on New Year's Day 1794, she lamented that the '"peace" and clemency which seemed to be dawning a few days ago, disappear again . . . I really believe that Europe will be in a state of convulsion, during half a century at least. Life is but a labour of patience.'[19]

Wollstonecraft's time, once preoccupied with debating the virtues and vices of the Revolution, was now spent contemplating life and death. Paris had become a blood bath. By the end of 1793, around 2,600 heads had fallen in front of 'Sainte Guillotine'.[20] But she had another reason to be disillusioned with life's upheavals: she was now five months pregnant. Just as the public executioner, Charles-Henri Sanson, was refining his skills on the scaffold – now taking only thirty-six minutes to cut off twenty-two heads – Wollstonecraft was devastated by a momentary thought that, because of her own ill health, she might be 'tormenting, or perhaps killing, a poor little animal, about whom I am grown anxious and tender, now I feel it alive, made me worse'.[21]

A new life was about to begin, but the land of liberty had turned into a slaughterhouse: What had gone wrong? Could she remember what principles she celebrated at the beginning of the Revolution? What were the origins of this despair? While thousands of French émigrés were fleeing the country, she remained withdrawn in a cottage outside Paris, contemplating these questions, and writing her *Historical and Moral View of the Origin and Progress of the French Revolution*.

Largely due to the popular writings of the French *philosophes* – those wits and radicals with whom the germ of revolution was thought (by some) to have originated – France was portrayed as the cradle of civilisation. Their message, shouted most loudly by the likes of Rousseau and Voltaire, was that enlightened civilisation needed to combat oppression. Such libertarian principles, shared by sympathisers including Wollstonecraft, advocated throwing off the yoke of despotism and eliminating the irrational superstitions of priestcraft and kingship. Wollstonecraft wrote with an air of relief that it was now time to 'get entirely clear of all the notions drawn from the wild traditions of original sin', old mythologies which had for too long maintained a stranglehold over humanity's emotions:

> the eating of the apple, the theft of Prometheus, the opening of Pandora's box, and the other fables, too tedious to enumerate, on which priests have erected their tremendous structures of imposition, to persuade us, that we are naturally inclined to evil.

Get rid of these oppressive weights, these strictures on belief, and 'we shall then leave room for the expansion of the human heart', leading to a happier, wiser, and more dignified society. This, at first, seemed to be happening. From enlightened hearts a 'new spirit has gone forth, to organise the body-politic'. 'Reason has, at last, shown her captivating face, beaming with benevolence ... liberty with maternal wing seems to be soaring to regions far above vulgar annoyance, promising to shelter mankind.'[22]

Wollstonecraft saw progress in the deflation of ancient myths; her message was a moral tale of the improving forces of modernity. Having for too long groaned under the weight of despotism, the people erupted in a frenzied fit of passion, hunger, and sorrow. Her *View of the French Revolution* was written to recover the heart of the matter, to provide a rational account of the character and conditions of rapid political change.

Corrupt political systems and the dominion of knavish tyrants granted power by hereditary honours, were holding civilisation hostage. From the prevalence of venal conduct amongst rulers was created a rank of overindulgent aristocrats. Extravagant displays of wealth in fashion, feasts, and *fêtes* fed the aristocratic appetite whilst leaving the Third Estate famished. What visitor to France would not notice the 'drapery of manners, which points out the *costume* of the age'? 'Their national character is,' opined a newly wide-eyed Wollstonecraft, 'more formed by their theatrical amusements, than is generally imagined: they are in reality the schools of vanity.'[23] Her description of the historical pre-conditions of the revolutionary spirit were laden with descriptive terms such as 'vice', 'intoxication', 'nocturnal orgies', 'flagitious immorality', 'obloquy', and eventually, '*deficit*'. (And these were merely in reference to Philippe, duc d'Orléans's regency period during Louis XV's minority, 1715–23.) Who, in this bacchanalian alliance, could claim to be in charge? 'Kings have been the dupes of ministers, of mistresses, and secretaries, not to notice sly valets and cunning waiting-maids, who are seldom idle.'[24]

The people of France, Wollstonecraft concluded, were simply demoralised. Their patience had been worn down by injuries and insults, they were 'determined to strike at the root of all their misery at once'. Europe, she imagined, would probably be for some time thrown into a state of anarchy. 'It is perhaps difficult to bring ourselves to believe, that out of this chaotic mass a fairer government is rising than has ever shed the sweets of social life on the world.' Initially, she had wanted to be there to see it happen.

But it *was* difficult to believe. While writing in rural solitude, veiled from the surrounding atrocities, her thoughts returned to the figure of Marie-Antoinette. And unlike the account she had published in reply to Burke three years earlier – where she registered her intolerance and disaffection for the monarchy in broad brushstrokes – she now rendered more humane the face of her ideological foe.

> The unfortunate queen of France, besides the advantages of birth and station, possessed a very fine person; and her lovely face, sparkling with vivacity, hid the want of intelligence. Her complexion was dazzlingly clear; and, when she was pleased, her manners were bewitching; for she happily mingled the most insinuating voluptuous softness and affability, with an air of grandeur, bordering on pride, that rendered the contrast more striking. Independence also, of whatever kind, always gives a degree of dignity to the mien; so that monarchs and nobles, with most ignoble souls, from believing themselves superior to others, have actually acquired a look of superiority.[25]

This was Wollstonecraft's way of restoring dignity to a woman whose liberty had been stripped from her. The 'gang of *banditti*' that thundered into the Queen's chambers at Versailles – that 'sanctuary of repose, the asylum of care and fatigue, the chaste temple of a woman' – had, she was now prepared to allow, 'violated [them] with murderous fury'.[26] These 'brutes' – shamefully 'dignified with the appellation of *the people*' – were '*not* to be confounded with the honest multitude, who took the Bastille'.[27] It was now clear to Wollstonecraft that the principles that had put Revolution into motion and once showed 'mother liberty' as a leader that women could follow, had now degenerated into maxims for murder.

For four years the Queen had been held captive, and had sat, for the better part of a year, in a filthy prison. Months had already passed since she last embraced her husband, and her future was in the hands of a vengeful tribunal who would also try her for treason. Wollstonecraft seemed to pity the prisoner, believing that the Queen's ultimate defect was her 'empty mind' and indifference to the necessities of her nation. 'The effect that adversity may have on her choked understanding time will show,' she wrote.[28] Wollstonecraft probably had little doubt what time would show – the Queen's fate was inextricably bound to the King's. Others certainly had no doubt. 'Unhappy woman!' wrote Lady Webster, upon earlier hearing of the Queen's confinement, when the 'melancholy tale' reached her at Aix-la-Chapelle. 'There is little hope of peace for her in this life.'[29] Shortly afterwards, to the roars of a huge crowd, the thirty-seven-year-old queen was executed.

Marie-Antoinette's gruesome end sent shivers up the spines of commentators across Europe – men and women equally.[30] Wollstonecraft wept and trembled. 'Oh France!,' she cried, imagining the flight of a soul once noble, 'hearing the snap of the *guillotine* at his heels'. What went wrong? 'Down fell the temple of despotism; but – despotism has not been buried in its ruins!' When would humanity emerge triumphant? 'Unhappy country! – when will thy children cease to tear thy bosom? – When will a change of opinion, producing a change of morals, render thee truly free?'[31] What a contrast this was to the events in 1793 and the aims of 1789!

But France, she was able to observe, was full of contrasts. By late January 1794, she arrived in Le Havre, to be reunited with her lover. After only a month together, Wollstonecraft suddenly found herself alone again after Imlay's business took him back to Paris. Wasting no time in finishing off her *View of the French Revolution*, she courageously sent the manuscript to her London publisher. It was daring because the French authorities were suspicious of all correspondence making its way to or from Britain – suspecting they might contain anti-revolutionary information. As she 'uncomfortably', perhaps even recklessly, wrote in a letter to her sister, the 'French are, at present, so full of suspicion that had a letter of James's [her brother], improvidently sent to me, been opened, I would not have answered for the consequence'. Wollstonecraft could have stuck to uncontroversial remarks, like her observation that the 'climate of France is uncommonly fine, the country pleasant, and there is a degree of ease'. But she could not restrain her pen.

'It is impossible for you to have any idea of the impression the sad scenes I have been a witness to have left on my mind,' she sorrowfully wrote. In contrast to the 'fine climate' of the country, 'death and misery, in every shape of terrour, haunts this devoted country'. The morbid events that were making history before her eyes would torment her memory; disquiet would forever violate her consciousness. Her heart ached for lost friends, whom she would 'call to mind when the remembrance is keen of the anguish it has endured for its fellow creatures, at large – for the unfortunate beings cut off around me – and the still more unfortunate survivors'.[32] This letter, showing how unsettled she had become with the course of the Revolution – which, if opened by an inspector, would no doubt have landed her in prison – was in the end never posted. The images it would have relayed would only have reconfirmed what another British woman who arrived in Paris in 1790 had also been struggling to come to terms with in her own letters home.

Paris, July 1790. In the weeks leading up to the first anniversary of the first revolutionary act, the storming of the Bastille, thousands of men, women and children of all classes offered their labour to prepare for the grand celebration. The Fête de la Féderation (now Bastille Day) on 14 July was to prove, as one commentator reported, the most 'astonishing and forever memorable spectacle of fraternity'.[33] The fête was to be a shining moment for the public that could openly and enthusiastically bask in the glory of their revolutionary achievements. From all around France, soldiers and national guardsmen, as well as labourers, women and children, travelled to Paris to join the party – in total somewhere between three and four hundred thousand souls.

The centre of the ceremony was organised by the municipality at Champ de Mars – the large area in front of the Ecole Militaire (where the Eiffel Tower now stands). Built around the sides was a huge tiered amphitheatre for the spectators, facing a massive elliptic arena in the centre of which rose the prominent 'Altar of the Fatherland', where an oath of loyalty to the King and constitution were to be taken (before the monarchy was completely overthrown by the attack on the Tuileries on 10 August 1792). A triple-arched Arc de Triomphe was erected as an entrance.

The day before the festivities, twenty-eight-year-old Helen Maria Williams arrived in Paris with her sister, Cecilia, on the invitation of Monsieur Augustin du Fossé, the husband of her French tutor. Augustin du Fossé had been born into an aristocratic and nobly titled family, but, due to complex family circumstances, renounced his title and became a fervent supporter of the Revolution. This gave Helen Williams, who (like Wollstonecraft) bemoaned the traditionalism of Edmund Burke, a privileged opportunity to absorb the excitement of the moment first hand.[34] Helen Williams came from an unremarkable background. Her father was an army officer and her mother a first-generation Huguenot immigrant, but she moved within leading literary, as well as resolutely dissenting, circles. She was acquainted with the contemporary London writer Charlotte Smith, whose novel *Desmond*, was itself a paean to the principles of the Revolution. In fact, the book's eponymous hero arrives in Paris just in time for the Fête de la Féderation, and Desmond's letters, around which the novel is structured, show remarkable similarities to the *Letters from Paris* that Helen Williams herself published in 1790.[35] In London she had already, by the late 1780s, gained popularity as a literary figure, translating some works, publishing her own poems, and penning a novel – *Julia* (1790) – which contained a panegyric to the French Revolution in a digressive poem, 'The Bastille: A Vision'.

But in 1790, Helen Williams was given the chance to play the part of the hero herself (even literally playing the part of 'Lady Liberty' in a play), anxiously travelling back to France, for 'had I not reached Paris at the moment I did reach it, I should have missed the most sublime spectacle which, perhaps, was ever represented on the theatre of this earth'.[36] Despite a torrential downpour of rain on that Wednesday morning, at half past eleven all the bells in the city began to ring, cannons were fired and hundreds of thousands of people paraded along the promenade, among pavilions and triumphal arches. It was a grand procession: mounted troops were led by the sound of trumpets, and the presidents of the districts were led by the beat of drums. In the middle was a battalion of children carrying a ceremonial flag reading: 'L'Esperance de la Patrie' – The Hope of the Country. Women, drenched but indifferent to the incessant rain, paraded in red bonnets and waved tricolour flags; elsewhere banners displayed classical symbols of regeneration above broken emblems of servitude.[37] When the time came for the King and the *fédérés* to take an oath of allegiance to the new constitution, bells simultaneously rang out in cities and towns across the country in a magnificent gesture of national unity.

Williams was awestruck. To her, the most poetic spectacle was the reaction of the 'exulting multitude'. 'Half a million people assembled at a spectacle,' she estimated, 'which furnished every image that can elevate the mind of man.'

> In the streets, at the windows, and on the roofs of the houses, the people, transported with joy, shouted and wept as the procession passed. Old men were seen kneeling in the streets, blessing God that they had lived to witness that happy moment. The people ran to the doors of their houses loaded with refreshments, which they offered to the troops; and crouds of women surrounded the soldiers, and holding up their infants in their arms, and melting into tears, promised to make their children imbibe, from their earliest age, an inviolable attachment to the principles of the new constitution.[38]

To witness the exulting multitude must have been breathtaking; to be amongst over 300,000 revellers packed in to the narrow streets.

Helen Williams was effusive in relaying the energy of the jubilee at which Lady Liberty was the guest of honour. France was young, fresh, alive: 'I joined the universal voice,' she wrote, 'and repeated with my heart and soul "Vive la nation!".' She relished the fact that she was floating in the heart of this heaving celebration, able to witness with her own eyes the sensational spectacle. 'While you observe from a distance,' she wrote in one of her letters, 'I am placed near enough the scene to discern every look and gesture of the actors.'[39]

There was an inescapable sense in her letters that here was an Englishwoman submerged in radical politics in a foreign country whose experiences were never intended to be solitary. She conscientiously wrote to a 'dear Friend' in England, sending 'once a week the details which I promised when we parted', being, however, 'well aware how very imperfectly I shall be able to describe the images which press upon my mind'.[40] It was the hindering limitation of writing descriptions that made being present in France so important to her. She did not wish to read anyone else's biased accounts (she was later to beg the public to rely on reports from those with 'a more intimate knowledge of French affairs than foreigners in general could find the means of obtaining' rather than the misleading newspapers).[41] Through her letters she tried to relay critical eyewitness accounts to inform her compatriots of the progress of the Revolution; they form one of the most complete records from a Briton ('The entire neighbourhood borrows Helen's latest publication from me,' complained Hester Piozzi, 'such that I have hardly had time to read it myself.')

But were these suitable 'images' for the sensitivities of an English-woman? And what of her *interpretation?* Other English witnesses to the revolutionary festivals were clearly nauseated by the way royal authority – which had ruled France for fourteen hundred years – had been usurped. The Scottish gardener Thomas Blaikie, for example, wrote bitterly of the 'many absurdities invented at that time to Amuse the people' and the 'Pamphlets vomiting all sorts of absurdities against the King'.[42]

But Helen Williams had a strong stomach for such political declarations. 'You will not suspect that I was an indifferent witness on such a scene,' she begged her friend. 'Oh no!' After all, this was not a time in which the distinctions of country were remembered. It was the triumph of human kind; it was man asserting the noblest privileges of his nature; and it required but the common feelings of humanity to become in that moment a citizen of the world. For myself, I acknowledge that my heart caught with enthusiasm the general sympathy; my eyes were filled with tears; and I shall never forget the sensations of that day, 'while memory holds her seat in my bosom'.[43]

The mere juxtaposition of the terms in this tribute made it clear where her sympathies rested. 'Human kind' – 'man' – triumphed over the monarchical privileges of the *ancien régime*. Any talk of '*noblest* privileges' now belonged to the 'nature' of humanity, who would assert the right to be, from then on, 'citizens of the world'. She widened the compass so she could be included in the Revolution, not just in proximity but in spirit. No national boundary would keep her away from gaining 'citizenship' in the new world order.

Neither would her gender exclude her. In fact, it was the significant role women played in the refashioning of the nation that excited Helen Williams's affections. The signatories of the famous *Cahiers des doléances* (notebooks of grievances) in 1789, which included a wide band of working-class women, was testimony of their involvement, as was the rise to prominence of women such as Madame Roland, Olympe de Gouges and Pauline Léon (who became president of the *Société des Citoyennes Républicaines Révolutionnaires*).[44] Of course, there were still some aristocratic women who saw no impropriety in the establishments of nobility – she met a few – but they were diminishing.

'Let me do justice to the ladies of France,' she declared – to clarify this point – in a letter home. 'The number of those who have murmured at the loss of rank, bears a very small proportion to those who have acted with a spirit of distinguished patriotism.' The generous affections that 'belong to the female heart' guided women to act in the 'common cause' and sacrifice their titles, fortune, and 'even the personal ornaments, so dear to female vanity'. When entering the shrine of liberty, off came the jewels which were given over as an example of the 'patriotic donation'. 'The women have certainly had a considerable share in the French Revolution,' she surmised; 'for, whatever the imperious lords of the creation may fancy, the most important events which take place in this world depend a little on our influence; and we often act in human affairs like those secret springs in mechanism, by which, though invisible, great movements are regulated'. 'Our influence,' 'we act': writing in the first person plural from France, she was able to ally herself with the revolutionary sorority – those invisible technicians of human affairs – that were coming out from the shadows *en masse*.

Even more of a privilege for Helen Williams was the fact that both she and her sister could visit the seat of national administration in person by attending the meetings of the National Assembly, formed by representatives of the Third Estate.[45] Here she was able to listen to the debates on forming the new constitution, and watch the work of the people who issue decrees which 'surrounding nations wait [for] in suspense'.[46] This was indeed close to the core of political colloquy. She imagined what eyebrows were raised amongst her countrymen, aware of her enthusiasm for French politics, and anticipated their concerns by addressing the question: would she be deleteriously affected by what she witnessed? Would she return to her own country a 'fierce republican'? Her defence was that she was moved by the general happiness in France (rather than some preconceived political notions) to sympathise with their pronouncedly enlightened goals. 'My love of the French Revolution,' she explained, 'is the natural result of this sympathy, and therefore my political creed is entirely an affair of the heart.' And why should visiting France at this singular moment in history be considered different from visiting any other country praised for its historical relics? Surely history-in-the-making was as important as the ancient curiosities that so many Grand Tourists were obliged to study for the improvement of their education? 'If I were at Rome,' she continued, would anyone be 'surprised to hear that I had visited, with the warmest reverence, every spot where any relics of her ancient grandeur could be traced? . . . Can you then expect me to have seen the Federation at the Champ de Mars, and the National Assembly of France, with indifference?'[47]

But it was precisely because it was *not* different that the guardians of Protestant probity back in Britain sounded their warning bells. She was in a Catholic country that had just revolted against its privileged rulers. Worse, she was a woman witnessing something that many critics thought women were best sheltered from: politics. Exposure to foreign customs and religious climes, argued evangelical enforcers, was dangerous. According to some, this was true for any Briton – man or woman – who wanted to travel abroad.

Helen Williams – a friend and confidante to leading revolutionaries and a suspected spy (albeit suspected of working both for Britain and for France) – was a prime candidate for political infection from abroad.[48] But, like Wollstonecraft, her effulgent support for the revolutionary fervour was tempered by its horrors. Leaving the Hôtel de Ville on her tour of Paris, she was shown an iron street lamp from which, she was told, 'for want of gallows, the first victims of popular fury were sacrificed'. Suddenly the suffering of the Revolution weighed in her mind.

> I own that the sight of La Lanterne chilled the blood within my veins. At that moment, for the first time, I lamented the revolution; and, forgetting the imprudence, or the guilt, of those unfortunate men, could only reflect with horror on the dreadful expiation they had made. I painted in my imagination the agonies of their families and friends, not could I for a considerable time chase these gloomy images from my thoughts.[49]

This was the beginning of a new level of comprehension of the humanitarian cost of revolution. And more so than any other witness who published their views, Helen Williams explored the depths of political agitation.

Helen Williams returned to England in September 1790 and quickly published an account of her trip. It was the first of a number of volumes on the French Revolution that she would publish – all based on eyewitness testimony, continuing the following year when she went back to Paris, never to return to Britain.

Paris became her new home, and soon after her arrival she began making new friends. In 1791 it was possible for many Britons to tour France. It became a kind of fashion to be in Paris – a naughty curiosity inspected by privileged foreigners. Not all gained good reputations for themselves. During the Peace of Amiens in 1802, Francis Jackson bitterly wrote to a friend reporting on the conduct of Englishwomen in Paris.

> I only wish you would extend the efforts of your police to keep at home a parcel of disorderly women who come abroad without bringing anything with them that does credit to the national character. There is Lady [Cholmondeley], who is one day taken up by the police and carried to the chief lock-up for persisting to drive in the Champs Elysées at forbidden hours and through forbidden roads. Another day she quarrels with people at the masquerade. A third she invites a dozen Frenchmen and women to her house and abuses them all for slaves. Then we have Lady [Monck], whose dear friend would welcome H[elen] M[aria] Williams and who gets into all the bad company in Paris. You must suppose it is very bad when *here* it is reckoned *mauvais ton* [bad manners]. You really should keep these people at home.[50]

Among those in Paris at this time were Lord and Lady Sheffield and their two daughters, Maria and Louisa. They were staying in comfort at the Hôtel de l'Université in Faubourg Saint-Germain: 'a suite of eight rooms very elegantly and perfectly clean, which is the first instance of the kind I have seen since I entered this Land of Liberty', Maria reported in her detailed letters to her aunt, Serena Holroyd. Among the people they ran into were Thomas Pelham and Sir Godfrey Webster – the latter about to leave Paris 'in a violent hurry', angry and jealous over the flirtations of his wife. Pelham became their tour guide. 'Nothing can pass pleasanter than our time does, under the direction of Mr. Pelham,' thought Maria. 'He lays out a plan for our mornings, goes to the Play and sups with us.' Like Williams, Maria and her family went to the National Assembly and listened to the rancorous debates, and afterwards attended the even noisier meetings of the Société de Jacobins, where she listened to 'warm debates' (as she euphemistically put it) about the King's future.[51]

At the beginning of 1793, Helen Williams befriended the recently arrived Wollstonecraft, who recognised a kindred spirit. 'Miss Williams has behaved very civilly to me and I shall visit her frequently,' wrote Wollstonecraft, 'because I *rather* like her, and I meet French company at her house.'[52] Wollstonecraft had the opportunity to meet many people (British and American as well as French) at Williams's apartment in the Rue Helvétius, because, just a couple of months earlier, Williams had established it as a weekly literary salon.

Salons were a prominent feature of Parisian intellectual life and were venues where women wielded considerable influence. Salon culture exemplified cosmopolitanism, where wit rather than landed wealth generated ideas intended to shape cultural tastes and (to a degree) political principles. As Mary Berry observed: 'Every saloon in Paris became an arena, where the arguments for the old and the new systems were brought forward with an extravagance on the one side, and repelled with a violence and contempt on the other, which the guillotine had not yet silenced.' One of these hot-spots was Anne-Catherine Helvétius's salon, which she kept with her husband, the *philosophe* Claude-Adrien Helvétius, until his death in 1771, then ran it herself until her death in 1800. Here, sociability and conversation passed on the values of gentility to those who were previously excluded from the *mondain* – noble culture.[53] By the mid-eighteenth century, there were salons for philosophic and scientific discussion, salons for artists and musicians, and for literary criticism. They promoted intellectualism and celebrated human achievement. Voltaire was a regular at Madame du Deffand's salon (established in the convent of Saint Joseph); the *Encyclopédistes* frequented the rue Saint Dominique salon of Julie de Lespinasse, and politicians attended Madame Helvétius's assemblies. During the early years of the Revolution they were wellsprings of political debate. Women such as Madame de Tesse, the Princess de Henin, and Madame de Tallien opened their doors.[54] Madame Necker (Suzanne Churchod) opened a leading literary salon (also a favourite of Voltaire) in the rue Michel-le-Comte, and later her daughter, Madame de Staël, followed suit. And then there was the salon of Madame Roland.

Madame Roland was heavily involved in revolutionary politics, especially after she and her husband, Jean-Marie Roland, moved from their home in Lyons and settled in Paris in 1791. At the Hôtel Britannique, on the Left Bank, in the spirit of dedication to republican principles, they opened a salon where many of the radical left could exchange ideas regarding the forming of the new state. Friendships led to positions of power in the new government that was established by the end of 1791. Many of the Rolands' salon guests suddenly held official posts, and in March 1792, Monsieur Roland became Minister of the Interior to the new government. They moved from the Hôtel Britannique to the luxurious mansion where Madame Necker ran her famous salon.[55] Now, twice a week, Madame Roland was a salonnière of status, and – despite the fact that at these meetings she abstained from active political debate – it was no secret that her astute political mind registered all the information necessary to manage her husband's political career.

One of Madame Roland's long-time friends was François-Xavier Lanthénas (a member of the Legislative Assembly) who introduced Helen Williams to the Rolands, and she became a regular visitor to their new salon. There were a number of aspects to Madame Roland's striking character that the likes of Williams or Wollstonecraft could identify with. She came from an ambitious middle-class background; her father was a master engraver whose business (geared for the luxury trade) was assisted by the management of his pious wife. A devotee of Rousseau, after the Revolution she eagerly attended the meetings of the National Assembly, where she listened to debates over the practicability of a constitutional monarchy. She also attended the meetings of the militant revolutionaries at the Jacobin Club, who were later to become an inspiring force for the more restless members of the revolutionary government. In Madame Roland, Williams had a distinct role model for the fashioning of her own salon.

Helen Williams's was thus another milestone in an illustrious history of salon culture – though unusual in that the hostess was an English woman. In no time at all her salon became a popular attraction, and was to remain so for the next twenty years. Besides Wollstonecraft, the soirees were attended by American diplomats and businessmen (including Gilbert Imlay), British dissenters, radical philosophers and poets (such as Thomas Paine, Joseph Priestley, William Godwin, William Wordsworth and, later, Wollstonecraft's daughter, Mary Shelley, and her husband). 'I believe she has a party every night,' the author and American public official Joel Barlow informed his wife, '30 or 40 or 50, chiefly English.' Thomas Poole (a friend of Thomas Paine) later recorded a more diverse social landscape, including 'Mr Livingstone (the American ambassador), Joel Barlow, Italian Princesses and German Princes, many of the *literati* of Paris, etc. etc.'[56] From the beginning, French politicians were there: 'The deputies of the Gironde and Barère passed most of their evenings at our house,' Williams wrote; among them, of course, were the Rolands.[57]

By the end of 1792, however, tensions had mounted between different factions of the French government: the moderate Girondins and the extreme Montagnards. The extremists – who marshalled the support of the labouring population – gained immense power and pursued new revolutionary aims, including the complete banishment of the monarchy and the establishment of a full republic. As a move to attain these aims, and despite the protests of the moderate Girondins, the King was executed. It was at this moment that Williams (like Wollstonecraft), sharing the concerns of her Girondin friends (including the Rolands), began to feel disillusioned by the dictatorship created by members of the more radical faction.

At the end of May 1793 everything was thrown into turmoil. The radical faction mounted an insurrection that led to the expulsion of the Girondins from government and the arrest of anyone suspected of being a counter-revolutionary. Many of those now in charge had for the past year been growing increasingly hostile to the Rolands and their allies. Friendship and political allegiance turned into fierce competition and political strife. Madame Roland now described Robespierre – who, once a regular at her salon, became the leader of the Montagnards – as 'fiery, jealous, hungry for popularity, envious of the success of others, domineering by nature'.[58] But her opinions were now to land her in the thick of adversity. On 31 May she was arrested and taken to the Abbaye prison 'for questioning'. The soldiers presented her with no grounds for arrest, but as her carriage pulled away from her home, she heard a shout from the gathered crowd: 'To the guillotine!'[59]

Girondins ran for cover. Madame Roland's husband fled and went into hiding. Rabaut Saint-Etienne (one of the patriotic clerics who survived the *ancien régime* and who was featured in David's *Tennis Court Oath*[60]) knew he was on the arrest list and, on the night Madame Roland was arrested, sought shelter in Helen Williams's home – 'pale, worn out and overcome with fatigue', she observed sympathetically. Having eschewed the formalities of issuing formal indictments against individuals, the arrested knew that protestations about legality were futile and that their fate was left to the desire of the accusers. The fear of exposure and the jeopardy to life felt among those suspected of being counter-revolutionary changed the mood on the streets. No one was quite sure who their enemies were.

Everyone knew radical politics were dangerous, not least Helen Williams, who as salon hostess was submerged in the heart-thumping anxiety aroused by the nature of the debates in her home. 'Often,' she wrote, 'conversation reached that certain pitch which only a feeling of personal danger could create.' The revolutionary spirit riled the patriotic. Emotions ran high for men and women – nationals and foreigners – alike. This was what made being in Paris – as an eyewitness, or, even more significantly, a participant in the activities – so enthralling. She recounted that once during a dinner with the mayor of Paris, Jerome Pétion, the

> conversation was lively and animated ... we hardly engaged in the ordinary chit-chat of society. The women

seemed to forget the task of pleasing, and the men thought less about admiring them . . . A mutual esteem, a common interest in the great issues of the day, were what manifested themselves most. We spoke of liberty in accents profound and sincere, which approached eloquence. The joy of this patriotic meal was augmented, rather than distracted, by the immense crowd that surrounded the Place de la Ville, and a thousand voices carried up to us the repeated cry, 'Pétion or death!'[61]

But now such meetings and conversations generated real 'feelings of personal danger' and fear for the safety of close friends. The currents of patriotism had somehow been sucked into an undertow of usurped power and the persecution of alleged counter-revolutionaries. On Sunday, 2 June 1793, the radical revolutionary leaders officially expelled the Girondin 'enemies of the people' and ordered the arrest of twenty-nine of their deputies. For Helen Williams, this represented the defeat of all that had been achieved since the beginning of the Revolution in 1789. 'From that fatal decree,' she wrote, 'may be dated all the horrors which have cast their sanguinary cloud over the glories of the Revolution.'[62]

'So here I was, in prison,' wrote Madame Roland, recording solemn moments in her memoir. But she was not alone. One after another, her friends were being hunted down and incarcerated. At first, Helen Williams offered as much comfort to them as she could. Twice she visited Madame Roland, as well as leading Girondins who were under house arrest. In the hope that one day 'the voice of innocence might be heard', Madame Roland smuggled into Williams's possession some papers – including her own notes, Girondin correspondence, and the papers of the famous educational writer Madame de Genlis – with the intention that they be made public. But she grew paranoid and, with regret, 'was compelled to destroy' them since their discovery 'would have been disastrous for us'.[63] It was bad enough to be *acquainted* with prisoners, let alone harbouring incriminating documents from them – even if, as Madame Roland suspected, 'ill-intentioned' people had plenty of opportunity to plant such evidence.[64]

Helen Williams wondered about her own fate. What kind of danger was she actually in? Would she, her mother and her sister, be spared from arrest on the grounds that they were merely a foreign 'family of women'? Unfortunately for her, 'neither sex nor age gave any claim to compassion'.[65]

It was now the beginning of October 1793. Passports to leave the country were refused and she heard that all English residing in France were to be arrested and their property confiscated. It was at this time that a pregnant Mary Wollstonecraft packed up from Paris and headed to Le Havre. Helen Williams was not so willing to flee. But finally, at 2 a.m. one restless night, she and her sister heard a banging at their hotel gate and immediately knew that this was 'the fatal sign of our approaching captivity'. Trembling, the sisters went to their antechamber and there they met two commissaries of the revolutionary committee, backed by guards with their swords drawn at the outer door. After gathering all they could manage to wrap up in a bundle of linen, they were escorted away.

Luxembourg Palace had been converted to a prison, and the gloomy state apartments, decorated with mattresses on floors, were now cells. This was Helen Williams's new home. In the apartments adjoining hers were two tea-table friends, the Marquis de Sillery (husband of Madame de Genlis who took his title in 1787) and Marc-David Lasource. Standing on a table one morning she managed to peer out of the iron-grated windows. The sun shone brightly, illuminating the brilliant autumn foliage in the beautiful gardens, set against a backdrop of Gothic spires and distant hills. What would be the future of freedom? How ironic it all seemed, including the names to each chamber inscribed over the locked doors – particularly the 'Chamber of Liberty', where certain prisoners were held *au secret*, in close confinement. More alarmingly, however, most of the names had once been illustrious citizens of ancient Greece or Rome, most of whom, she remembered, had been sentenced to death.[66]

At the end of October the English women prisoners were moved to the Couvent des Anglaises (English Conceptionist Convent). Here, in the company of her countrywomen and 'our sisters', she found some comfort and support. Patriotism and 'fraternity' were not defeated, only confined. It was this circumstance that 'tended to make our situation tolerable', she wrote – that 'spirit of fraternity that prevailed in our community, consisting of about forty female prisoners besides the nuns'.[67] Imagine how transformed and happy the world would be, she mused, if the mutual forbearance and amity that was found in a gloomy prison were extended to it. The prisons grew more crowded by the day although vast numbers were being shuffled out to their deaths at the scaffold. '*Suspect* was the warrant of imprisonment,' she wrote, 'and *conspiracy* was the watchword of murder.'[68] The reasons for it all she sought in vain.

After about two months, thanks to the efforts of a young Frenchman named Athanase Coquerel (who was enamoured with Helen's sister, Cecilia, whom he later married), they were set free. No sooner had they taken a few deep breaths in the open air when they abandoned their previous residence in the centre of town and sought shelter in a remote part of Faubourg Saint-Germain. Many of their friends, however, were not so fortunate. By the time of their release from prison, the centre of Paris had become a scene of carnage.

On 8 November, Madame Roland – her hair freshly cut to above her neck and her hands tied behind her back – was led with the other condemned 'enemies of the people' to the scaffold. From the crowd various people shouted: 'Here she comes! Here she comes!' Madame Roland was in front of a male prisoner who was on the verge of collapse. One witness reported seeing her calmly offer him support, and, as a sign of compassion, beg permission from the executioner to allow him to go first. Even at the scaffold, women were supposed to go first, but Sanson – her executioner – allowed it. It was a sign of some strength that she was able to watch the line of prisoners in front of her lie down one by one and have their heads cut off, as she awaited her turn. Helen Williams later wrote that Madame Roland's name 'will be recorded in the annals of history as one of those illustrious women whose superior attainments seem fitted to exalt her sex in the scale of being'. Indeed her famous last words have been enshrined in history: 'O Liberty! what crimes are committed in thy name!'[69]

Friends fell one by one. Two days after hearing about the death of his wife, Monsieur Roland left his hiding place in Rouen, wandered to the nearby woods and killed himself. A few weeks after Helen Williams was released from prison, in mid-December 1793, Rabaut Saint-Etienne – whom Williams considered 'one of the most enlightened and virtuous men whom the Revolution had called forth' – was put to death. So too were Monsieur and Madame Payzac who were found guilty of sheltering him (as indeed Williams had also done). Also guillotined were Helen Williams's salon regulars and ex-prisonmates the Marquis de Sillery and Lasource.

The following April, a new law was passed ordering all foreigners to leave Paris within ten days or be dragged to the scaffold. Leaving for Marly, north of Versailles, Williams and her family passed the Place de la Révolution, 'where we saw the guillotine erected, the crowd assembled for the bloody tragedy, and the *gens d'armes* on horseback, followed by victims who were to be sacrificed'.[70]

These were only a handful of the many who died between September 1793 and July 1794, when the tyrannical Robespierre was overthrown and executed. By that time, some 300,000 'suspects' had been arrested, and around 17,000 executed.

Many had managed to submit calmly to their fate. 'Rather death than slavery!' was the prison song. 'To die,' Helen Williams wrote, 'and get beyond the reach of oppression, appeared a privilege; and perhaps nothing appalled the souls of the tyrants so much as that serenity with which their victims went to execution.' Somehow comfort was found in knowing their souls too were about to be saved. Helen Williams soon began to realise the moral of her story – that not only does liberty have phantom guises, but one must be prepared to shed tears of compassion for those who died in search of it.

When the Terror was finally over, liberty, 'bleeding with a thousand wounds', could return and contact with the rest of the world could be restored. After 'a silence like that of death' and a separation which seemed 'as final as if we had been divided by the limits of "that country from whose bourn no traveller returns"', she was free to make contact with friends in Britain, and she had a wrenching story to tell.[71]

In 1790, even before France waged war against Europe, Horace Walpole was relieved that the Berry sisters had passed through that 'land of hyenas' and 'anarchy' as he liked to call it – and had made it to the safety of Florence. He worried, however, about certain defamatory remarks he had made against the French in his letters, fearing that these may have put Mary and her sister at further personal peril. 'Pray burn all my letters,' he implored the sisters. 'I trembled when they were ransacking y[ou]r trunks, lest they should meet with any of them.' It did not take much to upset the already deeply suspicious authorities searching for counter-revolutionaries. Indeed, Walpole knew that less than treasonable offences could easily incite the hostility of the national guard. He had recently heard that two Englishmen, in the company of two national guardsmen, had spent the night crammed into a sentry-box when one of the former happened to spit into the wind at an inopportune moment, hitting one of the guardsmen. This proved to the aristocratic Walpole that 'imprisonment is the characteristic of liberty, and when all men are equal, accidents are punished as only crimes used to be'.[72]

There seemed no end to the dangers to a traveller's life, purse, marriage and morals abroad, but the most daunting threat was that posed to one's political and religious faith in Catholic territory. As early as the seventeenth century Sir Fulke Greville had regretted that 'it is a vulgar scandall of *Travellers* that few return more religious than they went out', and at the beginning of the nineteenth, the Cambridge don John Cunningham issued his *Cautions to Continental Travellers*, likewise warning of the dangers. The concerns he had were 'whether our numerous travellers were of a class likely to be much influenced by the scenes they visit . . . [and] whether the evil, if proved to exist, admits of any remedy'. The author then argued that the evil did indeed exist, that the 'dangers are not of ordinary dimensions', and that they specifically relate to the exposure of travellers to 'diseased' Catholic states. The remedy? Read and re-read the Scriptures, know the dangers of popery, and never, no matter where in the world one travelled, neglect the Sabbath.[73]

Contagion – a potent cocktail of toxins and vices – was the metaphor used to describe continental dangers. Mary Berry thought that the early days of the Revolution, when the nation 'shook off the chains it had so long worn' and reclaimed citizens' rights, led to 'intoxication', which was 'immediately followed by a general fever of mind, a mental epidemic, accompanied by symptoms of delirium at once horrible and ridiculous'. From the 'centre of infection', the 'potent disease soon spread itself nationally and individually over the greater part of Europe . . .'[74] In the last years of the eighteenth century, threats to the moral probity of English travellers appeared only to diversify. Not only was religious toleration on trial, but the political turmoil created by the French Revolution threatened to propagate radical proposals for regal reform. It seemed to some travellers that there might not be an escape from such 'dangers'.

Political matters were not the only dimension of foreign life that was thought potentially to corrupt travelling souls. Polluters of religious principles or the contagion of irreligious, freethinking philosophical thought lingered abroad. The pious imagined that unsuspecting Grand Tourists were besieged by those whose minds and morals had been contaminated by the heretical ideas of Voltaire and Rousseau and well-wishers feared for their friends.

Sarah Tighe, however, was one adventurous woman who chose to ignore such attitudes. She asked her brother-in-law, 'who was a man of the world and had lived in the best literary society of London', what he thought of a learned education for women. Holding enlightened views, he cited a number of examples 'of learned ladies in the highest rank, who were better wives and mothers than those who had received a frivolous education', and so it was decided that Sarah's daughters would learn Latin.

When her eldest daughter, Caroline, was ten, Sarah decided to take her daughters to Italy. First she took them to the Bishop of London for their confirmation, where he expressed his disapproval of her plans. 'I never can forget the look he gave,' Caroline later recollected, 'shaking his head as much as to say Italy was a bad place for a young family, the influence of Rousseau and Voltaire having spread very wide.' They set off regardless, but – to the amplified apprehension of other friends – they went no further than Paris. There they were joined by a relative, William Tighe, and his friend, Frederick Hervey (later the 5th Earl, Lord Bristol – son of the inde-fatigable traveller of the same name after whom the Bristol Hotels are named). Caroline confessed that these men 'had both in some degree imbibed the principles of the French Philosophers but both, I rejoice to add, some years afterwards became convinced of the Truth of Christianity', and it appears Caroline herself managed to escape the clutches of the infidel philosophy.[75]

In 1792, the thirty-year-old London playwright Mariana Starke was resident in Nice. 'You will think us very unfortunate,' she wrote on her arrival in October, 'in having just reached Nice to see it captured; and you will, no doubt, be anxious to learn particulars.' Nice – formerly part of Piedmont-Sardinia, the kingdom of the house of Savoy – had just been annexed by France as it expanded its territories on the Alpine-Mediterranean front in preparation for war.[76] Accord-ing to Starke, after the Revolution many of the emigrants to Nice were not fleeing for their lives, but 'were in fact Republicans sent to disseminate revolutionary principles among the People'. As Nice filled with Piedmontese soldiers, the Bishop of Nice paid Mariana Starke's party a visit and warned them of an impending attack by the French. Sure enough, off the coast Mariana spotted sixteen French ships approaching. People frantically started burying their property and fleeing by foot to the mountains.

As more French troops poured into Nice (Mariana estimated around 25,000 in just over a week), the party heard soldiers breaking into surrounding houses in search of Italian troops in hiding. Within a few days, however, Mariana and her companions managed to pro-cure a passport from the commandant of the Sardinian troops to board an outbound vessel – along with others from the English consul – and escape. Suffering only a momentary assault from some hot-headed French soldiers, who 'jumped in considerable numbers upon our deck . . . swearing we were Aristocrats, and threatening to rob and murder us', they managed safely to sail into Italy.[77]

As rapidly as the situation deteriorated in France during the following year, the 'diseased principles' spread to other parts of Europe through the movements of the French army. When Lady Elizabeth Webster was back on the road to Italy after her brief return to England in 1793, she observed 'troops passing through, couriers coming and going. All too evidently proves the vicinity to the seat of war, but though a *little* alarming, yet one feels hurried on by an interesting curiosity' to see the sights. On every road, it seemed, soldiers were breathing down their necks. Lady Webster wanted to see as much as possible as quickly as possible, for who was to know what these inspiring places would look like in the event of war? 'We go tomorrow to Mayence' [Mainz], on the Rhine in Germany, 'which I expect to find a heap of ruins' due to French occupation. 'The road is all alive', she wrote outside of Mannheim, 'troops, recruits, baggage waggons, ammunition waggons, sick and wounded, stragglers, cavalry, all proclaim the direful din of arms is at hand'.[78]

Tensions grew between Italy and France. In January 1793, just after the execution of Louis XVI, the revolutionary government came into direct conflict with Pope Pius VI. Since its inception, he had condemned the Civil Constitution, which had forcibly reformed the French Church, and indeed the Revolution itself. He refused to take an oath of loyalty to the new regime, causing a rift between Rome and the revolutionaries. Furthermore he suggested that if the French who were resident in Rome planned to publicly flaunt their republican flags and tricoloured cockades, then they risked Italian retaliation. Cornelia Knight, in Rome at this time with her mother, witnessed the deterioration of relations. Unlike Wollstonecraft or Helen Williams, she had no sympathy for republican principles. She was a Tory and a Bourbonite; and had – she tells us – no intention of writing 'a history of the political events which occurred during our residence in Rome'. She and her mother remained in the city unmolested, until its occupation by General Berthier's forces in February 1798, when they escaped to Naples.[79]

During the reign of the Terror, Napoleon Bonaparte – who had once languished as an uninspired military cadet – swiftly attained the rank of general. Unmoved by claims for the sovereignty of the people or democratic will, he opted for reform backed by a bayonet. Curiously, this man of bellicose philosophy also became something of a salon luminary, attending Madame de Staël's salon, and even meeting his future wife, Josephine de Beauharnais, at Madame de Tallien's salon.

Some British women abroad also met Napoleon.[80] Helen Williams at first looked upon him with a 'glow of admiration', believing that he was a champion of liberty. When he became First Consul after a coup d'état on the eighteenth *Brumaire* (9 November), 1799, she wrote,

> the daystar of liberty seemed to rise on the vine covered hills of France. I dreamt of prison doors thrown open – of dungeons visited by the light of day, – of the peasant oppressed no longer – of equal rights, equal laws, a golden age, in which all that lived were to be happy.[81]

Shortly after, while riding horseback with a friend in the Bois de Boulogne, she was spotted by the leader himself. 'Bonaparte immediately joined us, and rode through the Bois at our side. He was extremely polite, and told me he had just read my description of the Naples revolution.' But her feelings soon wavered. Napoleon's self-aggrandisement and increasingly royalist pomp was certainly not to her taste. Her faith in the General was further eroded when, during the Peace of Amiens, she upset him by composing an ode in honour of England, and spent a further short stint in prison with the rest of her family.[82]

Another British woman who admired Napoleon was Mary Berry. 'What think you of the *man Buonaparte?*' she asked in a letter to a friend in 1800, 'absolute King of France, quietly established in the Tuileries! For my part I admire him, and think, if he can keep his place, he does his country a service.' What frustrated Mary were the British ministerial reports that 'vomited forth' all sorts of contradictory statements about the action Britain should take against France's new leader. 'Formerly they said we were fighting and aiding the other side [the allies of the first coalition against France] because it was imposs- ible to make peace with an absolutely democratical government; now that an absolutely aristocratical government is established, what is it to us' who is at its head? If peace and stability reigned, she thought (proving herself a poor prophet), why interfere? Surely this was better than the 'various tyrannies under which the French have laboured', she wrote. 'I confess that, as a citizen of enlightened Europe ... I should be sorry to see them return to their old original worn-out tyranny under the Bourbons.'

Now with the Peace of Amiens, Mary Berry had the first opportu- nity in years to return to Paris. On 5 April 1802, she watched a military parade from the privileged vantage point of a window in the Tuileries (where she was a guest of Josephine de Beauharnais). Here, as Napo- leon rode by the window on horseback, she set eyes on him for the first time. 'I saw enough to convince me he is not much like his busts,' she recollected, perhaps slightly disillusioned. 'But all I saw was a little man, remarkably well on horseback, with a sallow com- plexion, a highish nose, a very serious countenance, and cropped hair.' After surveying his troops and parading to the music, Napoleon dismounted his horse and disappeared. A few days later, Mary Berry was invited to a reception at the Tuileries, where she had the extra- ordinary opportunity of meeting him in person. By her account it is clear that he offered quick, artful words to his guests, and she also recorded his appearance in detail. He was short (five foot two), but

> his shoulders are broad, which gives his figure importance.
> His complexion, though pale and yellow, has not the
> appearance of ill-health. His teeth are good, and his
> mouth, when speaking, as I saw him, in good humour,
> has a remarkable and uncommon expression of sweetness

... His eyes are light grey, and he looks full in the face
of the person to whom he speaks. To me always a good
sign. Yet after all I have said of the sweetness of his countenance, I can readily believe what is said, that it is terrible
and fire-darting when angry, or greatly moved by any
cause.[83]

She could determine this not only from what 'is said' but what he
had done. After all, standing squarely in front of her for those brief
moments was the *homme terrible* who for the previous half decade
had won spectacular victories against the Austrians in Italy, begun
an invasion of the Middle East, and established himself as chief
public official of France – and public enemy number one in Europe.

But, like so many others, Mary Berry too believed that victory
bred vanity, and that Napoleon's megalomania had quashed the love
of liberty and equality that once inspired revolution.[84] The wits and
the *philosophes*, the cunning architects of reform, had failed in their
'foresight of what was likely to arise from the ruins they had made'.[85]
The political moral was that passionate endeavours to promote liberty
were all too easily corrupted by its own powers of seduction and
deception.

By 1798 Mariana Starke had reached a similar conclusion, as she
penned her history of Napoleon's plundering of Italy, identifying it
as a quest motivated by sheer greed, with the added incentive of
waging an economic campaign against Britain ('Buonaparte now flat-
tered himself the Mediterranean trade would be totally lost to Great
Britain . . .'). Italy 'was a mine replete with wealth', she observed. Its
citizens were 'dazzled by the specious promises, and fascinated by a
phantom falsely called Liberty, [and] were blind to the real intentions
of their Conqueror'. What were his 'real intentions'? A Milanese lady
posed the same question to Napoleon, who, in answer, picked up a
lemon, squeezed the juice from it, and threw it away.[86]

To Mary Berry – writing over twenty years later with all the
conviction that hindsight comfortably offers – tyranny was as prone
to emerge as was fungus on the forest floor. True liberty, her history
of France revealed, was certainly a tree that needed the nourishment

of the blood of tyrants.[87] Sadly for Mary, the age of the French Revolution did not carry the same promise of rectitude that she earlier thought characterised the Age of Voltaire.

Despite warnings issued to ladies and travellers alike about the dangers of contagion on the Continent, politics was at the forefront of many women's travel writings. Mariana Starke started her *Travels in Italy* by stating bluntly what she imagined would most interest her readers:

> Having witnessed the first entrance of the French into Italy, resided in Tuscany when they seized Leghorn and endeavoured to revolutionise Florence, and having been at Rome in March 1797, when they threatened to overthrow the papal Government, and in February 1789, when that threat was realised, I am tempted to give such a short account of these transactions as Persons on the spot only are capable of detailing.[88]

As eyewitnesses offering testimony on critical 'world' events, women gained a new authority as travellers and writers. They were able to speak about subjects from which they were previously excluded because they had been on the spot and could furnish readers and listeners with details not coloured by the propagandist's pen.

As one of the foremost authorities, Helen Williams asked herself an earnest question. Was there a fair representation of France to be found back in the English press? Were broadsheet reports exaggerated? When she briefly returned to England in 1790 she heard

> of nothing but crimes, assassinations, torture, and death. I am told that every day witnesses a conspiracy; that every town is the scene of massacre; that every street is blackened with a gallows, and every highway deluged with blood. I hear these things, and repeat to myself, is this the picture of France? Are these the images of that universal joy, which called tears into my eyes, and made my heart throb with sympathy?[89]

Helen Williams believed that – however sorrowful it was to accept it – a true republic needed to be founded on martyrs. The loss of so many friends during the Terror could only be stomached with the promise of future progress.[90]

Of course, not everyone reacted positively to Helen Williams's writings. Her letters did not propel her to stardom in England, largely because she remained abroad. 'What is she now?', asked a critic in 1817. 'If she lives (and if she does or not, few know and nobody cares), she is a wanderer – an exile, unnoticed and unknown.'[91] Her fascination for the French Revolution would never wane: 'The interest I once took in the French Revolution is not chilled,' she reported in the first page of her last book (*Letters on Events which have Passed in France since the Restoration in 1815*), 'and the enthusiasm I once felt for the cause of liberty still warms my bosom.'[92]

'Returned the best informed and most perfect creatures'

Bas Bleu Society & Lady Wits

Why, ye daughters of Britain, are so many of you insensible to those brightest glories of your sex? Where is your love for your native country, which, by thus excelling, you might so nobly serve? Where your emulation of those Heroic Women, that have in ancient days graced this happy land? How long will you be ambitious of flaunting French attire, of fluttering about with the levity of that fantastic people? When will you be satisfied with the simplicity of elegance, and the gracefulness of modesty so becoming in a nation like this, supported by trade, polished by taste, end enlightened by true religion? Say, when will you relinquish delusive pursuits, and dangerous pleasures, the gaze of fools, and the flattery of libertines, for the peaceful and solid study of whatever can adorn your nature, do honour to your country, reflect credit on your profession or Christianity, give joy to all your connections, and confer dignity on Woman-kind?[1]

James Fordyce, Sermons to Young
Women (1766)

I N 1755, THE NOVELIST and translator Frances Brooke praised
French women for looking beyond care for their appearances and
seeking to cultivate the arts and their own sense of taste. 'A French
woman of distinction,' she wrote in her short-run periodical *The Old
Maid*, 'would be more ashamed of wanting a taste for the Belles
Lettres, than of being ill dressed; and it is owing to the neglect of
adorning their minds, that our travelling English ladies are at Paris
the objects of unspeakable contempt, and are honoured with the
appellation of handsome savages.'[2]

The Duchess of Grafton too found foreign society entirely to her
satisfaction. She prefered Italian to English society, but in 1762 she
was unhappily returned to England by her husband. Back at home
she received a visit from Horace Walpole, who reported to Horace
Mann in Florence that he found the Duchess to be a changed woman:
'I was quite struck at seeing her so much altered. She wears no rouge,
and being leaner, her features, which never were delicate, seem larger.
Then she is not dressed French, but Italian, which is over-French.'
There seemed no end to how one could be improved by foreign
society. 'In one point,' Walpole continued, 'in which she cannot be
improved, she seemed so; being thinner, she looked taller.'[3] Writing
from the Continent in 1763, Elizabeth Montagu told her friend Elizabeth Vesey about a similar metamorphosis in her travelling companion, Elizabeth Carter:

With the same facility with which she translated Epictetus from greek into English she translated her native timidity into French airs, and French modes; bought robes trimmed with blonde and souci denton, Colliers, bouquets, des engageantes and all the most labour'd ornaments of dress; and as soon as she was equip'd, wish'd for a walk in the tuilleries more than she had ever done for one in the Portico. Instead of translating the memorable things of Socrates you may expect a lively and spirited translation of les amours and amourettes du Marquis de —, and instead of Plato's Republic, she will translate les égaremens du coeur et d'esprit of Crebillon.[4]

On returning to London, Elizabeth Montagu found that her friends scrutinised her for traces of continental caprice. 'After so long an absence,' she wrote, '[they] visited me with assiduity, my acquaintance with curiosity, they wanted to see whether I was germanised at Spa, Dutchified at the Hague, or frenchified by lodging two nights at the Lion d'argent at Calais.' Their verdict? 'I am not improved' nor 'metamorphosed.' In the past Elizabeth Montagu had been prone to complain about the quantity of rouge worn by Parisian women. Now she ventured to try it herself, 'to comply with the fashion', as she put it. Her assessment? She looked as though she had scarlet fever, but consoled herself with the belief that 'one is less looked at by wearing the uniform of the society one lives in'.

When her compatriot, Mrs Boscawen, learned that Elizabeth Montagu had gone native in France and was rapidly gaining in celebrity, she worried that England had altogether 'lost' one of its own. When Lady Anna Miller returned from her Grand Tour, the chattering wits of London cast on her a more favourable judgement. Horace Walpole, writing to the Countess of Ailesbury, remarked that she had returned 'a beauty, a genius, a Sappho, a tenth Muse, as romantic as Mademoiselle Scudéri, and as sophisticated as Mrs. Vesey'.[5]

Who knows what English society's reaction would have been had Hester Piozzi's reflections on herself been made public. 'I was looking at myself the other day,' she wrote to her daughter from Verona during her second continental voyage, in 1786, '& I thought I would tell you what a motley Creature I was become: for my Riding Habit was bought at *Rome* I recollected; my Hat & Shirt at *Naples*; my Shoes at *Padua*, my Stockings at *Brescia*, my Ruffles at *Genoa*, one of my Petticoats at *Milan*, & the rest of my dress in *England*. We sat for our Pictures at Rome as I said I would – but such *Objects!*[6]

Whilst foreign society had many features which travellers were keen to emulate, certain mannerisms or comportment were best avoided. Even Helen Williams, zealous in her enthusiasm for female Parisian intellectualism, warned her countrywomen against indiscreet slips in decorum:

> The manners of an English female are in danger of becoming contaminated, while she is only endeavouring to suffer without pain the customs of those she has been taught to consider as models of politeness ... so little are these people susceptible of delicacy, propriety, and decency, that they do not even use the words in the sense we do, nor have they any others expressive of the same meaning.[7]

This was a rare caveat from someone who was generally too concerned with revolutionary politics to care about 'feminine respectability'. Had the conservative critic Laetitia-Matilda Hawkins picked up on this, she would doubtless have added it to her arsenal to attack the idea that going abroad could yield *any* advantage to women, whom, she ventured, were created by God 'a *subordinate* class of beings'. Far from improving a woman, French society was a source of moral degradation, capable of upsetting the female psyche: 'whatever mad schemes may occupy the minds of *Frenchmen*', she wrote in her two-volume critique of Helen Williams's *Letters*, '*Englishwomen* are still in their sober senses', and she hoped they would remain so. How could a foreign land be defended that had such lax principles governing marital relations – where, Anna Barbauld was told by Richard Edgeworth (Maria Edgeworth's father), 'A married lady in France is allowed one lover, she is pardon'd for two; three is rather too many'?[8]

Mary Pendarves (the bluestocking luminary Mary Delany) was shocked by the malevolent gossip being spread about the sexual conduct of her aunt, Lady Lansdowne – recently returned from Paris. She was a woman who 'loved admiration – a most dangerous disposition in an agreeable woman. The libertine manners of France accomplished what her own nature was prone to. No woman could less justify herself than she could.'[9]

In her *Strictures on Female Education*, Hannah More wrote with similar prejudices against continental travel. Already horrified by Madame de Staël's declaration that coquetry is 'the flavour which gives to society its poignancy', she rolled up her sleeves with much to rebut. 'It may be also objected,' she wrote,

> that the opinion here suggested on the state of manners among the higher classes of our countrywomen, may seem to controvert the encomiums of modern travellers, who generally concur in ascribing a decided superiority to the ladies of this country over those of every other. But such is the state of foreign manners, that the comparative praise is almost an injury to *English* women.

Further, she could not understand why English parents were so desperate to obtain a French governess, in place of a 'pious' English education in which the child would have no patois in her French pronunciation. 'I', ventured More, 'would not offer up principle as a victim to sounds and accents,' especially whilst the shrieks of horror from the French Revolution resonated in English ears. She underscored her point with an evangelical and patriotic puff:

> for whatever disgrace it might once have brought on an English lady to have had it suspected from her accent that she had the misfortune not to be born in a neighbouring country, some recent events may serve to reconcile her to the suspicion of having been bred in her own: a country, to which (with all its sins, which are many!) the whole world is looking up with envy and admiration, as the seat of true glory and of comparative happiness: a country, in which the exile, driven out by the crimes of his own, finds

a home! A country, to obtain the protection of which it was claim enough to be unfortunate; and no impediment to have been the subject of her direct foe! A country, which in this respect, humbly imitating the Father of compassion, when it offered mercy to a suppliant enemy, never conditioned for merit, nor insisted on the virtues of the miserable as a preliminary to its own bounty!

Years later, in her last work, the *Moral Sketches of Prevailing Opinions and Manners* (1819), Hannah More returned to these themes in order to argue against what she called 'the epidemic French mania'. In her 'sketches of foreign manners', she examined the effects of visiting foreign climes, declaring that 'it is to be feared, that with French habits, French principles may be imported'. The increasing numbers of British travelling abroad after the end of the Napoleonic wars could only, she worried, have tragic consequences, going as far as to warn that: 'We are losing our national character.'[10] Elizabeth Montagu edged towards the same conclusion. 'Does not your brother think he is in Babel?' she wrote, inquiring about the first impressions of an Irish visitor to fashionable Royal Tunbridge Wells. 'How does he like English women in French dresses and French manners?'[11]

Not every returned traveller, of course, met with xenophobic sniggers or mockery. Homecomings could even be moments of celebration. When the exotic and extravagant Lady Spencer (mother of Lady Bessborough and the Duchess of Devonshire) returned to her home in Holywell in 1794 after an Italian sojourn the local villagers gave her a rousing reception: church bells rang and candles glowed in the villagers' windows.[12]

Once home, Grand Tourists were keen to reflect on the benefits of their travels. When Elizabeth Webster returned to England briefly in 1793, she wrote in her journal that she believed her manners had improved of late, and that the local celebrity she had acquired at social engagements must be due to the air of accomplishment 'as coming from abroad'.[13] Fearing that she might be constrained in British society, perhaps physically – subjected to the tantrums of her jealous husband – she was anxious to return to the Continent where life was different. If only things would change at home.

Many, in fact, dreamt of utopian changes at home. Sarah Scott was one. In 1751, inside a year of her abusive marriage to George Lewis Scott, she had left him and joined Lady Barbara Montagu in Batheaston, in what Sarah's sister joked was their 'convent', where she pursued a life of charitable enterprise.[14]

Sarah also wrote and had published a number of works of fiction and historical biography, including in 1762 her most well-known work, *A Description of Millenium Hall* – which presented an idealised vision of a society created and run by women. In the book, a gentleman traveller and his companion stumble across the community of women after being involved in a carriage crash. They find themselves in the midst of a charitable haven of feminised Christian culture; inspired, the gentleman traveller names the community Millenium Hall, in recognition of a new millennial reign of peace and prosperity. In what one of the women proprietors describes as 'this heavenly society', the residents study, paint, tend the gardens, and manage their own intellectual and economic affairs. 'Ay, indeed,' confirms one of the women taken into Millenium Hall's care, 'it is a most comfortable place. God bless the good ladies! I and my neighbours are as happy as princesses, we have everything we want and wish, and who can say more?'[15]

In the tale's sanguine conclusion, the gentleman traveller leaves, enlightened, and vows to replicate the model of the philanthropic sanctuary elsewhere.

Millenium Hall represented a microcosm of the values of a reformed nation, where the socially unjust condition of women in the 'outside world' (as represented in the personal histories of the proprietors of the Hall – all of whom, like Sarah Scott herself, had somehow been released from wretched marriages) was corrected through communal, collaborative effort.

Scott is said to have drawn her inspiration for *Millenium Hall* from her charitable life at Batheaston. But certain influences can also be seen in the characters of her bluestocking friends. Her sister Elizabeth Montagu's personal commitment to increasing the value of her husband's estates and mines in northern England, and towards developing philanthropic programmes benefiting its workers, mirrored many of the interests in estate management endorsed by the women of Millenium Hall.

Whereas Millenium Hall seemed a far-off fantasy, the Continent – or 'the paradise of lady wits', as Fanny Burney was enticingly informed[16] – was a more tangible source of inspiration.

In the 1760s, Elizabeth Montagu ran her own affairs and exercised a considerable degree of independence from her husband, even deciding to spend the fashionable season at her Hill Street home in London rather than at their country home in Sandleford, Berkshire, since 'London is the place for sinning', as she put it, and 'the country is for repentance – a twofold reason why fine Ladies prefer Town'. In town, especially during the winter, the bluestockings' soirées were in full swing, and Elizabeth was loath to miss them. Even when her husband retired to the country for Christmas, she remained at Hill Street, where 'I had parties of [bluestockings] to dine with me continually.'[17]

Her life changed in 1775, however, with the death of her husband – 'martyred by the gout'. The following year Elizabeth gathered together a travelling party – including her nephew, her friend Elizabeth Carter's nephew, their Swiss tutor, a Miss Gregory and a host of servants and footmen – and set off to experience 'the flutter of Paris'. There, she quickly acquired a busy schedule, socialising in salons and dining with the literati:

> at Madame de Guerchys, on Thursday at le Duc de Nivernois, on Friday at le Chateau de Meudon with Madame la Marechalle de Mirepoix. There a Comtesse de Cambysse shall sing some charming songs made by le Duc de Nivernois. After dinner la Marechalle shall carry you to see Belle Vue, a place made at immense expence by Madame Pompadour, and really very fine, but the Castle de Meudon

has a still finer prospect. The D: and Duchess de Nivernois and madame Rochefort were of ye party at madame de Guerchys; ye Duke and Madame de Rochefort at Madame de Mirepoix.[18]

By the end of all this she felt able to announce to Elizabeth Vesey that 'I am now quite a Parisian dame.' The Parisians, however, already knew who she was; her famous *Essay on the Writings and Genius of Shakespear* – in part a response to Voltaire's critique of the bard – had been published in its fourth edition earlier that year. In particular, Elizabeth enjoyed the company of the *salonnières* Susanne and Jacques Necker, whom she thought 'amiable and respectable as well as learned and ingenious'. It was not the first time they had met – months previously, Madame Necker had visited the Montagus' London home, and they again dined together with Diderot in Paris. Elizabeth felt exhilarated: 'I am often in society with the most celebrated beaux esprits,' she enthusiastically wrote. 'And they really are very captivating. I have not spent a dull or insipid hour in company since I came to Paris.'[19]

The French, she noted, had made conversation a superior art form. In Paris, learned men 'by their vivacity and politeness shew they have been used to converse much with women. The Ladies by being well informed and full of those graces we neglect when with each other shew they have been used to converse with men.' Maria Edgeworth shared a similar sentiment, hoping that, as in France, the English would learn to mix 'feminine and masculine subjects of conversation, instead of separating the sexes . . . into hostile parties, dooming one sex to politics, argument, and eternal sense, the other to scandal, dress, and eternal nonsense'. In Vienna, Hester Piozzi found the intellectual freedom given to women remarkable:

> The ladies here seem very highly accomplished, and speak a great variety of languages with facility, studying to adorn the conversation with every ornament that literature can bestow; nor do they appear terrified as in London, lest pedantry should be imputed to them, for venturing some-

times to use in company that knowledge they have acquired in private by diligent application.[20]

What struck Elizabeth Montagu most was the way in which women were included; she felt particularly honoured when invited to attend a meeting of the *Académie française* (although women were still prohibited from becoming members), where she listened to the discourses of academicians including the Marquis de Chastellux and the *philosophe* d'Alembert.

Elizabeth Montagu determined to fashion herself as a salon hostess at her newly built house in Mayfair – soon to be known as Montagu House. In 1776 she visited Paris in order to immerse herself in French etiquette and conversation. 'My great object in travelling there', she explained to her brother Morris Robinson 'has been to get well acquainted with the French character . . .' Her discoveries intrigued her. 'I find a greater difference from us in their sentiments, their tastes, their modes of life, than I had imagined.' Soon after returning to England, having relaxed and recovered from her journey, she reflected on the transformation of her outlook, summing up her views in a letter to an old family friend, Leonard Smelt.

> From a gay Parisian Dame visiting the Beau Monde, and conversing with the Beau Esprits of the Academies, I am at once metamorphosed into a plain Country Farmeress. I have the same love for my pigs, pride in my potatoes, solicitude for my Poultry, care of my wheat, attention to my barley, and application to the regulation of my dairy as formerly . . . I believe my friends at Paris would be amazed and scandalised at the joy I feel in this way of life, for they have not any taste of rural pleasures . . . The business of the toilette, the amusement of *les spectacles*, and the pleasure of conversation engross their whole attention; in the first, and the latter of these they shew skill and taste; as to their Spectacles I cannot commend them . . . Moliere is out of fashion, they have pretty comic pieces which are tolerably acted. The Dancers and scenery at the Opera are fine, but the musick bad, and the singers scream most insufferably. As the French Ladies dine at ½ after

two they have a long afternoon, and the spectacles are necessary to amuse the hours between dinner and supper. To me the most interesting object was the French themselves, and their conversation much the most agreeable thing I found at Paris, so that I went seldom to the Plays.[21]

Towards the end of 1778 she wrote to her close friend Elizabeth Vesey with excited anticipation of their spending the forthcoming season together in London:

Indeed my dear Friend it is not possible to tell you how happy I am in the hope of a most delightful winter in your Society, and in that blue room where all people are enchanted, tho the magic figure of the circle is vanished, thence; a Philosopher, a fine Lady, and a Gallant Officer form a triangle in one corner; a Maccaroni, a Poet, a Divine, a Beauty, and an Ottaheite Savage, a wondrous Pentagon in another; then the Coalition of Parties, professions, and characters which compose the group standing in the middle of the room; the flying squadrons of casual visitants that are ever coming in and going out! Great Orators play a solo of declamation; Witts lett off epigrams like minute guns; the Sage speaks sentences, every one does his best to please the Lady of the enchanting room, for all contend to win her grace whom all commend.

Another regular, Mrs Elwood, also found delight in Elizabeth Vesey's assemblies, noting that the host preferred guests to have wide-ranging conversation rather than gather around one speaker. 'Mrs Vesey had so great a horror of what was styled "a circle" from the stiffness and awe which it produced,' wrote Fanny Burney, a regular visitor,

that she was wont to push all the small sofas, as well as chairs, pell-mell about the apartments; and her greatest delight was to place the seats back to back, so that individuals could or could not, converse as they pleased, whilst she herself flitted from party to party, armed with an ear-trumpet (being exceedingly deaf), catching an occasional sentence here, or a word there, endeavouring to hear and to understand every thing that was passing around her.[22]

'Here, everything that is witty and everything learned is to be found,' wrote Hannah More, another visitor to Mrs Vesey's Tuesday evening assemblies. Here the ladies hobnobbed with the members of Dr Johnson's Literary Club, who would visit after their fortnightly dinner at the Turk's Head in Gerrard Street (Mrs Vesey's husband, Agmondesham, was a member of this literary and artistic club). Dr Burney (Fanny's father) described a typical soiree during which Sir William Hamilton described Pompeii, Elizabeth Carter and Hannah More discussed some new author, and Edmund Burke read aloud a pamphlet with 'incomparable eloquence'.[23]

Well-attended as Elizabeth Vesey's assemblies were, there was room for competition. Soon, Elizabeth Montagu's own flare for entertaining – according to Fanny Burney – seems to have made her salon even more favoured than her friend's. 'While to Mrs Vesey the Bas Bleu Society owed its origin and its epithet,' she explained, 'the meetings that took place at Mrs Montagu's were soon more popularly known by that denomination, for though they could not be more fashionable, they were far more splendid.' The only similarity between the two was that they were both 'houses of rendezvous' for the blue-stockings. 'Their grandeur or their simplicity, their magnitude or their diminutiveness, were by no means the principal cause of [their] difference.' Each salon had special qualities reflecting the hostess's discerning tastes, 'for though they instilled not their characters into their visitors, their characters bore so large a share in their visitors' reception and accommodation, as to influence materially the turn of the discourse'.

Whereas Mrs Vesey's home offered a cosy familiarity, Elizabeth Montagu, Fanny Burney felt, had drawn on her continental experiences to create an altogether different setting.

At Mrs Montagu's the semi-circle that faced the fire retained during the whole evening its unbroken form, with a precision that it seemed described by a Brobdingnagian compass. The lady of the castle commonly placed herself at the upper end of the room, near the commencement of the curve, so as to be courteously visible to all her guests; having the person of the highest rank or consequence, properly on one side, and the person the most eminent for talents, sagaciously, on the other side, or as near to her chair and her converse as her favouring eye and a complacent bow of the head could invite him to that distinction.[24]

Elizabeth Montagu had been inspired to have Montagu House built in Portman Square soon after returning from her continental sojourn. It was an architectural monument to a newly reinvigorated life, and her own tastes oversaw all aspects of its construction. The neoclassical architect James 'Athenian' Stuart was commissioned to superintend the decoration of Montagu House, which, upon its completion, duly impressed its visitors. 'I dined on Tuesday with the Harcourts, at Mrs Montagu's new palace and was much surprised,' wrote the ubiquitous critic Horace Walpole. 'Instead of vagaries, it is a noble simple edifice. Magnificent, yet no gilding. It is grand, not tawdry, not larded, and embroidered, and pomponned with shreds and remnants, and clinquant like all the harlequinades of Adam, which never let the eye repose an instant.'

The house was finished in 1781, and Elizabeth Montagu, at the age of sixty-one, felt she could settle. 'A good house is a great comfort in old age,' she proclaimed. It was perfect: 'so ample for the devoirs of Society, so calculated for Assemblies that it will suit all ones humours ... I congratulate myself every hour on having taken the trouble to build for myself.'[25]

The poet William Cowper described visiting Montagu House as going to 'Mrs Montagu's Academy' – a characterisation suggestive of the way that Elizabeth Montagu made the duties of a hostess resemble those of a schoolmistress: she controlled the assemblies – from topics of conversation to contributors.[26] Another commentator, writing in the periodical the *Observer*, wrote a caricature of the experience of attending one of Mrs Montagu's assemblies, referring to her with the pseudonym 'Vanessa', she:

> in the centre of her own circle, sits like the statue of the Athenian Minerva, incensed with the breath of philosophers, poets, painters, orators, and every art, science or fine speaking. It is in her academy, young noviciates try their wit and practice panegyric; no one like Vanessa can break in a young lady to the poetics, and teach her Pegasus to carry a side-saddle; she can make a mathematician quote Pindar, a master in chancery write novels, or a Birmingham hardware man stamp rhymes as fast as buttons.[27]

Bluestockings such as Elizabeth Montagu had replaced card playing with salon conversation, and as a rule it was the women of the house who now orchestrated these social occasions, reminiscent of Madame Necker's punctilious 'agendas for the day'.[28] The writer Jean-Françoise Marmontel – who kept a detailed journal of the salons he visited – once wrote that Julie de Lespinasse kept her guests 'in perfect harmony like the strings of an instrument tuned by a single hand' – a remark that could equally have been applied to the conduct of many of her English counterparts.[29]

Coterie and salon culture encouraged sociability between women of shared mutual interests and promoted enlightened relationships between men and women. That the muses were migrants from the Continent was famously remarked upon by Hannah More, who referred to the exemplary salon at the Hôtel de Rambouillet, whilst noting that she considered the British counterparts to be more sophisticated:

> O! how unlike the wit that fell,
> Rambouillet! At thy quaint Hotel;
> Where point, and turn, and equivoque,
> Distorted every word they spoke!
> All so intolerably bright,
> Plain Common Sense was put to flight;
> Each speaker, so ingenious ever,
> 'Twas tiresome to be quite so clever;

There twisted Wit forgot to please,
And Mood and Figure banish'd ease:
Poor exil'd Nature houseless stray'd,
'Till Sevigné receiv'd the maid.
Tho' here she comes to bless our isle,
Not universal is her smile . . .[30]

And even in her later years, when she flooded her publications with warnings against the mania for anything foreign, she was complimentary about British salon culture. Not only in foreign capitals, she wrote, but 'London also has had its select assemblies for conversation. They were neither trifling, dull, nor pedantic. If there were less display of wit, less pains to be easy, less study to be natural, less affectation of being unaffected, less effort to be unconstrained, there was more sincerity, integrity, and kindness.'[31] Other commentators remarked on the resemblance between the characters of the *salonnières*, such as the traveller Nathaniel Wraxall, who – commenting on Elizabeth Vesey, Hester Chapone, Mrs Boscawen, and other bluestockings in his *Historical Memoirs* – dubbed Elizabeth Montagu 'the Madame du Deffand of the English capital'.[32]

Ye belles, ye beaux, ye wits, and all,
From concert, cotillon, and ball,
Come, come with me, attend the call
Of Miller, at Batheaston.

No roof on earth with her's can vie
For mirth, and easy pleasantry;
Come, feast your ear, and please your eye,
With Miller, at Batheaston.

Old Tully's vase you there will find,
Replete with verse of every kind,
To form a wreath, the brow to bind
Of Miller, at Batheaston.

> Haste, haste then all, to celebrate,
> With jocund mirth and joy elate,
> The easy pomp and happy state
> Of Miller, at Batheaston.
>
> Pale Envy, keep thou far away,
> In town thou'lt find sufficient prey;
> Nor near the festive bower stray
> Of Miller, at Batheaston.
>
> But hither, pr'y thee hither flee,
> Ye Muses nine, and Graces three,
> And follow, follow, follow me
> To Miller, at Batheaston.
>
> *Poetical Amusements at a Villa near Bath*, I, 43

Soon after Anna Riggs married John Miller in Bath in 1765, they settled in nearby Batheaston (on the same road as Sarah Scott) where they built a quaint villa in the valley, facing the Avon, at a point where the river fell in a wide cascade, with several small rivulets running through their garden. It may have been 'diminutive' – as Horace Walpole, an early visitor to their house, described it – but, with views of meadows, scenes of the distant city, and the sound of babbling brooks, it was certainly picturesque. Here, in Walpole's view, was a 'new Parnassus', home of the muses, 'composed of three laurels, a myrtle-tree, a weeping-willow, and a view of the Avon', which, from the fantasy of seeing Batheaston grow into a sacred mountain for the Goddesses of inspiration, was a 'new christened Helicon'.[33]

Once their residence was established the couple, and old Mrs Briggs, took off to the Continent. Anna was taken with Paris. But, if we listen to Madame du Deffand, Parisian society did not take to her. 'Talk about boring,' du Deffand bluntly reported to Horace Walpole, 'some of your compatriots are here, a gentleman and two ladies who returned from Italy. They wanted to see me, I do not know why, but it would not be *them* who inspire in me a sense of anglomania.'[34] Harsh words from the *grande dame* of salon culture.

Seemingly unaware of the impression they had made on French

salon society, Anna and her husband were inspired to attempt to recreate at their home in Batheaston that which they enjoyed most on their continental travels. Hoping to 'contribute to the improvement of their own country', explained Walpole, 'they have introduced *bouts-rimés* [rhyming verse] as a new discovery'.

The concept drew many of the most fashionable from Bath to participate. 'I counted one morning above fifty carriages drawn up in a line from Bath Easton,' wrote one bemused visitor, who spotted amongst the crowd the Duchess of Cumberland, the Duchess of Northumberland, the Duchess of Ancaster, and the Duchess of Beaufort. The presence of the privileged bolstered the reputation of Anna Miller's assemblies; she invited 'few people who are not of rank or fame', noted Fanny Burney – herself among the talented few – and excluded 'all who are not people of character very unblemished'.

The idea of the *bouts-rimés* had its roots in the Millers' Italian excursion. In 1769 a labourer in Frascati – part of the ancient town of Tusculum – stumbled across an antique marble urn and sold it to the Millers, who brought it back to their villa in Bath and, fortnightly during the fashionable season (November and December), placed it on a pedestal in the bay window of their drawing room. Into the vase were placed the short poetical pieces, the brief 'mental exercises', composed by their guests about subjects assigned to them by Lady Miller.

One guest, for example, who had failed to appear at an assembly for most of one season, was required to write on the subject 'Delays are Dangerous'. Lord Miller's famous 'subject', however, was often the beauty of the women guests – Georgiana, the soon-to-be Duchess of Devonshire, receiving an inordinate amount of attention in his poetic effusions. Each guest read a *bout-rimé*, using assigned rhyming words to end the line of each poem:

> From Bath to Easton haste your flight,
> Prepare for scenes of sweet delight:
> MILLER, to please, exerts her power,
> And asks you to her charming bower,
> Where Nature joins, in concert meet,
> With Taste, to make the place complete:

May joy and mirth there ever glow,
As long as Avon's streams shall flow.

When each guest's *jeu d'esprit* was finished, reported one visitor, the
Reverend Richard Graves, 'some young nymph put in her delicate
arm, and took out a single poem, which the author, or some one
who either had, or fancied he had an agreeable elocution, read to the
assembly'. Graves summarised how the achievements of a morning's
musing were treated. After each poem was read,

> The gentlemen retired to a contiguous apartment; where
> amidst a profusion of jellies, sweetmeats, ice creams and
> the like, they decided on the merits of the several perform-
> ances; from which they selected three, which were deemed
> the best; and of course entitled to prizes; which her lady-
> ship distributed to the respective authors; a pompous bou-
> quet of flowers to the first, a myrtle wreath to the second,
> and a sprig of myrtle to the third. These were then usually
> presented, by the successful candidate, to some lady who
> wore them in her hair or her bosom, the next evening, to
> the publick rooms.[35]

In total, 235 poems were published in four volumes, titled *Poetical
Amusements at a Villa near Bath* (1775, 1776, 1777, and 1781), with over
sixty-five named contributors – the only notable one being the poet
Anna Seward. In the preface to the first volume, Lady Miller (writing
as an anonymous editor of the poems), offered an apology to the
public for the fact that the subject of Batheaston (and therefore
reflexive praise) was the focus of so many printed poems, which might
obscure the true talents of the authors themselves. 'Should politeness
to the Institution and Institutress be found to occupy too large a
portion of these sheets,' she wrote, 'the Editor must rest his justification upon the exclusion of many elegant and ingenious little pieces,
(from a mere motive of delicacy) that would have done equal honour
to the authors, as to the person and subject of their address.' The
authors of the Parnassean poetry might not rest on their laurels, but,
after all, the proceeds from the sales of the *Poetical Amusements* went
to the Bath Pauper Charity.[36]

In 1780, some seven seasons after the creation of 'The Vase', Anna Miller found herself in company with the party-hopping Fanny Burney – who was by now the famous author of *Evelina* (1778) – at a mutual acquaintance's house in Bath. Using Hester Thrale as an intermediary, Lady Miller requested an introduction to the novelist. 'Up I jumped and walked forward,' wrote Burney, recalling her first encounter with her; she 'said very polite things, of her wish to know me, and regret that she had not sooner met me'. Fanny Burney had heard of the fashionable Batheaston literary circle – recognising that Lady Miller tended to invite select company to keep its 'tonish'[37] appeal – and a week later was able to report on her own entertaining experience as a guest on a post-vase season 'public day' at Miller's villa.

Among the few in the company was 'a most prodigious fat old lady' – Anna Miller's mother, Mrs Riggs – who, star-struck at the sight of Fanny Burney, followed her around 'with an expression of comical admiration, fixed her eyes upon me, and for some time amused herself with apparently watching me'. Soon, Fanny realised that old Mrs Riggs was imagining she was watching the movements not of Burney, but of the author's fictional (but clearly inspirational) character, Evelina. When Burney rose from her seat to fetch a mislaid wrap for a chilled friend, Mrs Riggs 'followed me, laughing, nodding, and looking much delighted', periodically urging: 'That's right, Evelina! –Ah, look for it, Evelina! Evelina always did so – she always looked for people's cloaks, and was obliging and well-bred!' Soon after, Anna Miller's ten-year-old daughter treated Burney to an interrogation, having learned from listening to her mother read Burney's book aloud that Evelina was left at the end of the novel waiting for a chaise to return her to Berry Hill. Where, she pleaded, was Evelina now? ('I promised her I would inquire, and let her know', was Burney's tactful reply.)[38]

However, for all her efforts, Anna Miller's salon occupied a peripheral position in bluestocking culture. She was perceived more as a lady of leisure than a matron of enlightenment. It was felt she trivialised the *métier* of the *salonnières*, preferring parlour games to

political debate, her interests in prosaic entertainment leading
Madame du Deffand to divulge that the Millers did not 'instil in me
a sense of anglomania'.[39] In fact the Millers' parties, Fanny Burney
noted, were 'laughed at in London', although they remained remarkably popular amongst the gouty guests of Bath – where Miller herself
was seen as patron of the arts. When a literary figure of Fanny
Burney's stature arrived on the scene, it is not difficult to see how
admirers – young or old – could find themselves emotionally sub-
sumed by the author's oeuvre. No one in Miller's household literally
mistook Burney as anything but the author of a fictional creation,
but they saw in her a unique opportunity to reach the creative world
by engaging with the creator herself – as is captured in Mrs Riggs's
command to the novelist as she departed the villa – 'Set about
another!'

However scandalous the public considered the marriage of Lady
Elizabeth Webster to Henry Richard Fox, the 3rd Lord Holland, in
1797, a bond was sealed that would withstand all future calumnious
onslaughts. Lord Holland inherited a powerful political legacy from
his uncle, the Whig Charles James Fox, and became a prominent
debater in the House of Lords in his own right. Elizabeth adapted
perfectly to the role of political consort, and determined to make
Holland House in Kensington the base for the Fox family's political
ambitions. Not that a life in London dominated by English politics
was always the obvious choice. At one point when it seemed he might
have his pick of public offices under the patronage of his uncle, Lord
Holland immediately thought of some sort of ambassadorial duty,
which would be amenable to his wife. 'I added,' he later recollected,
'that Lady Holland's predilection for foreign modes of living would
make me prefer a diplomatick station to any other, and that the
embassy in Paris, when peace came, would of course be my ultimate
object in that line.'[40]

Elizabeth concentrated her interests in support of her husband's
political as well as personal affairs – even quickly defending her

cousin-in-law, Lord Edward Fitzgerald, when he was charged with murder during the planning of the Irish rebellion in 1798. 'These horrible times have had one good effect,' wrote Lord Holland to his sister, Caroline Fox, 'they have converted Elizabeth.'[41] Soon, Lady Holland's liberal views were aligned with many others in the Whig party circles who believed in middle-class improvement, promoted through enlightened government rule. Even years after the Hollands set up house together, acquaintances would remark on the strong-mindedness and independence which guided Lady Holland through her new life. She was, as the family friend and historian Thomas Babington Macaulay put it,

> A great lady, fanciful, hysterical and hypochondriachal, ill-natured and good natured, sceptical and superstitious, afraid of ghosts, and not of God – would not for the world begin a journey on a Friday morning and thought nothing of running away from her husband.[42]

It was her maverick manners and flamboyant free spirit that made her partnership with the politically minded Lord Holland so perfectly complementary. And Lady Holland found herself in her element. As she once told her friend and confidante, Lady Bessborough, 'all women of a certain age and in a situation to achieve it should take to Politicks'.[43]

In October 1797 Lord and Lady Holland moved back in to the refurbished Holland House – complete with carpets designed by the antiquarian Samuel Lysons from patterns imitating recently dis-covered Roman pavements. The agenda Lady Holland set for social life at Holland House was to turn her home into a political salon of considerable public influence. She saw herself less a bluestocking literary hostess, less *une femme du letters*, than a business woman, a sort of eighteenth-century *femme d'affaires*. But here (as with the bluestocking *salonnières*), foreign models (particularly the French salon, again provided the best examples. She was, of course, familiar with the celebrated culture of conversation on the Continent. In Florence in 1795, when, as Lady Webster, she was not spending languid days with Lord Holland casually reading Pope's translation of Homer's *Iliad*, she frequented the salon of Countess d'Albany – for many years a feature of social life at Florence:

> d'Albany preserves an excellent state of health and spirits. Her house is crowded with strangers of all countries; and although many of the English complain of the formality which reigns *chez elle*, all are presented to her with very few exceptions, and generally form the greater part of the society at her house . . . I have her library at my disposal. She receives all new books that are worth reading from England, France, and Germany.[44]

There she met Madame Germaine de Staël, who was five years her senior, and little esteemed by Lady Webster. Perhaps, it has been suggested, this was because of the many similarities to herself she saw in de Staël. The latter, like the future Lady Holland, was extremely strong-willed, pretentious, egocentric, the keeper of illicit lovers, and the mother of an illegitimate child. Like Madame de Staël, Lady Holland became a salon hostess with strong political views. So it must have been with a feeling of comfortable familiarity and empathy that Madame de Staël (and other *salonnières* such as Madame Recamier) later visited Holland House. Whatever their differences, they must have recognised in each other a shared desire to command conversation. 'Madame de Staël continues still the nine days wonder,' Lady Holland wrote during her visit.

> She is certainly very clever, but also very tiresome. One of the wittiest dialogues, in which however she only supplied the topics and was the cause of wit in others, occurred here at dinner between her and Lord Wellesley. Congreve could not have written a better scene. He parried inimitably well all her political queries and flowery harangues. She laughed very much on the wrong side of her mouth, as she has a mortal aversion to pleasantry in any shape.[45]

Lady Holland's new role as salon hostess was beginning to receive the kind of plaudits that English critics bestowed on French salonnières. There, observed the British philosopher David Hume, 'the females enter into all transactions and all management of church and state: and no man can expect success, who takes not care to obtain their good graces'. Lady Holland also had her critics. She was blamed for the stagnation of her husband's political career: Why had he been passed over as leader of the Whig party? Because, one associate suggested, 'He is completely under the dominion of his wife.'[46] But just as Lady Holland was able to ignore gossip about her sensational past, she also chose to disregard the disparaging remarks of political pundits. As Henry Holland (no relation) – an eminent London physician and a guest at Holland House – observed, she embraced her role with great self-confidence:

> Supreme in her own mansion and family, she exercised a singular and seemingly capricious tyranny, even over guests of the highest rank... Capricious it seemed, but there was in reality *intention* in all she did; and this intention was the maintenance of power, which she gained and strenuously used, though not without discretion in fixing its limits.[47]

As the years passed Lady Holland's self-fashioning became more grandiose. One visitor noted how '*Her Majesty*', Lady Holland, 'was seated on her throne, a pony chaise on the lawn, and there she received her subjects who came to be presented or to pay their respects. It was a much more formal ceremony than going to kiss the King's hands', while another quipped that Lady Holland's was 'the only really undisputed monarchy in Europe' – an association that would have been ill-received in the feverishly Whiggish atmosphere of Holland House.

In fact many believed that it was Lord and Lady Holland's private dinners and convivial meetings that kept the Whig party together. Regular guests at Holland House included Lord Holland's Oxford friends – Lords Morpeth, Boringdon, Digby and Granville Leveson-Gower, and Charles Beauclerk – who, a few years earlier, had been running wild on their Grand Tour in Naples.

But these were only a few of the regular stream of guests entertained at Holland House. A glance at the famous 'Dinner Books', which Lady Holland began keeping in the summer of 1799 (and which, as manuscript volumes, continue unbroken until 1875 – and even include the names of dinner guests received on trips abroad), show up to fifty guests a day visiting their home (though their dinners were usually restricted to about ten people).

Just as Lady Miller prescribed subjects of literary discussion and poetic expression in her salon, Lady Holland's guests were tactfully invited, according to their area of expertise, to contribute to a particular topic of debate. The focus at Holland House was set on British foreign policy, and specifically with eyes across the Channel. They were Francophiles. It was clear (even notorious) that here the principles of post-revolutionary France, the pursuit of liberty against monarchical tyranny, were being celebrated.

Holland House society strengthened the bonds between English and European politics in part because Lord and Lady Holland continued to spend as much time as they could abroad, visiting Paris during the Peace of Amiens, but also exploring the Iberian peninsula. Such was Lady Holland's impatience to tour again that she even broke with medical advice to travel when ill. 'I am uneasy, my dear Lady Holland,' wrote her friend, Sydney Smith, in 1814, 'at your going abroad.'

> Consider what it is to be well. If I were you, I would not stir from Holland House for two years: and then, as many jolts and frights as you please, which at present you are not equal to . . . Be wise, my dear Lady, and re-establish your health in that gilded room which furnishes better and pleasanter society than all the wheels in the world can whirl to you.

But they set off to Rome five days later.[48] Lord Holland was not surprised. 'She is always better travelling,' he had conceded years earlier, when she again expressed her determination to travel despite being virtually bed-ridden, 'the change of air & scene always agree with her'.[49]

European political representatives found themselves gathered together around the Holland House dinner table – including guests as varied as the ambassadors to Russia, Prussia, Austria, France, Sardinia and Portugal (the British Foreign Secretary Lord Palmerston in 1838 advised Lady Holland that inviting such guests would enable them to say 'that they had shared the hospitality, culinary and intellectual, of Holland House').[50] Lady Holland's adeptness at organising the dinners was widely applauded. 'None but a master hand,' wrote Dr Henry Holland, 'could have accomplished the result of so skilfully commingling English and Foreign Ministers and diplomats, men of learning and science, historians, poets, artists, and wits.'[51] But not everyone was happy about the assorted guests that gave Holland House its distinctly continental atmosphere. The famous German traveller Alexander von Humboldt, for one, expressed his distaste at the apparent favouritism shown to French, Spanish and Italian nationals. Even the house's servants were drawn from such milieux: the children's tutor in Italian was a refugee from Italy named Serafino Buonaiuti; their librarian was the ex-Pavian professor and Milanese writer Nicolo Ugo Foscolo, their hired hand was Guiseppe Binda, and there were a host of others who had fled Italy at times of foreign invasion.[52]

It was even claimed that Holland House achieved where the British government was failing in foreign affairs – although some viewed the Hollands' pursuit of political allies abroad as mischief-making. 'We din'd at Holland House yesterday,' wrote Lady Bessborough in 1813, complaining about the complexity of the political conversation. 'It was very pleasant, except for every now and then that tone of incredulity or indifference to our success [in the Napoleonic wars] – not in Spain, for I cannot make out the consistency of their views. They would defeat Bonaparte in Spain, and let him defeat the allies in Germany. This is beyond my politics.'[53] In fact, after 1789, much of Europe as a whole was beyond the political understanding of most Britons. Even though continental travel was still possible in the revolutionary and Napoleonic years, the numbers of Britons travelling abroad tailed off. Holland House – with its continental fashions, cosmopolitan guests,

and multi-lingual debates – brought Europe to England. Its signifi-
cance as a venue for Whig party debates (the famous 'Fox Club' was
established at a dinner there in 1813) could not be ignored, nor could its
influence on British politics and attitudes towards European politics,
which – as a centre of debate – lasted well into the nineteenth century.

On 22 October 1840, the partying ended: Lord Holland died aged
sixty-seven. 'This wretched day closes all happiness, refinement, and
hospitality within the walls of Holland House,' wrote Lady Holland,
who lived a further five years. Once menacing and stern, Lady Holland withdrew in her last years to a quiet life in London, nostalgic
about her adventurous past. Even Whig opponents knew that the
closing of Holland House would represent the end of a particular
epoch of social stimulation. 'Such is the social despotism of this
strange house,' reflected the politician Charles Greville (when a Tory),

> which presents an odd mixture of luxury and constraint,
> of enjoyment physical and intellectual with an alloy of
> désagréments [annoyance] . . . Though everyone who goes
> there finds something to abuse or to ridicule in the mistress
> of the house . . . all continue to go; all like it more or less;
> and whenever, by the death of either it shall come to an
> end, a vacuum will be made in society which nothing will
> supply . . . the world will suffer by the loss.[54]

'Home!' wrote Lady Holland to her sister-in-law Caroline Fox after
arriving back, alone, from a trip abroad in 1841. 'What a *word* for
me. To return to an empty House without all that formerly included
Home!'[55]

Home – once the place Lady Holland (when Elizabeth Webster)
referred to as 'the detested spot where I have languished in solitude
and discontent the best years of my life;'[56] home – the place she had
for so long wanted to escape from, which drove her abroad. Life had
come full circle.

'All this has ye air of a Novel'

A Legacy of Letters & the Grand Tour

*You are a wanderer, Lady Mary, like Cain, &
seem not to care for your own Country. You would
have liked it better, I believe, during the Hept-
archy, when we had more Kings & Queens than
there are in a Pack of Cards. If you should ever
write your Travels, and like Baron Polnitz give
a full account of all the gracious Sovereigns upon
Earth, I flatter myself you will honour the Strawberry Press with them. I promise you they shall be
printed on the best Imperial paper.*

Horace Walpole to Lady Mary Coke,
27 January 1771[1]

9

F<small>ROM</small> 1756–91 L<small>ADY</small> M<small>ARY</small> C<small>OKE</small> had been regularly received in royal households and courts across Europe. Her copious reflections on her continental travels formed a twenty-six volume journal, parts of which were subsequently published. The bulk of her writings, however, remained in manuscript form. So what of Walpole's playful suggestion that she might 'write [her] Travels' and publish them with his Strawberry Press – a vanity publishing house he set up in 1757 After all it was a standard enough course of action for returning male travellers. As the physician Henry Holland – who was planning to publish an account of his recent trip to Iceland – told Maria Edgeworth, 'Nobody, you know, travels now a days without writing a quarto to tell the world where he has been, & what he has beheld.' Everyone knew men liked to publish their travelling tales, but women, it seemed, were more reticent.

One exception was Lady Coke's friend and distant relative, Lady Mary Wortley Montagu, whose 'Embassy Letters' were written during travels after her husband was appointed Ambassador Extraordinary to the Court of Turkey, in about 1710. Collected into two manuscript volumes they were passed around privately, amongst circles of friends – as was customary for a woman of Lady Montagu's social status – and they gained widespread notoriety and appreciation. When in 1724 her friend, Mary Astell, had the 'Letters' in her possession, she was moved to add a preface to them, praising the fact that they offered a woman's perspective of foreign life, declaring her desire

that the World shou'd see to how much better purpose
the Ladys Travel than their Lords, and that whilst it is
surfeited with Male Travels, all in the same Tone, and
stuft with the same Trifles, a *Lady* has the skill to strike
out a New Path and to embellish a worn-out Subject with
a variety of fresh and elegant Entertainment.

Mary Astell assured future readers that they would find a fresh perspective on travel, 'a more true and accurate account of the customs
and manners of the several nations with whom this Lady conversed,
than he can in any other author'. The 'Embassy Letters' were eventually published posthumously, and against the wishes of Lady Montagu's daughter, in 1763.[2]

Lady Coke and Lady Montagu belonged to the older tradition of
women who chose to keep their personal views on foreign society
relatively private. By the end of the eighteenth century this trend was
changing, as women began to seek a wider and more public audience
for their views on foreigners and the wider, non-domestic world.

The bluestockings of the eighteenth century are not associated with
a body of published works – salon culture was on the whole less
concerned with turning talents into a profession than with promoting
social respectability for women. However, there were exceptions, and
early professional writers were inspirational to future women writers.
In Britain, there were authors such as Aphra Behn, Elizabeth
Inchbald, Eliza Haywood, Catharine Macaulay, or Anna Barbauld.
On the Continent, one could look to Madame de Sévigné, Madame
du Deffand, Julie de Lespinasse and Madeline de Scudéry.

Whether they wished to write salacious romances, scandalous
chronicles, poetry, history, or advice books, women could refer to
previous women for examples in the art of expression. This could
include letter writing, a literary form of its own which went beyond
entertainment to enforce intimate bonds between correspondents.[3]
The letters of Madame de Sévigné to her daughter, for instance, were
popularised both abroad and in Britain when reprinted in multiple

volumes throughout the 1780s in such editions as *Collection des meilleurs Ouvrages François, composées par des Femmes*.[4] By the mid-eighteenth century both male and female spectators were aware of how much more was being published by women. 'There never was perhaps an age wherein the fair sex made so conspicuous a figure with regard to literary accomplishments as in our own,' wrote one observer in the *Critical Review* in 1762, anxiously continuing with the worry that this meant women 'should get the upper hand of us'.[5]

It was gradually becoming acceptable to encourage women to write, as shown in the establishment of women's journals. In France, the *Journal des dames* not only displayed through its distribution the products of a woman's pen, but carried forth messages encouraging their education and declaring that women had the right to be informed about public issues.[6] In Britain, women's periodicals were ephemeral but popped up regularly throughout the century, from the *Female Tatler* (1709–10) to Eliza Haywood's *Female Spectator* (1744–46), Charlotte Lennox's *Ladies Museum* (1760–61), the *Ladies' Mercury* (founded 1693), the *Lady's Monthly Magazine* (1798–99), and the long-running *Lady's Magazine* (1770–1830). Many magazines provided women's perspectives on political and social matters, though – confronting critical opposition – occasionally they were turned into vessels for relaying moral messages about domestic contentment.[7]

Publishing opportunities were growing as were women's literacy rates – reaching an estimated 20 to 40 per cent both in Britain and the Continent. And while there may not have been consensus that women could pursue writing as a career, some did gain fame and wealth from their literary productions. Fanny Burney is of course a famous example, following the hugely successful publication of her novel *Evelina* in 1778, while the publication of *Camilla* (1796) added about another £2,000 to her income. Ann Radcliffe earned £500 from her *Mysteries of Udolpho* (1794) and £600 for *The Italian* (1797). Elizabeth Carter's friends organised a pre-publication subscription to support her translation of Epictetus, which raised £1,000. This is to say nothing of the less financially rewarding but critically acclaimed contributions to the literary world, such as Elizabeth Montagu's well-received *Essay on the Writings and Genius of Shakespear*. So, Mary Wollstonecraft's declaration that 'I am going to be the first of a new genus', when she published her first novel should be taken less as an assessment of the marketplace than the shaping of a burgeoning talent.[8]

'Feminine fiction' – novels preoccupied with domestic issues – is seen as an eighteenth-century creation, often leaving open the question of whether women considered exploring anything else. But women were also confident in tackling travel and adventure stories. Clearly Maria Edgeworth, who visited France twice, was inspired to draw on continental themes. Her novels, including *Leonora, Madame de Fleury, Emilie de Coulanges, Helen* and *Ormond* are populated by French people and set in scenic foreign locales. And a number of women characters travel as part of the narrative of the novel, written by men or women – such as Moll in *Moll Flanders*, Mrs Heartfree in Fielding's *Jonathan Wild*, or Arabella in Charlotte Lennox's *Female Quixote*.

Occasionally, we find that the woman as traveller was itself the subject of the story. In the novel, *Augusta; or the Female Travellers* (1787) we find an attractive and accomplished nineteen-year-old woman, Augusta, who relays accounts of her adventures. After escaping a life of domestic distress, she pursues the idea of living a tranquil and placid life in a convent abroad – 'a harbour wherein I may refit my shattered vessel before I continue on the voyage of life'.[9] So she sets off to Brussels, where she befriends another woman with whom she shares subsequent adventures throughout the Continent, eventually returning to a happier – yet once again 'domesticated' – life at home. This was a unique tale for an age increasingly outspoken about the 'separate spheres' of men and women, and it met with ambivalent reviews. One reviewer predicted it would be of interest to 'many readers', for the variety of entertaining incidents which twist the story rather than its commitment to 'present us with faithful images of men and things' – clever tales, but, another reviewer concluded, 'we have no inclination to open them again'.[10] The novel's mediocre moral or instructional merit did not matter, it was felt, since the author relayed a few good yarns, and the adventures of the admirable heroine were not overly 'heroic'. The author of *Augusta* was one Dr Andrews, a man.

Successful novels breed imitators, and Daniel Defoe's *Robinson Crusoe* (1719) is exemplary in this respect. Defoe himself exploited the success of *Robinson Crusoe*, not only benefiting financially – from the multiple editions of the book – but creatively, by adapting the storyline to dash off the *Farther Adventures of Robinson Crusoe* and the related adventures of *Captain Singleton*.[11] But in 1792 an intriguing variation appeared written by Charles Dibden: *Hannah Hewitt; or, the Female Crusoe*. Written as a diary in the first-person by the heroine, it tells of the adventures of a forty-year-old woman who is shipwrecked on her way to India, and, like Robinson, learns to live by her wits and senses, finding ways to adapt to the natural environment.[12] Unlike Augusta, Hannah Hewitt was a true heroine.

Perhaps unsurprisingly given the sentiment of the period, the book received mixed reviews. The *British Critic* introduced it as 'a series of most wonderful and improbable events' with, at the end, a good moral to the story. But the *Critical Review* lambasted the book, in part for its lacklustre reflection of the original tale ('it does not exhibit the one spark of genius displayed in that celebrated novel'), but also because the woman's adventures, in the reviewer's frank assessment, were 'grossly improbable' – as if those in the original were believable.[13] One could question whether it was because the adventurer was a woman that made it, to the reviewer's mind, 'improbable' and dismissible. And, one wonders, what 'moral' the former reviewer gleaned from the book to make it worthy of reading? After all, readers have declared a variety of morals to be found in Defoe's original tale. Jean-Jacque Rousseau recommended the book as a guide for natural education; Karl Marx used it to explain his theories of labour value.[14] For Gabriel Betteredge, the anxious butler in Wilkie Collins's *The Moonstone* (1868), opening *Robinson Crusoe* provided the answers for any end-of-day moral puzzle.

When women writers wrote about fictional women as travellers, there seemed to be much at stake in determining the moral of the story. Travel represented instability; it potentially altered one's perceptions of daily experience, whether social customs or religious beliefs. Travel was a direct and immediate way to confront cultural diversity, proving that, in the theatre of the world, diverse forms of human behaviour were defensible. One did not need to be a *philosophe* like Montesquieu (whose famous *Persian Letters* pressed this point) to see that travel could subvert the commonplace, the accepted norms, the banal routine of domestic life.

Complaints were only beginning about the fact that women were too preoccupied with fictional romances and corrupting novels that painted portraits of improbable affairs. Now, conservative commentators announced, women were letting loose their imaginations to recreate diverse, and even debauched, corners of society that travellers happen upon: a reality worse than fiction. Mary Ann Hanway, author of *Andrew Stuart, or the Northern Wanderer*, a story that followed the hero on a tour of Scotland, wrote with such attention to local idiosyncrasies and lifestyles that its candour made some readers uncomfortable. Her adaptation of colloquial jargon (referring, for example, to all the 'wee houses' seen on the road) was, to a writer for the *Critical Review*, barely tolerable; but when she allowed a character to describe himself as being 'a knowing one – up to a thing or two – a rum kiddy, that could gammon the deep ones', then the reviewer complained that 'we are sorry to find [such expressions] *even understood* by the softer sex'.[15]

Traveller's accounts were no mere postcard synopses proving their presence abroad, or reminding those at home of their absence. Letter writers strove to establish intimacy with their readers. Nothing in the act of travelling, or writing accounts of one's travels, was taken for granted. The inevitable risks involved with travel were evaluated against the potential rewards. Reading travellers' letters was reading about a physical and moral adventure. 'All this has ye air of a Novel,' Elizabeth Montagu quipped to her sister. It was hoped the reader would be compassionate, if also lenient and tolerant. 'I insist on your sympathising in every event,' she continued, 'for without the accompaniment of Sympathy a long narrative of frivolous matters is the most tiresome thing in the world.'[16]

When in 1776 the young Mary Hamilton made her first trip abroad with family friends, Lord and Lady Dartrey, she was happy to occupy her evenings writing detailed letters home. 'I should, my dearest Mama, write more particularly and acquaint you with *every* occurrence,' she wrote. Alas, her male guardian, who took the party to Spa ostensibly to improve his health, preferred her company for playing games. 'Lord Dartrey,' explained Mary, 'has made some gentle remonstrances against Lady Dartrey and I am spending too much time in scribbling letters, and when we settle for the evening he likes to play at dominoes or some round game.'[17] Lady Bessborough took advantage of her time in transit to pen her letters home from her carriage which was equipped with a portable table.[18]

Some recipients were relieved when the arrival of a letter proved the correspondent was still alive. In turbulent 1790, Horace Walpole begged Mary Berry to train her thoughts and pour the ink from her pen recounting her journey. 'Persons abroad, I know,' said Walpole, 'are often told by their correspondents, who have not the grace of friendship before their eyes, that they did not send them news, concluding they had better information.' But, he prayed, she should indulge his request to be kept abreast of their activities, even at the cost of adding some labour to an already tiresome day of tourism.

> You are young, have much to revisit, many pleasures, I fervently hope, to enjoy; many friends besides to write to, and your healths to re-establish. I certainly have nothing to do that I like half so well as writing to you two. Do but tell me in short notes yr stations, yr motions and intentions, and particularly how you both do, and I shall be content.[19]

Providing accounts of 'stations, motions, and intentions' was, in fact, usually the least that conscientious diarists and correspondents would bother to record. Most took the time and effort to note not only their itinerary, but also to assess and analyse what their trip meant to them, how travel affected their views, tastes, health and happiness. The letter was more than a source of information; it was testimony of the traveller's experiences. In this way, travel writing became an end in itself and the achievement of travelling. Some correspondents felt the burden of that responsibility to observe and record. In Paris in 1795, Helen Williams wrote in her *Memoirs*, 'My pen, wearied of tracing successive pictures of human crimes and human calamity, pursues its task with reluctance, while my heart springs forward to that fairer epoch which now beams upon the friends of liberty.'[20]

Commentators such as Helen Williams or Mary Wollstonecraft, while in the minority as women writers of foreign political affairs, realised that although excuded from formally participating in government, the world of print gave them an opportunity to establish their views. Travel and travel writing provided a powerful platform for such women who wanted their presence in the public domain to be recognised and respected.

Mary Berry – whose everlasting esteem for France was qualified with mixed views about the future of its political and humanitarian principles – put down much that she had learned from over fifty years of travelling in two major publications, her *England and France: A Comparative View . . . from the Restoration of Charles the Second to the French Revolution* (two volumes, published in 1828) and *Social Life in England and France from the Revolution in 1789, to that of July 1830* (1831).[21] While these were the culmination of her travels, she had, some thirty years earlier, declared her intention to chronicle the changing times. 'I am resolved for the future,' she wrote in May 1797, 'to make memoranda of the remarkable circumstances and characters that pass either immediately under my own eyes and knowledge, or . . . such accurate observers, as may satisfy even the steady search and unquenchable desire of truth which has ever existed in my mind.' The great changes occurring throughout Europe – the new systems of social order being forged and the prevailing 'heedless enthusiasm of novelty' – could not go unnoticed, or without historical reflection.

How, she wondered, would her own country fare in this intemperate climate – only 'a hundred years after its complete embellishment' (the restoration of Charles II in 1660). Mary Berry thought the questions, the history, the analysis, and the predictions 'spellbinding'. However, 'my sex and situation condemning me to perfect insignificance, and precluding all possibility of my ever taking an active part', she had only the option of being an observer and recorder. Perhaps, she thought – catching a whiff of the authority she could aspire to – enforced distance would make her 'the more fit to record what I see'.[22]

Distance always helped the traveller clarify her perspective and prose. Offering one's observations to the public was not an automatic intention when reopening the travel diary, nor was moving from personal reflections to public reading straightforward. Preparing for publication – that is, preparing to represent oneself as an observer, a critic, and a travel *writer* – involved considerable editorial intervention. The route to becoming a travel writer involved retracing and *re-writing* the steps that made one a traveller first of all.

When Hester Piozzi announced in a letter from Paris in 1784, during her second continental journey, 'Well! now am I a professed Traveller', she was only half the traveller that she would eventually become. It was not until she gave the public an account of her journey that her identity as a traveller was complete. After returning to England in 1787 following the publication of her *Anecdotes* of Samuel Johnson, the London press was eager to know what she planned to publish next. Perhaps something more on Johnson, they predicted. But what would be very 'curious', thought the *World* (a paper edited by a friend of Hester Piozzi's, Charles Este) on 9 March 1787, 'would be a publication of her travelling anecdotes and observations!' Still waiting a year later, the same newspaper again wrote in anticipation of a publication, but this time – having then recently finished off her *Letters to and from Dr Johnson* (published March 1788) – she was planning to fulfil the prophesy. 'I will write my Travels & publish them – why not?' she asked herself. ''Twill be difficult to content the Italians & the English but I'll try it – & tis something to do.' A leisurely summer trip through Bath and down to Exmouth might just give her the necessary time to prepare her travel journals for publication.

So in June 1788 she sat down with what amounted to seven fresh folio notebooks and began transcribing her foreign journals, which were written into two large, quarto notebooks. By November she had finished the first draft, at which point she neatly recopied the text, making additional revisions, and eventually handing the large, 400-page manuscript to her publisher, Cadell – a publisher with a long list of travel books – which paid 500 guineas for it.[23] In June of 1789, her *Observations and Reflections made in the Course of a Journey through France, Italy, and Germany* was published in two volumes, totalling about 800 pages.

The published *Observations and Reflections* assumed the style of a well-ordered travel diary, with chapters divided by both time and space. But the published account was produced only after a laborious process of borrowing, adapting, rewriting and editing her old journals and the materials collected from others' publications.[24] The exact order of local excursions presented in the written account could not always be taken as the literal path of the traveller. Also questionable at times was the travel writer's claims that their own visit to a foreign city allowed them to penetrate beyond generalisations, since theirs was purportedly a first-hand account. Were reflections, or adjustments in attitude, actually made on the spot, or created retrospectively? When did a traveller assess what she (or he) had learned from their experiences abroad? Answering such questions allows us to glimpse at how the lady of letters established her *authority* as a traveller and travel writer, as was accomplished by Hester Piozzi.

In her 1789 *Observations* Hester Piozzi contemplated the standard of living in Paris and the 'irremeable boundary' that divided the classes of society. Interrupting her thoughts, she declared that her 'Reflections must now give way to facts'. These she then presented, revealing a noisy, compact, shadowy and altogether contradictory Paris. 'Few

English people want to be told that every hotel here, belonging to people of condition,' that is, for the wealthy, are

> shut out from the street like our Burlington-house, which gives a general gloom to the look of this city so famed for its gaiety: the streets are narrow too, and ill-paved; and very noisy, from the echo made by stone buildings drawn up to a prodigious height, many of the houses having seven, and some of them even eight stories from the bottom.

Further contrasting the gloom and gaiety of the city, she wrote of walking through the streets and finding 'a countess in a morning, her hair dressed, with diamonds too perhaps', and in the next street a '*femme publique*, dressed avowedly for the purposes of alluring the men, with not a very small crucifix hanging at her bosom'. Perhaps not wanting to sound overly judgmental, Hester informed her readers that 'I have, however, borrowed Boccage's Remarks upon the English nation, which serve to damp my spirit of criticism exceedingly'. Madame Boccage's *Lettres sur l'Angleterre* was written during a stay in London that 'was longer than mine in Paris', Hester wrote. 'Yet, how was she deceived in many points!' Realising that a French visitor to London presented an inaccurate picture of that town, she was careful not to rush to do the same herself. 'I will tell nothing that I did not *see*,' she assured her readers.[25]

What she did not tell her readers when communicating her 'facts' about what she saw of the contrasts of Pairs in both street life and architecture was that these comments were lifted almost verbatim from the pages of her travel journal, written during her first trip to Paris in 1775 – thirteen years earlier. It was in an entry in her earlier journal dated 1 October 1775 that she first confirmed the opinion of her (then) friend and travelling companion Giuseppe Baretti that 'the Extremes of Magnificence & Meanness meet at Paris', and where she recorded that 'Yesterday I was shewn a Femme Publique dress'd out in a Theatrical Manner for the Purpose of attracting the Men with a *Cricifix* on her Bosom.' Continuing her observations that same day, she described how 'their great Houses are shut off from the

Street in the manner of Burlington House & are said to be princely. I have not yet seen any. Their streets are more noisy than those of London, being narrower one hears every carriage on both sides the way, & there being no Terrace for Footpassengers, they come up close to one's door. The Houses too are so very high that they make an Echo, & every Sound is so reiterated that it stuns one.' And, in fact, it was – according to her 1775 journal – the day before this that she personally met Madame Boccage, and the following morning read through her 'Letters on the English Nation', prompting Hester to determine that 'I will relate only what I see – which can hardly fail of being true.'[26]

Hester had performed an editorial sleight of hand. The thirteen-year discrepancy suggests that what she meant by 'relating only what I see' was that she would provide a synthesis, collecting her assorted observations to create a composite portrait of Parisian society. To this she added the influence of external sources – from James Howell's *Instructions for Forreine Travell* (1642), to Joseph Addison's *Remarks on Several Parts of Italy* (1705), to Martin Sherlock's *Letters from an English Traveller* (1780), and a number of others.[27] She was, of course, not unique in drawing from, verifying, or contradicting other travellers' published accounts. In the flourishing marketplace for travel literature in the latter half of the eighteenth century, travellers literally covered the same ground and consulted the same texts in preparation of their volumes.

Hester Piozzi's account is distinguishable from others in some respects however. First, she was one of only a small clutch of women travel writers – sharing company with Lady Mary Wortley Montagu (*Turkish Embassy Letters*, 1763), Lady Anna Miller (*Letters from Italy*, 1776); Elizabeth Justice (*A Voyage to Russia* 1739); Mrs Vigor (*Letters from a Lady, who Resided some Years in Russia* 1775); Jemima Kindersley (*Letters from the Island of Teneriffe* 1777), and in the same year as Hester Piozzi's *Observations*, 1789, Lady Elizabeth Craven published *A Journey through the Crimea to Constantinople.*[28] She was also distinct in her narrative style. Whereas many other available travel accounts were essentially guidebooks intended to be taken on the road by young gentlemen (the titles are telling: Taylor's *Gentleman's Pocket Companion for Travelling into Foreign Parts* (1722) or Martyn's *Gentleman's Guides* through Italy or France, 1787), Hester wrote about her own experiences. Using the first person singular pronoun throughout, she made it clear that her observations, her views, were what mattered. By publishing her account she declared that she, regardless of how many others have written about the Continent, was an authority.

She had earlier deliberated whether to present herself as an individual travel writer and diarist or as a member of a group. At one point in her 1775 journal written in Paris, she recalled the day's tour through art galleries, which, she wrote (correcting herself), 'had filled ~~my~~ our Eyes with delight among the Duke of Orlean's Pictures where the School of Titian had for an hour's Time or two glow'd *in ~~my~~ our Sight & Triumphed in ~~my~~ our Soul* – they led ~~me~~ us to a grand Gallery – for the conclusion – the bonne bouche as they call'd it . . .'. She may have believed that by presenting her words as the views of a group, rather than a lone female, they gained greater authority.[29]

By and large Hester Piozzi's *Observations and Reflections* contains less 'observation' – descriptive accounts of scenery or objects – than 'reflections', where she enthusiastically tells the reader what she thought of her experiences. Whereas male travel writers seemed more concerned with analysing the politics and topography of the countries they visited–what they called *viaggiono con profitto* (travel for improvement) – ladies of the Grand Tour had other, less affected, interests. As the Duchess of Northumberland's observations show, they saw and noticed what men did not; they paid attention to people, especially to the lifestyles of foreign women. This is why Mary Astell celebrated Lady Mary Wortley Montagu's 'Embassy Letters', which bestowed heartfelt praise on Turkish women ('who are', Montagu wrote, 'perhaps, freer than any ladies in the universe').[30]

Hester Piozzi's account was likewise intimate in its portrayal of the people she met. When she and her husband settled in a comfortable house in Milan for the winter of 1784, she expressed her delight at what she immediately saw as a 'chance to gain that insight into every day behaviour, and common occurrences, which can alone be called knowing something of a country'; this, she thought, was much better than 'counting churches, pictures, palaces', and so forth, such as was done 'by those who run from town to town'. When she went on to recall her insights into 'every day behaviour', however, she wrote with a particular audience in mind. After a brief discussion of the role of birth and culture in ascertaining a man or woman's rank in Italian society, she stopped – apparently considering who her readers would be. 'But my country-women would rather hear a little of our *intérieur*,' she declared, 'or, as we call it, family management,' whereby she described how Italian women were less involved in the organisation of domestic affairs than she expected.

Women, she was gradually learning, commanded a different measure of respect in Italian society; there was 'attention paid to the wife that no Englishwoman can form an idea of', she wrote. Repeatedly she offered particular observations of women's behaviour and customs. But in Milan she was corrected by her Italian servant and made to understand the difference, in colloquial parlance, between a *dama* – a lady, and a mere woman of wealth. Observing a rich banker's wife and, 'contemptuously smiling at [Hester's] simplicity', he explained to his mistress that the woman in question was 'no lady'. 'If you look' he said, 'the servants carry no velvet stool for her to kneel upon, and they have no coat armour in the lace to their liveries: *she* a lady! Repeated he again with infinite contempt.'

Hester was also surprised by Venetian attitudes towards the wearing of make-up: Venetian women 'are not behind-hand in the art of gaining admirers', she observed, but 'they do not, like their painters, depend on *colouring* to ensure it'. Like Lady Mary Wortley Montagu seventy years earlier, Hester Piozzi never quite came to terms with the Italian custom of *cicisbeism* – when a married woman had a male companion accompany her to social outings, and was even sometimes her lover ('Well!', she concluded on that topic, 'we will not send people to [Italy] to study delicacy or very refined morality to be sure').[31] Arguably Hester's care in portraying the Italian people in detail was because her husband was Italian. '*I*,' she stressed, 'ought to learn that which before us lies in daily life, if proper use were made of my demi-naturalization.' But she also repeatedly made it clear that she was writing with special regard to the interests of women readers back home.[32]

Some of Piozzi's readers found her narrative style annoying, however. The intimacy and frankness of her 'observations and reflections' seemed to many to violate publishing etiquette. Within the flutter of reviews of her work that appeared in the newspapers and monthly magazines, her book was variously criticised for being pretentious and packed with 'ungraceful terms' (*Monthly Review*), 'colloquial barbarisms' (*Town and Country Magazine*), and, hyper-critically, 'such mean and vacant terms as "*to be sure*", "*sweet creature*", "*lovely theatre*", "*though*", "*vastly*", "*exactly*", "*so*", "*charming*", "*dear, dear*", and many others' (*European Magazine*).[33] Horace Walpole, never a fan of Hester Piozzi, repeatedly condemned the 'vulgarity' of the book. He took the opportunity to renew his critique a few years later when Piozzi was preparing to publish a book on English synonyms, offering to Mary Berry: 'Methinks she had better have studied them before she stuffed her travels with so many vulgarisms!'[34]

Hester Piozzi received a mixed reception from the bluestockings. Hannah More wrote to Elizabeth Montagu (who had been godmother to Piozzi's youngest daughter, who died in 1783 at four years old), a month after its publication, 'I have finished Madame Piozzi and found in almost every page amusement and disgust; very sprightly and shining passages debased by the most vulgar colloquial barbarisms; much wit spoilt by much affectation; some learning rendered disgusting by insufferable pedantry.'[35] Elizabeth Montagu then received a letter from Elizabeth Carter, who thought Piozzi 'writ with spirit, acuteness, and much sensible observation. The style is sometimes elegant, sometimes colloquial and vulgar, and strangely careless in the grammatical part, which one should not expect from the writer's classical knowledge'.[36] The poet Anna Seward was also disturbed by what she considered compositional laziness from a writer with more professional capabilities. In late December 1789 she wrote to Piozzi offering qualified praise of the book. 'Suffer me now to speak to you of your highly ingenious, instructive, and entertaining publication with the sincerity of friendship.' She continued:

> No work of the sort I ever read possesses, in an equal degree, the power of placing the reader in the scenes, and amongst the people it describes. Wit, knowledge, and imagination illuminate its pages – but the infinite inequality of the style! ... those strange *dids*, and *dos*, and *thoughs*, and *toos*, which produce jerking angles, and stop-short abruptness, fatal at once to the grace and ease of the sentence ... With what pleasure should I see this your cluster of intellectual jewels, appearing through future editions, in cloudless brilliance! That done, and The Travels of Mrs. Piozzi will be one of the first ornaments of that class of reading.[37]

The book also met with unqualified praise: the *London Chronicle*, for example, was eager to print regular excerpts from 'this entertaining work', as did other papers. One sympathetic soul was William Cowper, who, when reading Piozzi's publication to an after-supper group, commented that 'It is the fashion, I understand, to condemn them. But we who make books ourselves are more merciful to book-makers.'[38]

Indeed, criticism was expected by all authors, and Piozzi was not alone in receiving it. Her predecessor, Lady Anna Miller, was not exempt when she published her *Letters from Italy*. The bluestocking Mary Delany was told that her work was considered 'very conceited ... and not worth buying'. The pernickety Horace Walpole was bothered by the number of grammatical and linguistic errors that confounded the text. 'The poor Arcadian patroness[39] does not spell one word of French or Italian right through her three volumes of Travels,' he complained in a letter to Sir Horace Mann.[40]

But the lady of letters knew how to handle criticism. Travel writing was not just about how the woman wrote, but about how she chose to live her life.[41] This Hester Piozzi managed well, and even antici- pated the natural trajectory of her book's career. 'You will like the description of Naples best,' she wrote to a friend, after just finishing off the first draft, 'but there will be great Censure upon the whole, *that* I expect and shall willingly compound for. The first thing for a book is to be *read*, the second to be *praised*, the third to be criticised – but the irremediable Misfortune is – *to be forgotten*.'[42] Happily, her book was not forgotten, and Piozzi was quite happy with its reception. Six months after the publication of her book, she entered into her diary 'I think my Observations & Reflections in Italy, &c., have been, upon the whole, exceedingly well liked, and much read'.[43]

Whatever the petty complaints and criticisms, there was support to be found from the emerging women's literary community, and travel writing potentially stimulated other aspiring authors. Just as Piozzi had read Lady Mary Wortley Montagu's writings, so the future travel writer Ann Radcliffe read Piozzi, and was said to have culled from it the geographical detail that provided the scenery for 'marvellous Italy' in her *The Mysteries of Udolpho* (1794).[44] That same year Radcliffe went abroad for the first time, travelling with her husband through Holland to Germany (where, despite hopes of reaching Switzerland, they were forced to return home under suspicion of being spies), and in 1795 she published her own travel book, *A Journey Made in the Summer of 1794*.

Hester Piozzi was also one of the first of many to experience the delights of success as a woman travel writer. Mariana Starke's two-volume *Letters from Italy*, published in 1800, was only a precursor to the multiple editions of her informative guide books, *Travels on the Continent*, which were issued throughout the nineteenth century. These books, in which she graded the degree to which she recommended sites by the amount of exclamation points next to their names, established her identity and career as a travel writer, and give her publisher, John Murray, the idea of launching his own guide books to the Continent.[45]

With the nineteenth century came the boom in women's published travel writing. These later generations of women had different opportunities to their predecessors. 'There are peculiar powers inherent in ladies' eyes,' wrote Lady Elizabeth Eastlake in an 1845 article titled 'Lady Travellers', 'that power of observation which, so long as it remains at home counting canvass stitches by the fireside [is not apt to be considered very shrewd] but which once removed from the familiar scene, and returned to us in the shape of letters of books, seldom fails to prove its superiority.' Men now had literary rivals, with women rapidly capturing the interest of readers who were growing bored with an all-male view of the world. Simply compare the travel books written by each, Lady Eastlake suggested. The 'gentleman's [are] either dull or matter-of-fact, or off-hand and superficial', while 'the lady's – all ease, animation, vivacity, with the tact to dwell upon what you most want to know, and the sense to pass over what she does not know herself'.[46]

The stock of knowledge continued to increase. Women such as Louisa Stuart Costello (now known as the 'first professional lady travel writer'[47]), Lady Sydney Morgan, or even Marianne Colston (who published an account of her honeymoon trip through Europe with a Paris press in 1822) were amongst the many women who were publishing more and more accounts of their world-wide travels. These later women travel writers owe much to their eighteenth-century predecessors who went one step beyond mere travelling to create an identity for themselves as ladies of letters. But men and women alike can appreciate their expressions – for everyone is a traveller and on a road to enlightenment. As Serena Holroyd wrote to her niece, Maria (daughter of Lord Sheffield), on her eighteenth birthday:

> I shall mark it down in my book of Events, that in the year 1789, not only the 'Lord Sheffield,' but also his dear little Sloop 'Maria' was launched upon the uncertain Ocean of the world, where she escaped the 'Rocks of Folly,' and gently steered aright to the 'Harbour of Peace,' without loss or damage, in full enjoyment of all her best tackle. May her Voyage through Life be equally happy![48]

Dramatis Personae

MARY BERRY (1763–1852): sister of Agnes (1764–1852) and daughter of Robert Berry. Her mother died in childbirth. After receiving an ignominious inheritance from her uncle upon the death of her great-uncle in 1783, she, Agnes and their father set off for the Continent. In 1788 she befriended Horace Walpole, whose 'literary remains' she edited and published in five volumes in 1798. Her career as an author and editor continued with an ill-starred comedy *Fashionable Friends* (1802); *Letters of Madam du Deffand* (1810); *A Biographical Account and Selected Letters of Rachel, Lady Russell* (1815) and her *Comparative Social Life in England and France* (1828). Mary and her sister were known in London society for their fashionable salon, run first at Audley Street, then Curzon Street, whose patrons included the Duke of Wellington. Mary and her sister remained unmarried. She travelled to the Continent five times: 1783–5; 1790–1; 1802; 1802–3 and 1816.

LADY BESSBOROUGH: *see* Lady Harriet Duncannon

ELIZABETH CARTER (1717–1806): was taught Greek, Latin and Hebrew by her father, the Revd Dr Nicholas Carter. She befriended Samuel Johnson and contributed to his periodical *The Rambler*. She was the author of *Poems for Peculiar Occasions* (1738), *An Ode to Wisdom* (1761) and in 1758 translated the complete works of Epictetus. She was close friends with other bluestocking women, including Catherine Talbot and Elizabeth Montagu. She never married and was famed for taking snuff to stay awake during long hours of study.

LADY MARY COKE (1726–1811): the fifth and youngest daughter of
John Campbell, 2nd Duke of Argyll and Jane Warburton. In 1747
she married Edward, Viscount Coke, heir apparent to the 1st
Earl of Leicester. The marriage, however, was a disaster; they
separated in 1749 and Edward died four years later. She was a
regular visitor to court, but after the death of the Duke of York
(with whom there was speculation – partly encouraged by Lady
Coke – she had been having an affair) she spent much time
travelling on the Continent.

FRANCES CREWE née Greville (1760–1818): the eldest of the six
daughters of Fulke Greville and Frances McCartney. She travelled
to Paris in 1772 and again in 1785–6. In the 1784 general election
she helped Lady Harriet Duncannon and Georgiana, Duchess of
Devonshire, to canvas for Charles James Fox for his Westminster
constituency. By 1791 her political views were closer to those of
Edmund Burke and henceforth she supported the Portland
Whigs. In 1806 her husband, John, was created 1st Baron Crewe.

LADY HENRIETTA (HARRIET) FRANCES DUNCANNON, née
Spencer, later Lady Bessborough (1761–1821): daughter of Lord
and Lady Spencer and sister to Georgiana, Duchess of Devonshire. In November 1780 she married Frederick, Viscount
Duncannon, but had a largely unhappy marriage due to his abusive behaviour, her love affairs (including a liaison with Richard
Brinsley Sheridan) and their debts. Upon the death of her father-
in-law in 1793, they inherited the title Lord and Lady Bessborough, along with an income which considerably improved their
situation. They had four children: John William Ponsonby
(b.1781), Frederick (b.1783), Caroline (b.1785) and William (b.1787).
With her lover, Lord Granville Leveson Gower she had a daughter, Harriet Stewart (1800–1852) and a son, George Stewart
(d.1870). She wrote a novel, *Ada Regis* (1804) and travelled to the
Continent three times between 1791 and 94 and again in 1802,
1803, 1816 and finally in 1821, to Florence, where she died.

MARIA EDGEWORTH (1768–1849): the eldest of twenty-two children. At the prompting of her father, Richard Lovell Edgeworth, she wrote the educational tracts *The Parents' Assistant* (1796) and *Moral Tales for Young People* (1798) and collaborated with him to produce *Practical Education* (1798). Championing domesticity, she was not a radical feminist but nevertheless favoured education for both sexes. She never married (despite being taken to France by her father in the hope of finding a suitor), preferring to remain with her father and extended family at their estate in Edgeworthstown, Ireland. In 1802, during the Peace of Amiens, she travelled to Paris. She also wrote several novels including *Castle Cockrent* (1800), *Ennui* (1809) and *The Absentee* (1812). Upon her father's death in 1817 she declared that 'her motivation for writing had gone'. Nevertheless, she edited his memoirs in 1820 and produced a final novel, *Helen* (1834).

MARY 'HAMMY' HAMILTON (1756–1816): the niece of Sir William Hamilton, British Ambassador to Naples. At the age of twenty she travelled to Flanders and Belgium. A year later she joined the court of Queen Charlotte as sub-governess to her daughters, where she was pursued by an infatuated Prince of Wales. Upon leaving court in 1782 she befriended the Veseys and became involved in the bluestocking circle. In 1785 she married John Dickenson.

LADY HOLLAND: *see* Lady Webster

ELLIS CORNELIA KNIGHT (1757–1837): chiefly educated by her father, an admiral, she published her first novel, *Dinarbus*, in 1790. She spent sixteen years living in Italy before returning to England to become lady companion to the aged Queen Charlotte. She then spent a year, less happily, in the service of Princess Charlotte. In 1814 she resumed the life of a continental traveller. After the restoration of the Bourbons, she toured France and Italy; she died in Paris in 1837. Her other works included the novels *Marcus Flamnus* (1792) and *Sir Guy de Lusignan* (1833). Her autobiography was published posthumously in 1861.

LADY ANNA MILLER (1741–81): with her husband, John, built a house in Batheaston. Following their return from the Continent, they opened their house to fashionable visitors to Bath who participated in *bouts-rimés* parties. Her three-volume *Letters from Italy* was published in 1776 and 1777, and she edited four volumes of collected poems composed during the parties. In 1778 her husband was made Baronet of Ireland and the title 'Lady' was extended to Anna as a courtesy.

ELIZABETH MONTAGU (1720–1800): daughter of Thomas Robinson and Elizabeth Duke. She was educated at home, first by her father but later by Dr Congers Middleton ('the best judge of prose in his day', according to Alexander Pope). In 1742 she married a man nearly thirty years her senior, Edward Montagu of Allerthorp, the fifth son of the 1st Earl of Sandwich. Their only son died in infancy. On the death of her husband in 1774 she inherited a vast estate, including a property in Sandleford, Berkshire, which she had rebuilt in the Gothic style on the advice of her friend Horace Walpole, and she also had built Montagu House in Portman Square in London. As the 'Queen of the Bluestockings', she was a much admired *femme d'esprit*, leading Dr Beattie to pronounce: 'I have known several ladies in literature, but she excelled them all; and in conversation she had more wit than any other person, male or female.' Her most significant work was the *Essay on the Writings and Genius of Shakespear* (1769), but she also contributed to Lord George Lyttleton's *Dialogues of the Dead* (1760). She was a noted philanthropist, holding an annual May Day dinner for the chimney sweeps of London. She died during a 'fainting fit', apparently brought on by an 'immoderate dose of eau de luce'.

HANNAH MORE (1745–1833): the fourth daughter of Jacob More and Mary Grace, she was educated by her father, a headmaster, in order that she and her four sisters could support themselves by founding a day school. In 1786 she wrote the poem 'Bas Bleu; Or, Conversation', in celebration of the salon society headed by Elizabeth Montagu. She later befriended members of the evangelical Clapham Sect, including the philanthropist William Wilberforce, who persuaded her to join the anti-slavery movement. Her works range from plays (such as *The Search After Happiness*, 1773), to political tracts (*Village Politics*, 1792, in which she criticised Thomas Paine) – to religious works (*Practical Piety*, 1818). In *Strictures on the Modern System of Female Education* (1799), she advocated full education for both sexes.

LADY NORTHUMBERLAND, ELIZABETH SEYMOUR PERCY, later the Duchess of Northumberland (1716–1776): daughter and only surviving child of Algernon, 7th Duke of Somerset and Frances Thynne. In 1740 she married Sir Hugh Smithson (who became 1st Duke of Northumberland, third creation in 1766). Sir Hugh, an agricultural improver, gained the favour of King George III, and was appointed to the post of Lord Chamberlain to Queen Charlotte. He died in 1786. The Duchess of Northumberland was for many years a lady of the bedchamber to Queen Charlotte during which time she kept detailed diaries of court life. Eventually she fell out of favour with the Queen, and in 1770 resigned her position and travelled through Europe with her dog Tizzy.

HESTER PIOZZI, earlier Thrale, née Salusbury (1741–1821): her early poems were published anonymously in the *St James Chronicle*. In 1762 she married Henry Thrale, a brewer; they had twelve children. She travelled abroad for the first time in 1775 with her husband, her friend Dr Johnson and her eldest daughter Queeny. Widowed in 1781 she married the Italian musician, Gabriel Piozzi, to the grave disappointment of her friends, who included Oliver Goldsmith, Elizabeth Montagu and Fanny Burney. She and her new husband left England for Italy in 1784 and returned in 1787. Two years later she had published *Observations and Reflections on a Journey Through France, Italy and Germany.* In 1795 the couple retired to Wales and she went on to write the political pamphlets 'Three Warnings to John Bull Before He Dies' (1798) and 'Retrospect' (1801).

MARIANA STARKE (*c.*1762–1838): born in Surrey, she grew up in Madras, India, where her father was governor at Fort St George. Her plays *The Sword of Peace* (1788) and *The Widow of Malabar* (1798) were both based on her experiences in India. In 1792 she set out for Italy, accompanying a sick relative who hoped the warm southern climes would help relieve the effects of consumption. In 1800 the first of her travel writings were published: the two-volume *Letters from Italy Between the Years 1792 and 1798*, in which she provided practical details for tourists' survival on the road. From the 1820s onwards she frequently returned to the Continent to update her research and thereon published a series of companion guides, entitled *Travels on the Continent*, which ranked sites of interest with exclamation points, and provided tips for travellers on hotels, prices, transport and foreign phrases. These guides set the standard for the genre, including her publisher's own highly successful tourist books, the famous *Redbooks* by John Murray. She died in Milan, on a journey from Naples to England, aged seventy-six.

ELIZABETH VESEY (1715–91): the daughter of the Bishop of Ossory, she was first married to William Handcock and then to Agmondesham Vesey MP. In 1756 she met Elizabeth Montagu, a friend and rival *salonnière*, in London.

LADY WEBSTER, née Vassall, later Lady Holland (1771–1845): daughter of Jamaican-born Richard Vassall and May Clark. In 1786 she married Sir Godfrey Webster, thirty-four years her senior. One year later she travelled to the Continent for the first time. Acutely unhappy in her marriage she spent most of her time travelling abroad. During the course of her various travels she met Lady Bessborough, beginning a close friendship. With Lord Webster she had two children, Godfrey (b.1789) and Henry (b.1792). With her lover, Thomas Pelham she had a daughter (Harriet Frances, b.1794). In 1797 she was divorced from Lord Webster and married Henry Richard Fox, 3rd Lord Holland, with whom she had already had an illegitimate son (Charles Richard Fox, b.1796); they had three more children (Henry Edward Fox, b.1802, Mary Fox, b.1806 and Georgina, b.1809). As a divorcee she was never received at court. Lord and Lady Holland prioritised their political activities and foreign travel over their family life, which led to long absences and alienation from their children. ('I hate my son; I don't like my daughter,' she allegedly declared to Lord John Russell in defence of her callous last will and testament.) She died five years after her husband.

HELEN MARIA WILLIAMS (*c.*1761–1827): daughter of a British army officer and a first generation French Huguenot immigrant to Scotland. Her most enduring legacy remains her voluminous letters from France which reveal a deep-rooted belief that 'Enlightenment' would emerge out of the French Revolution – which 'she loved'. She took up residence in Paris in 1791. Like Mary Wollstonecraft (who admired Williams as a writer before meeting her in Paris in early 1793), she became politically disillusioned and her attitudes changed when she witnessed the horrors of the Terror. Her reflections are charted in her eight-volume *Letters Containing a Sketch of the Politics of France* (1794). She was also a minor novelist, essayist, translator and poet. With the exception of a six-month stay in Switzerland during the Terror, she stayed in Paris, running her salon, which remained popular until the early nineteenth century.

MARY WOLLSTONECRAFT (1759–1797): the eldest of six daughters. She and her sisters suffered considerably at the hands of their drunken and violent father, Edward Wollstonecraft, a silk weaver and failed farmer. After a brief spell as a lady's companion to

Mrs Dawson of Bath, she founded a day school in Islington in 1783 and four years later produced *Thoughts on the Education of Daughters*. Greatly influenced by the French Revolution she wrote *The Vindication of the Rights of Man* (1790), and in response to Edmund Burke she wrote the polemical tract *The Vindication of the Rights of Woman* (1792). In December 1792 she travelled to Paris and witnessed the Terror first hand. Whilst there she began a love affair with the American entrepreneur, Gilbert Imlay, which resulted in the birth of a daughter, Fanny. Imlay deserted her in 1795 and she returned to London, where she attempted suicide by jumping off Putney Bridge. A year later she married the socialist and feminist writer William Godwin when pregnant with his child. She died of an infection caught during the birth of their daughter, the future Mary Shelley, who herself became a traveller and travel writer.

Notes

Chapter Two: Education & Improvement

1 This phrase has been introduced by various authors: see Chard, *Pleasure and Guilt on the Grand Tour*, p. 10; also Langdon, 'The Imaginative Geographies of Claude Lorrain', in Chard and Langdon (eds), *Transports*, pp. 151–78, which develops a theme of painters' metaphors in the depiction of classical landscapes.

2 Bloom and Bloom (eds), *The Piozzi Letters*, p. i, 176. Most of Gibbon's six-volume *Decline and Fall of the Roman Empire* (1776–88) was in print at this time.

3 Tillyard, *Aristocrats*, p. 252, for Caroline Lennox's Grand Tours; also, The Earl of Ilchester (ed.), *Journal of Elizabeth Lady Holland*, i, pp. 135–6.

4 Piozzi, *Observations and Reflections*, p. 118.

5 For a discussion of a lady's educational potential in the seventeenth century, see George, *Women in the First Capitalist Society*, particularly chapter 14.

6 Lewis, (ed.), *Journals and Correspondence of Miss Berry*, ii, p. 313.

7 Ibid., i, p. 4.

8 The following biographical account is taken from Mary Berry's autobiographical notes, reproduced in ibid., i, pp. 1–15, and the supplementary account from Melville, (ed.), *The Berry Papers*, pp. 1–11.

9 Lewis, (ed.), op. cit., i, pp. 9–10.

10 British Library, MSS Add. 37726, f. 7.

11 Lewis, (ed.), op. cit., i, p. 10.

12 Ibid., i, pp. 5, 10.

13 Gay, *The Enlightenment: The Science of Freedom*, p. 24.

14 Berry, *Social Life in England and France*, ii, p. 94.

15 Though, as Acomb points out in *Anglophobia in France*, we should recognise that despite the existence of French critics of the *ancien régime* who celebrated England's liberalism, there did also emerge an 'anti-Anglophile party'.

16 Tomaselli, 'Enlightenment Debate on Women'.

17 Quoted in Tinker, *Salon and British Letters*, p. 55.

18 Lewis (ed.), *Horace Walpole's Correspondence*, xxxi, p. 76.

19 Adams, *The Paris Years of Thomas Jefferson*, p. 215; Hemlow (ed.), *Journals and Letters of Fanny Burney*, v, p. 73.

20 Quoted in Mowl, *Horace Walpole*, p. 250.

21 Lewis (ed.), *Journals and Correspondence of Miss Berry*, i, pp. 8, 11.

22 Ibid., i, p. 134.

23 For a list of notable encounters drawn from the entries in her travel diary see Melville (ed.), op. cit., pp. 205–6.

24 See the fascinating biographical reference work, de Beer, *Travellers in Switzerland*, for different types of tourists.

25 Lewis, (ed.), op. cit., i, p. 131.

26 Walpole to Lady Ossory, 11 October 1788, in Melville (ed.), op. cit., p. 14.

27 Lewis (ed.), op. cit., ii, p. 313.

28 Anson and Anson (eds.), *Mary Hamilton*, pp. 249–50.

29 Hufton, *The Prospect Before Her*, pp. 82–3.

30 Climenson, *Elizabeth Montagu*, ii, p. 79.

31 Blunt (ed.), *Mrs. Montagu*, i, p. 321.

32 Ibid., ii, p. 53, in a letter to Benjamin Stillingfleet from Spa, 9 August 1763.

33 William Spencer Cavendish to Mary Berry, 30 January 1803, in Lewis (ed.), op. cit., ii, p. 235.

34 Bell (ed.), *The Hamwood Papers*, p. 65, 139.

35 Anson and Anson (eds), op. cit., p. 225, 231.

26 Brewer, *Pleasures of the Imagination*, pp. 78–9.

37 For a discussion of women's clubs and same-sex sociability see Clark, *British Clubs* and Roberts, 'Pleasures Engendered by Gender'.

38 See Myers, 'Learning, Virtue, and the Term "Bluestocking"', and also her extended survey of the use of the term to the present day in *The Bluestocking Circle*.

39 Horace Walpole quoted in Bodek, 'Salonnières and Bluestockings', p. 194; Ford, *Hannah More*, pp. 65–9.

40 Chapone, *Letters on the Improvement of the Mind*. Her reading regimen is cited in Scott, *Bluestocking Ladies*, p. 76.

41 See Taylor, 'Introduction', pp. xi–xii.

42 Wollstonecraft, Mary, *Vindication of the Rights of Woman*, chapter 5.

43 Goodwin, *Friends of Liberty*; Philip (ed.), *French Revolution and British Popular Politics*.

44 Mary Berry, having read one immediately after the other, commented on the 'amazing' points of agreement between Hannah More and Mary Wollstonecraft,: Lewis (ed.), op. cit., ii, pp. 91–2.

45 More, *Strictures on Female Education*, i, p. 183.

46 Roberts, *Life and Correspondence of Hannah More*, ii, p. 372.

47 More, op. cit., i, pp. 63–4.

48 More, op. cit., ii, p. 28, and More, 'A Comparative View of Both Sexes', p. 14.

49 More, *Strictures on Female Education*, ii, 'The Practical Uses of Female Knowledge', pp. 1–2.

50 Edgeworth, *Letters to Literary Ladies*, p. 2.

51 Reviewer in the *Monthly Review*, June 1758, quoted in Myers, op. cit., pp. 169–70. See also her chapter 6 on Elizabeth Carter's achievements as an essayist, translator and poet.

52 Kowaleski-Wallace, *Their Fathers' Daughters*, pp. 99–107.

53 Edgeworth, op. cit., p. 26.

54 Home (ed.), *Letters and Journals of Lady Mary Coke*, ii, p. 234 and iii, pp. 4, 53.

55 This collection is mentioned in Blank and Todd, introduction to Charlotte Smith's *Desmond*, p. xxii. See also Rogers, *Feminism in Eighteenth-Century England*, p. 27.

56 The Earl of Ilchester (ed.), op. cit., i, pp. 158–9, 192.

57 Bury, *Diary of a Lady-in-Waiting*, i, p. 29.

58 Freemantle (ed.), *Wynne Diaries*, i, pp. 174–5.

59 Anson and Anson (eds), op. cit., p. 236.

60 Contemporary observation quoted in Foote, 'Sir Humphry Davy'.

61 The Earl of Ilchester (ed.), op. cit., ii, p. 52.

62 Findlen, 'Translating the New Science'.

63 Shteir, 'Botanical Dialogues', pp. 309–10.

64 Lazarus to Edgeworth, 6 January 1827, in MacDonald, *Education of the Heart*, p. 114.

65 Fordyce, *Sermons to Young Women*, i, p. 89.

66 Urania from Hannah More's play, quoted in Ford, *Hannah More*, p. 13.

67 Sarah Dickenson to Mary Hamilton, 21 January 1771, cited in Anson and Anson (eds), op. cit., p. 9.

68 William Napier to Mary Hamilton, August 1772, in ibid., p. 17. Her secret had already been revealed: 'Don't be alarmed,' wrote Sarah Dickenson, 'if I tell you that your learning Latin is no

secret, Mr. Lawton mentioned it to me, but without any reflections, as he has the highest opinion of you imaginable.' But, she went on to advise her friend not to dispense with her social duties by living in a dead poet's society: 'do not study as to hurt your health, remember we are creatures formed for Society & that we must not so wholly converse with old Authors, as to neglect the cheerful conversation of our acquaintance.'

69 Anne Damer to Mary Berry, February 1791, in Lewis (ed.), op. cit., i, pp. 334–5.

70 Fulford (ed.), *Autobiography of Miss Knight*, pp. 25–6.

71 Mangin quoted in Hayward (ed.), *Autobiography*, i, p. 49, who mentioned that Hester Thrale did not know Greek.

72 Gray, *Papers and Diaries*, pp. 257–8.

73 See Cohen, *Fashioning Masculinity*, for more on this point, particularly with regard to 'accomplishment' in learning languages.

74 Myers, 'Learning, Virtue, and the term 'Bluestocking', p. 281.

75 Chapone, op. cit., p. 187.

76 More, *Strictures on Female Education*, i, p. 140.

77 Ibid., i, pp. 136, 142.

78 Ibid., i, pp. 40–41.

79 Lewis (ed.), op. cit., ii, p. 262.

80 Michaelson, 'Women in the Reading Circle'.

81 The Earl of Ilchester (ed.), op. cit., i, pp. 206, 236.

82 Edgeworth, op. cit., p. 27.

83 Lewis (ed.), op. cit., ii, p. 313.

84 See Bermingham, 'Culture and self-image', for what she refers to as 'the customs of display associated with the marriage market'.

85 Vickery, *Gentleman's Daughter*, p. 269, discusses the idea that marriage 'liberated women from the burden of chaperonage'. Maria Edgeworth did, in fact, receive her only marriage proposal while on that trip to France in 1802, but she turned the Swedish 'royal secretary' down: see Colvin,

Maria Edgeworth in France and Switzerland, p. x.

86 I have developed this point elsewhere, arguing that the last decades of the eighteenth century witnessed the 'death' of the Grand Tour for gentlemen, when travel and travel writing about Europe became focused on scientific and natural historical concerns; see Dolan, *Exploring European Frontiers*.

87 Eustace, *Tour through Italy*, i, p. xix.

88 More, op. cit., i, p. 31; More, *Moral Sketches*, p. 18. Though Hannah More did suggest that a carefully selected reading list could be acceptable: 'History, well-chosen travels, select biographical works, furnish not only harmless, but profitable reading.' She did not, however, suggest titles; More, ibid., p. 225.

89 More, *Strictures on Female Education*, i, pp. 44, 192, 163–4.

90 *Imperial Review*, i (1804), p. 631.

91 For an analysis of how classical discourse of the enlightenment contributed to 'women's suppression', see Salvaggio, *Enlightened Absences*.

Chapter Three: Liberty & Independence

1 Quoted in Taylor, 'Introduction', p. vii.

2 Wollstonecraft, *Vindication of the Rights of Woman*, p. 69.

3 Quoted from Rousseau's *Emile*, in ibid., p. 93.

4 Ibid., p. 60.

5 Ibid., p. 51.

6 Ibid., p. 169.

7 Ibid., p. 201.

8 Wardle (ed.), *Collected Letters of Mary Wollstonecraft*, p. 218.

9 For the relationship between Wollstonecraft's life and writings, see Todd, *Mary Wollstonecraft*; also Poovey, *The Proper Lady and the Woman Writer*.

10 Wardle (ed.), op. cit., p. 159.

11 Ibid., p. 152.

12 Ibid., p. 173.

13 Ibid., p. 186.

14 Wardle, *Mary Wollstonecraft: A Critical Biography*, p. 174.

15 Todd, op. cit., p.185. I am indebted to Professor Janet Todd for drawing my attention to this point.

16 From Godwin's *Memoir*, partly reprinted in Wollstonecraft, op. cit., *Vindication of the Rights of Woman* (Tauchert, ed.), p. 322.

17 Todd, op. cit., pp. 195, 199.

18 Wardle (ed.), *Collected Letters of Mary Wollstonecraft*, p. 230.

19 Ibid., p. 230 n4.

20 Ibid., p. 218.

21 Ibid., p. 233.

22 But see, for example, Labbe, 'A Family Romance'.

23 Piozzi, *Observations and Reflections*, p. xxvi.

24 More, *Strictures on Female Education*, p. 107.

25 Quoted in Stone, *The Family, Sex and Marriage*, p. 217.

26 Of course, there were many other sorts of employment for women in the eighteenth century – from servants to agrarian labourers – that fall short of the more privileged choices I here refer to. For background analysis on this, see Hill, *Women, Work, and Sexual Politics in Eighteenth-Century England*.

27 Edgeworth, *Letters for Literary Ladies*, p. 20.

28 Chapone, *Letters on the Improvement of the Mind*, p. 111.

29 Historians such as Peter Gay, but most vociferously Lawrence Stone, have argued that the eighteenth century saw the demise of the patriarchal family and the rise of the friendly, companionate, egalitarian nuclear family. Other historians have taken issue as to whether the new family structure was unique to the eighteenth century, stressing continuities with the seventeenth century and criticising the supposed causal links in the demographic conditions that allegedly gave rise to the nuclear family. I do not suggest that marriages based on mutual affection and emotional ties did not exist, nor do I take the extreme opposite position and argue that only mercenary marriages existed. Rather, here I choose to underscore how, in the eighteenth century, companionship in marriage was an Enlightenment ideal representing secular values and rational management of the emotions. This point is further developed below. See Gay, *The Enlightenment: The Science of Freedom*, pp. 31–3; Stone, *Family, Sex and Marriage*, especially chapter eight for 'The Companionate Marriage'; one recent critique of Stone's thesis of the rise of the nuclear family in the eighteenth century is Vickery, *Gentleman's Daughter*, chapter two, p. 306 n5.

30 Chapone, *Letters on the Improvement of the Mind*, p. 112; for the role of conduct books in mediating pleasure, see Jones, 'Seductions of Conduct'.

31 Porter, 'Diseases of Civilisation'.

32 Quoted in Gay, op. cit., p. 32; Harth, 'The Virtue of Love'.

33 See Montesquieu's *Persian Letters* (1721; 1973), for his views on marriage as a distinguishing characteristic of civil over natural society, for example, 'Letter 129'.

34 Quoted in Stone, op. cit., p. 219; I, however, do not take this statement at face value, as Stone does, as evidence that 'companionship' in marriage replaced 'the near-absolute authority of the husband over the wife'. The ideal of the 'companion', I believe, needs to be related more sensitively to individual circumstances. Gregory might have held women in such regard, but others would have disagreed, or at least have been sceptical of his position.

35 Wollstonecraft, op. cit., p. 112, emphasis added. Unless otherwise indicated, all references to the *Vindication of the Rights of Woman* are the Everyman 1995 reprint.

36 Bucholz, *Augustan court*; see chapter 7, 'Court Life and Culture' for an overview of some of the activities.

37 Quoted in Somerset, *Ladies-in-Waiting*, p. 232.

38 Greig (ed.), *Diaries of a Duchess*, p. 78.

39 Anson and Anson (eds), *Mary Hamilton*, pp. 132–3.

40 Hedley, *Queen Charlotte*, p. 123.

41 Anson and Anson (eds), *Mary Hamilton*, pp. 77, 83.

42 The recovery of which, in addition to his sordid love letters, cost the King £5,000, plus another £800 in a lifetime annuity for the actress and her daughter. Ayling, *George the Third*, p. 223.

43 Chisholm, *Fanny Burney*, chapter 8; Somerset, *Ladies-in-Waiting*, p. 240.

44 For court hierarchy, see Hedley, *Queen Charlotte*, pp. 48–9; Thoms, *Book of the Court*.

45 Quoted in Chisholm, *Fanny Burney*, p. 134.

46 Quoted in Somerset, *Ladies-in-Waiting*, p. 240.

47 Quoted in Hill, *Fanny Burney*, p. 128.

48 Burney, *The Wanderer*, ii, p. 62; iii, pp. 110, 266, 338; for Burney's friends recommending she travel after leaving court, see comments in Scott, *Bluestocking Ladies*, p. 158.

49 As reported by Lady Mary Coke, Home (ed.), *Letters and Journals of Lady Mary Coke*, i, p. 142, 144.

50 See Myers, *Bluestocking Circle*, chapter six for discussion of Elizabeth Carter's work; comment about Epictetus on p. 159.

51 Pennington (ed.), *Memoirs*, i, p. 184.

52 Bury, *Diary of a Lady-in-Waiting*, p. 17.

53 Anson and Anson (eds), *Mary Hamilton*, p. 162, 127, respectively.

54 Quoted in Somerset, *Ladies-in-Waiting*, p. 233; Greig, *Diaries of a Duchess*, p. viii.

55 Greig, *Diaries of a Duchess*, p. 97.

56 Ibid., p. iii; Bucholz, *Augustan court*.

57 Pennington (ed.), *Letters from Elizabeth Carter to Montagu*, i, p. 28;

see Frances Thynne's correspondence with Henrietta Louisa, Countess of Pomfret, Bingley (ed.), *Correspondence*.

58 Greig, *Diaries of a Duchess*, p. 99.

59 Ibid., p. 100.

60 Home (ed.), op. cit., p. 210.

61 The most thorough biographical memoir of Lady Mary Coke remains the memoir written in 1827 by Lady Louisa Stuart, daughter of Lord Bute, great-granddaughter to John, 2nd Duke of Argyll. It is reprinted as the introduction to Home (ed.), op. cit., i, pp. xv–cxxii (hereafter cited as Stuart, 'Memoir').

62 British Library, MSS Add. 22629, f. 139.

63 Ibid., ff. 142, 143.

64 Ibid., ff. 160, 161.

65 *Evans v. Evans* (1790), quoted in Stone, *Road to Divorce*, p. 203.

66 British Library, MSS Add. 22629, f. 159.

67 Ibid., f. 180. The problem, as her lawyer put it, was in determining 'What particular excesses or ill usage was he guilty of to Lady Mary, and by whom, or how, can they be proved?'

68 Stuart, op. cit., p. xci.

69 Greig (ed.), *Diaries of a Duchess*, pp. 79–80.

70 Home (ed.), op. cit., i, pp. 168–9.

71 Stuart, op. cit., p. lxxxviii; Walpole quoted in Ayling, *George the Third*, p. 211.

72 Home (ed.), op. cit., ii, p. 145.

73 Ibid., ii, p. 144.

74 Ibid., i, p. 10.

75 Stuart, op. cit., p. xciv.

76 Home (ed.), op. cit., ii, p. 157.

77 Ibid., iii, p. 143.

78 Ibid., iii, p. 184.

79 Ibid., iii, p. 146.

80 Myers, *Bluestocking Circle*, p. 154.

81 Home (ed.), op. cit., iii, p. 170. She did, however, collect as much information about the descendants of Madame de Sévigné as she could, and relayed it to her mother in a series of letters: iii, pp. 170–77.

82 Ibid., iii, p. 161.

83 Foreman, *Georgiana*, p. 12.

84 Home (ed.), op. cit., iii, p. 199.

*Chapter Four: Fashionable Society &
Foreign Affairs*

1 Blunt (ed.), *Mrs Montagu*, i, p. 25.
Two years later, Elizabeth Robinson
married a cousin of Lady Mary
Wortley Montagu's husband, and
became Elizabeth Montagu – the
future bluestocking traveller.

2 The Earl of Ilchester (ed.), *Journal of
Elizabeth Lady Holland*, i, p. 1

3 From *A Father's Legacy to his
Daughters*, in Jones (ed.), *Women in
the Eighteenth Century*, p. 49.

4 Catharine Macaulay Graham, *Letters
on Education* (1790), part one, letter
xxiv; *A Letter of Genteel and Moral
Advice to a Young Lady* (1740), in
Jones (ed.), *Women in the Eighteenth
Century*, p. 116; 30.

5 *Trials for Adultery*, preface to volume
1; 'Philogamus', *The Present State of
Matrimony: or, the Real Causes of
Conjugal Infidelity and Unhappy
Marriages* (1739), in Jones (ed.), *Women
in the Eighteenth Century*, p. 78.

6 Hill, *Women, Work and Sexual Politics*,
p. 180.

7 Stone, *Family, Sex, and Marriage*,
p. 331; Foreman, *Georgiana*, pp. 72, 268.

8 Tillyard, *Aristocrats*, pp. 263–8;
pp. 281–5.

9 This was part of the mentality that
thought it honourable for men to
require more 'perfection' from their
wives than from themselves – a
situation that Keith Thomas and
subsequent historians refer to as 'The
Double Standard'.

10 Stone, *Road to Divorce*, p. 188.

11 See discussion of the ambiguous status
of 'Private Separation Deeds' and
court-sanctioned divorces in ibid.; also
see Trumbach, *Rise of the Egalitarian
Family*, pp. 156–7.

12 Chisholm, *Fanny Burney*, pp. 170–72.

13 Adeane (ed.), *Girlhood of Maria
Josepha Holroyd*, p. 229.

14 Home (ed.), *Letters and Journals of
Lady Mary Coke*, iii, p. 52; Trumbach,
op. cit., i, p. 157.

15 Home (ed.), op. cit., iv, pp. 126–7.

16 Lord Holroyd writing to his mother,
quoted in *Gibbon's Italian Journal*,
p. 20 n7.

17 Brooke, *History of Emily Montague*, i,
letter 36; ii, letter 62.

18 Greig (ed.), *Diaries of a Duchess*,
p. 148.

19 Granville (ed.), *Lord Granville Leveson
Gower*, pp. i, 40, 73.

20 'Civicus' in *London Journal*, 7 August
1731, quoted in Black, *The British
Abroad*, p. 190.

21 The Earl of Ilchester (ed.), op. cit., i,
p. 5.

22 Ibid., i, p. 5; for biographical
background, from which the following
sketch is chiefly drawn, see Keppel,
The Sovereign Lady.

23 Quoted in Scott, *Bluestocking Ladies*,
pp. 20–22.

24 Rogers, *Feminism in
Eighteenth-Century England*, pp. 12–13.

25 Quoted in Brown, 'Domesticity,
Feminism, and Friendship', p. 408.

26 The Earl of Ilchester (ed.), op. cit,
pp. 53–4.

27 Adeane (ed.), *Girlhood of Maria
Josepha Holroyd*, p. 64; Keppel, *The
Sovereign Lady*, p. 16.

28 Lewis (ed.), *Journals and
Correspondence of Miss Berry*, i, p. 179,
36.

29 Bessborough and Aspinall (eds), *Lady
Bessborough*, p. 23.

30 Hamilton in Anson and Anson (eds),
Mary Hamilton, pp. 306–7.

31 Blunt (ed.), *Mrs. Montagu*, p. ii, 160,
273.

32 The Earl of Ilchester (ed.), op. cit., i,
p. 5.

33 Foreman, op. cit., chapter 16. The
following account of the conditions
that affected Lady Duncannon's
decision to travel in 1791 is interwoven
with the affairs of her sister, the
Duchess of Devonshire. I recommend
Foreman's biography to the reader for
a rich exposition on Georgiana's side

of the story. See also the discussion of this in Hodge, *Passion & Principle*, chapter 3.

34 Granville (ed.), *Lord Granville Leveson Gower*, i, pp. 117–18; Foreman, *Georgiana*, p. 260.

35 Foreman, op. cit., pp. 132, 167, 197, for affairs; pp. 396–8 for marriage to the Duke.

36 For cloaked acknowledgement of Harriet's 'admirers', see Bessborough and Aspinall (eds), *Lady Bessborough*, pp. 8–9.

37 Bessborough and Aspinall (eds), *Lady Bessborough*, p. 37.

38 Quoted in Foreman, op. cit., p. 239. Sheridan's sister, 'Betsy', was also keen to see her brother's attraction to Lady Duncannon ended once and for all; 'Lady Duncannon is, thank God, gone to Bruxelles', she wrote in 1790, 'I should not be sorry to hear she was drown'd on her way thither': LeFanu (ed.), *Betsy Sheridan's Journal*, p. 195.

39 Foreman, op. cit., p. 244.

40 Damer to Mary Berry, 21 June 1791, in Melville, Lewis (ed.), *The Berry Papers*, pp. 42–3.

41 Bessborough and Aspinall (eds), *Lady Bessborough*, pp. 33–4.

42 Quoted in Foreman, op. cit., pp. 74, 87.

43 Damer to Mary Berry, 21 June 1791, in Melville, Lewis (ed.), *The Berry Papers*, p. 42.

44 Foreman, op. cit., p. 262.

45 Bessborough and Aspinall (eds), *Lady Bessborough*, pp. 62, 64.

46 Ibid., *Lady Bessborough*, p. 75.

47 Ilchester (ed.), op. cit., i, p. 6.

48 Ibid., i, pp. 9, 13–14 for quotations; Adeane (ed.), *Girlhood of Maria Josepha Holroyd*, p. 43; Keppel, op. cit., p. 19, for Sir Godfrey's character.

49 Ilchester (ed.), op. cit., i, p. 19.

50 Ibid., i, p. 26.

51 Ibid., i, p. 29; Otter, *Life and Remains of Edward Daniel Clarke*, i, pp. 135–65.

52 Ilchester (ed.), op. cit., i, p. 38.

53 Bessborough and Aspinall (eds), op. cit., pp. 87–95 for Harriet's debts; Foreman, op. cit., p. 253. In today's figures, Harriet's debt was in the

region of £200,000, Georgiana's about £4 million.

54 Holcombe, *Wives and Property*, p. 30.

55 Quoted in Stone, op. cit., p. 166.

56 Home (ed.), op. cit., iii, p. 30.

57 *Collet* v. *Collet* (1770), from *Trials for Adultery*, all divorces in this seven-volume compilation (published 1779–80) were granted, since their publication was intended to act as a deterrent by instilling a 'fear of shame' in its readers; since all save a handful were cases of wifely adultery (the others concerning impotence or desertion), it is clear who was intended to be afraid. In none of the cases is the woman's defence presented.

58 Ilchester (ed.), op. cit., i, p. 67.

59 Adeane (ed.), *Girlhood of Maria Josepha Holroyd*, p. 239: 'André' seems to have been replaced with another manservant referred to as 'wild and staring Antonio' as commented on by Sydney Smith (Smith, *Letters of Sydney Smith*, i, p. 202); Keppel, op. cit., pp. 42–3.

60 Granville (ed.), *Lord Granville Leveson Gower*, i, p. 52.

61 Ilchester (ed.), *Journal of Elizabeth Lady Holland*, i, pp. 116–17.

62 Ibid., i, p. 119.

63 Ibid., i, pp. 70–71, 86.

64 In the context of this chapter it is interesting to note that one of Charles James Fox's passions was opposing the bills proposed to prevent wives divorced for adultery from marrying their lovers.

65 Ilchester (ed.), op. cit., i, p. 121.

66 Granville (ed.), op. cit., i, pp. 88–9; Colley, *Britons*, chapter 7.

67 Ilchester (ed.), op. cit., i, p. 126, for birth and christening; Keppel, op. cit., pp. 56, 51–2 for Pelham quotations, pp. 41, 52 for paternity.

68 Ilchester (ed.), op. cit., i, pp. 263–4 for Lady Webster's later confession; Keppel, op. cit., p. 67.

69 Trumbach, *Rise of the Egalitarian Family*, p. 154.

70 Keppel, op. cit., p. 70.

71 Granville (ed.), op. cit., i, pp. 123–5.
72 Mitchell, *Holland House*, p. 20.
73 Sir Godfrey's suicide led to a legal battle regarding the redistribution of the Vassall family wealth between Elizabeth's children to Sir Godfrey and Lord Holland, which rendered the previous divorce settlement defunct and therefore the wealth of Lord and Lady Holland more difficult to calculate precisely.
74 Granville (ed.), op. cit., i, p. 162.
75 Tillyard, *Aristocrats*, pp. 260–68, 292.
76 As Stella Tillyard, the biographer of the Lennox sisters, nicely summed it up in ibid., p. 310.
77 *Horneck v. Horneck* (1775) and *Degen v. Degen* (1777), from *Trials for Adultery*.
78 For Carter and Clarges's travels and relationship, see Rizzo, *Companions Without Vows*, chapter 12.
79 Stone, op. cit., pp. 181, 285; for an account of the rise and fall of the 'criminal conversation' suit, see his chapter 9.
80 Stone, *Family, Sex and Marriage*, p. 277.

Chapter Five: Sea Breezes & Sanity

1 Daniel Drake, from *Western Medical and Physical Journal* 1 (1827), p. 305.
2 Starke, *Travels in Italy*, ii, pp. 263–5.
3 Blunt (ed.), *Mrs Montagu*, p. ii, 315–16.
4 Fulford (ed.), *Autobiography of Miss Knight*, p. 73; see Black, *The British Abroad*, chapter four for further discussion of road conditions.
5 Miller, *Letters from Italy*, ii, p. 4.
6 Fulford (ed.), *Autobiography of Miss Knight*, p. 44.
7 Black, *The British Abroad*, pp. 98, 103, 105; Hibbert, *The Grand Tour*, p. 31.
8 Gray, *Correspondence*, i, p. 128.
9 Quoted in Kirby, *Grand Tour*, p. 38.
10 Piozzi, *Observations and Reflections*, p. 23.
11 Ilchester (ed.), *Journal of Elizabeth Lady Holland*, i, pp. 40, 33, 62, 75, 67; Keppel, *The Sovereign Lady*, p. 29.
12 Miller, op. cit., i, p. 162.

13 Starke, op. cit., ii, pp. 259–60.
14 Home (ed.), *Letters and Journals of Lady Mary Coke*, i, p. 7.
15 Quoted in Hibbert, *The Grand Tour*, p. 229; see the same for comments about the amount of luggage often taken on the road by Grand Tourists, p. 19.
16 Quoted in Steedman, 'A woman writing a letter', p. 127.
17 Blunt (ed.), op. cit., ii, p. 328.
18 Home (ed.), op. cit., iii, p. 147.
19 Ibid. iv, p. 241.
20 Ibid. iv, p. 272; for speculation about the relationship between Maria Theresa and Lady Coke, see Lady Stuart's comments, i, pp. ciii–civ.
21 Home (ed.), op. cit., iv, p. 302.
22 Rousseau, 'Nerves, Spirits and Fibers'. The term was coined by Thomas Willis in the seventeenth century; 'neurosis' (referring to specific diseases of the nervous system causing sensory-motor problems) about one hundred years later by William Cullen.
23 Porter, *Mind Forg'd Manacles*, pp. 47–54.
24 Bernard Mandeville's *A Treatise of the Hypochondriack and Hysterick Passions* (1711), was one such advocate of the 'talking cure' for nervous disorders; Porter, *Mind Forg'd Manacles*, p. 172.
25 Home (ed.), op. cit., iv, p. 247; Joseph's second wife died of smallpox.
26 Ibid., iv, p. 261.
27 Brown, *Estimate of the Manners and Principles of the Times*, p. 88; quoted in Porter, *Mind Forg'd Manacles*, p. 82; Tyson and Guppy (eds), *French Journals of Mrs Thrale*, p. 224.
28 Romanell, *John Locke and Medicine*, pp. 129–32.
29 Burton, *Anatomy of Melancholy*, p. 338.
30 Cullen, *First Lines in the Practice of Physick*, p. 531.
31 King-Hele (ed.), *Letters of Erasmus Darwin*, p. 273.
32 Greig (ed.), *Diaries of a Duchess*, p. 178.
33 Fulford (ed.), *Autobiography of Miss Knight*, pp. 139–40.

34 Chapman (ed.), *Letters of Samuel Johnson*, iii, p. 106.

35 Bloom and Bloom (eds), *The Piozzi Letters*, i, p. 344.

36 Ibid., i, p. 119.

37 'Gambling exists here, it is unfortunately true', reported a nineteenth-century writer on European spas, but it was 'not the sole business of the place, as in Baden-Baden and Hamburg'; Madden, *The Spas*, p. 95.

38 Blunt, op. cit., ii, p. 56.

39 Home (ed.), op. cit., ii, p. 63.

40 Ibid., iii, p. 205.

41 Anson and Anson (eds), *Mary Hamilton*, pp. 33–5.

42 Ibid., pp. 270, 326.

43 Gisborne, *Enquiry into the Duties of the Female Sex*, p. 209.

44 Climenson, *Montagu*, i, p. 92.

45 This story is relayed in Dewhurst, *Dr Thomas Sydenham*, pp. 53–4.

46 Chapman (ed.), *The Letters of Samuel Johnson*, iii, pp. 498–9; quoted in Porter and Porter, *Patients' Progress*, p. 43.

47 Quoted in Porter and Porter, *In Sickness and in Health*, pp. 156, 157.

48 Home (ed.), op. cit., iv, pp. 86–7.

49 Barrett (ed.), *Diary and Letters*, ii, p. 265.

50 Piozzi to Burney, 6 August 1784, in Bloom and Bloom (eds), op. cit., i, p. 107.

51 Swinburne, *Courts of Europe*, i, p. 53.

52 Bamford (ed.), *Dear Miss Heber*, pp. 46–7.

53 Home (ed.), op. cit., ii, p. 63.

54 Ibid., iii, p. 203.

55 Fulford (ed.), op. cit., p. 65.

56 Ilchester (ed.), op. cit., i, p. 55.

57 Lewis (ed.), *Journals and Correspondence of Miss Berry*, i, pp. 246–7.

58 Bloom and Bloom (eds), op. cit., i, p. 175.

59 Hannaway, 'Environment and Miasmata'.

60 Bloom and Bloom (eds), op. cit., i, p. 201.

61 Or, sometimes, vice versa. When Frances Macartney, wife of Fulke Greville, envoy extraordinary to the Elector of Bavaria (1765–9) accompanied her husband abroad on diplomatic residency, she grew unwell and moved home two years early. Lady Coke heard that she had complained 'that the climate of the Country has greatly hurt her health, which is the reason She returns to England' (Home (ed.), op. cit., ii, p. 56.

62 Macculloch, *On Malaria*, p. 6; see also Wrigley, 'Infectious Enthusiasms'. The collection of essays in Wrigley and Revill (eds), *Pathologies of Travel* is also useful here. Later travellers were more conscientious about the pathologies of the environment ('I know not whether it be incipient illness', exclaimed Anna Jameson from Naples, 'or the enervating effects of this soft climate, but I feel unusually weak . . .'), but no less lured by its promise of self-fulfilment: 'Why am I not in Italy', Mary Shelley ached to know when lamenting the death of her husband, 'Italian sun & airs & flowers & earth & hopes – they are akin to love enjoyment freedom – exquisite delight'; discussion of these later travellers in Chard, *Pleasure and Guilt on the Grand Tour*, pp. 196, 185.

63 Bell (ed.), *The Hamwood Papers*, pp. 315–6.

64 Lewis (ed.), op. cit., i, pp. 197–214.

65 Fitzgerald (ed.), *Correspondence of Emily, Duchess of Leinster*, i, p. 574.

66 Home (ed.), op. cit., ii, p. 338; iv, p. 283.

67 Ilchester (ed.), op. cit., i, p. 132.

68 Piozzi, *Observations and Reflections*, p. 206.

69 Tyson and Guppy (eds), *French Journals of Mrs Thrale*, pp. 224–5.

Chapter Six: Fine Art & Fashion

1 Anson and Anson (eds), *Mary Hamilton*, p. 35.

2 Isherwood, *Farce and Fantasy*, pp. 161–5.

3 Tyson and Guppy (eds), *French Journals of Mrs Thrale*, pp. 110, 91.

4 Greig, *Diary of a Duchess*, pp. 105–6.

5 Sébastien Mercier quoted in Roche, *The People of Paris*, p. 16.

6 It was not until the nineteenth century, as Alain Corbin reminds us, that a 'deodorised bourgeoisie' grew distinct from the 'foul-smelling masses', in his *The Foul and the Fragrant*.

7 Piozzi, *Observations and Reflections*, p. 98.

8 Black, *British Abroad*, pp. 39–40.

9 Tyson and Guppy (eds), op. cit.

10 Ibid., p. 102, 232. 'Tom' referred to the servant, whose name was Thière.

11 British Library MSS Add. 37926, f. 32.

12 Tyson and Guppy (eds), op. cit., p. 130; Redford, *Letters of Samuel Johnson*, ii, p. 272.

13 Miller, *Letters from Italy*, pp. 6, 372, 54, 161, 14.

14 Tyson and Guppy (eds), op. cit., p. 103; the editors' references here deal with the subsequent history of the collection.

15 Ibid., pp. 103–111.

16 Climenson, *Elizabeth Montagu*, i, p. 128.

17 Quoted in Ashelford, *The Art of Dress*, p. 123.

18 Hufton, *Prospect Before Her*, p. 85.

19 See Ashelford, op. cit., p. 133, for an illustration of a lady's travelling petticoat.

20 Roche, *History of Everyday Things*, chapter eight, discusses these themes.

21 Crewe, British Library, Add. MSS 37926, f. 23.

22 Greig, *Diaries of a Duchess*, p. 66; see the similar observations by Mary Hamilton, in Anson and Anson (eds), op. cit., p. 38.

23 Thus in eighteenth-century Poitou, which had an economy based on hemp, clothes were dull and coarse – a stark contrast to city silk.

24 Fulford, *Autobiography*, p. 41.

25 Alger, *Napoleon's British Visitors*, p. 165.

26 The Earl of Ilchester, *Home of the Hollands*, p. 189.

27 Tyson and Guppy (eds), op. cit., p. 101.

28 *The World*, 3 May 1753; 19 July 1753.

29 Roche, *History of Everyday Things*, pp. 204–5.

30 See Johns, 'The Entrepôt of Europe', which is the introduction to the fantastic Bowron and Rishel (eds), *Art in Rome in the Eighteenth Century*; for the artistic community and numbers of visitors, see Bowron, *Pompeo Batoni*.

31 Piozzi, op. cit., p. 91.

32 Ford, 'The Dartmouth Collection'.

33 Lewis (ed.), *Journals and Correspondence of Miss Berry*, i, p. 61.

34 Ibid. i, p. 68.

35 The Earl of Ilchester (ed.), *Journal of Elizabeth Lady Holland*, i, pp. 19, 25, 137.

36 Ibid., i, p. 45.

37 Quoted in Allen, 'The Travellers', p. 51.

38 Lewis (ed.), op. cit., i, p. 71.

39 Ibid., i, p. 77.

40 Miller, *Letters from Italy*, i, pp. 17, 34.

41 The gendered readings of *Hercules* is nicely discussed by Chloe Chard in 'Effeminacy, pleasure and the classical body'.

42 Miller, op. cit., i, p. 324.

43 Ibid., ii, p. 7.

44 From the unpaginated 'advertisement' for ibid.

45 Ibid., ii, p. 285.

46 Samuel, *Remarks on the Utility of Drawing*, p. 15; see also Bermingham, *Learning to Draw*.

47 Piozzi, op. cit., p. 87. She is referring to Giovanni Antonio Canal, called Canaletto (1697–1768), praised for his detailed representations of the scenes and activity of Venice.

48 Home (ed.), *Letters and Journals of Lady Mary Coke*, ii, p. 83.

49 Bell, *Hamwood Papers*, p. 331.

50 Fulford (ed.), op. cit., p. 27.

51 Home (ed.), op. cit., iv, p. 373.

52 Anson and Anson (eds), op. cit., p. 155; Mankowitz, *The Portland Vase*, p. 29.

53 See particularly the articles in

54 Bloom and Bloom (eds), *Piozzi Letters*, i, p. 270.
55 Anson, Elizabeth and Florence (eds), *Mary Hamilton*, p. 218.
56 Piozzi, *Observations and Reflections*, p. 86.
57 Ibid., p. 63.
58 Bloom and Bloom (eds), op. cit., 11 May 1786.
59 Bessborough and Aspinall (eds), *Lady Bessborough*, p. 104; Lewis (ed.), op. cit., ii, pp. 271–2.
60 The Earl of Ilchester (ed.), op. cit., ii, p. 6.
61 Ibid., ii, p. 19.
62 Bloom and Bloom, op. cit., i, p. 222.
63 Ibid.
64 Fulford, op. cit., p. 54.
65 Home (ed.), op. cit., iv, p. 402.
66 More, *Moral Sketches*, p. 13.

Chapter Seven: Revelation & Revolution

1 Adams, 'Miss Williams', p. 104.
2 Burke, *Reflections on the Revolution in France*, p. 71; Schama, *Citizens*, p. 467.
3 Kelley, *Women of the French Revolution*, p. 38.
4 For the problem of Burke's inconsistency in his views, see Macpherson, *Burke*, chapter one.
5 Wollstonecraft, *Vindication of the Rights of Men*, p. 15, 18, 26; Burke, *Reflections on the Revolution in France*, p. 75.
6 Paulson, *Representations of Revolution*, chapter 3; for an interpretation that emphasises Burke's attempt to make a Queen into a symbol of man's desire for a feminine ideal, see Nixon, *Mary Wollstonecraft*, pp. 62–4.
7 Quoted in Paulson, op. cit., p. 85.
8 For the broader history of political activism, see Hufton, *The Prospect Before Her*, particularly chapter twelve.
9 For an eyewitness account of the royal family's life in prison, from the king's own servant, see Cléry, *A Journal of the Terror*.
10 Wardle (ed.), *Collected Letters of Mary Wollstonecraft*, p. 227; for an additional account of the king's demeanour at this moment, see Jordan, *The King's Trial*, p. 129; Todd, *Wollstonecraft*, p. 205.
11 Jordan, op. cit., p. 127.
12 A view that was new to Paris. 'In London', wrote Sébastien Mercier in the 1780s, 'they speak of the majesty of the English people: in Paris we don't know what to call *le peuple*'. Quoted in Roche, *The People of Paris*, p. 55.
13 Jordan, op. cit., p. 220.
14 See Burley, *Witness to the Revolution*, pp. 179–80, who cites the opinion (from which I quote) of the American commercial agent Gouverneur Morris on this point.
15 Quoted in Nixon, op. cit., p. 109.
16 Wollstonecraft, from 'Letters to Imlay', pp. 369–70.
17 Ibid., p. 372.
18 Ibid., pp. 372–3.
19 Ibid., p. 376.
20 Connelly, *The French Revolution*, p. 132.
21 Wollstonecraft (6 January 1794), op. cit., p. 378; for Sanson see Schama, op. cit., p. 804.
22 Wollstonecraft, *View of the French Revolution*, pp. 21–2.
23 Ibid., p. 25.
24 Ibid., p. 35.
25 Ibid., pp. 72–3.
26 Ibid., p. 209.
27 Ibid., p. 197, emphases added.
28 Ibid, p. 73; see p. 85 for 'pity' of vanquished monarchy; Todd, op. cit., p. 219.
29 The Earl of Ilchester (ed.), *Letters and Journals of Elizabeth, Lady Holland*, i, p. 85.
30 Colley, *Britons*, pp. 255–6.
31 Wollstonecraft, op. cit., p. 85.
32 Wollstonecraft (10 March 1794), in

Bermingham and Brewer (eds), *Consumption of Culture*; also discussions of consumerism in Vickery, *Gentleman's Daughter*; Roberts, 'Gender, Consumption, and Commodity Culture'.

Wardle (ed.), *Collected Letters*, pp. 250–1.

33 Kennedy, *Cultural History of the French Revolution*, p. 330.

34 Bray, 'Helen Maria Williams and Edmund Burke', for an analysis of Williams's rhetoric in her *Letters from France* relative to the general discourse of English radicalism.

35 See the remarks on this in the introduction to the reprint of Smith, *Desmond*, by Blank and Todd, pp. xxix–xxx, where they point out Smith's familiarity with Williams's publications but the extent to which they knew each other is uncertain. Smith did, however, write a letter of introduction to Williams for William Wordsworth.

36 Williams, *Letters Written in France*, pp. 1–2; for her thespian role, see ibid., pp. 203–4.

37 Parker, *Portrayals of Revolution*, chapter 2; see also Thompson (ed.), *English Witnesses of the Revolution*, pp. 82–5, for additional contemporary comments.

38 Williams, op. cit., pp. 5–6, 9–10.

39 For the theme of Williams as eyewitness, within a literary analysis of her *Letters* as a 'sentimental memoir', see Favret, *Romantic Correspondence*, chapter 3.

40 Favret, *Romantic Correspondence*, p. 60.

41 Williams, *Memoirs*, p. 166.

42 Thompson, *English Witnesses of the French Revolution*, p. 82.

43 Williams, *Letters Written in France*, p. 14.

44 Roessler, *Out of the Shadows*.

45 'Third Estate' comprised the commoners; in September 1791 the Legislative Assembly replaced the National Assembly.

46 Williams, op. cit., p. 45.

47 Ibid., pp. 66–7.

48 Favret, 'Spectatrice as Spectacle', for the complex setting of Williams at her 'home' in Paris.

49 Williams, op. cit., p. 81.

50 Quoted in Alger, *Napoleon's British Visitors*, p. 162.

51 Adeane (ed.), *Girlhood of Maria Josepha Holroyd*, pp. 41–6.

52 Wardle (ed.), *Collected Letters of Mary Wollstonecraft*, p. 226.

53 Landes, *Women and the Public Sphere*, p. 25. Indeed it was an aristocratic criticism that sometimes dismissed the *précieuse* – the affected woman of the Parisian salon – as merely managing elegant brothels.

54 Bodek, 'Salonières and Bluestockings', pp. 188–9; see also discussion of the role of French salons as models for English women's literary and political assemblies in the next chapter.

55 May, *Madame Roland*, p. 205.

56 Quoted in Adams, 'Miss Williams and the French Revolution', p. 89.

57 Favret, 'Spectatrice as Spectacle', for further discussion of Williams's salon.

58 May, op. cit., p.214.

59 Roland, *Memoirs*, p. 40.

60 Kennedy, *A Cultural History of the French Revolution*, p. 251.

61 Williams quoted in Favret, 'Spectatrice as Spectacle', p. 288.

62 Williams, quoted in Kennedy, 'Spectacle of the Guillotine', p. 98. This Jacobin-inspired insurrection and the expulsion of the Girondins from government by Montagnard leaders is, of course, a much more complicated affair than represented here, so I refer interested readers to the detailed study by Slavin, *The Making of an Insurrection*.

63 Roland, op. cit., p. 42. Williams, *Memoirs*, pp. 97–8; Favret, 'Spectatrice as Spectacle', p. 274; Wyndham, *Madame de Genlis*, p. 128.

64 Roland, op. cit., pp. 39–40.

65 Williams, op. cit., p. 25.

66 This is a summery of some of the circumstances as described by Williams in op. cit., chapter one.

67 Williams, op. cit., p. 90.

68 Ibid.

69 Ibid., p. 99; Taylor, *Life of Madame Roland*, chapter 27.

70 Williams, *Memoirs*, pp. 120–21.

71 Ibid., p. 23.

72 Lewis (ed.), *Journals and*

Correspondence of Miss Berry, i, pp. 253–4. As if the Berrys did not have enough to worry about even in terms of physical safety on the road. Bologna, Mary reported, 'is one of the towns in Italy where there are the most frequent attempts to murder and stab people – our books of travel said much above a hundred every year. Everybody we questioned upon the subject owned there might be above fifty or sixty. We tried in vain to buy a stiletto, or what is called from its length a *sept and demi*, but their sale is prohibited, and we could not meet with one', ibid., pp. 50–51.

73 Cunningham, *Cautions to Continental Travellers*, p. 29.

74 Berry, *England and France: A Comparative View*, i, p. 267.

75 Bell (ed.), *The Hamwood Papers*, pp. 330–31.

76 Overviews of these campaigns can be pursued in Ford, *Europe 1780–1830* and Esdaile, *Wars of Napoleon*.

77 Starke, *Travels in Italy*, pp. 25–45.

78 The Earl of Ilchester (ed.), op. cit., i, pp. 80–81.

79 Knight, *Autobiography*, pp. 100–103.

80 When rumours made it to Fleet Street that Lady Georgina Gordon, who was in Paris during the Peace of Amiens, frequently danced with Napoleon's stepson, the broadsheets embellished the tale. 'It is certain,' reported *The Times* on 12 January 1803, 'that some of our travelling Nudes of Fashion intended to conquer the Conqueror of the Continent. What glory would it have brought to this Country, if it could have boasted of giving a Mistress, or a Wife, to the First Consul. How pretty would sound Lady G— (we mean Lady GODIVA) BONAPARTE?'

81 Williams, *A Narrative of the Events*, p. 8; see also Adickes, *The Social Quest*, chapter 3.

82 See the introduction to Williams, *Memoirs*, by F. Funck-Brentano, p. 19.

83 Melville (ed.), *The Berry Papers*, pp. 207–8.

84 'Anglomania' meant the 'crazed' admiration for England, which – as popularised by Voltaire in his *Lettres philosophiques* – was portrayed as a nation that was rich, happy, and free.

85 Berry, *England and France: A Comparative View*, i, p. 269.

86 Starke, *Travels in Italy*, pp. 112–13. Her characterisation of Napoleon links the corruption of his principles to the freethinking radicalism of philosophers such as Voltaire, which is one place Starke's moral history of the revolutionary era differs from that of Williams or Berry, for example. 'I cannot finish this sketch of the most rapid and brilliant conquests ever gained in so short a period,' she wrote, 'without lamenting, that a Man whose great and amiable qualities at once excite our wonder and our praise, a Man whose persuasive eloquence and consummate policy taught Italy to call her rapacious and despotic Conqueror the Parent of her happiness and freedom, should have been betrayed, by the False principles of a French education, to establish the dominion of Blasphemers, Regicides, and Robbers, dimming the lustre of his courage, by deriving it from ideas of predestination, and eclipsing the splendour of his victories by the wickedness of the cause they were gained to support. To that branch of French philosophy, however, termed FREE-THINKING, may we attribute the errors of BUONAPARTE, and the growth of those licentious maxims and manners, which have brought an unoffending Monarch to the guillotine, destroyed the peace of Society, and deluged Europe with blood,' ibid., pp. 153–4.

87 The metaphor is borrowed from Thomas Jefferson's 1787 expression.

88 Starke, *Travels in Italy*, p. iii.

89 Williams, *Letters from France*, p. 217.

90 Parker, *Cult of Antiquity*, develops this point.

91 Quoted in Favret, *Romantic Correspondence*, p. 55.

92 Quoted in Adams, 'Miss Williams and the French Revolution', p. 113.

Chapter Eight: Bas Bleu Society & Lady Wits

1 Fordyce, *Sermons*, p. 18; quoted in Kelley, 'Bluestocking Feminism', p. xi.

2 *The Old Maid*, No. 3, 29 November 1755.

3 Doran, *'Mann and Manners*, ii, p. 90.

4 Blunt (ed.), *Mrs Montagu*, p. i, 49.

5 Ibid., pp. i, 89, 324; Scott, *Bluestocking Ladies*, p. 70; Tinker, *The Salon*, p. 119 (for Miller).

6 Bloom and Bloom (eds), *Piozzi Letters*, i, p. 215.

7 Browne, *Feminist Mind*, p. 126.

8 Hawkins, *Letters on the Female Mind*, ii, p. 208; Le Breton, *Memoir of Mrs. Barbauld*, p. 94.

9 Scott, op. cit., p. 24.

10 More, *Moral Sketches*, p. 10.

11 Climenson, *Montagu*, i, pp. 159–60.

12 Aspinall, *Lady Bessborough*, p. 107.

13 Keppel, *Sovereign Lady*, p. 44.

14 Gonda, 'Sarah Scott'; Kelly, 'Introduction: Sarah Scott'.

15 Scott, *Millenium Hall*, p. 65.

16 Comment by Dr Delop to Hester Thrale in 1779, who then relayed it to Burney: Barrett, ed., *Diary and Letters*, i, p. 197.

17 Blunt (ed.), op. cit., pp. ii, 16, 5.

18 Ibid., pp. i, 321.

19 Ibid., pp. i, 326.

20 Rogers, 'View from England', p. 360; Piozzi, *Observations*, pp. 373–4.

21 Blunt (ed.), op. cit., i, p. 339.

22 Scott, op. cit., p. 17.

23 Jones, *Hannah More*, p. 58; Clark, *British Clubs*; *Memoirs of Dr Burney*, p. 192.

24 Scott, op. cit., p. 17; Brobdingnag is one of Gulliver's destinations in Swift's tale.

25 Blunt (ed.), op. cit., ii, p. 103.

26 Tinker, *The Salon*, 187; Putnam, *The Lady*, 269, for Montagu as school mistress.

27 Scott, op. cit., p. 194.

28 For Madame Necker's preparation for her salon meetings, see Goodman, *The Republic of Letters*, p. 79.

29 Renwick, *Marmontel mémoires*; Bodek, 'Salonières and Bluestockings', p. 372.

30 More, 'Bas Bleu', p. 27.

31 More, *Moral Sketches*, p. 67.

32 Blunt (ed.), op. cit., ii, p. 38.

33 Hesselgrave, *Lady Miller*, pp. 4–5.

34 A propos d'ennuyeux nous avons ici de vos compatriotes qui ne sont pas divertissants, un monsieur et deux dames qui reviennent d'Italie. Ils ont voulu me voir, je ne sais pourquoi, mais ce ne serait pas eux qui me donneraient l'anglomanie.

35 Hesselgrave, *Lady Miller*, p. 25.

36 Ibid., p. 35, notes that the 'ostensible' reason was to raise money, through subscription, to the Bath Pauper Charity'.

37 From *bon-ton*, a French phrase meaning polite or fashionable society, introduced to England in the mid-eighteenth century.

38 Hesselgrave, op. cit., p. 13.

39 See Goodman, *Republic of Letters*, p. 74, for conversation about the self-assigned roles of French *salonnières*.

40 Holland, *Memoirs of the Whig Party*, i, p. 232. The fact that the 'Foxite creed' incorporated support for the emancipation of slaves created a somewhat awkward situation with regard to the fact that Lady Holland's wealth was – and to a degree continued to be – gained from her family's slave-run Jamaican plantations.

41 26 May 1798, British Library, Add. MSS 51735, f. 37; for the political context, see Tillyard, *Citizen Lord*, pp. 279–85.

42 Mitchell, *Holland House*, p. 18.

43 Ibid., p. 21.

44 The Earl of Ilchester, *Home of the Hollands*, p. 136.

45 Quoted in ibid., p. 283.

46 Mitchell, op. cit., p. 31.

47 Sanders, *Holland House Circle*, p. 62.

48 Austin (ed.), *Letters*, ii, p. 119.

49 Lord Holland to Caroline Fox, July 1798, British Library Add. MSS 51753, f. 56.

50 The Earl of Ilchester, *Chronicles of Holland House*, p. 238.

51 Sanders, op. cit., p. 62.

52 The Earl of Ilchester, *Home of the Hollands*, chapter 14; Mitchell, op. cit., pp. 203–5.

53 Ilchester, op. cit., p. 288.

54 Mitchell, op. cit., p. 307.

55 15 May 1841, British Library Add. MSS 51747, f. 189.

56 Quoted in Ilchester, op. cit., p. 123.

Chapter Nine: A Legacy of Letters & the Grand Tour

1 Lewis (ed.), *Yale Edition of Horace Walpole's Correspondence*, p. xxxi, 154. 'Baron Polnitz' refers to Karl Ludwig, Freiherr von Pöllnitz, who published his letters and memoirs, with reflections on the principal courts of Europe.

2 Grundy, *Lady Mary Wortley Montagu*, pp. 241, 612, 625–6.

3 Redford, *The Converse of the Pen*, studies the art and aims of eighteenth-century letter writing.

4 Edited by Mademoiselle de Keralio; see *Monthly Review* 79 (1788), p. 696, for comments about their merit.

5 This quotation begins the introduction to Jones (ed.), *Women and Literature*, i, a recent volume which can be used as an initial guide to the substantial literature now available on the history of women's writing.

6 Landes, *Public Sphere*, p. 58.

7 Ballaster, et al., *Women's Worlds*, chapter 2, develops this argument.

8 Wardle, *Letters*, p. 164; Todd, *Wollstonecraft*, p. 124.

9 Andrews, *Augusta*, i, p. 146.

10 Reviews from *Monthly Review* 78 (1788), pp. 530–31; *Critical Review* 65 (1788), p. 237.

11 West, *Daniel Defoe*, p. 248.

12 Dibden, *Hannah Hewitt*.

13 Reviews from *British Critic* 8 (1796), pp. 305–6; *Critical Review* 23 (1798), p. 114.

14 West, op. cit., p. 403.

15 *Critical Review* 32 (1801), p. 231, emphasis added.

16 Blunt (ed.), *Mrs Montagu*, i, pp. 315, 320.

17 Anson and Anson (eds), *Mary Hamilton*, p. 36.

18 Aspinall, *Lady Bessborough*, p. 104.

19 Lewis (ed.), *Journals and Correspondence of Miss Berry*, i, pp. 230–31.

20 Williams, *Memoirs*, p. 152.

21 The original title of the former work, published in one volume in 1825, was *A Comparative View of the Social Life of England and France, from the Restoration of Charles the Second, to the French Revolution*; the title was changed when the second volume was published in 1828 to *England and France: A Comparative View of the Social Condition of Both Countries*. In 1831, she then published a single-volume sequel to this work, titled (confusingly similar to the publication of 1825) *Social Life in England and France from the French Revolution in 1789, to that of July 1830*.

22 Lewis (ed.), op. cit., ii, p. 22; it appears that Berry later repeated her commitment to keeping a journal, being particularly inspired by the travel writings of her friend, Bertie Greatheed. See Bury and Bloom (eds), *An Englishman in Paris*, p. xix.

23 Piozzi to Cadell, 14 November 1788, in Bloom and Bloom (eds), *Piozzi Letters*, p. 286.

24 Adams, *Travellers and Travel Liars*, for an account of these tall tales.

25 Piozzi, *Observations and Reflections*, pp. 10–11.

26 Tyson and Guppy (eds), *French Journals of Mrs. Thrale*, 93–4.

27 See the brief remarks in Herbert Barrow's introduction to Piozzi, *Observations and Reflections*, for

additional discussion on other authorities available to Piozzi. See also Appendix 2 in Bloom and Bloom (eds), *Piozzi Letters*, for material that Piozzi edited out of her published travel account.

28 For an extensive bibliography of women's travel books over a few centuries, see Robinson, *Wayward Women*; an abbreviated but telling sample of the available literature by men compared to women in the eighteenth century is provided by Jeremy Black in his *The British Abroad*.

29 Tyson and Guppy (eds), op. cit., p. 115; this seems to be the only place where she changed the text to indicate she was in fact in the company of others; throughout the journal she reflects on both her independent activities and those of the group she was with – most likely reflecting when she went about 'alone' (or, without her English travelling companions, as she often did) or with them.

30 Montagu, *Turkish Embassy Letters*, p. 134; Grundy, *Lady Mary Wortley Montagu*, p. 241, for her comments about Mary Astell's 'feminist celebration' of Montagu's letters.

31 Piozzi, op. cit., pp. 35, 52, 53, 94, for quotations.

32 So, after describing a philosophical discussion with the curator of a natural history collection, she apologised: 'Well! these are unpleasant reflections: I would rather, before leaving the plains of Lombardy, give my country-women one reason for detaining them so long there', whence she traced the origin of certain London fashions to Padua; ibid.,

pp. 35, 69–70; for Piozzi's nationalism and the strategy she uses to show how pleased she was with Italy – in juxtaposition to the more common trope by English writers registering their *displeasure* with foreign terrain, see McCarthy, *Hester Thrale Piozzi*, chapter six.

33 Critics discussed in Clifford, *Hester Lynch Piozzi*, pp. 343–4.

34 Lewis (ed.), op. cit., i, p. 412.

35 Bloom and Bloom (eds), *Piozzi Letters*, i, 300.

36 Pennington, *Letters from Mrs Elizabeth Carter*, iii, p. 314.

37 Quoted in Conger, 'Fellow Travellers', p. 115.

38 Clifford, op. cit., p. 345.

39 Walpole's characterisation of Lady Miller as an 'Arcadian patroness' refers to her emulation as arbiter of the literary competitions that began at the Academy of Arcadia in late seventeenth-century Rome – where mental competitions imitated the physical of the ancient Olympic games.

40 Hesselgrave, *Lady Miller*, p. 6.

41 Showalter, *Literature of their Own*; Mills, *Discourses of Difference*, chapter one.

42 Bloom and Bloom (eds), op. cit., i, p. 270.

43 Hayward (ed.), *Autobiography*, i, p. 323.

44 Hamalian (ed.), *Ladies on the Loose*.

45 Robinson, *Wayward Women*, p. 195.

46 Quoted in Robinson (ed.), *Unsuitable for Ladies*, p. xiii.

47 By Jane Robinson in her indispensable reference book, *Wayward Women*, p. 177.

48 Adeane, *Miss Holroyd*, p. 24

Select Bibliography

Acomb, Frances, *Anglophobia in France 1763–1789: An Essay in the History of Constitutionalism and Nationalism* (Durham, NC: Duke University Press, 1950).

Adams, M. Ray, 'Helen Maria Williams and the French Revolution', in Earl Leslie Griggs (ed.), *Wordsworth and Coleridge: Studies in Honour of George McLean Harper* (Princeton: Princeton University Press, 1939).

Adams, Percy, *Travellers and Travel Liars, 1660–1800* (London: Constable, 1980).

Adams, William Howard, *The Paris Years of Thomas Jefferson* (New Haven and London: Yale University Press, 1997).

Adeane, J.H. (ed.), *The Girlhood of Maria Josepha Holroyd (Lady Stanley of Alderley): Recorded in Letters of a Hundred Years Ago: From 1776 to 1796* (London: Longmans, Green and Co., 1896).

Adickes, Sandra, *The Social Quest: The Expanded Vision of Four Women Travelers in the Era of the French Revolution* (New York: Peter Lang, 1991).

Alger, John Goldworth, *Napoleon's British Visitors and Captives 1801–1815* (Westminster: Archibald Constable, 1904).

Allen, Brian, 'The Travellers', in Wilton, Andrew and Bignamini, Ilaria (eds), *Grand Tour*.

Andrews, Dr, *Augusta; or the Female Travellers*, 3 vols (London, 1787).

Anson, Elizabeth and Florence (eds), *Mary Hamilton, Afterwards Mrs John Dickenson, at Court and at Home, From Letters and Diaries 1756 to 1816* (London: John Murray, 1925).

Ashelford, Jane, *The Art of Dress: Clothes and Society 1500–1914* (London: The National Trust, 1996).

Austen, Jane, *Sanditon* (unfinished novel, completed by 'Another Lady' [Marie Dobbs]: London: Arrow, 1998).

Ayling, Stanley, *George the Third* (London: Collins, 1972).

Ballaster, Ros, Beetham, Margaret, Frazer, Elizabeth, and Hebron, Sandra, *Women's Worlds: Ideology, Femininity and the Woman's Magazine* (Basingstoke: Macmillan, 1991).

Bamford, F. (ed.), *Dear Miss Heber* (London: Constable, 1936).

Barrett, Charlotte (ed.), *Diary and Letters of Madame D'Arblay*, 4 vols (London: George Ball, 1891).

Bedfordshire County Record Office, *Aristocratic Women: the Social, Political, and Cultural History of Rich and Powerful Women, Part 1: The Correspondence of Jemima, Marchioness Grey (1722–97) and her Circle* (Wiltshire: Adam Matthew, 1995).

Bell, (ed.), *The Hamwood Papers* Benedict, Barbara, *Framing Feeling: Sentiment and Style in English Prose Fiction, 1745–1800* (New York: AMS Press, 1994).

Benkovitz, Miriam, 'Some Observations on Woman's Concept of Self in the Eighteenth Century', in Fritz, Paul and Morton, Richard (eds), *Woman in the Eighteenth Century.*

Bermingham, Ann and Brewer, John (eds), *The Consumption of Culture 1600–1800: Image, Object, Text* (London and New York: Routledge, 1995).

Bermingham, Ann, 'Elegant Females and Gentlemen Connoisseurs: The Commerce in Culture and Self-Image in Eighteenth-Century England', in Bermingham, Ann, and Brewer, John (eds), *The Consumption of Culture 1600–1800: Image, Object, Text* (London and New York: Routledge, 1995).

Bermingham, Ann, *Learning to Draw: Studies in the Cultural History of a Polite and Useful Art* (New Haven & London: Yale University Press, 2000).

Berry, Mary, *England and France: A Comparative View of the Social Conditions of Both Countries*, 2 vols (London, 1828–31; republished 1844).

Bessborough, Earl of and Aspinall, A. (eds), *Lady Bessborough and Her Family Circle* (London: John Murray, 1940).

Birdsall, Virginia Ogden, *Defoe's Perpetual Seekers: A Study of the Major Fiction* (London and Toronto: Associated University Presses, 1985).

Black, Jeremy, *The British Abroad: The Grand Tour in the Eighteenth Century* (London: Alan Sutton, 1992).

Blunt, Alison, *Travel, Gender, and Imperialism: Mary Kingsley and West Africa* (New York: Guilford Press, 1994).

Blunt, Reginald (ed.), *Mrs Montagu: 'Queen of the Blues': Her Letters and Friendships From 1762 to 1800*, 2 vols (London: Constable and Company, 1923).

Bodek, Evelyn Gordon, 'Salonnières and Bluestockings: Educated Obsolescence and Germinating Feminism', *Feminist Studies* 3 (1976), pp. 185–99.

Bohls, Elizabeth, *Women Travel Writers and the Language of Aesthetics, 1716–1818* (Cambridge: Cambridge University Press, 1995).

Bowron, Edgar Peters and Rishel, Joseph J. (eds), *Art in Rome in the Eighteenth Century* (London: Merrell, in association with Philadelphia Museum of Art, 2000).

Bowron, Edgar Peters, *Pompeo Batoni (1708–1787) and His British Patrons* (London: Greater London Council, 1982).

Bray, Matthew, 'Helen Maria Williams and Edmund Burke: Radical Critique and Complicity', *Eighteenth-Century Life* 16 (1992), pp. 1–24.

Brewer, John, *The Sinews of Power: War, Money and the English State 1688–1783* (London: Routledge, 1989).

—— *The Pleasures of the Imagination: English Culture in the Eighteenth Century* (London: HarperCollins, 1997).

Brockliss, L.W.B., 'The Development of the Spa in Seventeenth-century France', in Roy Porter (ed.), *The Medical History of Waters and Spas* (*Medical History*, Supplement 10; London: Wellcome Institute for the History of Medicine, 1990), pp. 23–47.

Brooke, Frances, *History of Emily Montague* (London, 1769).

Brown, Irene Q., 'Domesticity, Feminism, and Friendship: Female Aristocratic Culture and Marriage in England, 1660–1760', *Journal of Family History* 7 (1982), pp. 406–24.

Brown, John, *Estimate of the Manners and Principles of the Times*, 2nd edition (London, 1757).

Browne, Alice, *The Eighteenth Century Feminist Mind* (Brighton: Harvester Press, 1987).

Bucholz, R.O., *The Augustan Court: Queen Anne and the Decline of Court Culture* (Stanford: Stanford University Press, 1993).

Burke, Edmund, *Reflections on the Revolution in France* (edited with an introduction by Mitchell, L., Oxford: Oxford University Press, 1993).

Burley, Peter, *Witness to the Revolution: American and British Commentators in France 1788–94* (London: Weidenfeld & Nicolson, 1989).

Burney, Frances, *Evelina* (1778; reprint London: Penguin, 1994).

Burton, Robert, *The Anatomy of Melancholy*, edited by Dell, Floyd and

Jordan-Smith, Paul (New York: Tudor Publishing Company, 1927).

Bury, Lady Charlotte, *The Diary of a Lady-in-Waiting: Being the Diary Illustrative of the Times of George the Fourth Interspersed with Original Letters from the Late Queen Caroline and from other Distinguished Persons*, 2 vols, edited by Stuart, A. Francis (London: John Lane, 1908).

Bury, J.P.T. and Berry, J.C. (eds), *An Englishman in Paris: 1803. The Journal of Bertie Greatheed* (London: Geoffrey Bles, 1953).

Busse, John, *Mrs Montagu: Queen of the Blues* (London: Gerald Howe Ltd, 1928).

Campbell, Gerald, *Edward and Pamela Fitzgerald: Being an Account of their Lives Compiled from the Letters of Those who Knew Them* (London: Edward Arnold, 1904).

Chapone, Hester, *Letters on the Improvement of the Mind, Addressed to a Young Lady*, 2 vols (Dublin, 1773; reprint London: William Pickering, 1996).

Chard, Chloe and Langdon, Helen (eds), *Transports: Travel, Pleasure, and Imaginative Geography, 1600–1830* (New Haven and London: Yale University Press, 1996).

Chard, Chloe, 'Effeminacy, pleasure and the classical body', in Perry and Rossington (eds), *Femininity and Masculinity in Eighteenth-Century Art and Culture*, pp. 142–61.

—— *Pleasure and Guilt on the Grand Tour: Travel Writing and Imaginative Geography 1600–1830* (Manchester: Manchester University Press, 1999).

Chisholm, Kate, *Fanny Burney: Her Life, 1752–1840* (London: Vintage, 1999).

Clark, Peter, *British Clubs and Societies 1580–1800: The Origins of an Associational World* (Oxford: Clarendon Press, 2000).

Cléry, Jean-Baptiste, *A Journal of the Terror: Being an Account of the Occurrences in the Temple during the Confinement of Louis XVI, by M. Cléry the King's Valet-de-Chambre, together with a Description of the Last Hours of the King, by the Abbé de Firmont*, edited by Sidney Scott (London: The Folio Society, 1955).

Clifford, James L., *Hester Lynch Piozzi (Mrs. Thrale)* (first edition, 1941; Oxford: Clarendon Press, 1987).

Climenson, Emily J., *Elizabeth Montagu: The Queen of the Blue-Stockings, Her Correspondence from 1720 to 1761*, 2 vols (London: John Murray, 1906).

Cohen, Michèle, *Fashioning Masculinity: National Identity and Language in the Eighteenth Century* (London: Routledge, 1996).

Colley, Linda, *Britons: Forging the Nation 1707–1837* (London and New Haven: Yale University Press, 1992).

Colvin, Christina (ed.), *Maria Edgeworth in France and Switzerland: Selections from the Edgeworth Family Letters* (Oxford: Clarendon Press, 1979).

Conger, Sydney McMillen, 'Fellow Travellers: Eighteenth-Century Englishwomen and German Literature', *Studies in Eighteenth-Century Culture* 14 (1985), pp. 109–128.

Conrad, Lawrence, Neve, Michael, Nutton, Vivian, Porter, Roy and Wear, Andrew, *The Western Medical Tradition: 800 BC to AD 1800* (Cambridge: Cambridge University Press, 1995).

Cook, Harold J., *The Decline of the Old Medical Regime in Stuart London* (Ithaca and London: Cornell University Press, 1986).

Corbin, Alain, *The Foul and the Fragrant: Odor and the French Social Imagination* (Cambridge, MA: Harvard University Press, 1986).

Cottom, Daniel, *The Civilized Imagination: A Study of Ann Radcliffe, Jane Austen, and Sir Walter Scott* (Cambridge: Cambridge University Press, 1985).

Cranston, Maurice, *The Noble Savage: Jean-Jacques Rousseau (1754–1762)* (London: Allen Lane, 1991).

Cullen, William, *First Lines in the Practice of Physick*, 4 vols (Edinburgh: William Creech, 1778–84).

Cunningham, John William, *Cautions to Continental Travellers* (Cambridge, 1818).

De Beer, G.R., *Travellers in Switzerland* (London: Oxford University Press, 1949).

De Koven, Anna Farwell, *Horace Walpole and Madame du Deffand: An Eighteenth-Century Friendship* (New York and London: D. Apelton, 1929).

Derry, John W., *Charles James Fox* (London: Batsford, 1972).

Dewhurst, Kenneth, *Dr. Thomas Sydenham (1624–1689): His Life and Original Writings* (Berkeley and Los Angeles: University of California Press, 1966).

Dibden, Charles, *Hannah Hewitt; or, the Female Crusoe, Being the History of a Woman . . . who became the sole inhabitant of an Island*, 3 vols (London, 1792).

Dolan, Brian, *Exploring European Frontiers: British Travellers in the Age of Enlightenment* (Basingstoke: Macmillan, 2000).

Doran, John, *'Mann' and Manners at the Court of Florence, 1740–1786: Founded on the Letters of Horace Mann to Horace Walpole*, 2 vols (London: Richard Bentley, 1876).

Edgeworth, Maria, *Letters for Literary Ladies; to which is Added An Essay on the Noble Science of Self-Justification* (1795; reprint London: Everyman, 1993).

Eger, Elizabeth (ed.), *Bluestocking Feminism: Writings of the Bluestocking Circle, 1738–1785: Volume 1, Elizabeth Montagu* (London: Pickering & Chatto, 1999).

Elias, Norbert, *The Civilizing Process: The History of Manners and State Formation and Civilization* (first published 1939; translated by Edmund Jephcott, Oxford: Basil Blackwell, 1994).

Esdaile, Charles, *The Wars of Napoleon* (London: Longman, 1995).

Eustace, John Chetwode, *A Tour through Italy, Exhibiting a View of its Scenery, its Antiquities, and its Monuments; Particularly as they are Objects of Classical Interest and Elucidation: With an Account of the Present State of its Cities and Towns; and Occasional Observations on the Recent Spoliations of the French*, 2 vols (London, 1813).

Favret, Mary A., 'Spectatrice as Spectacle: Helen Maria Williams at Home in the Revolution', *Studies in Romanticism* 32 (1993), pp. 273–95.
—— *Romantic Correspondence: Women, Politics and the Fiction of Letters* (Cambridge: Cambridge University Press, 1993).

Febvre, Lucien, 'Civilisation: evolution of a word and group of ideas,' in Peter Burke (ed.), *A New Kind of History: From the Writings of Febvre*, translated by Folca, K. (London: Routledge and Kegan Paul, 1973), pp. 219–257.

Fitzgerald, Brian (ed.), *Correspondence of Emily, Duchess of Leinster (1731–1814)*, 3 vols (Dublin: Stationary Office, 1949–57).

Fitzgerald, Brian, *Emily, Duchess of Leinster 1731–1814: A Study of her Life and Times* (London: Staples Press, 1949).

Foote, G.A., 'Sir Humphry Davy and his Audiences at the Royal Institution' *Isis* 43 (1952), pp. 6–12.

Ford, Brinsley, 'The Dartmouth Collection of Drawings by Richard Wilson' *The Burlington Magazine* 90 (1948), pp. 337–48.

Ford, Charles Howard, *Hannah More: A Critical Biography* (New York: Peter Lang, 1996).

Ford, Franklin, *Europe 1780–1830* (London: Longman, 1970).

Fordyce, James, *Sermons to Young Women*, 2 vols (London, 1770).

Foreman, Amanda, *Georgiana, Duchess of Devonshire* (London: HarperCollins 1998).

Foster, Shirley, *Across New Worlds: Nineteenth-century Women Travellers and their Writings* (London: Harvester Wheatsheaf, 1990).

Freemantle, Anne (ed.), *The Wynne Diaries 1789–1820*, 3 vols (London, 1935–40).

Fritz, Paul and Morton, Richard (eds), *Woman in the Eighteenth Century and Other Essays* (Toronto and Sarasota: Samuel Stevens, 1976).

Fruchtman, Jack (ed.), *An Eye-Witness Account of the French Revolution by Helen Maria Williams: Letters Containing a Sketch of the Politics of France* (New York: Peter Lang, 1994).

Fulford, Roger (ed.), *The Autobiography of Miss Knight: Lady Companion to Princess Charlotte* (London: William Kimber, 1960).

Gay, Peter, *The Enlightenment, An Interpretation: The Rise of Modern Paganism* (1966; New York and London: W.W. Norton, 1977).

—— *The Enlightenment, An Interpretation: The Science of Freedom* (1969; New York and London: W.W. Norton, 1977).

Gerbod, Paul, *Voyages au pays des mangeurs de grenouilles: La France vue par les Britanniques du XVIIIe siècle à nos jours* (Paris: Albin Michel, 1991).

George, Margaret, *Women in the First Capitalist Society: Experiences in Seventeenth-Century England* (London: Harvester Press, 1988).

Gilbert, Sandra and Gubar, Susan, *The Madwoman in the Attic: The Woman Writer and the Nineteenth-Century Literary Imagination* (New Haven: Yale University Press, 1979).

Gisborne, Thomas, *An Enquiry into the Duties of the Female Sex* (London, 1797).

Goldsmith, Elizabeth (ed.), *Writing the Female Voice: Essays on Epistolary Literature* (Boston: Northeastern University Press, 1989).

Gonda, Caroline, 'Sarah Scott and "The Sweet Excess of Paternal Love"', *Studies in English Literature* 32 (1992), pp. 511–35.

Goodman, Dena, *The Republic of Letters: A Cultural History of the French Enlightenment* (Ithaca: Cornell University Press, 1994).

Goodwin, Albert, *The Friends of Liberty: The English Democratic Movement in the Age of the French Revolution* (London: Hutchinson, 1979).

Granville, Castalia (ed.), *Lord Granville Leveson Gower (First Earl Granville): Private Correspondence 1781 to 1821*, 2 vols (London: John Murray, 1916).

Gray, Mrs Edwin, *Papers and Diaries of a York Family 1764–1839* (London: Sheldon Press, 1927).

Greatheed, Bertie, *An Englishman in Paris*, edited by Bury, J.P.T., and Barry J.C. (London: Geoffrey Bles, 1953; originally published 1803).

Grundy, Isobel, *Lady Mary Wortley Montagu* (Oxford: Oxford University Press 1999).

Halsband, Robert, 'Women and Literature in Eighteenth Century England', in Fritz, Paul and Morton, Richard (eds), *Women in the Eighteenth Century*.

Hamalian, Leo (ed.), *Ladies on the Loose: Women Travellers of the Eighteenth and Nineteenth Centuries* (South Yarmouth, MA: John Curley & Associates 1981).

Hamlin, Christopher, 'Chemistry, Medicine, and the Legitimization of English Spas, 1740–1840', in Roy Porter (ed.), *The Medical History of Waters and Spas* (*Medical History*, Supplement 10; London: Wellcome Institute for the History of Medicine, 1990), pp. 67–81.

Hannaway, Caroline, 'Environment and Miasmata', in Bynum, W.F. and Porter, R. (eds), *Companion Encyclopaedia of the History of Medicine* Vol 1, (London: Routledge, 1993).

Harth, Erica, 'The Virtue of Love: Lord Hardwicke's Marriage Act', *Cultural Critique* 9 (1988), pp. 123–54.

Hawkins, Laetitia-Matilda, *Letters on the Female Mind, its Power and Pursuits addressed to Miss H.M. Williams*, 2 vols (London, 1793).

Hayward, A. (ed.), *Autobiography, Letters and Literary Remains of Mrs Piozzi (Thrale)*, 2 vols (London, 1861).

Hedley, Olwen, *Queen Charlotte* (London: John Murray, 1975).

Hemlow, J. (ed.), *Journals and Letters of Fanny Burney*, 5 vols (Oxford: Oxford University Press, 1973).

Hesselgrave, Ruth Avaline, *Lady Miller and the Batheaston Literary Circle* (New Haven: Yale University Press, 1927).

Hibbert, Christopher, *The Grand Tour* (London and New York: Spring Books 1974).

Hill, Bridget, *Women, Work and Sexual Politics in Eighteenth-Century England* (Oxford: Basil Blackwell, 1989).

Hill, Constance, *Fanny Burney at the Court of Queen Charlotte* (London and New York: John Lane, 1912).

Hodge, Jane Aiken, *Passion and Principle: The Loves and Lives of Regency Women* (London: John Murray, 1996).

Holcombe, Lee, *Wives and Property: Reform of the Marries Women's Property Law in Nineteenth-Century England* (Oxford: Martin Robertson, 1983).

Holland, Lord (Henry Richard Fox), *Memoirs of the Whig Party during my Time* (London, 1852–4).

Home, J.A. (ed.), *The Letters and Journals of Lady Mary Coke*, 4 vols (Edinburgh: David Douglas, 1889).

Hufton, Olwen, *The Prospect Before Her: A History of Women in Western Europe Volume I: 1500–1800* (London: HarperCollins, 1995).

Hunter, Jean, 'The Eighteenth-Century Englishwoman: According to the Gentleman's Magazine', in Fritz, Paul and Morton, Richard (eds), *Woman in the 18th Century*, 73–88.

Ilchester, The Earl of (ed.), *Elizabeth, Lady Holland, to her Son 1821–1845* (London: John Murray, 1946).

—— *The Journal of Elizabeth Lady Holland (1791–1811)*, 2 vols (London: Longmans, Green, and Co., 1908).

—— *Chronicles of Holland House, 1820–1900* (London: John Murray, 1937).

—— *The Home of the Hollands 1605–1820* (London: John Murray, 1937).

Isherwood, Robert, *Farce and Fantasy: Popular Entertainment in Eighteenth-Century Paris* (Oxford and New York: Oxford University Press, 1986).

Johns, Christopher M.S. 'The Entrepôt of Europe: Rome in the Eighteenth Century', Bowron, Edgar Peters and Rishel, Joseph J. (eds), *Art in Rome*.

Jones, M.G., *Hannah More* (Cambridge: Cambridge University Press, 1952).

Jones, Vivien (ed.), *Women and Literature in Britain 1700–1800* (Cambridge: Cambridge University Press, 2000).

—— (ed.), *Women in the Eighteenth Century: Constructions of Femininity* (London: Routledge, 1990).

—— 'The Seductions of Conduct: Pleasure and Conduct Literature' in Porter, Roy and Roberts, Marie Mulvey (eds), *Pleasure in the Eighteenth Century* (Basingstoke: Macmillan, 1996).

Jordan, David P., *The King's Trial: Louis XVI vs. the French Revolution* (Berkeley and London: University of California Press, 1979).

Kavanagh, Julia, *English Women of Letters: Biographical Sketches*, 2 vols (London: Hurst and Blackett, 1863).

Kelly, Gary, 'General Introduction: Bluestocking Feminism and Writing in Context', in *Bluestocking Feminism: Writings of the Bluestocking Circle 1738–1785*, Vol 1 (London: Pickering & Chatto, 1999).

—— 'Introduction: Sarah Scott, Bluestocking Feminism, and Millenium Hall', in Sarah Scott, *A Description of Millenium Hall*, pp. 11–43.

Kelly, Linda, *Women of the French Revolution* (London: Hamish Hamilton 1987).

Kennedy, Deborah, 'Spectacle of the Guillotine: Helen Maria Williams and the Reign of Terror', *Philological Quarterly* 73 (1994), pp. 95–113.

Kennedy, Emmet, *A Cultural History of the French Revolution* (New Haven and London: Yale University Press, 1989).

Keppel, Sonia, *The Sovereign Lady: A Life of Elizabeth Vassall, third Lady Holland with Her Family* (London: Hamish Hamilton, 1974).

King-Hele, Desmond (ed.), *The Letters of Erasmus Darwin* (Cambridge: Cambridge University Press, 1981).

Kirby, Paul Franklin, *The Grand Tour in Italy (1700–1800)* (New York: S.F. Vanni, 1952).

Kowaleski-Wallace, Beth, 'Milton's Daughters: The Education of Eighteenth-Century Women Writers', *Feminist Studies* 12 (1986), pp. 275–93.

—— *Their Fathers' Daughters: Hannah More, Maria Edgeworth, and Patriarchal Complicity* (New York and Oxford: Oxford University Press, 1991).

Labbe, Jacqueline, 'A Family Romance: Mary Wollstonecraft, Mary Godwin and Travel', *Genre* xxv (1992), pp. 211–28.

Landes, Joan B., *Women and the Public Sphere in the Age of the French Revolution* (Ithaca and London: Cornell University Press, 1988).

Le Breton, Anna Letitia, *Memoir of Mrs Barbauld* (London: George Bell, 1874).

LeFanu, William (ed.), *Betsy Sheridan's Journal: Letters from Sheridan's Sister 1784–1786 and 1788–1790* (Oxford: Oxford University Press, 1986).

Lefebvre, Georges, *The French Revolution from 1793 to 1799* (London: Routledge and Kegan Paul, 1964).

Lennox, Charlotte, *The Female Quixote; or, The Adventures of Arabella* (originally published 1752; London: Oxford University Press, 1970, edited by Margaret Dalziel).

Lewis, Judith Schneid, *In the Family Way: Childbearing in the British Aristocracy 1760–1860* (New Brunswick, NJ: Rutgers University Press, 1986).

Lewis, Lady Theresa (ed.), *Extracts of the Journals and Correspondence of Miss Berry from the Year 1783 to 1852*, 2 vols (London: Longmans, Green, and Co., 1865).

Lewis, W.S. (ed.), *The Yale Edition of Horace Walpole's Correspondence*, volume 31 (New Haven: Yale University Press, 1961).

Macculloch, John, *On Malaria: An Essay on the Production and Propagation of this Poison, and on the Nature and Localities of the Places by which it is Produced: with an Examination of the Diseases caused by it, and of the Means of Preventing or Diminishing them, both at Home and in the Naval and Military Service* (London, 1827).

MacDonald, Edgar (ed.), *The Education of the Heart: The Correspondence of Rachel Mordecai Lazarus and Maria Edgeworth* (Chapel Hill: University of North Carolina Press, 1977).

Macintyre, Sylvia, 'Towns as Health and Pleasure Resorts: Bath, Scarborough and Weymouth, 1700–1815' (D Phil Thesis: University of Oxford, 1973).

Macpherson, C.B., *Burke* (Oxford: Oxford University Press, 1980).

Malcomson, A.P.W., *The Pursuit of the Heiress: Aristocratic Marriage in Ireland 1750–1820* (Belfast: Ulster Historical Foundation, 1982).

Mangin, Edward, *Piozziana; or, Recollections of the Late Mrs Piozzi* (London 1833).

Mankowitz, Wolf, *The Portland Vase and the Wedgwood Copies* (London: Deutsch, 1952).

Marshall, Roderick, *Italy in English Literature 1755–1815: Origins of the Romantic Interest in Italy* (New York: Colombia University Press, 1934).

Mavor, Elizabeth (ed.), *The Grand Tours of Katherine Wilmot: France 1801–3 and Russia 1805–7* (London: Weidenfeld and Nicolson, 1992).

May, Gita, *Madame Roland and the Age of Revolution* (New York and London: Columbia University Press, 1970).

McCarthy, William, *Hester Thrale Piozzi: Portrait of a Literary Woman* (Chapel Hill and London: University of North Caroline Press, 1985).

McKendrick, Neil, John Brewer, and J.H. Plumb, *The Birth of a Consumer Society: The Commercialization of Eighteenth-Century England* (London: Europa, 1982).

Melman, Billie, *Women's Orients: English Women and the Middle East, 1718–1918: Sexuality, Religion, and Work* (London: Macmillan, 1992; 2nd edition 1995).

Melville, Lewis, *The Berry Papers,* ?? Michaelson, Patricia, 'Women in the Reading Circle,' *Eighteenth-Century Life* 13 (1989), pp. 59–69.

Miller, Lady Anna, *Letters from Italy, Describing the Manners, Customs Antiquities, Paintings, &c of that Country, In the Years MDCCLXX and MDCCLXXI, to a Friend residing in France*, 3 vols (London, 1776).

Mills, Sara, *Discourses of Difference: An Analysis of Women's Travel Writing and Colonialism* (London and New York: Routledge, 1991).

Mitchell, Leslie, *Holland House* (London: Duckworth, 1980).

Montagu, Lady Mary Wortley, *Turkish Embassy Letters* (originally published 1763; London: William Pickering, 1993, edited by Malcolm Jack).

Montesquieu, Charles-Louis de Secondat, Baron de, *Persian Letters* (1721; trans. C.J. Betts, Harmondsworth: Penguin, 1973).

Moravia, Sergio, *Il pensiero degli Idéologues: Scienza e filosofia in Francia (1780– 1815)* (Florence: La Nuova Italia, 1974).

More, Hannah, 'Bas Bleu', in Hole, Robert (ed.), *Selected Writings of Hannah More* (London: William Pickering, 1996).

More, Hannah, *Strictures on the Modern System of Female Education; with a View of the Principles and Conduct Prevalent among Women of Rank and Fortune* 2 vols (London, 1799; reprint Oxford and New York: Woodstock, 1995).

More, Hannah, *Moral Sketches of Prevailing Opinions and Manners, Foreign and Domestic*, 5th edition (London, 1820).

Morton, R.E. and Browning, J.D. (eds), *Religion in the Eighteenth Century* (New York & London: Garland, 1979).

Mowl, Timothy, *Horace Walpole: The Great Outsider* (London: John Murray 1996).

Murray, Venetia, *High Society in the Regency Period 1788–1830* (Harmondsworth: Penguin, 1998).

Myers, Sylvia, 'Learning, Virtue, and the Term "Bluestocking",' *Studies in Eighteenth-Century Culture* 15 (1986), pp. 279–88.

—— *The Bluestocking Circle: Women, Friendship, and the Life of the Mind in Eighteenth-Century England* (Oxford: Clarendon, 1990).

Nixon, Edna, *Mary Wollstonecraft: Her Life and Times* (London: J.M. Dent & Sons, 1971).

Nussbaum, Felicity A, *Torrid Zones: Maternity, Sexuality, and Empire in Eighteenth-Century English Narratives* (Baltimore and London: The Johns Hopkins University Press, 1995).

Otter, William, *The Life and Remains of Edward Daniel Clarke, Professor of Mineralogy in the University of Cambridge*, 2 vols (London, 1825).

Parker, Noel, *Portrayals of Revolution: Images, Debates and Patterns of Thought on the French Revolution* (London: Harvester Wheatsheaf, 1990).

Paulson, Ronald, *Representations of Revolution (1789–1820)* (New Haven and London: Yale University Press, 1983).

Pennington, Montagu (ed.), *Letters from Mrs Elizabeth Carter to Mrs Montagu Between the Years 1755 and 1800, Chiefly upon Literary and Moral Subjects* 3 vols (London, 1817).

—— *Memoirs of the Life of Mrs Elizabeth Carter*, 2 vols (3rd edition, London, 1816).

Perry, Gill and Michael Rossington (eds), *Femininity and Masculinity in Eighteenth-Century Art and Culture* (Manchester: Manchester University Press, 1994).

Philip, Mark (ed.), *The French Revolution and British Popular Politics* (Cambridge: Cambridge University Press, 1991).

Piozzi, Hester Lynch, *Observations and Reflections Made in the Course of a Journey Through France, Italy, and Germany* (originally published 1789; edited by Herbert Barrows; Ann Arbor: University of Michigan Press, 1967).

Pollen, Thomas, *The Fatal Consequences of Adultery, to Monarchies as* well as to Private Families, with a Defence of the Bill, Passed in the House of Lords in the Year 1771 (London, 1772).

Poovey, Mary, *The Proper Lady and the Woman Writer: Ideology as Style in the Works of Mary Wollstonecraft, Mary Shelley, and Jane Austen* (Chicago and London: University of Chicago Press, 1984).

Porter, Dorothy and Porter, Roy, *Patient's Progress: Doctors and Doctoring in Eighteenth-century England* (Stanford, CA: Stanford University Press 1989).

—— *In Sickness and in Health: The British Experience, 1650–1850* (London: Fourth Estate, 1988).

Porter, Roy and Brewer, John (eds), *Consumption and the World of Goods* (London: Routledge, 1993).

Porter, Roy, *Mind-Forg'd Manacles: A History of Madness in England from the Restoration to the Regency* (Cambridge, MA: Harvard University Press 1987).

—— *The Medical History of Waters and Spas* (*Medical History*, Supplement 10; London: Wellcome Institute for the History of Medicine, 1990).

—— 'Diseases of Civilisation', in Bynum, W.F. and Porter, Roy (eds), *Companion Encyclopedia of the History of Medicine*, Vol 1 (London and New York: Routledge, 1993).

—— *Health for Sale: Quackery in England, 1660–1850* (Manchester and New York: Manchester University Press, 1989).

Raven, James, *Judging New Wealth: Popular Publishing and Responses to Commerce in England, 1750–1800* (Oxford: Clarendon Press, 1992).

Redford, Bruce (ed.), *The Letters of Samuel Johnson*, 5 vols (Princeton: Princeton University Press, 1992).

Reid, Loren, *Charles James Fox: A Man for the People* (London: Longmans, 1969).

Renwick, John, *Marmontel Mémoires*, 2 vols (Paris: L'Institut d'Etudes du Massif Central, 1972).

Rizzo, Betty, *Companions Without Vows: Relationships Among Eighteenth-Century British Women* (Atlanta and London: University of Georgia Press, 1994).

Roberts, William, *Memoirs of the Life and Correspondence of Mrs Hannah More*, 2 vols (New York: Harper & Brothers, 1835).

Roberts, Marie Mulvey, 'Pleasures Engendered by Gender: Homosociality and the Club', in Porter, Roy and Roberts, Marie

Mulvey (eds), *Pleasure in the Eighteenth Century* (Basingstoke: Macmillan, 1996).

Robinson, Jane, *Wayward Women: A Guide to Women Travellers* (Oxford and New York: Oxford University Press, 1990).

—— (ed.), *Unsuitable for Ladies: An Anthology of Women Travellers* (Oxford and New York: Oxford University Press, 1994).

Roche, Daniel, *France in the Enlightenment* (Cambridge, MA: Harvard University Press, 1998).

—— *The History of Everyday Things: The Birth of Consumption in France, 1600–1800* (Cambridge: Cambridge University Press, 2000).

—— *The People of Paris: An Essay in Popular Culture in the Eighteenth Century* (Leamington Spa: Berg, 1987).

Roessler, Shirley Elson, *Out of the Shadows: Women and Politics in the French Revolution, 1789–95* (New York: Peter Lang, 1998; orig. 1996).

Rogers, Katharine M., 'The View from England', in Spencer, Samia I. (ed.), *French Women and the Age of Enlightenment* (Bloomington: Indiana University Press, 1984).

—— *Feminism in Eighteenth-Century England* (Brighton: Harvester Press, 1982).

Romanell, Patrick, *John Locke and Medicine: A New Key to Locke* (New York: Prometheus Books, 1984).

Rousseau, G.S., 'Nerves, Spirits and Fibers: Towards Defining the Origins of Sensibility', *The Blue Guitar* 2 (1976), pp. 125–53.

Russell, Mary, *The Blessings of a Good Thick Skirt: Women Travellers and their World* (London: Collins, 1988).

Salvaggio, Ruth, *Enlightened Absence: Neoclassical Configurations of the Feminine* (Urbana: University of Illinois Press, 1988).

Samuel, Richard, *Remarks on the Utility of Drawing and Painting* (London: 1786).

Sanders, Lloyd, *The Holland House Circle* (London, 1908).

Schaffer, K., *Women and the Bush: Forces of Desire in the Australian Cultural Tradition* (Cambridge: Cambridge University Press, 1989).

Schama, Simon, *Citizens: A Chronicle of the French Revolution* (London: Penguin, 1989).

Schnorrenberg, Barbara Brandon, 'Medical Men of Bath', *Studies in Eighteenth-Century Culture* 13 (1984), pp. 189–203.

Scott, Sarah, *A Description of Millenium Hall and the Country Adjacent* (1762; edited by Gary Kelly, Peterborough, Ont: Broadview Press, 1995).

Scott, Walter S., *The Bluestocking Ladies* (London: John Green, 1947).

Showalter, Elaine, 'Women Writers and the Double Standard', in Gornick, V. (ed.), *Women in Sexist Society* (New York: Basic Books, 1971).

—— *A Literature of Their Own* (London: Virago, 1977).

Shteir, Ann, 'Botanical Dialogues: Maria Jacson and Women's Popular Science Writing in England', *Eighteenth-century Studies* 23 (1990), pp. 301–17.

Shuckburgh, Evelyn (ed.), *The Memoirs of Madame Roland* (London: Barrie & Jenkins, 1989).

Slavin, Morris, *The Making of an Insurrection: Parisian Sections and the Gironde* (Cambridge, MA: Harvard University Press, 1986).

Smith, Charlotte, *Desmond* (1792; reprinted with introduction by editors Blank, Antje and Todd, Janet, London: Pickering & Chatto, 1997).

Smith, P. Nowell (ed.), *The Letters of Sydney Smith*, 2 vols (Oxford: Clarendon Press, 1953).

Somerset, Anne, *Ladies-in-Waiting from the Tudors to the Present Day* (London: Weidenfeld and Nicolson, 1984).

Spencer, Samia I. (ed.), *French Women and the Age of Enlightenment* (Bloomington: Indiana University Press, 1984).

Spender, D., *Women of Ideas and What Men have Done to Them: From Aphra Behn to Adrienne Rich* (London: Routledge, 1982).

Starke, Mariana, *Travels in Italy, Between the Years 1792 and 1798; Containing a View of the Late Revolutions in that Country . . . with Instructions for the Use of Invalids and Families*, 2 vols (London: R. Phillips, 1802).

Steedman, Carolyn, 'A Woman Writing a Letter', in Earle, Rebecca (ed.), *Epistolary Selves: Letters and Letter-Writers 1600–1945* (Aldershot: Ashgate, 1999).

Stone, Lawrence, *The Family, Sex, and Marriage in England 1500–1800* (London: Weidenfeld & Nicolson, 1977).

—— *Road to Divorce: England, 1530–1987* (Oxford: Oxford University Press, 1990).

Stuart, Lady Louisa, 'Memoir of Lady Mary Coke' (1827), in Home (ed.), *Letters and Journals of Lady Mary Coke*, i, pp. xv–cxxii.

Swinburne, Henry, *The Courts of Europe at the Close of the Last Century*, 2 vols (London, 1841; edited by C. White).

Taylor, Barbara, 'Introduction', to Wollstonecraft, Mary, *A Vindication of the Rights of Woman* (1792; edited by Barbara Taylor, London: Everyman 1992), pp. vii-xxxi.

Taylor, I.A., *Life of Madame Roland* (London: Hutchinson, 1911).

Thomas, Keith, 'The Double Standard', *Journal of the History of Ideas* 20 (1959).

Thompson, J.M., (ed.), *English Witnesses of the French Revolution* (Oxford: Basil Blackwell, 1938).

Tillyard, Stella, *Aristocrats: Caroline, Emily, Louisa and Sarah Lennox 1740–1832* (London: Chatto & Windus, 1994).

—— *Citizen Lord: Edward Fitzgerald, 1763–1798* (London: Chatto & Windus 1997).

Tinker, Chauncey Brewster, *The Salon and English Letters: Chapters on the Interrelations of Literature and Society in the Age of Johnson* (New York: Guardian Press, 1967).

Todd, Janet, *Mary Wollstonecraft: A Revolutionary Life* (London: Weidenfeld & Nicolson, 2000).

—— (ed.), *Mary Wollstonecraft: Political Writings* (London: William Pickering, 1993).

Tomaselli, Sylvana, 'The Enlightenment Debate on Women', *History Workshop Journal* 20 (1985), pp. 101–24.

Toth, Karl, *Woman & Rococo in France, Seen through the life and works of a contemporary, Charles-Pinot Duclos* (translated by Roger Abingdon; London: George C. Harrap, 1931).

Trials for Adultery: or, The History of Divorces, Being Select Trials at Doctors Commons, for Adultery, Fornication, Cruelty, Impotence, &c, From the Year 1760, to the Present Time . . ., by 'A Civilian', 7 vols (London, 1779–80; facsimile reprint, New York and London: Garland Publishing, 1985).

Trumbach, Randolph, *The Rise of the Egalitarian Family: Aristocratic Kinship and Domestic Relations in Eighteenth-Century England* (New York: Academic Press, 1978).

Tyson, Moses and Guppy, Henry (eds), *The French Journals of Mrs Thrale and Doctor Johnson* (Manchester: Manchester University Press, 1932).

Varey, Simon, *Space and the Eighteenth-Century English Novel* (Cambridge: Cambridge University Press, 1990).

Vickery, Amanda, *The Gentleman's Daughter: Women's Lives in Georgian England* (New Haven and London: Yale University Press, 1998).

Wardle, Ralph M., (ed.), *Collected Letters of Mary Wollstonecraft* (Ithaca and London: Cornell University Press, 1979).

Watson, Nicola, *Revolution and the Form of the British Novel 1790–1825: Intercepted Letters, Interrupted Seductions* (Oxford: Clarendon Press, 1994).

Williams, Helen Maria, *Memoirs of the Reign of Robespierre*, Funck-Brentano, F. (ed.) (London: John Hamilton, 1929).

Wilson, Arthur, '"Treated Like Imbecile Children" (Diderot): The Enlightenment and the Status of Women', in Fritz, Paul and Morton Richard (eds), *Woman in the Eighteenth Century*.

Wilton, Andrew and Bignamini, Ilaria (eds), *Grand Tour: The Lure of Italy in the Eighteenth Century* (London: Tate Gallery Publishing, 1996).

Wollstonecraft, Mary, 'Letters to Gilbert Imlay', reproduced in Todd, Janet and Butler, Marilyn (eds), *The Works of Mary Wollstonecraft*, 7 vols (London: William Pickering, 1989), Vol 6.

—— *A Vindication of the Rights of Men, in a Letter to the Right Honourable Edmund Burke* (1790), reprinted in Janet Todd (ed.), *Political Writings*.

—— *A Vindication of the Rights of Woman* (1792; edited by Ashley Tauchert London: Everyman, 1995).

—— *An Historical and Moral View of the Origin and Progress of the French Revolution* (1794), reprinted in Janet Todd and Marilyn Butler (eds), *The Works of Mary Wollstonecraft*, 7 vols (London: William Pickering, 1989) Vol 6.

Wrigley, Richard and Revill, George (eds), *Pathologies of Travel* (Amsterdam and Atlanta, GA: Rodopi, 2000).

Wrigley, Richard, 'Infectious Enthusiasms: Influence, Contagion, and the Experience of Rome', in Chloe Chard and Helen Langdon (eds), *Transports: Travel, Pleasure, and Imaginative Geography, 1600–1830* (New Haven and London: Yale University Press, 1996).

Wyndham, Violet, *Madame de Genlis: A Biography* (London: André Deutsch, 1958).

Index